Rationale Management in Software Engineering

Allen H. Dutoit · Raymond McCall · Ivan Mistrík ·
Barbara Paech (Eds.)

Rationale Management
in Software Engineering

With 92 Figures and 18 Tables

 Springer

Allen H. Dutoit
Technische Universität München
Institut für Informatik / I1
85748 Garching bei München
Germany
allen.dutoit@computer.org

Ivan Mistrík
Fraunhofer Institut für
Integrierte Publikations- und Informationssysteme
Dolivostr. 15
64293 Darmstadt
Germany
mistrik@ipsi.fraunhofer.de

Raymond McCall
University of Colorado at Boulder
College Architecture & Planning
314 UCB
Boulder, CO 80309-0314
USA
Mccall@colorado.edu

Barbara Paech
Institut für Informatik
Universität Heidelberg
Im Neuenheimer Feld 326
69120 Heidelberg
Germany
paech@informatik.uni-heidelberg.de

ISBN 978-3-642-06816-4

Springer is a part of Springer Science + Business Media
springer.com

© Springer-Verlag Berlin Heidelberg 2006
Softcover reprint of the hardcover 1st edition 2006

Production: SPI Publisher Services, Pondicherry

Cover design: KünkelLopka, Heidelberg, Germany

Printed on acid free paper   45/3100/SPI   5 4 3 2 1 0

To the memory of Horst Rittel,
who pioneered the field of design rationale.

Foreword

Thirty years ago, I first entered the dark realm of software engineering, through a prior interest in documentation. In those days, documentation pretty much meant functional specifications. The idea that stakeholders in a system (its implementers, its end-users, its maintainers, and so forth) might want something other than an alphabetic list of function definitions was just taking hold. There was an exciting (to me) vision of stakeholders accessing and contributing to explanations of how and why aspects of a system work as they do, tradeoff analysis of concomitant downsides, and perhaps even accounts of why other possible approaches were not followed.

There were many challenges to overcome in achieving this vision. The most formidable is the belief that people do not like to create or use documentation. This negative image of documentation is (unfortunately) more than just the bias of a few incorrigible system developers. It is more like a deep truth about human information behavior, about how human beings construe and act towards information. Humans are, by default, active users of information; they want to try things out, and get things done. When documentation is interposed as a prerequisite between people and a desired activity, they try to skip through it, circumvent it, or undermine it. Designing information to suit the needs and interests of its users is an abiding challenge, but we have come a long way from functional specifications as the only answer.

A second formidable challenge is that some of the most important information about systems is tacit. Tacit knowledge is typically conveyed among people through enactment; for example, the way that office colleagues show one another how to configure and manage a printer in the course of just doing it. Exchanging tacit knowledge through the course of joint endeavor can be highly effective with respect to organizing workplace learning and performance. However, it does not produce an explicit rendering of what was shared, and therefore it does not document critical concepts, techniques, and practices. If or when current participants move on, tacit knowledge is lost to the organization. Nowadays, this is sometimes called the challenge of knowledge management.

Twenty years ago, I first encountered the term design rationale as a label for the reasons and the reasoning that supports a design. In the latter 1980s, design rationale became a rallying concept for a diverse set of contributions to the new vision of system documentation, and to a view of system design as a process of managing knowledge. Design rationale research, at that time, drew upon and integrated the insights of Alexander, Rittel, Schön and Simon into design problem solving. It asked a variety of fairly basic questions, such as "What kinds of rationale can there be?", "How can tradeoffs be usefully represented?", "Who will create design rationale documentation and who will use it?", "Can rationale help designers generate novel ideas?", "Can it help different stakeholder groups communicate more effectively?", "How will people create and use design rationale, and how will they be motivated?", and "How much rationale is enough, and of what kind?"

A huge amount of technical progress and cultural evolution has occurred through the past two decades. It is not unusual now for software organizations to expect developers to explain their designs in ways useful to themselves and to other stakeholders, and to cultivate organizational knowledge as a substantive asset created in the system development process. The traditional and onerous goal of generating (and then not using) more system documentation, has been overtaken by the objective of creating better documentation. We have clearly moved a long way towards a culture of the software development enterprise that is less craft-like, and ever more like a science of software design, to use a current touchstone of the US National Science Foundation.

Ten years ago, with Tom Moran, I edited a book entitled "Design Rationale." I think that book has held up quite well, though a decade onward it does seem a bit prefatory – conceptual and methodological analysis, discussion of notations and ontologies, small experiments and relatively focused field studies. It is past time for another detailed summary of research on design rationale. Allen Dutoit, Ray McCall, Ivan Mistrík, and Barbara Paech have done an excellent job of this in "Rationale management in software engineering." The chapters in this volume show how design rationale can be incorporated into the heart of the software development process – into requirements engineering, software architecture, and code design. The issue of capture seems particularly well developed, relative to 10 years ago.

I am delighted to see that the rethinking of system documentation and the emergence of design rationale as a new paradigm has not lost any steam, but has developed greater depth and breadth.

John M. Carroll
Edward M. Frymoyer Professor of Information Sciences and Technology
Penn State University, USA
ACM CHI Lifetime Achievement Award

Preface

A.H. Dutoit, R. McCall, I. Mistrík, B. Paech

Successful software engineering is contingent on the decision-making abilities of the stakeholders involved. Rationale is the justification behind decisions and is indispensable for communicating decisions. This book collects the current status of capturing and using rationale for software engineering as a resource and an incentive for all software engineers who strive to enhance their ability to make decisions.

Introduction

Nowadays, software engineers are busy keeping pace with the ever-growing wealth of technologies (e.g., web-oriented, components, application frameworks), and process models (e.g., agile, risk-oriented, model-driven). These new technologies and process models reflect the challenges of today's software engineering (SE): building more complex software in distributed teams, faster, and at a lower cost. However, the emphasis on technologies and process models obscures the fact that SE is primarily a human-based activity and that the success of a project or product is contingent on the decisions made during engineering. Due to the nonmaterial nature of software, the development process is characterized by a step-wise reduction of uncertainty, mutual learning, continuous consensus building, and many interdependent creative construction and accurate control activities. This can only be balanced by a transparent and convincing decision making process which supports all stakeholders in making their decisions explicit, in convincing each other of the value of these decisions, and in sharing the work of implementing (in the most general sense) these decisions.

Rationale management (RM) is concerned with just this: supporting explicit decision making by capturing and using the rationale, i.e., the justifications behind decisions. RM has been explored since 1970 in many application domains, most prominently for political debates and engineering activities. In the 1980s, software engineers started to adapt the first approaches to their needs. It soon became apparent that it is time-consuming to capture rationale, that it can be disruptive, and that there is not just one convenient way to express rationale. This led to a wealth of approaches for RM in specific SE activities. However, none of these approaches supports even half of the overall project activities. In other words, we are far away from having integrated RM support for SE decision making. However, by looking at these approaches in detail, we can develop an understanding of what it means to capture and use SE rationale. We think that it is now time to draw a picture of RM for SE research and practice, to look for similarities and synergies, and to start building an integrated baseline.

The aim of this book is to encourage software engineers to explore different ways for RM in research and practice and help to make RM a well-recognized ingredient for successful software engineering.

Book Overview

This book begins with an editorial chapter, followed by four parts. The editorial chapter provides a historical survey of rationale approaches, both in general and for SE in particular. Part 1 describes fundamental problems of RM and how some of them might be solved. This part should be read right after the editorial chapter. The other parts focus on the three most prominent uses for RM in SE today and can be read in any order. The three uses are: RM during requirements, where the decisions on the scope and functional and nonfunctional properties are made; RM during software architecting, where the fundamental decisions on the construction are made, and finally, RM for organizing reusable bodies of knowledge.

Part 1: Fundamentals – Rationale Representation, Capture, and Use

To many early researchers in design rationale, the obvious value of recorded rationale meant that RM systems would soon be in widespread use in real-world projects. In reality, there was little such use. It became clear that researchers working in many different application domains had badly underestimated the difficulties of making RM practical.

It now seems that there is a core of domain-independent problems that confront any attempt to apply RM to real-world projects. These problems concern the capture of rationale as well as its representation and use. Part 1 deals with these problems and how they might be solved in SE.

Part 1 contains four chapters that address issues of RM in SE projects. One of these chapter inventories the problems that an RM system must solve to be effective. Two chapters argue for diametrically opposed approaches for solving the worst problem confronting the field: rationale capture. The fourth proposes a new use for design rationale and thus indirectly supports capture by providing greater motivation for doing it.

Part 2: Rationale Management for Requirements Engineering

Requirements engineering exemplifies the concept of "wicked problem" that RM aims to address: different stakeholders with conflicting views and different frames of reference must agree on a problem that is not well understood. Once a solution is formulated (i.e., the requirements for the future system) leading to a shared understanding of the problem, the initial problem changes, resulting in new requirements, possibly conflicting with earlier requirements. To make matters more challenging, requirements engineering, more than other areas of SE, is inherently creative and insight driven.

Part 2 contains five chapters dealing with RM approaches adapted to deal with these challenges, such as supporting different stakeholders achieving shared understanding of the problem under consideration, consensus over the scope of the solution, capture the origins of the requirements, or supporting reconceptualization and reformulation of requirements after new insights have been gained.

Part 3: Design Rationale and Software Architecting

The importance of capturing and managing knowledge for architectural decisions has been recognized by many researchers and practitioners. It has also been acknowledged that the quality requirements are heavily influenced by the architecture of the system and capturing the relationship between architectural design decisions and quality attributes provides an important new role for rationale.

Part 3 primarily contains articles dealing with rationale in the context of software architecture. One chapter brings the message that a certain level of uncertainty in real-world software results always exists. Another chapter on software maintenance covers the important issue of determining the impact of potential changes on what already exists. Topics covered in this part include a framework for capturing and managing architecture design knowledge, capturing and using rationale for software architecture, software maintenance using rationale, role of rationale in design of product line architectures, role and impact of assumptions in SE and its products, and using design decisions to bridge rationale and architecture.

Part 4: Rationale for Organizing Bodies of Knowledge

Rationale for organizing bodies of knowledge comprises knowledge and justifications for decisions to be reused in any kind of software engineering project. It is more widespread than rationale for individual projects and products, as it can be used by many different people and thus the effort for its capture is more generally accepted. Furthermore, it is often easy to access, e.g., in open repositories or textbooks.

Part 4 contains four chapters dealing with such universal rationale. One chapter generalizes the notion of design spaces and shows how this alleviates architectural decision-making in industry. There are two chapters on capturing and using process rationale in terms of patterns. These patterns describe typical activities during software engineering, in one case focusing on agile processes, in the other case focusing on requirements engineering conflict situations. Another chapter shows how to capture and use rationale during process improvement to enhance the understanding and buy-in of the process participants.

Acknowledgments

Many people have supported us during this project. First, we thank the authors for their commitment and hard work in this endeavor, making this book a success. We are especially grateful to Jack Carroll for his stimulating foreword. We would also like to thank Doris Keidel-Müller for her support in formatting the book. Ralf Gerstner and Ulrike Stricker of Springer Germany provided invaluable advice in publishing matters. At the Technische Universität München, Prof. Bernd Brügge sponsored Allen Dutoit for the duration of this project. Finally, this book would not have been possible without the patience of our families.

Contents

Contributors

Michael Atwood
College of Information Science
and Technology
Drexel University
Philadelphia, PA 19104, USA
atwood@drexel.edu

Muhammad Ali Babar
Empirical Software Engineering
National ICT Australia
Alexandria, NSW 1435, Australia
Muhammad.AliBabar@nicta.com.au

Eric Barboni
LIIHS-IRIT
University Paul Sabatier
31062 Toulouse Cedex 9, France
barboni@irit.fr

Len Bass
Software Engineering Institute
Carnegie Mellon University
Pittsburgh, PA 15213, USA
ljb@sei.cmu.edu

Rémi Bastide
LIIHS-IRIT
University Paul Sabatier
31062 Toulouse Cedex 9, France
bastide@irit.fr

Barry Boehm
Center for Software Engineering
Department of Computer Science
University of Southern California
Los Angeles, CA 90089, USA
boehm@cse.usc.edu

Jan Bosch
Software and Application Technologies
Nokia Research Center
00045 Nokia Group, Finland
Jan.Bosch@nokia.com

Teodora Bozheva
European Software Institute
Parque Tecnológico Edif. 204
48170 Zamudio (Bizkaia), Spain
teodora.bozheva@esi.es

Holger Breitling
C1 WPS GmbH and University of Hamburg
Vogt-Kölln-Str. 30
22527 Hamburg, Germany
holger.breitling@c1-wps.de

David C. Brown
Department of Computer Science
Worcester Polytechnic Institute
Worcester, MA 01609, USA
dcb@cs.wpi.edu

Simon J. Buckingham Shum
Knowledge Media Institute
The Open University
Milton Keynes, MK7 6AA, UK
sbs@acm.org

Janet E. Burge
Department of Computer Science and
Systems Analysis
Miami University
Oxford, OH 45056, USA
burgeje@muohio.edu

John M. Carroll
Information Sciences and Technology
The Pennsylvania State University
University Park, PA 16802, USA
jcarroll@ist.psu.edu

Paul Clements
Software Engineering Institute
Carnegie Mellon University
Pittsburgh, PA 15213, USA
clements@sei.cmu.edu

Jeff Conklin
CogNexus Institute
1037 Juarez St.
Napa, CA 94559, USA
jeff@cognexus.org

Allen H. Dutoit
Institute for Informatics / I1
Technische Universität München
85748 Garching, Germany
allen.dutoit@computer.org

Juan Fernández-Ramil
Faculty of Maths and Computing
The Open University
Milton Keynes, MK7 6AA, UK
J.F.Ramil@open.ac.uk

Maria Elisa Gallo
European Software Institute
Parque Tecnológico Edif. 204
48170 Zamudio (Bizkaia), Spain
mariaelisa.gallo@esi.es

Ian Gorton
Empirical Software Engineering
National ICT Australia
Alexandria, NSW 1435, Australia
ian.gorton@nicta.com.au

Lars Hagge
Deutsches Elektronen-Synchrotron
Information Management,
Processes, Projects (IPP)
22607 Hamburg, Germany
lars.hagge@desy.de

Charles B. Haley
Department of Computing
The Open University
Milton Keynes, MK7 6AA, UK
c.b.haley@open.ac.uk

Steven R. Haynes
School of Information Sciences and Technology
The Pennsylvania State University
University Park, PA 16802, USA
shaynes@ist.psu.edu

Wiebe Hordijk
Faculty of Electrical Engineering,
Mathematics and Computer Science
University of Twente
7500 AE Enschede, The Netherlands
hordijkwtb@cs.utwente.nl

John Horner
Information Science and Technology
Drexel University
Philadelphia, PA 19104, USA
john.horner@drexel.edu

Frank Houdek
DaimlerChrysler AG
Research and Technology
89081 Ulm, Germany
frank.houdek@daimlerchrysler.com

Anton G.J. Jansen
Mathematics and Computer Science
University of Groningen
9700 AV Groningen, The Netherlands
a.g.j.jansen@cs.rug.nl

Hasan Kitapci
Center for Software Engineering
Department of Computer Science
University of Southern California
Los Angeles, CA 90089, USA
hkitapci@cse.usc.edu

Barbara Kitchenham
Empirical Software Engineering
National ICT Australia
Alexandria, NSW 1435, Australia
barbara.kitchenham@nicta.com.au

Jens Knodel
Fraunhofer Institute for Experimental
Software Engineering
Fraunhofer-Platz 1
67663 Kaiserslautern, Germany
knodel@iese.fraunhofer.de

Andreas Kornstädt
C1 WPS GmbH
Vogt-Kölln-Str. 30
22527 Hamburg, Germany
andreas.kornstaedt@c1-wps.de

Xavier Lacaze
LIIHS-IRIT
University Paul Sabatier
31062 Toulouse Cedex 9, France
lacaze@irit.fr

Kathrin Lappe
Deutsches Elektronen-Synchrotron
Information Management,
Processes, Projects (IPP)
22607 Hamburg, Germany
kathrin.lappe@desy.de

Meir M (Manny) Lehman
School of Computing
Middlesex University
The Boroughs, Hendon London, NW4 4BT,
UK
mml@mdx.ac.uk

Raymond McCall
College of Architecture and Planning
University of Colorado
Boulder, CO 80309, USA
mccall@colorado.edu

Ivan Mistrík
Fraunhofer Institute for Integrated
Publication and Information Systems
Dolivostr. 15
64293 Darmstadt, Germany
mistrik@ipsi.fraunhofer.de

Dirk Muthig
Fraunhofer Institute for Experimental Software Engineering
Fraunhofer-Platz 1
67663 Kaiserslautern, Germany
muthig@iese.fraunhofer.de

David Navarre
LIIHS-IRIT
University Paul Sabatier
31062 Toulouse Cedex 9, France
navarre@irit.fr

Lemai Nguyen
School of Information Systems
Deakin University
211 Burwood Highway
Burwood, Victoria, Australia 3125
lemai.nguyen@deakin.edu.au

Jos A. G. Nijhuis
Mathematics and Computer Science
University of Groningen
9700 AV Groningen, The Netherlands
j.a.g.nijhuis@rug.nl

Robert L. Nord
Software Engineering Institute
Carnegie Mellon University
Pittsburgh, PA 15213, USA
rn@sei.cmu.edu

Bashar Nuseibeh
Department of Computing
The Open University
Milton Keynes MK7 6AA, UK
B.A.Nuseibeh@open.ac.uk

Barbara Paech
Mathematics and Computer Science
University of Heidelberg
69120 Heidelberg, Germany
paech@informatik.uni-heidelberg.de

Philippe Palanque
LIIHS-IRIT
University Paul Sabatier
31062 Toulouse Cedex 9, France
palanque@irit.fr

Bhavani Palyagar
Information and Communication Sciences
Macquarie University
Sydney, NSW 2109, Australia
bpalyaga@ics.mq.edu.au

Mike Pidd
Department of Management Science
Lancaster University
Lancaster, LA1 4YX, UK
M.Pidd@lancaster.ac.uk

Debbie Richards
Department of Computing for Bhavani
Palyagar
Information and Communication Sciences
Macquarie University
Sydney, NSW 2109, Australia
richards@ics.mq.edu.au

John Rooksby
Computing InfoLab21
Lancaster University
Lancaster, LA1 4WA, UK
rooksby@comp.lancs.ac.uk

Joachim Sauer
C1 WPS GmbH and University of Hamburg
Vogt-Kölln-Str. 30
22527 Hamburg, Germany
joachim.sauer@c1-wps.de

Kurt Schneider
FG Software Engineering
Universität Hannover
30167 Hannover, Germany
Kurt.Schneider@Inf.Uni-Hannover.de

Albert M. Selvin
Knowledge Media Institute
The Open University and Verizon
(White Plains, NY 10604, USA)
Milton Keynes, MK7 6AA, UK
alselvin@gmail.com

Maarten Sierhuis
Research Institute for Advanced Computer
Science
NASA Ames Research Center
Moffett Field, CA 94035-1000, USA
msierhuis@mail.arc.nasa.gov

Ian Sommerville
Computing InfoLab21
Lancaster University
Lancaster, LA1 4WA, UK
is@comp.lancs.ac.uk

Judith A. Stafford
Software Engineering Institute
Carnegie Mellon University
Pittsburgh, PA 15213, USA
and
Department of Computer Science
Tufts University
Medford, MA 02155, USA
jas@cs.tufts.edu

Paul A. Swatman
School of Computer and Information
Science
University of South Australia,
Adelaide, Australia
Paul.Swatman@unisa.edu.au

Jan Salvador van der Ven
Department of Mathematics and Computer
Science
University of Groningen
9700 AV Groningen, The Netherlands
Salvador@cs.rug.nl

Roel Wieringa
Faculty of Electrical Engineering,
Mathematics and Computer Science
University of Twente
7500 AE Enschede, The Netherlands
roelw@cs.utwente.nl

1 Rationale Management in Software Engineering: Concepts and Techniques

A.H. Dutoit, R. McCall, I. Mistrík, B. Paech

Abstract: Rationale is the justification behind decisions. It is captured and used in many different forms during software engineering. While it has not achieved widespread use in practice, several approaches have emerged and successfully been used in selected projects. The goal of this chapter is to review the current state-of-the art of rationale management approaches and tool support in software engineering, and map future research directions.

Keywords: design rationale, rationale management, software engineering, software architecting, software requirements

1.1 Introduction

Rationale[1] is the justification behind decisions. It is captured and used in many different forms during software engineering (SE). The availability of rationale increases the developers' understanding of the system, making it easier to adapt or maintain. Being able to explain past decisions also facilitates the training of new members in a development team. However, rationale is often only captured partially and informally, often as natural language in design documents and in communication artifacts, making it difficult to access and maintain.

In the 1980s, the SE community, along with several others, started using rationale approaches. Process-based approaches, such as the use of Issue Based Information System (IBIS) described by Conklin and Burgess-Yakemovic [9], represent rationale as decision-making steps, capturing the argumentation behind designs as it occurs. Structural approaches, such as Questions, Options, and Criteria (QOC) [38], represent rationale as a space of alternatives and evaluation criteria, reconstructing rationale after decisions are made. In both cases, capturing rationale entails the elicitation

---

[1] Historically, much reasearch about rationale focuses on design and, hence, the term design rationale is most often used in the literature. In Sects. 1.1–1.5, which cover fundamentals of rationale management, we use the term *design rationale*. However, in Sects. 1.6–1.8, we use the term *software engineering rationale* to emphasize that rationale models are used during all activities of development, including requirements engineering, architectural design, implementation, testing, and system deployment.

and formalization of tacit knowledge, potentially introducing much overhead and disruption in the development process [4]. Rationale also features many elements and interdependencies, making it often difficult to keep up to date.

A rationale management system (RMS) is one that aims to address the above-stated issues. RMSs enable the capturing and accessing of rationale. The potential benefits of employing the services of an RMS include the following:

- Providing greater support to project management
- Improving dependency management
- Providing greater design support
- Helping support collaboration
- Supporting downstream users of design
- Allowing more detailed documentation
- Helping in requirements engineering
- Aiding in design reuse and ultimately provide a learning tool for evaluating design [36]

The complete rationale for even a small system is impossible to represent; consequently, developers are faced with selecting which rationale to represent in an RMS. Other implementation issues raised by researchers [46] are the formality (or informality) of the design rationale (DR) representation [21], and the approach to capturing rationale (e.g., reconstruction, apprentice shadowing, automatic generation). An RMS also aims to address the disruption caused by capturing rationale, recording rationale as a side effect of other activities, such as requirements elaboration, risk management, or process enactment.

The goal of this chapter is to review the current state-of-the art of rationale management approaches and tool support in SE, and map future research directions. Section 1.2 defines DR concepts. Section 1.3 discusses the fundamental DR approaches, such as IBIS, DRL, and QOC, from a historical perspective. Section 1.4 identifies and categorizes uses of design rationale. Section 1.5 identifies inherent limitations of DR approaches and proposes possible remedies. Section 1.6 discusses rationale in the specific context of SE, in terms of opportunities and a survey of the current state of the art. In Sect. 1.7 we synthesize our observations of Sect. 1.6 and propose an architectural framework for RMSs in SE. We conclude and discuss future research directions in Sect. 1.8.

1.2 Design Rationale Fundamentals

Systematic documentation of rationale for practical decisions began more than 35 years ago with work on rationale for design [30], in particular, design of buildings and cities. In the 1980s, interest in rationale spread to other fields involved with design, including SE and mechanical engineering. In recent years, researchers in SE have begun to look at rationale for activities other than design, and we argue later that this is an essential trend for the future of the field. Nevertheless, rationale for design remains the dominant theme in rationale research in SE. To understand the history and current state of the field, it is essential to understand the work done on design rationale. This section therefore defines the term *design rationale* and introduces fundamental characteristics of DR approaches.

1.2.1 Definitions

Our definitions are meant to accommodate many points of view about DR. The definitions we have chosen are similar to those given by MacLean et al. [38]:

1. We start by defining a *design process* as one that aims at devising an appropriate *design* for an artifact. A *design* we define as an artifact description that is detailed enough for use in implementing (constructing) that artifact. We consider a design *appropriate* if the artifact described would satisfy requirements while not being unacceptable in other ways, e.g., by producing an unacceptable set of side- and after-effects. Two major categories of *artifacts* are (1) physical artifacts, such as buildings, cities and computer hardware, and (2) cognitive artifacts, such as notation systems and software.
2. We define a *designer* to be anyone participating in a design process. This definition depends on how the term *participating* is defined and leaves open the possibility that users and clients could be designers.
3. *Design rationale (DR)* is the reasoning that goes into determining the design of the artifact. It can include not only direct discussion of artifact properties but also any other reasoning influencing design of the artifact. Note that our definitions do not imply that design starts only after requirements have been fully determined. During requirements specification many design decisions are made and these are relevant for design rationale. Similarly, design does not stop before implementation begins. Feedback from implementation and testing could be part of the design rationale.

1.2.2   Making Sense of the Varieties of DR Approaches

There are already many different approaches to DR, and more are coming into existence on a regular basis. This multiplicity of approaches shows that the DR field is healthy, but it also creates the need to make sense of this variety by finding organizing principles. In this section, we will therefore look at some ways of characterizing DR approaches to facilitate comparison, reveal trends and highlight issues. Describing even briefly the many approaches used is beyond the scope of this chapter, but we will describe some approaches that are frequently used and others that challenge widely held assumptions.

There are three ways of characterizing approaches to DR that reveal fundamental differences and similarities among them. One is to look at the way in which DR is *represented* and *processed* in an approach. Another is to describe the extent to which approaches are *descriptive or prescriptive* with respect to design. The third is to describe their *intrusiveness* in the design process.

Representation and Process Implementation

It is useful to characterize DR approaches by how they represent rationale and by how they implement basic DR processes.

- *DR representation form.* Almost invariably, DR is represented by being divided up into *chunks* that are assigned certain properties and/or relationships. By far, the most common way of doing this is through use of a DR schema, i.e., a fixed, semi-formal, conceptual schema that represents the types of elements (chunks), properties and relationships in terms of which DR is represented. An alternative approach to DR representation involves linking DR chunks to features of the artifact they discuss. Yet another approach is to link DR chunks to steps in a description of the process of using the artifact.
- *DR process implementation.* Using a DR approach involves making commitments about how to implement three basic processes:
  o   Capturing rationale, the process of eliciting rationale from designers and recording it
  o   Formalizing rationale, the process of transforming rationale into the desired representation form, such as a DR schema
  o   Providing access to rationale, the process of getting recorded rationale to the people who need it

A given rationale approach typically indicates how each of these processes is to be implemented. It indicates which entities perform processes, i.e., whether they are done by computers or humans, and, if humans, which by which humans. It also indicates when the processes are carried out, e.g., during design or afterwards.

Capturing rationale might be done in different ways. Designers might do it themselves or have it done by nondesigners who are specialists in DR documentation. A third possibility is to extract DR from records of communication among participants in a project. A fourth is to capture it as a side-effect of the use of design-support software.

Traditionally, capturing and formalizing rationale were combined in a single operation. In recent years, however, alternative approaches separate the formalizing of rationale from its capture. One way of implementing formalization is to have it done by the same people who state the rationale. An alternative is to have it formalized by personnel specially trained in formalizing rationale. Yet another approach is to use software tools that partially or completely formalize informally stated rationale.

The most common approach to accessing DR is through use of a system that lets users browse a hyperdocument containing the rationale. Conventional information retrieval (IR) search techniques can also be used. A third approach to accessing DR uses knowledge-based critics that alert users to the existence of DR they might need.

Descriptive or Prescriptive

– *Descriptive approaches.* Some approaches to DR are aimed only at describing whatever thinking processes designers might choose to use. Such approaches make no attempt to alter designers' reasoning. They might, however, use records of DR to improve processes outside of design, such as implementation, maintenance, or reuse of designed artifacts. They might also use DR to bring new members of a design team up-to-date. Such approaches are only interested in DR as a *descriptive model* of designers' thoughts, utterances or actions.
– *Prescriptive approaches.* On the other hand, some approaches are aimed at *improving design processes* by improving the reasoning of designers. They typically attempt to remedy perceived deficiencies in design reasoning by making it more correct, more consistent and more thorough. As with descriptive approaches, prescriptive approaches can create records of DR that are used to improve processes outside of design. It should also be noted that the descriptive and prescriptive are not always mutually exclusive. For example, some approaches are primarily descriptive in intent yet also have some prescriptive goals.

Intrusiveness

Another useful way of characterizing DR approaches is by their intrusiveness in the design process. This includes not only how intrusive they are but in what respects they intrude. Thus, an approach might be highly nonintrusive during capture of DR but relatively intrusive during retrieval and display of rationale. Measures of intrusiveness can include the degree to which a DR approach dictates the way design is done as well as the amount of extra effort required to use the approach. And the acceptability of intrusiveness may differ for capture, formalization and access.

- *More-intrusive approaches.* Most proposed DR approaches are highly intrusive with respect to DR capture in that they intervene in the design process to guide the way rationale is elicited from designers. Typically such interventions use a DR schema that defines what types of elements of rationale should be elicited from designers and how these elements should be linked together.
- *Less-intrusive approaches.* Over the past 15 years, a number of researchers have sought less intrusive ways of capturing and formalizing DR. This is due to concern about difficulties experienced in getting rationale capture to work in design projects. Specifically, many of these researchers believe that intrusiveness has been a central obstacle to effective capture of rationale, though there have been few complaints about intrusiveness as a barrier to accessing it.

One might imagine that prescriptive approaches were generally intrusive while descriptive modes were nonintrusive, but the actual story is not so simple. For example, QOC [38] is a highly intrusive yet primarily descriptive, while use of domain-oriented issue bases in Procedural Hierarchy of Issues (PHI) [17] is prescriptive yet highly nonintrusive. It is true, however, that descriptive approaches sometimes facilitate use of nonintrusive means to capture DR. Examples include the capture of DR from CAD usage [47] and use of natural language processing to structure computer mediated communication in design [45].

By itself, no representation scheme, such as a DR schema, is intrusive. It only becomes intrusive when used with an intrusive processing implementation mode, as when a schema is used to guide rationale elicitation. In such cases, however, different schemas can have different levels of intrusiveness. Generally, a more fine-grained schema will be more intrusive, because it makes designers perform more categorization and linking tasks. In addition, schemas that organize rationale in a way that is different from the way designers would intuitively organize it create a cognitive dissonance that adds to the cognitive overhead that designers must cope with.

1.3 Approaches to Design Rationale

This section focuses on three argumentative approaches to DR: IBIS, QOC, and Decision Representation Language (DRL). It thereby gives an introduction into the most prominent issues in providing DR support. It also contrasts argumentative approaches with problem-based, scenario-based, and generative approaches.

1.3.1 Three related approaches to argumentation – IBIS, QOC, and DRL

The most commonly used way of treating DR is as a type of *argumentation* that is structured according to a given schema. There are many ways in which DR argumentation might be structured, but there have historically been two major branches of thought. One branch uses some variant of the schema for argument structure devised by Toulmin [63]. The other uses one of a group of DR schemas having IBIS, QOC, and DRL as its most prominent members. Interest in the former branch seems to have faded over the past 15 years, while the latter continues as perhaps the dominant trend in the field. We will concentrate exclusively on the latter approach to argumentation. In particular, we will examine the similarities and differences among IBIS, QOC, and DRL.

IBIS

Historically, the DR movement began with Rittel's IBIS (Issue-Based Information System), which was not a software system but a way of modeling argumentation [30]. By 1967, Rittel had become convinced that design problems were *wicked problems* and fundamentally different from the well-defined problems of science [7, 54]. He called for an "argumentative approach" to wicked problems and used IBIS to implement this approach [55]. In the 1970s and 1980s he applied IBIS to large-scale projects in planning and policy making for the United Nations, the Commission of European Communities and the West German government. Other researchers applied IBIS to architecture and planning [41].

In the mid-1980s Conklin discovered Rittel's writings on *wicked problems* and saw this theory as a way of understanding the profound difficulties that software design had run into. He then contacted Rittel, who told him about IBIS [53]. Conklin then adapted IBIS for use in SE and created the graphical IBIS (gIBIS) hypertext system to support this use of IBIS [8, 9].

Rittel's IBIS had the following elements:

- Issues
- Positions
- Arguments
- Resolutions

In addition, there was a variety of inter-element relationships.

IBIS considers the pros and cons of *positions*, which are proposed alternative answers to questions, which are called *issues*. Positions are evaluated on the basis of *arguments* about the relative merits of the positions as well as the merits of other arguments. In principle, these arguments can range in size from a brief sentence to many paragraphs, though typically they are one to three sentences in length. Issue discussion often involves a multilevel structure of arguments for and against positions as well as arguments for and against other arguments. The decision on which position to accept is called the *resolution* of the issue.

Rittel's IBIS used several relationships to link different issue discussions. These included *more general than, logical successor to, temporal successor to, replaces* and *similar to*. Variants of IBIS developed by others often used relationships that differed from Rittel's to lesser or greater degrees.

Rittel looked at IBIS as a way of representing debate of controversial questions that arise in design. In fact, he intended IBIS to be a means for promoting debate of such questions from many different points of view. He was much less interested in the treatment of noncontroversial design questions, which were labeled *trivial issues* and not dealt with by IBIS.

Rittel's approach was from the outset both prescriptive and intrusive, as were almost all of his IBIS projects. Other researchers, however, have sought much less intrusive ways of using IBIS.

PHI

Procedural hierarchy of issues (PHI) [40, 41] extended IBIS to noncontroversial issues and rethought the relationships between issues. The centerpiece of PHI is the *subissue* relationship, where one issue's resolution depends on the resolution of another. In PHI a design project is a quasi-hierarchical structure of subissues that resembles a *calling structure* of subroutines in procedural programming. (A quasi-hierarchy is a directed acyclic graph with some added cyclical structures.) This is in contrast to the "spaghetti" structure of issue networks in Rittel's original version of

IBIS. PHI was intended to facilitate the creation of larger and more comprehensive models of design reasoning. While Rittel's IBIS typically dealt with 30–50 issues in a project, PHI typically dealt with 200–400 issues.

PHI also revised IBIS to better reflect actual practice in the IBIS community in the 1970s. The term *answer* was adopted (instead of *position*), since this term was widely used in this community. Also, the concept of *subanswer* was added so that hierarchies of answers could be represented. Such hierarchies were also in widespread use by IBIS practitioners, yet had no formal status in IBIS. PHI extended this naming scheme to arguments: the arguments on other arguments got labeled *subarguments*. This meant that hierarchies of issues, answers, and arguments could all be dealt with using a uniform naming scheme.

Originally PHI was both prescriptive and intrusive. Over the past 20 years, however, PHI has been used in ways that are increasing nonintrusive. The central tenet of PHI was that the key to improving design reasoning is to *raise more subissues*. In other words, the attitude behind PHI was that better treatment of an issue means thinking about what other issues its resolution depends on. For example, a house designer might raise the issue, "How many stories should the house have?" You can do a better job resolving this issue if you consider what other issues (*subissues*) the resolution depends on. For example, the number of stories for a house might depend on the following subissues:

- How much land is available for the house?
- How many people will live in the house?
- Will elderly or disabled people be living in the house? (since such people may have difficulty with stairs)

A number of hypertext systems were created to support PHI, starting with PROTOCOL [41] in the late 1970s. This was succeeded by MIKROPLIS [39, 44] in the early 1980s, which in turn evolved into PHIDIAS [42, 43] in the 1990s. In this period, the JANUS [17] system was also created to support delivery of PHI-based rationale to designers.

A crucial application of PHI is to create *domain-oriented issue bases*. These are structured collections of issues, answers, and arguments that have a high degree of recurrence in different projects in a given problem domain, e.g., design of houses. An issue's rationale might not include its resolution, since this varies from project to project. There is no claim that an issue base contains all the rationale for a project; instead, it is merely a convenient starting point for creating that rationale. Typically, much more work goes into designing a domain-oriented issue base than it is reasonable to spend on DR design in a single project. This extra work pays off when an issue base is used to inform many design projects within a domain.

QOC

A second schema for argumentative DR is used by the QOC approach to DR. While *QOC* stands for Questions, Options, and Criteria, it actually has six major types of elements:

- Questions
- Options
- Criteria
- Assessments
- Arguments
- Decisions

In addition, QOC has relationships between elements, including inter-question relationships. Since QOC's schema appears similar to IBIS's, it will be useful to point out the differences between the two as we explain QOC. Like IBIS, QOC centers DR on the discussion of questions. A crucial difference between QOC and IBIS is that while IBIS's questions, i.e., *issues*, can concern any design topic, *QOC's questions deal exclusively with features of the artifact being designed*. An example of a QOC question given by MacLean et al. is, "How should the scrollbar be displayed?" This, of course, would also count as an issue in IBIS. While QOC potentially deals only with a subset of the questions that an IBIS might deal with, QOC has the advantage of not allowing the designer to ignore questions about features of the artifact. IBIS, by contrast, does not mandate that such questions be dealt with, though they typically are.

Alternative answers to QOC questions are called *options*. Options represent possible features of the artifact being designed. These are identical to *positions* on IBIS issues that deal with the features of the artifact. The following are examples of options adapted from an account by MacLean et al. [38]:

1. Have the scroll bar permanently fixed to the edge of the window
2. Have the scroll bar invisible normally but visible when the cursor 'rolls over' the edge of the window

Questions and their options in QOC together constitute the design space, which corresponds to the set of possible alternative designs for the artifact. The use of QOC is referred to as design space analysis.

One crucial respect in which QOC differs from IBIS is in the way in which the alternative answers to questions are evaluated. QOC, first of all, requires use of explicitly stated *criteria* to evaluate proposed answers (*options*). Criteria indicate desirable properties of options or requirements they should satisfy. Second, QOC requires that answers be linked by positive or negative links to criteria, a positive link indicating that an option does well according to a criterion and a negative link indicating that it does poorly. The links of criteria to options are called *assessments*. IBIS does not require this sort of consistent evaluation. It only asks for arguments for or against the answers (*positions*). Nevertheless, each assessment in QOC could be represented in IBIS as an argument for or against a position.

Like IBIS, QOC can have *arguments* that challenge or support any element. In QOC emphasis is given to arguments on assessments. As with IBIS, argumentative structures can have multiple levels of arguments on arguments. Finally, QOC has *decisions* indicating which options to accept for each question. These correspond to *resolutions* of issues in IBIS.

In summary, there are two main things that distinguish QOC's schema from IBIS's. One is that QOC's questions always have possible answers (*options*) that describe properties of the artifact being designed, whereas *issues* in IBIS can include these questions as well as the many other questions that arise in a design project. QOC has no way of dealing with the multilevel *subissue* structures that are the hallmark of the PHI version of IBIS. On the other hand, the IBIS schema cannot guarantee that QOC-type questions are addressed. The second thing distinguishing the schemas is that QOC uses *assessments* indicating how answers (*options*) perform with respect to explicit *criteria*. While these assessments can be stated in IBIS as arguments, IBIS has no explicit representation of criteria as elements.

The goals of QOC approach are primarily descriptive, in that the main purpose of the system is to create a description of designers' rationale that is sufficiently detailed to inform other phases of the artifact lifecycle. QOC's *process implementation mode* is intrusive in its use of designers' time to guarantee that the description is thorough.

The authors of QOC have not created software to support QOC, though a number of other researchers have incorporated such support into their systems.

DRL

Decision Representation Language (DRL) [34] began as an extension of the Potts and Bruns model of DR [49], which was itself an extension of IBIS. Lee and Lai [35] argue that DRL is more expressive than other argumentation schemas in the sense that it enables the answering of a broader range of questions that might arise in various phases of the artifact lifecycle. What this claim primarily boils down to is having DRL provide a finer level of granularity in certain parts of its schema. Lee and Lai do not claim that DRL provides more comprehensive coverage of DR than other approaches. They state that their schema is for *decision rationale* and does not deal with all aspects of *design* rationale, such as deliberations on how to generate design alternatives. IBIS can deal with these aspects.

The primary elements of DRL are as follows:

- Decision problems
- Alternatives
- Goals
- Claims
- Groups

DRL also has various relationships between these elements. Many of these elements and relationships correspond to the aspects of QOC and IBIS.

A *decision problem* is something to be decided. Lee and Lai claim that a decision problem is equivalent to both a question in QOC and an issue in IBIS, but they appear not to recognize that a QOC question is not equivalent to an IBIS issue. It seems, however, that a decision problem actually corresponds to a QOC question rather than an IBIS issue because *alternatives,* i.e., the alternative solutions to decision problems, are always artifact features. An *alternative* is the same as an *option* in QOC and can be represented as a *position* in IBIS. A *goal* is used for comparative evaluation of alternatives and corresponds to a *criterion* in QOC, but has no explicit representation in IBIS. Alternatives can be linked to goals by *achieves* relationships, which correspond to *positive assessments* in QOC. Alternatives are evaluated by *claims* about the *achieves* relationships between alternatives and goals, a scheme that mirrors QOC's use of arguments to discuss its *assessment* relationships between *options* and *criteria*. These can be modeled as IBIS arguments, but doing so buries the *goals* in texts rather than explicitly representing them as elements. Further claims can be linked to other claims by *support* or *deny* relationships, which are semantically identical to relationships in both QOC and IBIS.

So far DRL looks nearly identical to QOC, but DRL has some features not found in QOC or IBIS. One is a *presupposes* relationship between claims. In addition, each claim has three attributes: *evaluation, plausibility,* and *degree,* the value of the evaluation attribute being determined from the values of the plausibility and degree attributes. *Plausibility* represents the likelihood that the claim is true, and *degree* represents the degree to which it is true. DRL also allows the creation of *goal–subgoal* hierarchies. DRL also includes a *subdecision* relationship between decision problems that corresponds to a *subissue* relationship among issues in PHI. Also DRL's *claims* represent a sentential level of granularity for argumentation, whereas IBIS *arguments* provide only a syllogistic level of granularity.

The stated goal of making DRL more expressive than other methods suggests that the system is primarily descriptive, but a number of the questions that Lee and Lai list in defining DRL's expressiveness have implications for improving design. So DRL appears to be more prescriptive than QOC, though less prescriptive than IBIS.

Lee created SYBIL, a knowledge-based hypertext system to support collaborative use of DRL [32, 33]. SYBIL is built on ObjectLens [31], a general tool for building CSCW applications.

IBIS, QOC, and DRL Compared

DRL's schema seems to correspond to a superset of QOC's, because every QOC feature appears to correspond to a DRL feature, though not the other way around. Both QOC and DRL are more expressive than IBIS in that they provide more fine-grained models of the argumentation that directly deals with evaluation of artifact features. But IBIS is more comprehensive in that it can represent the discussions of some design questions (*issues*) that neither QOC nor DRL treats. Lee and Lai state that DRL deals only with *decision rationale* and that this does not include all of *DR*. Since DRL is a superset of QOC, this limitation would also apply to QOC. Neither Rittel's IBIS nor its PHI variant has this limitation.

What aspects of DR are left out of *decision rationale*? Lee and Lai give only one example: discussions related to generating feature alternatives. In PHI there are two major classes of subissues: those that help in *evaluating* alternative answers (*positions*) and those that help in *generating* them. Lee and Lai are, in effect, saying that the latter cannot be represented in DRL, and, by implication, QOC. A simple example of an alternative-generating subissue might be, "How have multiple 'screens' of information been displayed in other software systems?" Such an issue identifies possible alternatives for artifact features, such as, "by scrolling" and "by showing multiple 'cards' of information, as in NoteCards and HyperCard." Yet such an issue it is not a *decision problem*, because answering the issue *does not decide which feature alternative to adopt*. Neither DRL nor QOC has any explicit way of dealing with such issues.

QOC, however, can deal with certain design questions that do not have alternative answers that are artifact features, for some criteria in QOC are represented as questions. Such questions would clearly count as issues in IBIS (and subissues in PHI); but criteria in QOC (goals in DRL) only deal with things, such as requirements, that can be used to directly evaluate alternative artifact features. One example of questions that neither count as QOC *questions* or *criteria* is found in an example of an area of design discussion where MacLean et al. acknowledge that the "overlap" with

Design Space Analysis "is relatively weak." In this example from an empirical study software designers say the following:

What is causing the long queue[?] Is it people just going through these steps, or is it people adding options to other services, and then using the other option?

MacLean et al. describe the process of addressing such questions as building an ad hoc *theory*, something that QOC does not handle. IBIS requires no special new way of handling such questions; they are simply *issues*.

Originally, both the IBIS and QOC schemas were used in intrusive DR approaches. But over the past 15 years, research on the PHI has sought to devise nonintrusive means for capture, formalization and delivery.

The QOC approach concentrates on the *design of rationale* rather than *recording the processes of rationale generation*, such as in *the process implementation mode* in the use of IBIS described by Conklin and Burgess-Yakemovic [9]. Apparently, on the basis of this difference MacLean et al. have claimed IBIS is restricted to capturing rationale "on the fly" and therefore only records a history of a design process, whereas QOC records the "logical argumentation." Actually, over its 35-year history IBIS has often been used in the same way QOC is used, i.e., to create "logical argumentation." For example, using PHI to create domain-oriented issue bases [17] is entirely concerned with designing "logical" rationale and leaves no record of the process by which the rationale is produced. In other words, the schemas of Rittel's IBIS and its PHI variant have been used with different DR *process implementation modes*.

Here, it is important to point out a fact that makes it difficult to compare DRL with QOC: writings on DRL generally contain little information about *process implementation mode*. DRL seems not so much a DR approach as a schema that might be used in various DR approaches.

It is perhaps surprising that there are so few significant differences in the schemas of IBIS, QOC, and DRL. The differences that do exist appear to be features of one schema that could profitably be added to the other two. In fact, MacLean et al. state that they would like to make QOC more like DRL, and Lee and Lai say that they see DRL as extending the changes that PHI made in IBIS. This suggests that it might be both possible and useful to combine the three schemas.

1.3.2 Approaches to DR that Go Beyond Argumentation

Problem-Based Evaluation

Lewis et al. [37] present a novel approach for evaluating alternative features of an artifact. They describe their own software design process as using a suite of problems for conceptual evaluation of different proposals for a computational environment they devised. Their experiences may sound familiar to other software designers, and yet no other DR approach has taken such experiences into account. Among other things, their work suggests that argumentation alone may not be the only, or even the best, means of evaluating alternatives, and this, in turn, challenges the sufficiency of existing argumentative approaches to DR. Implications of the Lewis–Riemann–Bell insight for other types of design, including other types of software design, need to be looked into. How their work might augment an argumentative approach to DR also needs to be worked out.

Scenario-Based Evaluation

Carroll and Rosson [6] propose a way of evaluating software features that does not document the reasoning of designers but rather the potential reasoning of users in hypothetical scenarios of human–computer interaction. While this is fundamentally different from standard argumentative approaches, a potential point of connection with argumentative DR is that the four examples of scenarios that Carroll and Rosson provide are all *question-answering processes*. Another connection is that scenario-based design involves the analysis of *claims*. Carroll and Rosson emphasize, however, that the claims they study deal only with the psychological consequences of artifact features and are "embodied" in, and thus inferable from, the artifact and its use. They see their work as a more abstract version of the problem-based approach of Lewis, Riemann, and Bell. They also see it as similar to QOC in some ways, but as being at a higher level of analysis and more connected to use situations.

Generating DR from Data and Models

Gruber and Russell [23] argue that argumentative schemas do not include all the rationale that designers use, because all of them are prescriptive about what information is relevant. No collection of DR, they claim, could answer all of the questions that might be raised about the rationale for an artifact. Rather than having designers elicit highly detailed models of their rationale, it would be better to collect engineering data and models and then later use these to infer DR in response to questions that arise about it.

1.4 Uses of DR and DR Methods

There are many potential uses of DR, some aimed at improving design, others at improving other phases of the artifact life cycle. Frequently proposed uses are listed below. Note that there are some overlaps and dependencies among items in this list. We group them into four main categories: the first focuses on collaboration, the second on reuse and change, the third on quality improvement, and the fourth on knowledge transfer.

1.4.1 Supporting Collaboration

Promoting Coordination in Design Teams

DR can help to coordinate many aspects of a design team's work. Different members of a team can use a common repository of DR to understand what others in the team are doing and what the consequences are for their own work. This can promote the identification of both potential conflicts between team members and opportunities for mutual support.

Exposing Differing Points of View

One use of DR is to expose differing points of view. Sometimes these are merely differences of opinion on detailed issues, but sometimes they are also profound differences of worldview on fundamental topics, e.g., open-source vs. de facto commercial standards. Sometimes they arise from differences in domain expertise in a functionally differentiated design team. Sometimes they arise from the different goals of different stake-holders in a project. Exposing differing points of view and the reasoning behind them was a central goal in Rittel's use of IBIS. Not all DR approaches share Rittel's aim of promoting debate. Some are more aimed at promoting a rapid convergence on agreement.

Facilitating Participation and Collaboration in Design

DR can be used to promote both collaborative and participatory design. Rittel argued that participation by users in design is often inhibited because they do not understand what rationale designers are using, what questions they are addressing, what alternative answers they are considering, what arguments they are using. He looked at IBIS as a way of making designers' reasoning transparent, i.e., a glass box rather than a black box, and thus empowering users to ask questions and to make comments and suggestions.

Similarly, he saw collaboration as also being inhibited when members of a design team did not understand the rationale being used by other members. DR approaches other than IBIS can also be used this way.

Building Consensus

Many users of IBIS have complained that it lacks adequate means for promoting consensus and reaching decisions. Other DR methods might be better for creating consensus for the simple reason that they do not go to such lengths as IBIS goes to promote debate.

1.4.2 Supporting Reuse and Change

Supporting Future Changes

The most commonly mentioned reason for using DR in SE is to support future changes in software, a problem that is perhaps more pressing in this field than in any other design or engineering field. This does not necessarily require a prescriptive approach to DR. This goal might be well served by approaches that merely record what designers happened to think. People who want to make future changes need to understand the effects of those changes; knowledge of the rationale for the design can help in achieving that understanding. Sometimes that rationale may also reveal that some planned changes are actually inappropriate. It is not uncommon that a design feature that seems wrong to a new designer was originally arrived at, through a painful process of trial-and-error in which all the "intuitive" approaches failed. Without a record of the rationale, this painful process might have to be repeated, perhaps many times.

Supporting Reuse

Software reuse is often considered the "holy grail" of software design. But before software can be reused it needs to be understood and/or modified. This requires knowing the reasoning behind its original design. DR can also help to identify parts of software that might be extracted and reused.

1.4.3 Improving Quality

Increasing Consistency of Decisions

Often it is only by making rationale explicit that consistency can be achieved. For example, it is not uncommon in large projects for the same decision tasks to be done by different groups within the design team. Recording rationale makes it easier to identify this fact and to make sure that decisions are mutually consistent. This use of DR is prescriptive, for it seeks to change the way designers think, i.e., making it more consistent. Though this use of DR requires methods that go beyond mere historical description of designer's rationale, such description may be of value because it exposes designers' reasoning to critical scrutiny.

Verifying Designs (Supporting Traceability)

This use of DR requires an explicit linking of requirements criteria to the descriptions of artifact features that satisfy these criteria. In the case of software, it also suggests the desirability of linking the criteria to actual features of the implemented software. This requires a schema that makes criteria explicit, as QOC and DRL do, rather than schemas where criteria are embedded in larger arguments, as is the case with IBIS.

Supporting Maintenance

One possible use of DR is to support debugging, fixing problems, and extending the functionality of an artifact. This problem is probably more critical with software than with any other type of artifact. DR can be used to spot conceptual errors in design as well as implementation errors, and errors of omission as well as errors of commission.

1.4.4 Supporting Knowledge Transfer

Learning from the Past

To learn from the past, we need to understand the reasoning behind past decisions. Most DR researchers maintain that this can best be done through explicit recording of the rationale for those decisions, something that requires nothing more than a descriptive model of whatever it was that the designers were thinking when they made decisions. Gruber and Russell [23], however, have presented evidence that designers are often able to effectively reconstruct the rationale for past designs from data other than an explicit record of rationale. These authors even suggest that it may be more useful to record such data rather than the rationale itself.

Validating Designs

To maximize learning from the past, we need to be able to compare designers' expectations about the consequences of their decisions with the actual consequences. This requires more than an understanding of the reasoning behind past decision; it requires evaluation of artifacts in use. One approach to doing this is found in case-based reasoning (CBR) projects by Kolodner [29]. Especially interesting is the ARCHIE project, which records the experiences of users of artifacts (buildings) and links these experiences to representations of the artifact.

Organizing and Delivering Reusable Knowledge

The issue of learning from the past is also fundamentally connected to the reuse of knowledge. Reuse can be thought of not only as using the success-ful ideas and rationale from the past, but also a matter of preserving records of what not to do. There is no point in reinventing the wheel, but it makes even less sense to reinvent the square wheel. Thus, the blunders of past designers represent an important type of reusable knowledge.

There are two basic approaches to the reuse of knowledge: *the case-based approach*, mentioned above, and what we might call *the gener-alized approach*. The latter term is intended here as an umbrella term for a number of approaches that try to put knowledge in a generalized form that goes beyond the mere annotation of individual cases. There are currently a number of generalized approaches, including patterns and issue bases.

Patterns, as used in SE, constitute one of the most heavily used approaches for organizing reusable knowledge [19]. Integrating rationale more completely into such patterns could be an important way of making rationale reusable. The patterns used in SE ultimately derive from Alexander's concept of *pattern* used in his work on architecture and urban planning [1]. This pattern concept has rationale explicitly built in, though this rationale is relatively unstructured.

Domain-oriented issue bases have only been created with PHI. Such issue bases contain hierarchies of issues, positions, and arguments that are commonly raised in projects in the domain. Most issues are left unresolved and designers are invited to make their own minds up on the issues. Wher-ever the software technology permits, issue bases are extensible by designers, who can add to them and even edit them for use in specific projects.

Supporting Training

One use of DR is to bring new members of a design team up-to-date on work in a current project. DR can function as a sort of larger-scale version of an FAQ, so that a new member can understand the rationale for the current state of the artifact's design before suggesting changes to it.

Providing External Design Memory

DR is useful as a memory aid for members of a design team. This is especially important where projects go on for long periods of time and where designers leave the team. It is very important when designers leave a project that all knowledge of their project rationale does not leave with them.

1.5 Limitations of Current DR Approaches and Software

Despite the many approaches to DR suggested and the many software systems devised, DR has not found ongoing use in real-world design. There are cases where DR has been applied successfully; but these often depend on special circumstances, such as the presence of a "DR champion" [9], that cannot be expected to exist in the majority of cases.

There are a number of ways in which DR methods can fail to be used in practice. One is the use for eliciting and recording rationale from designers, which is generally known as *capturing DR*. The other way is for retrieval and display of recorded rationale, what we shall call *providing access to DR*. We will focus here on the former, because it has been the central obstacle to the practical applications of DR. In fact, so little DR has been captured to date that has been relatively little opportunity to investigate the problem of DR access in real-world settings.

1.5.1 The Capture Problem

There seems to be a broad consensus that DR capture has generally not worked in practice. Designers have typically resisted rationale capture. Why they resist is a central question in research on DR capture and one of the most important issues in the DR field. If we were certain of how to answer this question, we would know the conditions, if any, under what the capture problem is solvable and how to begin solving it.

There are a number of possible explanations for resistance to DR capture. Some researchers point to its intrusiveness as the problem. One kind of intrusiveness is due to the work required for capture. Most capture involves designers writing up their rationale in a given DR schema. This requires a great deal of work in addition to the normal work of design.

Other reasons for resistance to capture can include political and legal factors. Designers might not want their bosses or the public to know the real reasons for their decisions. They might also want to protect themselves from potential law suits. There is also the problem that any argument can be a double-edged sword that provides others with a way to attack decisions made.

For descriptive approaches, the extra work of DR capture can be a fundamental problem. Since such approaches do not aid design, those who record the rationale are unlikely to be the ones who use it. Designers might thus have little motivation to do the capture. Descriptive approaches run afoul of Grudin's principle that collaborative systems tend to fail when those who do the work are not the beneficiaries of that work [24, 25].

Grudin argues that in developing commercial off-the-shelf (COTS) software DR capture might not pay off at all for later phases. COTS projects are failure prone, because (1) most products fail commercially and (2) up to 90% of projects are not completed. Failed projects do not need DR, and using resources for its capture could make failure more likely.

Grudin also suggests that in COTS development design decision making is often highly distributed. Experts and stakeholders of many types shape the design. There is often no way of compelling these individuals to share their rationale, much less to use a DR software system.

Grudin analyzes DR capture in three additional development contexts. For *in-house development in organizations* and *competitively bid contract development* he finds that incentives for DR capture offset some of the disincentives he found in COTS development. For *customized software development*, however, the only real disincentive he finds is that the firms doing it are often small and lack resources to invest in new software tools.

Another possible explanation for resistance to DR capture is that the quantity of work required for capture is greater in time than designers have for in a project even if they want to do it. Design is an intense activity that tends to absorb all the resources of time and personnel available.

For prescriptive approaches, there is supposedly a benefit to designers for capturing DR, so designers should be more motivated to do it. Yet even here, it has not succeeded. A simple reason for this might be that investing resources in DR capture has less benefit than investing it in design.

Another possible reason for the failure of DR capture in both descriptive and prescriptive approaches is that DR capture might actually be detrimental to design in ways that go beyond its cost in resources. For example, Fischer et al. [17] use Schön's theory of Reflective Practice [56] to argue that DR can actually disrupt designers' thinking. Schön sees design as involving two very different cognitive processes: an intuitive process of skillful action, which he calls *knowing-in-action,* and a reasoned process of reflection, which he calls *reflection-in-action*. He sees design as continually alternating between the two. The two processes cannot be done simultaneously, because reflection disrupts knowing-in-action. Reflection is only productive when intuition fails to cope with some new circumstance arising in design. To Fischer et al. this means that the explicit argumentation of DR is only appropriate for reflection-in-action. This in turn implies that rationale capture can actually degrade the quality of design if it is *intrusive into the intuitive processes of knowing-in-action*.

A more radical position on intrusiveness is taken by Shipman and Marshall [57]. They argue that semi-formal schemas are themselves the problem. As they see it, all such schemas are obstacles to capture information. They advocate doing away with structured user input and using only informal input.

Another possible explanation for the resistance to capture is that we still are not collecting the right information. The work of Gruber and Russell, Lewis, Riemann, and Bell as well as that of Carroll and Rosson suggest that argumentation by itself may not be enough to account for designers' reasoning. There are enough dissenters from the argumentative view of DR to leave room to doubt that we are capturing the right information. Nevertheless, there is little evidence to date that differences in information recorded have made any difference to the success of DR capture in practice.

1.5.2 Approaches to Solving the Capture Problem

Traditionally, DR literature has emphasized that devising the right schema, i.e., one that captures the right information and structures it correctly, is the way to solve the problems of DR usage. Yet designers' resistance to DR capture exists regardless of what schema is used. Solving the capture problem will require research on more than schema design.

One direction taken by researchers working on solving the capture problem is to try to reduce the intrusiveness of DR capture, either by reducing the work of DR capture or reducing its disruptiveness in design or both. The MIKROPLIS [39, 44] and gIBIS [8] hypertext systems reduced the work of managing DR by providing extensive support for browsing, modification, and retrieval. This, by itself, however, was not enough. The cognitive overhead of DR capture remained daunting.

One approach to reducing the cognitive overhead of capture is to use the strategy of *differential description*, in which designers only need to describe how the rationale for the current project differs from other rationale. One way to do this uses domain-oriented issue bases in PHI [18]. These contain rationale commonly used in projects in a given domain, including commonly raised issues, positions and arguments. Designers need to add only the missing information, including their decisions on the issues.

There are other ways in which differential description might be implemented. One would be by using rationale-annotated cases of similar projects, such as those provided by the ARCHIE system [29]. Another way might be to use design patterns annotated with rationale.

Of course, differential description only works for domains where previous design work has been done and where someone has built collections of issue-based discussion, precedent cases, or design patterns. By definition, this approach is not useful for unprecedented problems. It should also be noted here that Rittel's theory of wicked problems, which led to the first DR method, included the notion that design problems are "essentially unique," and thus not easily solved by looking to precedents [54].

A number of researchers have explored ways of capturing DR without use of any schema, either because schemas are too labor intensive to use or because they interfere cognitively with capture. For example, Shipman and his collaborators from Xerox PARC built "spatial hypertext systems" [61] that enable informal input of information in a 2D space and then infer the structure of that information from its spatial arrangement, work inspired in part by gIBIS's graphical representation of IBIS structure. Reeves [52] also created a system that uses a schema-free approach to capture. With his system designers write their rationale as textual notes in the graphical representation of a physical artifact in a CAD system. The design history of the artifact then becomes the means by which rationale is structured. A different schema-free and completely nonintrusive approach is used by Myers et al. [47]. They add semantic information to a CAD system's symbol library and then infer the DR from the designer's use of the system. This approach, however, does not produce argumentation as such.

The idea of abandoning use of an explicit schema is controversial in the DR field. On one side of the debate, there are MacLean et al. [38] arguing for intrusive, schema-based approach to DR capture. At the opposite end are Shipman and Marshall [57, 58, 59] arguing for nonintrusive approaches that abandon use of schemas.

Another approach to facilitating DR capture tries to find when rationale is naturally elicited as part of design communication [60]. In these cases eliciting DR is not an extra task for designers and does not interfere with design. It is instead an already existing and accepted part of the design process. In fact, it is the means by which collaboration takes place in design. There are two approaches that can be taken in using design communication as the basis for DR capture. One is to structure that communication using a schema. Another approach is to record it in its natural, informal form and then structure it retroactively, for example, by using natural language processing [45].

1.6 Rationale Management in Software Engineering

This section focuses on rationale-based approaches specific to software engineering (SE). First, we describe different types of SE projects where the use of rationale could have the most benefits, that is, in which addressing the limitations described in the previous section could yield a significant return on investment. In Sect. 1.6.2, we analyze for each SE activity how rationale can be captured and used. Using the SPICE process standard as a framework for discussing activities [http://www.sqi.gu.edu.au/spice/], we conclude that the concept of DR is too limited to encompass all the rationale-based processes of SE. We suggest that the concept of *SE rationale (SER)* is more general and more useful for discussing rationale management in SE. In Sect. 1.6.3, we present representative SER management approaches. Finally, we summarize the different SER approaches by activity, usage, schema, and original features.

1.6.1 Opportunities for Rationale in Software Engineering

Despite the challenges to the capture of rationale discussed in Sect. 1.5, there are also specific contexts in SE where the benefits of rationale capture could outweigh the costs. Below we list four contexts suitable for the four categories of uses introduced in Sect. 1.4.

- *Distributed projects*. A current trend of SE projects is the outsourcing of development, sometimes to organizations that are in different time zones. This leads to a breakdown in informal communication, where rationale is usually communicated peer-to-peer. Thus, approaches that use rationale to support collaboration could help here.
- *Product-line projects*. As products become instances of a product line, the life cycle of the product line becomes longer and the number of products that impact its design is high. Rationale can then be used to relate features of the product lines to specific product needs. It also can be used to externalize knowledge to guard against staff turnover. This could be alleviated by rationale uses focusing on reuse and change.
- *Safety critical systems*. Traceability of decisions is an important prerequisite for high-quality decisions, in particular when dealing

with change requests. Some organizations such as EUROCONTROL require this explicitly. Rationale can support this traceability. Clearly, rationale focusing on quality is most valuable here. Furthermore, in this context the high cost of failure changes the perception of the cost involved in rationale management.

- *COTS-based or mobile systems.* When systems are assembled from existing parts (either at deployment time of even at execution time in case of mobile systems) rationale can be useful to externalize knowledge between customer and supplier. Approaches focusing on knowledge transfer are most valuable here.

1.6.2 Supporting Software Engineering with Rationale

As described in Sect. 1.4, there are many different uses of rationale. Clearly, rationale can be provided on all decisions during SE. According to the sketch of the new version to be published in summer 2006, SPICE distinguishes the following process areas:

- Acquisition and supply (CUS1 and CUS2)
- Engineering (CUS3, ENG1, and ENG2)
- Operation (CUS 4)
- Support Processes (SUP1 to SUP8)
- Management (MAN1 to MAN4)
- Reuse (ORG6)
- Process improvement (ORG1, ORG2, and ORG5)
- Resource and infrastructure (ORG3 and ORG4)

In the following, we describe these process areas and analyze how rationale management could support ongoing or future activities.

When we defined DR in Sect. 1.2.1, we used a broad definition of the design process. But no reasonable definition of design is broad enough to encompass all the processes described in SPICE. Many of these processes involve decision making that is not part of design. If we consider carefully how the rationale associated with these decisions is generated and used, it becomes clear that the concept of *DR* is not broad enough to include all the rationale that needs to be managed in SE

We have defined the term *DR* in a way that corresponds to how it is typically defined in the literature. In this definition, DR includes two things: (1) rationale generated by designers, regardless of who makes use of that rationale and (2) rationale used by designers, regardless of who generates that rationale. Thus, if rationale generated by designers is used by software maintenance personnel, it is typically called DR. If rationale generated by software maintenance personnel is used by designers, e.g., to design a future version of the software, then it is also typically called design rationale.

This definition of DR might seem to suggest that the only rationale in SE is design rationale. But we can see that this is not so by looking carefully at decisions taken in the nondesign processes of an SE project, for example, decision made in software maintenance. The people who make such decisions often do so, on the basis of explicitly stated rationale. Some of this rationale might be useful for design, as indicated earlier, and we could, according to our definitions, count this as DR. It is quite possible, however, that some of the rationale is only useful for maintenance, e.g., for keeping track of which maintenance decisions have been made and what the justification was for these decisions. In this case, the label *DR* is not appropriate. We would have to call this something like *maintenance rationale*. Once we acknowledge the legitimacy of such a term, however, it seems that some of what we have called *DR* might with equal justification be labeled *maintenance rationale*. By extension we can see that every process within SE has an equal claim to having rationale of its own.

Since design is only one of many SE processes, the term *DR* is not general enough to encompasses all the types of rationale that a rationale management systems needs to deal with in SE. In the following sections we will therefore use the term *software engineering rationale* (SER) to encompass all these different types of rationale. We use the term *rationale* when we do not specifically address the difference between SER and DR.

There is every reason to expect that the discussion on DR (SER for design) presented in the previous sections will be true for every other kind of SER. There may, however, turn out to be additional facets.

Acquisition and Supply

Acquisition encompasses the preparation (in terms of definition of criteria and provision of resources), the selection of a supplier, the monitoring of the supplier during engineering, and the acceptance of the product through the customer. Supply mirrors these activities on the side of the supplier. SER on the current customer system and on the supplied components supports the communication between customer and supplier.

During acquisition preparation, SER of the current customer system could help to understand the current software and its limitations (both by the customer and the supplier). In particular, the decision about whether to extend the current system or to buy a new one would be facilitated.

During supplier selection, SER of the supplied components could be used to justify how the components satisfy the acquisition requirements. The same holds true during supplier monitoring and the acceptance test.

Engineering

Engineering encompasses the entire development process including software requirements analysis, software design, construction, and integration, as well as software testing, system integration, and testing, as well as system and software maintenance.

In this process area SER essentially improves the communication between stakeholders and the quality of the products (Fig. 1.1). By communication, we mean in particular elicitation of knowledge, any kind of negotiation and structuring of meetings. With quality we mean consistency and correctness of decisions with respect to decision criteria, including automatic checks.

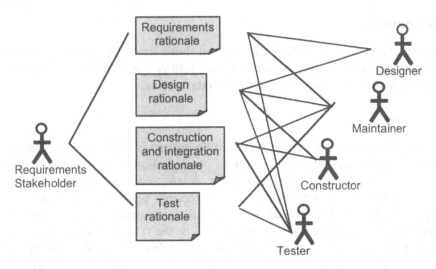

Fig. 1.1. Engineering rationale use

As for acquisition, preparation rationale about the current system supports the shaping of requirements on a new system. Rationale on the elicited requirements supports communication between the requirements stakeholders and to the designers, maintainers, and testers. SER of the design supports the (automatic) verification of the design against the requirements, and the communication between the designers and the constructors, maintainers, and testers. Similarly, SER of the construction supports the (automatic) verification of the construction against the design and the communication between constructors and the maintainers and testers. In the same manner, integration can be verified against requirements and design, and needs to be communicated between customers and suppliers (in particular, testers). During testing, SER can be captured with respect to test coverage decisions. This can be used to verify that tests cover all requirements and to support communication between testers and to maintainers. Maintenance is one of the most popular rationale usage areas so far. As discussed in [12, 15] maintenance decisions concern sensitivity analysis with respect to possible changes, pretraceability to identify what prompted the change in the system element, posttraceability to identify what is influenced by the system element and impact analysis to identify the consequences of a change. All of these decisions profit from SER about the system being maintained. In addition, SER rationale on the maintenance actions helps to verify that the changed system meets its requirements and supports the communication between customers and suppliers on the changes.

Operation

During operation, both the customer and those supplying support need to understand how the system will behave. Both can be aided in gaining this understanding by SER captured during engineering.

Support

Support encompasses a number of specific processes within the engineering process area, namely, documentation, configuration management, quality assurance, verification, validation, joint review, audit, and problem resolution. As mentioned with respect to engineering, verification is supported by rationale. The same holds true for validation, which tries to show that the systems meets the user expectations. For the review of a product (e.g. requirements or design) the rationale concerning the product facilitates understanding by the reviewers. Similarly, for the audit of a process, the rationale about that process facilitates understanding by the assessors. As a special case, quality assurance ensures that the processes required by the customer were followed and the required artifacts were produced. SER could be used to justify why specific processes were not executed or why certain artifacts were not provided. As SER is particularly well suited for making alternatives explicit, it could facilitate configuration management by making configuration options explicit and enabling automatic configuration. Furthermore, SER helps to make argumentation from differing points of view explicit. This could be used to generate documentation for people with fundamentally different perspectives on the SE process, e.g., different stakeholders.

Management

SER captured in the above-mentioned process areas can be used to support communication with management, as management needs to understand the forces that have lead to special project situations. For example, the number of unresolved issues or the priority of certain requirements can serve as indicators of project status. SER produced during project management could focus on risks. This would support both the communication about and the evaluation of those risks.

Reuse

Software reuse is another popular usage of rationale. The SER of any artifact produced or of any process step can indicate the situations in which the artifact or step is reusable and in what way it is reusable. This kind of SER is typically consolidated to enable quick and informed reuse decisions. One popular example where SER is crucial for a reusable artifact is a design pattern.

Process Improvement

Clearly, SER is very beneficial during process improvement. During process establishment, SER for specific process facets can increase the acceptance of the process. During process assessment, SER will support understanding by the assessors. Consolidated SER (e.g., as a part of patterns) can be used to suggest new process steps (see also reuse).

Resource and Infrastructure

Finally, the SER of any artifact or process step part of the current project helps newcomers to understand the current situation. This is particularly helpful for new employees to become quickly involved in the team.

1.6.3 Survey

In Sect. 1.6.2, we analyzed the potential use of SER for each SE activity. In this section, we present selected rationale approaches for SE, illustrating the current state-of-the-art for each activity. Our goal is not to provide a complete survey, but rather to select representative examples illustrating how the limitations described in Sect. 1.5 can be addressed. While most SE activities could benefit from SER, current research has focused mostly on engineering, management, reuse, and process improvement.

Engineering

Eliciting Requirements – SCRAM
SCRAM [62] is a requirements elicitation approach combining several techniques, including scenario-based requirements elicitation and QOC. To elicit requirements, end users are presented a mockup of the system in the context of a usage scenario. Next, SER of key aspects of the mockup is shown to end users as a QOC model, emphasizing its advantages and weaknesses compared to other alternatives with respect to a set of criteria that have been identified so far. By making the SER explicit to the end users, requirements engineers not only can evaluate the current solution, but also elicit additional criteria and priorities among criteria. In general, the presentation of several options provided more discussion opportunities for end users and resulted in more kinds of information being elicited. Thus, collaboration and knowledge transfer is enhanced. SCRAM differs from Design Space Analysis in that recording SER is not a long-term goal in itself, but rather, a short-term means for eliciting additional knowledge from the client.

Elaborating Requirements – Inquiry Cycle
The Inquiry Cycle is a general process model for requirements elaboration [50]. It includes three activities, *expression, discussion,* and *commitment,* which are repeated in sequence. During the expression activity, stakeholders acquire domain-related knowledge, propose new requirements or scenarios. During the discussion activity, stakeholders comment and annotate the proposed requirements. During the commitment activity, stakeholders make decisions, generate change requests, or commit to find missing information. The cycle is repeated as often as necessary. Tool support for the Inquiry cycle included IBIS-like support for discussions, allowing stakeholders to track questions, answers, reasons, and requirements within the same tool. Like SCRAM, rationale is used for eliciting more information from stakeholders (as opposed to capturing long-term rationale). Unlike SCRAM, the Inquiry Cycle focuses on asynchronous and ad hoc use of SER, as opposed to post hoc use of a design space.

Refining Nonfunctional Requirements – NFR Framework
The NFR Framework [10] is a method for tracking the relevant nonfunctional requirements for each decision, evaluated alternative, and interaction among nonfunctional requirements. Nonfunctional requirements are

treated as goals to be met. To address the difficulty that nonfunctional requirements are usually high-level and subjective, goals are refined and clarified by decomposing them into subgoals. Goals and subgoals are represented as nodes in a goal graph. Decomposition relationships are represented as directed arcs. The NFR Framework provides two types of decompositions:

- *AND decomposition.* A goal can be decomposed into subgoals, all of which need to be met to help the parent goal.
- *OR decomposition.* A goal can be decomposed into alternative subgoals, any one of which needs to be satisfied to help the parent goal.

The top-level goals (specified by the client and the users) are hence refined by developers into lower-level and more concrete goals. Note that a single subgoal can be related to more than one parent goal. Moreover, the NFR Framework provides additional types of links to capture other relationships. For example, correlation links between two goals indicate how one goal in the graph can support or hinder the other goal. Since nonfunctional requirements are rarely qualities that are either met or not, links in a goal graph represent how much a goal contributes to or hinders another goal. A goal is satisficed (as opposed to satisfied) when the selected alternative meets the goal within acceptable limits. Otherwise, the goal is said to be denied. Root nodes represent high-level goals specified by the client. As these goals are refined into more concrete ones the refinement activity moves toward system features. Goals that represent system features are called operationalizing goals.

The NFR framework enables stakeholders to evaluate trading off different options against a set of conflicting criteria. By the end of the refinement process, the stakeholders can record the selected option as well as the explored alternatives and their reasons for not selecting them.

Tracing to Human Sources – Contribution Structures
Contribution structures [22] record the authors of requirements and their role in shaping the requirement, so that the originators of requirements can be identified, or, minimally, their intent better understood, when requirements are changed. The contribution structures framework distinguishes three capacities:

- The *Principal* motivates the requirement and is responsible for its effects and consequences.
- The *Author* develops the requirements' structure and content and is responsible for its form and semantics.

- The *Documentor* records or transcribes the requirements' content and is responsible for its appearance.

Recording the role of a contributor with respect to a requirement provides a simple way to document the commitment and responsibility of the contributor. Although contribution structures do not capture an explicit intent in the way IBIS or QOC does, traceability to human sources enable change requirements prioritization and change requests to be directed to the right contributor, based on the nature of the change and the requirements being changed.

Post-Traceability – REMAP
REMAP is a conceptual model extending IBIS to include requirements and design elements to process knowledge during requirements engineering [51]. A prototype of REMAP was built to demonstrate how requirements, design elements, design decisions, constraints, and argumentation are captured in a graph, representing the process by which requirements and design were generated and negotiated. Using a truth maintenance system, the REMAP prototype propagates constraints and the validity (or invalidity) of assumptions through the graph, illustrating the benefit of traceability from requirements through SER and design elements. REMAP is in essence similar to DRL.

Requirements Checking – C-ReCS
C-ReCS is a tool for supporting collaborative requirements and recording decisions [27, 28]. It enables users to specify requirements and their SER in a formal language, a semantic net composed of predefined entities. The tool then provides users a suite of tools for detecting, diagnosing, and proposing resolutions for exceptions, such as consistency, completeness, and correctness problems. Once an exception is detected, the diagnosis attempts to explain to the user the underlying cause of the exception, using a predefined decision tree.

For example, C-ReCS detects inconsistencies based on the propagation of constraints in the requirements graph. A diagnosis would then present the propagation trace and the two constraints that are in conflict. This in turn serves as a basis for suggesting that the user relaxes one or the other constraint. When changing the requirements to remove the inconsistency, the user can link to the diagnostic as SER for the change.

Design Checking – SEURAT
SEURAT is a tool for recording and using SER of the system under construction at the level of source code [5]. SEURAT is integrated into the development environment, making it easier to switch back and forth

between development and documentation tasks. It is based on an extension of DRL, allowing the representation of detailed arguments and dependencies. It also provides a rich ontology of arguments, making it easy for the developer to reuse arguments. The ontology, combined with rules for syntactic and semantic checking, enables SEURAT to automatically identify inconsistencies or omissions in the rationale.

The rich and extensible argument ontology aims at lowering the effort for developers to capture SER, while increasing its accuracy. Making it accessible in a development environment, and providing services that are similar to standard style and consistency checking on source code, SEURAT also aims at increasing the short-term incentives for developers to use the SER they provided.

Long-term Collaboration – Sysiphus
Sysiphus provides a simple and integrated solution to manipulate system models and SER, embedding only minimal process specific knowledge [14,16]. This allows different development processes and the use of SER for a broad range of activities. Sysiphus includes a tool suite centered on a repository, which stores all models, SER, and user information. The repository controls access and concurrency enable multiple users to work at the same time on the same models. SER elements are first class objects (as opposed to buried notes or comments) and are accessed the same way as system model elements. The tool puts equal focus on the system and the SER. The end user can browse back-and-forth between SER and system models. Changes made by the end user are propagated synchronously to other end users working on the same model, enabling users to collaborate synchronously. When overlaps are discovered, the end user is prompted by the system to merge conflicting changes.

Sysiphus adopts a similar approach to SEURAT for lowering the threshold for capturing SER and increasing short-term developer incentive. However, Sysiphus focuses on the modeling and collaboration environment while SEURAT focuses on the development environment.

Management

WinWin
WinWin [3] is an approach where SER is used in support of risk management. WinWin resulted from the observation that satisfying all key stakeholders is a necessary condition for project success. Often, the issue of dealing with conflicting success criteria is not only to reconcile conflicting views, but also to identify the key stakeholders of the system and to clarify their success criteria. Once these criteria are known to all, it is much easier

to identify conflicts and to resolve them by negotiating compromise alternatives.

The WinWin negotiation model, similar to the QOC model described in Sect. 1.3, includes four elements. *Win conditions* are criteria, originated by stakeholders that, if not met, result in the failure of the project. *Issues* represent areas of disagreements typically a conflict between Win conditions that need to be further clarified or negotiated. *Options* represent alternatives for resolving issues, and *Agreements* represent decisions for closing an issue. Finally, Win conditions and agreements are classified into taxonomy categories. The taxonomy is specific to the system under construction and is used to relate large numbers of win conditions and agreements to broad requirements categories.

WinWin is tightly integrated into Boehm's spiral model. For the each iteration, critical stakeholders are identified and the win conditions relevant to the current iteration are elicited and reconciled. Win conditions are prioritized and scheduled to iterations based on risk. For example, a strong area of disagreement can result in a small set of win conditions being addressed in an early iteration, to ensure that an area of agreement can be found and to build trust among stakeholders.

Reuse

Augmenting Design Patterns with Rationale – DRIMER
DRIMER is a software development process and tool for applying design patterns [48]. Developers can search a design pattern catalog based on their intents, and examine specific examples of use of the design pattern. SER for each example is also provided following the DRIM schema, making it easier for a novice developer to understand unfamiliar patterns and for the experts to validate their usefulness. DRIM is similar to DRL, provides elements for representing intents, proposals, recommendations, justifications, and context of decisions. By integrating the process of finding reusable solutions with the process of recording experiences, DRIMER aims to create short-term incentives for developers to provide SER information while lowering the effort involved with capturing it.

Process Improvement

CoMoKit
CoMoKit is a process modeling and enactment tool that automatically records dependencies among products [11]. A process model specifies how products are generated and used by tasks. Tasks can be refined into subtasks, all of which need to be completed for the parent task to be

completed. The process model can include several methods for accomplishing the task, each possibly resulting in different products.

The approach assumes that there is a causal relationship between the input products of a task and its outputs. When the process model is enacted (i.e., when the user executes tasks, selects methods to create products), the tool records causal dependencies between products and decisions. Moreover, the user can add additional justifications for or against decisions.

When decisions or products are invalidated, CoMoKit automatically retracts other decisions and products that were derived from the newly invalidated element.

CoMoKit is similar to REMAP, in that it captures dependencies between products and decisions, and uses a truth maintenance system to propagate validity. Unlike REMAP, CoMoKit captures some dependencies automatically and provides a unified representation for both user-specified and generated rationale.

1.6.4 Summary

A summary of the SER approaches surveyed in this section is given in Table 1.1. Much progress has been made on the development of such

Table 1.1. Summary of SER approaches

Approach	Schema	SE activity	rationale use
SCRAM (1995)	QOC	requirements elicitation	collaboration
Inquiry Cycle (1994)	IBIS	requirements elaboration	collaboration
NFR Framework (1999)	Goal graph	nonfunctional requirements refinement	improve quality
Contribution structures (1994)		requirements change	collaboration
REMAP (1992)	IBIS++	requirements management	improve quality
C-ReCS (1997)	DRCS	requirements elaboration	improve quality
SEURAT (2004)	DRL++	development	improve quality
Sysiphus (2001)	IBIS/QOC	any	collaboration
WinWin (1994)	IBIS	risk management	collaboration
DRIMER (1996)	DRIM		reuse
CoMoKit (1996)		process improvement	improving quality

approaches and tools since the early 1980s. A number of important proto-types have been developed, but few rationale management systems have made it into practical use in industry. Recent research tends to combine these systems with other forms of design support systems [2, 26].

1.7 Tool Support for Rationale Management

This section describes an ideal tool support for rationale management in SE (rationale management system, RMS for short). In Sect. 1.7.1 ,we describe the life cycle of SER knowledge, which is used to deduce the functional requirements of an RMS. In Sect. 1.7.2, we discuss further requirements to overcome the challenges identified in the earlier sections. In Sect. 1.7.3, we describe a generic RMS in terms of an architectural framework populated by a set of components.

1.7.1 Rationale Life Cycle

In Sect. 1.4, we described the uses of rationale, that is, the ways in which rationale adds value to a development project. When developing tool support for rationale management, however, we need to consider the entire lifecycle of rationale knowledge, from planning to preservation. In view of general knowledge management, we can identify the following rationale management tasks [13]:

- Rationale goal definition
- Rationale measurement
- Rationale identification
- Rationale acquisition
- Rationale development
- Rationale distribution
- Rationale use
- Rationale preservation

Rationale goal definition, measurement, and rationale identification are critical for identifying the kind of rationale needed, but they are strategic planning activities and, thus, are typically not supported by an RMS. However, the outcome of these activities is a critical prerequisite for deploying an effective RMS. We discuss this further in Sect. 1.7.2.

All the other tasks can be directly supported by an RMS. In the following, we list the required features:

- Rationale acquisition is most often called *rationale capture*. Here the major question is how rationale is captured, for example, through reconstruction, apprentice shadowing of designers, or automatic generation. Other possibilities include capture during communication and reasoning.
- Rationale development *structures and packages rationale*. The major question is how to represent rationale. Lee [36] identifies three layers as representative of a generic structure of an RMS:
  o A decision process layer which stores the rationale, e.g., into five sublayers: issue, argument, alternatives, evaluation, and criteria
  o A design artifact layer which links the rationale to the development process artifacts, e.g., a product-process model
  o A design intent layer: meta-information underlying design decisions, such as intents, strategies, goals, and requirements

Further questions are whether representations are informal, semi-formal, or formal and is visual modeling used [20, 21].

- Rationale distribution makes the *rationale available for concurrent users*. An important issue here is ease of retrieval e.g., through a user-adaptable feature to browse, view, and filter the rationale. This should also enable the answering of questions and the review of similar design cases. Another important issue is collaboration, as rationale is often captured during collaboration.
- To support rationale use, the RMS must be *closely integrated into the tool support for the SE tasks*. Furthermore, it should support reasoning about the available rationale and the development artifact, for example, evaluation of given artifacts based on their rationale or suggestions for enhancements and modifications of artifacts based on available rationale.
- To allow *long-term usage of the rationale*, the RMS should support *rationale preservation*, for example, by filtering out redundant rationale or by giving priority to rationale that has been critical during development.

The above features must be adapted to the context in which the RMS is used. For example, development could be more process-oriented or more feature-oriented at different development stages. In fields with a relatively high degree of understanding of problems, solution technologies and standardization of artifacts, the feature-oriented approach can be used to give logical representation of artifacts, to follow the rules of the process.

In development where the problems or solution technology are poorly understood and where there is little standardization of artifacts a process-oriented approach can provide historical representation of artifacts [9].

Ideally, the RMS should support these features throughout all SE activities. So far, however, RMSs have been most successful when adapted to specific activities and specific goals. These goals depend mostly on the rationale usages identified in Sect. 1.4.

1.7.2   Dealing With Rationale Challenges

In addition to supporting rationale tasks, an RMS must deal with the limitations discussed in Sect. 1.5. In particular, strategic decisions made during the rationale goal definition and rationale identification tasks can significantly impact the selection and tailoring of the framework components.

– *Assessing cost vs. benefits.* The project or organization must a priori identify areas in which the use of rationale can yield a return on investment. For a project developing a safety critical system, rationale may facilitate the safety analysis of the design. For a COTS-based project, selecting a COTS with its available rationale may reduce the effort for integrating it into the system.
– *Addressing the capture problem.* In addition to identifying what kinds of rationale should be captured, a means and incentive for capturing it must also be identified. This can range from schema-free capture and automated structuring using natural language processing or inference to demonstrating compliance with review certification criteria. Developers capturing rationale should have a clear short-term use or benefit for capturing it.
– *Dealing with scale and complexity.* The scale and complexity of captured rationale depends on the selected granularity, the scale and complexity of the system and application domain, and on the rate of change of decisions. Accordingly, the RMS needs to account for these issues, by providing the necessary traceability links, search, versioning, filtering, and customization features. Automating syntactical and semantic checks, such as in SEURAT, enforces a higher level of consistency in the captured rationale, especially when many end users are involved.

1.7.3   An Architectural Framework for Rationale Management

Tool support for rationale has been often viewed as a stand-alone system. A monolithic tool supports the capture, representation, and use of rationale, either as a general-purpose tool such as gIBIS or a tool specialized to an activity, such as CoMoKit for process enactment. Instead, we view a rationale system as supporting designers in handling designs within a framework. An RMS is mostly transparent, appearing as an extension of the design environment, adaptable to the specific project situation.

In system terms, we propose that tool support for rationale should be viewed as a framework of components, each supporting a different activity and able to produce outcomes compatible with other components. In this section, we describe such a framework, its components, its interfaces to the design environment, and the constraints it must satisfy (Fig. 1.2).

Capture Components

An RMS supports rationale acquisition with a number of capture components for recording rationale from developers, extracting it from artifacts, or inferring it from developer actions. Such components might support:

- *Rationale capture by supporting collaboration.* Systems such as gIBIS, WinWin, or Sysiphus support project participants for communication and collaboration by providing a structured set of actions and entities for exchanging their opinions and criteria. In effect, the tool structures the collaboration to elicit the rationale to be captured and to reduce the overhead for structuring it. To increase collaboration through the component, many such SER components also provide a complete range of groupware features, such as group awareness, synchronous and asynchronous modes of communication, and support for multimedia.
- *Rationale extraction from artifacts.* An alternative approach is to extract rationale from communication or design artifacts after the fact. Natural language processing approaches identify key issues and arguments from natural language text, removing the burden from the participants to follow predefined schemas.
- *Rationale capture in design reasoning.* Systems such as SEURAT provide design support, either on their own or integrated into a larger development environment. This enables the capture of traceability links and inference of knowledge from the actions of the developer.
- *Rationale as justification.* Developers currently document rationale for decisions that are not obvious or that could impact other decisions. Systems like CoMoKit recognize the need for explicit capture of justifications and relate them with rationale captured or inferred by other components.

We expect that the most development projects will require a combination of the above components, depending on project-specific opportunities and constraints for capturing rationale.

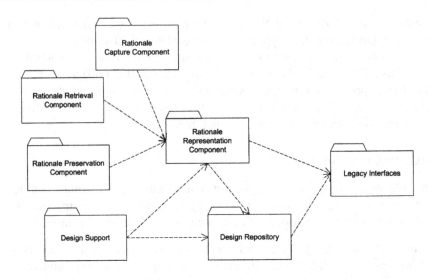

Fig. 1.2. RMS component overview

Representation Component

Even if the input of rationale is schema free and its formalization automated (see Sect. 1.5), an RMS supports rationale development with a representation component that provides a schema for storing and relating the rationale to other artifacts. A minimum amount of structuring is necessary for making it easier for developers to maintain, search, or relate to the design context. Most RMSs provide their own proprietary representation component, based on the specific SE activity that they support. A general RMS spans many activities and, as such, requires an open and extensible representation so that rationale can be captured at different levels of detail or be categorized according to different ontologies, based on the project context and activities supported. Such a representation could be used to enable different activities in the same environment to use either IBIS or QOC, organize issues hierarchically as in PHI, and capture intents as in DRL. A critical feature of the representation component is its ability to relate captured rationale to design artifacts, in particular, specific versions or configurations of the software, documents, or models.

Retrieval Components

An RMS supports access to rationale with retrieval components whose task is to derive information from rationale to facilitate their current task. Retrieval components range from simple generic components for navigating the rationale to specialized components that check for design rule violations or that evaluate designs:

- General-purpose components
  - Retrieve by query
  - Navigate rationale
  - Visualize rationale
- Specialized components
  - Formulate design documents
  - Answer designer's questions
  - Identify similar design cases
  - Design reasoning
  - Evaluate design

Preservation Components

An RMS supports rationale preservation with components for restructuring and reformulating rationale for long-term use. For example, rationale captured from communication is often incomplete. Terminology evolves and specializes over the course of the project, making initial requirements rationale more difficult to understand. There is a need for explicit preservation components. There has been little research in this dimension of RMSs so far, because the attention has been focused so heavily on rationale capture.

Interfaces to Legacy Components

The primary focus of a designer is on the plan leading to the artifact. Developers produce system designs that lead to the construction of software. A project manager produces task plans that lead to the consumption of resources and the production of economic value for the project. Rationale is a support function and is not the main focus of the designer. Consequently, there has been a trend towards tight integration of design rationale representations with other design representations [5, 14, 27] with the RMS being treated as an extension of the design system. An RMS must be able to interface with many external artifacts and tools (Fig. 1.3):

- *Product history.* Rationale evolves with the system under construction. As the system changes, developers need to justify changes and update rationale already captured. Consequently, they need to link to the design repository, that means different versions and configurations of the system and its design when formulating justifications.

– *Knowledge base.* Organizations accumulate knowledge that lives across individual projects, in terms of guidelines, lessons learned, and standards. Such knowledge finds its source in actual cases and also serves as the basis for decisions in subsequent projects. An RMS should also provide the ability to link to and from this knowledge.
– *Patterns base.* Developers refine pattern solutions for recurring design problems. As such pattern solutions become more general and refined, it becomes necessary to document its possible usage and trade-offs encountered during their uses. By attaching rationale to pattern solutions, developers can more easily identify which pattern to apply and how to refine it. Similarly, linking design decisions with a patterns base avoids repeating this rationale in the design.
– *Process models and enactment.* Recording rationale (justification behind process-level decisions, as for example in CoMoKit [11]) similarly enables organizations to reuse and evolve processes. While we do not expect process and product rationale to overlap significantly, using a uniform environment for capturing both would reduce training overhead and increase familiarity among project participants.

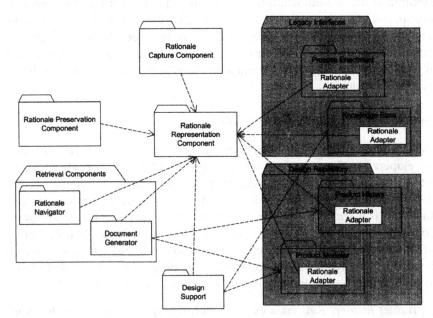

Fig. 1.3. An example of RMS architecture with legacy interfaces

1.8 Conclusion

In this chapter, we reviewed the state-of-the-art in rationale management in SE. We first provided a historical perspective by examining DR research in general. We then identified challenges and limitations faced by rationale approaches in SE. We also explained that to describe the rationale for all the processes of SE we need a more general term than *DR*; and for this purpose we adopted the term *SER*. We then discussed selected rationale approaches applied to SE, illustrating how specific challenges could be overcome. Finally, we presented an architectural framework for rationale management tool support.

Over the past decades, the research community has achieved some consensus on selected rationale research issues. For example, it is now widely accepted that having developers formalize the rationale for their decisions as they work is disruptive and that collaborative or post hoc approaches have better chances of capturing rationale. While general-purpose methods have not been widely adopted, specialized approaches addressing narrow problems have emerged, such as providing rationale with design patterns to facilitate their reuse, both in terms of design and DR.

As solutions are found for front-end issues, we anticipate that the research focus will include rationale preservation issues. For example:

Activity cross-pollination. Approaches presented in Sect. 1.6 often focus on a single use or activity of rationale. As rationale is used across several activities, the cost of capturing and training developers will be lower, relative to benefits. It is unclear, however, how to manage such overlaps.

Development environment integration. Parts of the research community have come to the consensus that rationale support should be tightly integrated into the development environment. First, rationale supports design and could be captured as a side-effect of the design methodology. Second, as system models and decisions are revisited, their accompanying rationale needs to be re-examined. This entails strong traceability between rationale and system models. There is a consensus that there should be a tight integration, but it is unclear, how to achieve it beyond specialized cases.

Rationale maintenance. An often-advertised benefit of rationale is to support changes, across time, staff turnover, and organizational boundaries. This means that rationale knowledge is also long-term knowledge that needs to be updated and consolidated as systems and designs evolve, and that contains obsolete knowledge that should be retired. Surprisingly, there is little research on rationale maintenance. As capture and structuring methods become more successful, rationale maintenance in particular, and rationale preservation in general, will need to be explicitly addressed.

Rationale management research has made inroads in a broad variety of disciplines, both within and outside the field of SE. As the confronted issues become more systemic, the interdisciplinary character of rationale research will be a critical asset in finding solutions that work beyond specialized situations.

Acknowledgments. We are grateful to David Brown, Janet Burge, Manny Lehman, Philippe Palanque, and Debbie Richards for their constructive and detailed feedback. All remaining errors are our own.

References

[1] Alexander C, Ishikawa S, Silverstein M, King I, Angel S, Jacobson M (1977) A Pattern Language: Towns, Buildings, Construction. Oxford University Press, Oxford

[2] Banares-Alcantara R, King JMP (1997) Design support systems for process engineering – design rationale as requirement for effective support. Comput. Chem. Eng. 21(3): 202–212

[3] Boehm B, Egyed A, Kwan J, Port D, Shah A, Madachy R (1998) Using the WinWin spiral model: A case study. IEEE Computer 31(7): 33–44

[4] Burge J (1998) Design rationale. Technical Report, Worcester Polytechnic Institute, Computer Science Dept., In: http://www.cs.wpi.edu/Research/aidg/DRRpt98.html (accessed: 02/17/2005).

[5] Burge J, Brown DC (2004) An integrated approach for software design checking using rationale. In: Gero, J (ed) Design Computing and Cognition '04. Kluwer Academic Publishers, Netherlands, pp. 557–576

[6] Carroll JM, Rosson MB (1996) Deliberated evolution: Stalking the view matcher in design space. In: Moran T P, Carroll J M (eds.) Design Rationale: Concepts, Techniques, and Use. Lawrence Erlbaum Associates, Mahwah, NJ, pp. 107–145

[7] Churchman CW (1967) Wicked problems. Guest editorial, Manage. Sci., 14 (4): 141–142

[8] Conklin J, Begeman M (1988) gIBIS: A hypertext tool for exploratory policy discussion. ACM Trans. Off. Inform. Syst. 4: 303–331

[9] Conklin J, Burgess-Yakemovic K C (1991) A process-oriented approach to design rationale. Hum.–Comp. Interact. 6: 357–391

[10] Chung L, Nixon BA, (1996) Dealing with change: An approach using non-functional requirements. Requir. Eng. J. 4: 238–260

[11] Dellen B, Kohler K, Maurer F (1996) Integrating software process models and design rationales. In: Proceedings of 11th Knowledge-Based Software Engineering Conference (KBSE '96) September 25–28, Syracuse, NY, pp. 84–93

[12] Dutoit AH, Paech B (2000) Supporting evolution: Rationale in use case driven software development. In: Proceedings of the International Workshop on Requirements Engineering: Foundations of Software Quality (REFSQ'2000), Stockholm, June, pp. 99–112

[13] Dutoit AH, Paech B (2001) Rationale management in software engineering. In: Chang SK (ed.) Handbook of Software Engineering and Knowledge Engineering. Vol. 1. World Scientific, Singapore

[14] Dutoit AH, Paech B (2002) Rationale-based use case specification. Requir. Eng. J. 1: 3–9

[15] Dutoit AH, Paech B (2003) Eliciting and maintaining knowledge for requirements evolution. In: Aurum A, Jeffery R, Wohlin C, Handzic M (eds.) Managing Software Engineering Knowledge. Springer, Berlin, pp. 135–156

[16] Wolf T, Dutoit AH (2004) A rationale-based analysis tool. 13th International Conference on Intelligent and Adaptive Systems and Software Engineering, July 1–3, Nice, France

[17] Fischer G, Lemke A, McCall R, Morch A (1996) Making argumentation serve design. In: Moran TP, Carroll JM (eds.) Design rationale: Concepts, techniques, and use. Lawrence Erlbaum, Mahwah, NJ, pp. 267–294

[18] Fischer G, McCall R, Morch A (1989) Design environments for constructive and argumentative design. In: Proceedings of the SIGCHI Conference on Human Factors in Computing Systems: Wings for the Mind, March, ACM New York, pp. 269–275

[19] Gamma E, Helm R, Johnson R, Vlissides J (1995) Design patterns. Addison-Wesley, Reading, MA

[20] Ganeshan R, Garrett J Jr, Finger S (1994) A framework for representing design. Int. J. Design Stud. 1 : 59–84

[21] de la Garza J, Alcantara P (1997) Using parameter dependency network to represent design rationale. J. Comput. Civil Eng., 2(2): 102–112

[22] Gotel O, Finkelstein A (1995) Contribution structures. In: Proceedings International Symposium on Requirements Engineering, IEEE, York, pp. 100–107

[23] Gruber TR, Russell DM (1996) Generative design rationale: Beyond the record and play paradigm. In: Moran TP, Carroll JM (eds.) Design Rationale: Concepts, Techniques, and Use. Lawrence Erlbaum, Mahwah, NJ, pp. 323–349

[24] Grudin J (1988) Why CSCW applications fail: problems in the design and evaluation of organization of organizational interfaces. In: Proceedings of the 1988 ACM Conference on Computer-supported Cooperative Work, ACM, New York, pp. 85–93

[25] Grudin, J (1996) Evaluating opportunities for design capture. In: Moran TP, Carroll JM (eds.) Design Rationale: Concepts, Techniques, and Use., Lawrence Erlbaum, Mahwah, NJ, pp. 453–470

[26] King JMP, Banares-Alcantara R (1997) Extending the scope and use of design rationale. Artificial Intelligence for Engineering Design, Analysis and Manufacturing, 11(2): 155–167

[27] Klein M (1993) DRCS: An integrated system for capture of designs and their rationale. In Gero J (ed.) Artificial Intelligence in Design '92. Kluwer Academic Publishers, Boston, pp. 393–412

[28] Klein M (1997) An exception handling approach to enhancing consistency, completeness and correctness in collaborative requirements capture. Concurrent Engineering Research and Applications, 5(1): 37–46

[29] Kolodner J (1993) Case-based reasoning. Morgan Kaufmann, San Mateo, CA

[30] Kunz W, Rittel H (1970) Issues as elements of information systems. Working Paper 131, Center for Urban and Regional Development, University of California, Berkeley.

[31] Lai K, Malone T, Yu K (1989) Object lens: A 'Spreadsheet' for cooperative work. ACM Transaction on Office Information Systems, 6(4): 332–353

[32] Lee J (1990) SIBYL: a tool for managing group design rationale. In: Proceedings of the ACM Conference on Computer-supported Cooperative Work, ACM, New York, pp. 79–92

[33] Lee J (1990) SIBYL: A qualitative decision management system. Artificial intelligence at MIT expanding frontiers. MIT Press, Cambridge, MA

[34] Lee J (1991) Extending the Potts and Bruns model for recording design rationale. In: Proceedings of the 13th International Conference on Software Engineering (ICSE'13), IEEE Computer Society Press, Los Alamitos, CA, pp. 114–125

[35] Lee J, Lai K (1996) What is design rationale? In: Moran TP, Carroll JM (eds.) Design Rationale: Concepts, Techniques, and Use. Lawrence Erlbaum Associates, Mahwah, NJ, pp. 21–52

[36] Lee J (1997) Design rationale systems: Understanding the issues. AI in Design, IEEE Expert, May/June: 78–85

[37] Lewis C, Rieman J, Bells B (1996) Problem-centered design for expressiveness. In: Moran TP, Carroll JM (eds.) Design Rationale, Concepts, Techniques and Use, Lawrence Erlbaum Associates, Mahwah, NJ, pp. 147–184

[38] MacLean A, Young RM, Bellotti VME, Moran T (1996) Questions, Options and Criteria. In: Moran TP, Carroll JM (eds.) Design Rationale, Concepts, Techniques and Use, Lawrence Erlbaum Associates, Mahwah, NJ, pp. 53–106

[39] McCall R (1989) MIKROPLIS: A hypertext system for design. Des. Stud. 10(4): 228–239

[40] McCall R (1991) PHI: a conceptual foundation for design hypermedia. Des. Stud. 1: 30–41

[41] McCall R (1979) On the structure and use of issue systems in design., Doctoral Dissertation 1978, University of California, Berkeley, University Microfilms

[42] McCall R, Bennett P, d'Oronzio P, Ostwald J, Shipman F, Wallace N (1990) PHIDIAS: A PHI-based design environment integrating CAD graphics into dynamic hypertext. In: Rizk A, Streitz N, André J (eds.), Proceedings of the European Conference on hypertext (ECHT'90), INRIA, France, Cambridge University Press, New York, NY, pp. 152–165

[43] McCall R, Bennett P, D'Oronzio P, Oswald J, Shipman FM III, Wallace N (1992) PHIDIAS: Integrating CAD graphics into dynamic hypertext. In: Streitz N, Rizk A, André J (eds.), Hypertext: Concepts, Systems and Applications, Cambridge University Press, New York, NY, pp. 152–165

[44] McCall R, Mistrík I, Schuler W (1981) An integrated information and Communication system for problem solving. In: Proceedings of the Seventh International CODATA Conference, Kyoto, Japan, pp. 107–115

[45] McCall R, Mistrík I (2005) Capture of software requirements and rationale through collaborative software development. In: Maté JL, Silva A (eds.) Requirements Engineering for Sociotechnical Systems. Information Science Publishing, pp. 303–317

[46] Moran TP, Carroll JM (1996) Design Rationale: Concepts, Techniques and Use, Lawrence Erlbaum Associates, Mahwah, NJ

[47] Myers KL, Zumel NB, Garcia PE (1999) Automated rapture of rationale for the detailed design process. In: Proceedings of the Eleventh National Conference on Innovative Applications of Artificial Intelligence (IAAI-99), AAAI Press, Menlo Park, CA, pp. 876–883

[48] Pena-Mora F, Vadhavkar S (1996) Augmenting design patterns with design rationale. Artificial Intelligence for Engineering Design, Analysis and Manufacturing, 11: 93–108

[49] Potts C, Bruns G (1988) Recording the reasons for design decisions. In: Proceedings of the 10th International Conference on Software Engineering (ICSE'10). Los Alamitos, CA, pp. 418–427

[50] Potts C, Takahashi K, Anton A (1994) Inquiry-based requirements analysis. IEEE Software, March,: 21–32

[51] Ramesh B, Dhar V (1992) Supporting systems development by capturing deliberations during requirements engineering. IEEE Trans. Softw. Eng. 18 (6): 498–510

[52] Reeves B, Shipman FM III (1992) Supporting communication between designers with artifact-centered evolving information spaces In: Proceedings of the 1992 ACM Conference on Computer-supported Cooperative work, November 1–4, Toronto, Ont., Canada, pp. 394–401

[53] Rittel H (1985) personal communication

[54] Rittel H, Weber M (1973) Dilemmas in a general theory of planning. Policy. Sci. 4: 155–169

[55] Rittel HWJ (1972) On the planning crisis: Systems analysis of the first and second generations. Bedriftsokonomen, Norway, 8:390–396

[56] Schön D (1983) The reflective practitioner. How professionals think in action. Temple Smith, London

[57] Shipman FM III, Marshall CC (1999) Formality considered harmful: Experiences, emerging themes, and directions on the use of formal representations in interactive systems. Comput. Support. Cooperat. Work 8(4): 333–352

[58] Shipman FM III, McCall R (1994) Supporting knowledge-base evolution with incremental formalization. In: Proceedings of the SIGCHI Conference on Human Factors in Computing Systems, Boston, Massachusetts, US, pp. 285–291

[59] Shipman FM III (1993) Supporting knowledge-base evolution with incremental formalization. PhD dissertation, Technical Report CU-CS-658-93, Department of Computer Science, University of Colorado, Boulder

[60] Shipman FM III, McCall R (1997) Integrating different perspectives on design rationale: Supporting the emergence of design rationale from design communication. Artif. Intell. Eng. Des., Anal., Manuf., 11(2): 141–154
[61] Shipman FM III, Marshall C (1999) Spatial hypertext: An alternative to navigational and semantic links. ACM Computing Surveys, ACM, New York, 31(4es): 14
[62] Sutcliffe A, Ryan M (1998) Experience with SCRAM, a scenario requirements analysis method. In: Proceedings of the 3rd International Conference on Requirements Engineering, Colorado Springs, CO, pp. 164–173
[63] Toulmin S (1958) The Uses of Argument. Cambridge University Press, UK

Part 1
Fundamentals – Rationale Representation, Capture, and Use

R. McCall

This part focuses on basic issues of rationale management in software engineering, including the following:

- How to capture rationale, i.e., how to elicit it and record it
- What form to represent rationale in
- How to formalize rationale, i.e., get it into the desired representational form
- How recorded rationale can be used
- What the potential barriers are to capture, representation, formalization, and use

A newcomer to the subject of rationale management (RM) might be surprised to find that issues so basic remain unresolved, and in some cases hotly disputed, more than 35 years after research on design rationale began. The reason for this situation is that extraordinary difficulties have plagued attempts to create RM systems that are effective in real-world projects, and these difficulties appear to have a lot to do with the basic issues listed here.

In the early days of research on design rationale many expected that RM would rapidly find widespread practical application. Certainly, no one foresaw how hard it would be to devise approaches and systems that worked in practice. Nowadays, researchers on RM in software engineering are aware of these problems, and much of their work is aimed at understanding and solving them. The four chapters in this part share this aim.

Many problems of RM are not unique to the domain of software engineering (SE). For example, there appears to be widespread agreement that effectively capturing rationale is the single greatest problem facing RM in SE. This same problem is the main barrier to successful RM applications in mechanical and civil engineering, as well as in building design, urban design, and policy making. In fact, it now seems clear that there is a core of domain-independent problems that must all be solved for the rationale management to be practical in any field.

While many of the problems confronting RM in SE are domain independent, solving these problems may well depend on exploiting feature specific to the SE domain. In fact, there is a good reason to think that SE has decisive advantages over other domains that seek to create practical RM systems. For one thing, there is a crucial difference between the role of the computer in SE and in other design domains. In other domains computers typically support design by creating a *model* of the artifact, e.g., a digital model of a building. But in SE it is *the artifact itself*, i.e., the software, that is created on the computer. In fact, SE is perhaps the only domain where the computer is used not only for design of an artifact but also for its implementation and use. Since the computer is also the best tool for capture, representation, and delivery of rationale, there exists a unique potential for connecting rationale with the software artifact itself and for integrating RM into every stage of the software lifecycle.

The first paper in Part 1 is Chap. 2, "Three Studies of Design Rationale as Explanation," by Steven Haynes. This chapter centers on studies in which software systems were created to address specific needs. The purpose of these studies was to explore the practical difficulties and advantages of using design rationale as a basis for constructing explanations that can help users to better understand complex systems. Along the way, Haynes encounters a number of basic issues of capture and representation of rationale.

One study extracted rationale from transcripts of free-wheeling discussions at design meetings, and put the rationale into QOC [5] format. This nonintrusive approach to rationale capture was used so as not to disrupt design discussion, but it resulted in the captured rationale being inadequate in a number of respects. Haynes concludes that the costs of not disrupting design were excessive. He concludes that it might have been better to use an intrusive approach that guided the discussion with an explicit rationale schema, but he also acknowledges that designers have often resisted this.

The two other studies had greater success, using a scenario-and-claims approach to rationale [1] as a basis for creating explanations of the software systems. The third study owed its positive result in part to using a semi-structured technique to guide elicitation of rationale in the form of scenarios and claims. This, like the first study, argues for the value of using intrusive techniques of guided elicitation to capture higher quality rationale.

Chapter 3, "Effective Design Rationale: Understanding the Barriers," by John Horner and Michael Atwood is an inventory of the many problems that design rationale approaches must solve if they are to be sucessful. Researchers who have applied such approaches in real-world projects typically know a lot about the many difficulties of doing so sucessfully; yet it is hard to find much indication of this in the literature. There is a tendency for articles in the field to acknowledge the existence of problems only when their authors think they have a way of solving them.

There is also the so-called "rectifier effect" that results in the publication almost exclusively of "successes" of RM and the suppression, however, unintentional, of accounts of the many failures of RM. These and other factors have resulted in a general tendency to under-report the difficulties of making RM work in practice. Chap. 3 is a valuable corrective for that tendency.

Horner and Atwood approach the subject of *barriers to effective design rationale* not as advocates of design rationale, but as "outsiders" who seek to keep the "insiders" honest about the challenges they face. While many of the barriers they describe will be familiar to those who have used design rationale, seeing them listed at length in Chapt. 3 is a sobering reminder of the work that remains to be done.

Chapter 4 is "Rationale as a By-Product" by Kurt Schneider, and Chap. 5 is "Hypermedia Support for Argumentation-Based Rationale: 15 Years on from gIBIS and QOC" by Simon Buckingham Shum, Albert Selvin, Maarten Sierhuis, Jeffrey Conklin, Charles Haley, and Bashar Nuseibeh. These two chapters represent fundamental opposites in several respects. Schneider is one of those researchers who, at some time in the past dozen years or so, have come to believe that *intrusiveness* of rationale capture is the most significant barrier to making RM work in practice. His chapter describes prototypes he has created in an attempt to capture and formalize rationale with minimal intrusion on software design. On the other hand, Buckingham Shum et al. remain committed to an intrusive approach to rationale capture and formalization. This approach, which has its roots in Rittel's use of IBIS [4] in the 1970s, has been described as, "constructively disruptive" of design processes because it improves the quality of the designed artifact. The Compendium system they describe is not a mere prototype; it is a software system mature enough for use in industrial settings.

Schneider lists the goals and principles of his "by-product" approach and then describes two system prototypes created to demonstrate its feasibility. Schneider's approach to formalization eschews use of a schema for representing design rationale. He instead structures rationale by the structure of the software processes to which it relates. He thus exploits the fact that design, implementation, and use of software can all take place on the same device (the computer) that is used for rationale capture and delivery. He acknowledges that some of his techniques for formalization might not provide adequate indexing for retrieval, but he argues that this is really a task better left to the people who are motivated to retrieve the rationale.

Shum et al. describe the sophisticated functionality of the Compendium system, which uses a graphical approach to representing rationale that has its roots in gIBIS [2]. They then describe three different practical applications of Compendium to capture argumentative rationale. The first application involved constructing *satisfaction arguments* [3] in the analysis of system security. The second two applications involve use of IBIS. The first of these applications used IBIS for Y2K risk assessment, while the second used it to index videos of meetings. With its ten-year history and its use in 100 projects, Compendium may well have the best claim to making RM a practical reality.

The four chapters contained in Part 1 provide only a small sample of the ongoing discussion of the basic issues of rationale management listed earlier. They do, however, give some idea of the nature of this discussion and some indication of why the debates on many of these issues remain unresolved. While few can doubt the sophistication of the Compendium system and its successful application to practical problems, a number of researchers continue to have doubts about the traditional, schema-driven rationale elicitation, and formalization that is the basis for use of Compendium. At the same time, it is clear that the development of alternatives to this approach is still in their early stages and too early to know yet whether they will prove viable in the long run. It is also clear that whatever success RM systems have had to date, these successes have yet to live up to the lofty expectations of the pioneers of the field. Much remains to be done, but researchers continue to generate innovative ideas about how to make RM a practical reality in SE.

References

[1] Carroll, JM (1995) Scenario-based design: Envisioning work and technology in system development, Wiley, New York
[2] Conklin J, Begeman ML (1988) gIBIS: A hypertext tool for exploratory policy discussion. ACM Trans. on Off. Inform. Syst., 4(6): 303–331
[3] Haley CB, Laney RC, & Nuseibeh B. (2005). Arguing security: Validating security requirements using structured argumentation, TR 2005/04. Department, of Computing, The Open University, UK
[4] Kunz W, Rittel HWJ (1970) Issues as Elements of information systems, Working paper 131, Center for urban and regional development, University of California, Berkeley
[5] MacLean A, Young R, Bellotti V, and Moran T (1991) Questions, options and criteria: Elements of design space analysis. Hum.–Comput. Interact., 6: 201–250

2 Three Studies of Design Rationale as Explanation

S.R. Haynes

Abstract: Prior research has pointed out the potential for design rationale to act as a base of explanatory knowledge about an evolving or completed design. One of the benefits of design rationale and its associated techniques and tools is that they help to answer questions about *why* a particular design possesses the structure and behaviors that it does. Answers to these *why* questions are explanations. To date, little empirical work has investigated the challenges and opportunities that emerge when attempting to realize the utility of design rationale as explanations. The three short case studies reported here describe examples of research that explores the use of design rationale as a means to enhance communication and comprehension among the stakeholders in complex systems projects. Lessons learned from the three studies are provided and some areas for future research are identified.

Keywords: design rationale, explanation, case studies, usability

2.1 Introduction

This chapter examines the relationship between the rationale that emerges in the systems design and development context and the explanations constructed in the context of system development, evolution, and use. Motivating this work is the proposition that as systems become more pervasive, complex, and intelligent, better means of explaining their structure and behavior will be required to ensure adoption and effective use. The use of design rationale (DR) as the basis for system explanations is an important part of the DR value equation. Justifying the cost and effort of DR capture involves developing ways to use the products of these efforts more effectively. Access to DR may be particularly important in more complex systems, intelligent, distributed systems, for example, because of the degree of understanding and trust required between these systems and their users as they work together in a problem domain.

DR captures the intentions underlying creation of a system artifact, and the issues, questions, argumentation, and decisions made in the process of navigating a given design space. The knowledge base represented by DR provides the raw material for active construction of system explanations in these contexts. As Dutoit et al. ([12], Chap. 1 in this book) point out there is a range of different uses for DR including, importantly, knowledge transfer among different stakeholders in a systems development project. DR is about helping to make explicit much of the assumed, tacit knowledge that underlies shared understanding between stakeholders in the same and in different roles. The studies reported here describe three example "use cases" of DR as explanation.

DR as explanation is both a descriptive and a prescriptive thesis. DR is about capturing and communicating the "why" underlying the structure and behavior of a system. DR as explanation is therefore a descriptive idea; it is the essence of the rationale-centric approach to the thinking about the design knowledge. To really leverage the potential power of these explanations, however, requires acknowledging the communicatory power and value of rationales. Explanations are pervasive in the use of DR. Whether among designers or between designers and other project stakeholders, explanations based on the underlying rationale of particular design are the means by which systems are comprehended, adopted, used effectively, enhanced, reused in new settings, and so on. Software engineering is a team-oriented and knowledge-intensive enterprise; DR is the currency that facilitates exchange of knowledge among the project team members.

The chapter first explores complex system explanations and frames these relative to the capabilities provided by access to DR. Prior research in knowledge-based systems and in software engineering has suggested a role for DR as the basis for system explanations, and this work is reviewed in support of the chapter's main arguments. Section 2.2 describes three specific cases of DR as explanation. In the first of these, the *Questions–Options–Criteria* (QOC, [17]) approach was employed to support development of the system help content. In the second, scenarios and claims analysis [7,8,9] are being used to construct a technology transfer package designed to assist potential technology adopters in comprehending the technology and how it might fit with their own organizational objectives and priorities. In the third, scenarios and claims were again employed, this time as a means for evaluating a collaborative system in the field. This last case shows how evaluation results can be transformed into retrospective DR, and how these can be used to develop new design meta-criteria for future system developers.

2.2 Explanations of Complex Systems

Mirel [19] describes complex systems as those used to help structure and solve ill-structured problems. She defines the domains and tasks that give rise to complex systems development as characterized by some core attributes including:

- Indeterminacy of both task goals and criteria for task completion
- Requiring higher order cognitive skill and integrating knowledge from different areas
- Requiring advanced learning and instruction for effective performance

Design for systems created to meet these challenges is correspondingly complex. The indeterminacy of task goals requires the design of flexible systems that rely on abstract software components. The higher the level of abstraction from a particular behavioral or structural requirement, the more difficult it becomes for developers and end users to reconstruct this process of abstraction later, and thereby relate the abstraction to the design deliberations, or rationale, that gave rise to it [3]. The integration of different knowledge in design and use, and the assumption of variable cognitive skills on the part of end users introduce additional complexity to the task of understanding how a particular system form emerges from a particular set of requirements. That these systems require advanced learning on the part of their users raises questions about where they obtain the information needed to facilitate this learning.

Today, many routine computing tasks are supported by *high-functionality applications* (HFAs, [29]), which typically include hundreds or even thousands of features and are used to manage large volumes of heterogeneous information. Each feature of such a system may be realized by a number of complexly interacting software components [1]. Intra- and inter-component interactions, as well as the distributed, intersystem interactions that increasingly define the modern computing milieu, make comprehending these systems difficult because of the cognitive load introduced when attempting to comprehend their structure and functionality.

The nature of complex systems suggests that the kinds of explanations required to convey understanding go beyond relatively simple, descriptive knowledge to include *how* and, especially, *why* a design assumes a particular structure and set of behaviors. Explanation requests, compared to, say, requests for instructions, are usually concerned with acquiring some deep knowledge of the event or entity in question. Explanations are provided in response to *why* questions that appeal to the causal chain that resulted in occurrence of the event or existence of the entity.

In the design context, this causal chain can potentially include a large, heterogeneous network of factors and influences that combine to inform the design decisions being made, in other words, the DR. For example, the second of the three development cases reported later in the chapter involved selection and implementation of certain decision-theoretic tools to support antiterrorism planning. The rationale for why a particular set of tools was selected, and how important domain concepts were translated into working software has proven to be of considerable interest to project stakeholders.

Providing even the briefest explanation of a complex system is a knowledge intensive activity. Providing a parsimonious explanation typically requires awareness of substantial implicit and tacit factors including the purpose motivating the explanation request, the current task at hand, what the explanation requestor already knows, and other contextual details that point to the essential information required to fulfill the explanation request [13]. People have adapted to inferring this detail from the environment and do it almost effortlessly. Computer-based information systems, however, are largely unable to ascertain the contextual detail needed to provide focused explanations to even the most well-formed explanation-seeking questions. Section 2.3 discusses related work on identifying appropriate explanation content for complex systems.

2.3 Design Rationale as Explanation Content

Swartout [26, 27] first identified the potential utility of DR as explanation content. His work on the explainable expert system (EES) project was an attempt to address some of the explanation content deficiencies identified in early expert system research. In this earlier work, especially Mycin [4] and derivative projects [10], researchers found significant gaps between the problem-solving strategies systems built to replicate or enhance, and the structural properties of the systems created to realize these strategies. Clancey [10, 11] identified this missing link as the detailed *support knowledge* representing the translation of domain requirements into functional software systems. The nature of this support knowledge presented a knowledge engineering conundrum because it represented a huge and seemingly intractable base of knowledge that was not germane to the application domain per se, but which was required to explain to domain users how system functionality emerged in relation to their domain requirements.

Swartout's attempt to mitigate the effects of this knowledge gap involved construction of an automatic expert system generator that tracked and logged decisions made by the system as it produced rules and control logic based on input in the form of relatively abstract, domain-specific problem-solving goals. The early XPLAIN system and later work on the EES relied on the existence of a domain model and problem-solving principles to translate goals into a system of productions, or rules. The log of automatic design decisions served as justifications for why the resulting system was appropriate given the domain model and principles and the problem-solving goals as expressed by the system developer.

One of the challenges faced by the EES developers was to elucidate the link between domain-independent, strategic concepts and the domain-specific or instance-specific information that is needed to apply a strategic concept in a particular goal scenario. For example, a design principle such as "simplify wherever possible" might be instantiated in a software design as "we can combine these two modules into one with no loss of cohesion." The EES attempts to solve this linkage problem through the concept of *capability descriptions*, which relate system goals to operationalized plans to achieve those goals. Capability descriptions are used to define what the plan does, its competencies. System goals are mapped to plans and associated methods used to achieve those goals through these capability descriptions. The EES was thereby designed to 'understand' the goals that it might be called upon to explain.

Several researchers outside the intelligent and knowledge-based systems community have since highlighted the potential for DR to act as an explanatory knowledge base [14, 15, 18, 20]. These works point to the potential utility of DR as the basis for informed discussion between system designers and system users, and between designers and external stakeholders. Some have claimed that DR's primary benefit is as a facilitator of this cross-party communication, rather than as a cognitive aid to designers or as a form of documentation, as it is often assumed [24].

DR helps to narrow the "gulf of understanding" [21] that exists between users who are domain experts and designers who understand how a particular system was intended to operate within a domain. DR is a critical element in the portfolio of communications tools that are employed in a complex development project. The techniques and tools developed to support DR capture and transfer are communications and organizational memory devices that can help to bridge the knowledge gap between what a given system "knows" about the domain, tasks, and user, and what users know about the complex tools that they use [28].

2.4 Three Cases of Design Rationale as Explanation

Prior research discussed in Sect. 2.3 highlights the potential for DR to improve the understanding of end users and other stakeholders external to the development team on a complex systems project. Despite this promise, relatively little work has empirically investigated this potential. In the sections that follow, I describe three condensed case studies that explore various aspects of these ideas. The first study was carried out with graduate student participants in a partially controlled environment. The second and third are field studies where DR was captured and is being used, in the first as a vehicle for a technology transfer and in the second as the basis for system evaluation and iterative redesign. The three cases reveal some of the challenges to harnessing the explanatory potential of DR, but also the opportunities for DR to contribute to the comprehensibility of complex systems.

2.4.1 A Transparent User Interface: VentureQuery

The first case is the VentureQuery project, which explored whether concepts and techniques of DR could be leveraged to provide an implementable model of embedded explanations for a software application. As discussed earlier, the theory underlying this research is that DR-based explanations may help to make more transparent the structure of a system by exposing design team deliberations including system requirements, envisioned use scenarios, and the technical, cognitive, organizational, and other constraints applied in the development process.

The VentureQuery project involved analysis, design, and construction of a software system to create and automatically publish electronic questionnaires on the web. A goal of the research design was to provide a project of realistic complexity to act as a source for DR, and to capture and structure the DR in a system capable of providing it back to system users. The team decided that the target application would consist of a web-based question–answer system in the form of a venture capital-seeking "game". The application was intended to help to educate novice e-business entrepreneurs in the venture capital-seeking process.

The project team consisted of 12 graduate students drawn from a Masters of Science course at a UK university. About half of the project team had significant systems development experience and all had a strong interest in the process of system design. Twenty-one meetings of the core design team were recorded on audiotape. An additional three meetings between members of the design team and various project reviewers and potential users were also recorded in full. Meetings averaged 90 min. Tapes were transcribed to text files resulting in over 400 pages of design meeting dialog. In addition to the design meeting tapes, other project artifacts were analyzed for their contribution to the DR including domain analysis documents, design documents (e.g., flip chart drawings), various Unified Modeling Language (UML) diagrams, meeting agendas and notes, and e-mail between team members.

Design meeting transcripts were analyzed using the Atlas/ti (www.atlasti.de) qualitative analysis software package. Coded transcript fragments were fairly coarse-grained to ensure that the context of a given design deliberation was not lost in analysis. Based on word counts, approximately 52% of the content of the design meetings related directly to design of the application. Design deliberations were coded, extracted, and then captured as DR in a database developed to act as a knowledge base for the systems explanation facility.

The Questions, Options, Criteria (QOC), DR semi-formalism [17] was used as the representational medium for the study. This selection was made based on QOC's balance of ease of use with representational fidelity. QOC is a relatively simple and sparse method for representing DR. This simplicity was deemed an essential trait in the context of this study, as it was felt to most closely parallel the selection criteria likely to be applied in applied project settings, where practitioners are unlikely to invest time learning a potentially more richly expressive, but necessarily more complex and difficult to use formalism.

In the QOC notation, *Questions* highlight issues that have been identified as relevant to the design, *Options* are the potential solution approaches that have been identified to address a given question, and *Criteria* are the reasons that are considered for or against each of the identified options. Whether a criterion is considered a positive or negative factor in the evaluation of a given option is represented in the links, known as *Assessments*, between Options and Criteria. Assessments in QOC are not assigned weights to represent their relative importance to the argument for an Option. Criteria may be instances of *Metacriteria* (such criteria are called bridging criteria by QOC's designers), though this relationship is not required. Finally, Questions may be derived from Options (the Consequent Questions of QOC) as a particular design issue is discussed. In addition, the framework was elaborated with the code *QOC Outline*, which was used to relate a particular element of the DR to the specific application component (generally, a Java class). The code set used and data counts appear in Table 2.1.

Table 2.1. QOC code set and data counts

QOC element	# captured
QOC outline elements	25
total questions	151
total options	339
total criteria	122
meta-criteria	21
bridging criteria	87
consequent questions	32
new questions that arose as a result of a selected option.	
assessed option–criterion Pairs	114
option–criterion pairs for which an explicit assessment, + or –, was derivable directly from the meeting transcripts and other materials.	
un-assessed option–criterion pairs	322
option–criterion pairs for which no explicit assessment, + or –, was derivable directly from the meeting transcripts and other materials.	

After being coded as QOC, elements of the DR were cross-coded to identify the explanatory information represented by each QOC component. The code set used was based on a taxonomy of explanation types derived from prior research on the philosophy of explanation see [15]. The purpose of this cross-coding was to identify the types of explanations provided by DR and to serve as a schema for explanation delivery at application runtime. Explanation types are divided into two types: *operational* explanations that provide basic information about the design, and *why* explanations conforming more closely to conceptions of explanation content as appealing to deeper knowledge about the application domain. Both the operational and *why* explanation code sets and data counts appear in Tables 2.2. and 2.3.

Though the operational explanation types are straightforward, the *why* explanation types require further definition. Deductive-nomological (law-based) explanations are those based on the constraints (laws) imposed by the underlying technical aspects of the system and from the need to conform to standards and legislative statutes. Functional explanations are those that relate directly to the purpose or requirement of a system or component, for example, use scenarios and desired outcomes from use.

Table 2.2. Operational explanation code set and data counts

operational explanations	count (%)	examples
What is it?	56/37	what is user answer?
		what are the attributes of user answer?
how do I use it?	35/23	what user answer input formats are supported?
		can question wording be varied?
how does it work?	54/36	how are user answers validated?
		how are question dependencies managed?
other	6/4	who will system test the application?
		who will own the rights to the application?

Table 2.3. *Why* explanation code set and data counts

why explanations	count (%)	Examples
D–N (law-based) explanation	14/11	*we are constrained by http*
		EU privacy laws prevent us from storing that
functional explanation	108/89	*what is the purpose of user answer?*
		we need user square path to tailor questions based on prior responses

Discussion and Lessons Learned

One of the most important results from the VentureQuery case study was that much of the design deliberation, including crucial assessments of criteria against design options, as well as the actual process of deciding on elements of a final design, were not made explicit in the design process, as shown in Table 2.1. Though this retrospective approach to rationale capture did help to work around some of the design process disruption associated with integrating QOC into a project "ecology" [5], in the context of explanation content capture the costs of not following the approach appear to be too great. The decision not to follow an explicit DR process meant that deliberations on a particular design issue did not always result in a complete QOC structure, with, for example, multiple Options generated for each Question, and each Criterion explicitly applied to the evaluation of each Option. This finding lends weight to Schön's argument [23] that deliberate techniques must be applied in technological design in order to promote explicit consideration and reflection during the design problem solving process.

Though it has been claimed that the most significant issues in any software project are discussed in design meetings, rather than informal discussions or not at all [24], it is also possible that certain implementation decisions are made in isolation by individual members of the project team, and therefore, never deliberated and never recorded as part of the rationale. Such "rationale ambiguity" may be an unavoidable, even essential characteristic of technological design and construction [2]. If large, complex design and development projects are to be completed within their inherent resource constraints, not every decision and relevant factor can be deliberated, and the challenge becomes one of defining an acceptable level of ambiguity rather than eliminating it altogether. That said, this ambiguity poses a significant challenge to providing comprehensive explanations.

Another problem that emerged was that of explanatory completeness with respect to design *questions* and how they appear to be answered in practice. Analysis of full-text meeting transcripts suggests that design options sometimes emerge almost mystically from design discussions. It was sometimes difficult to see the chain of reasoning that led to a particular design option being proposed and then being either accepted or rejected. This problem was especially acute in situations where a design option took the form of a high-level design object, for example, a class, and then candidate object components were enumerated in rapid succession. We might expect such cases to generate a rich set of rationales, but the conversation moved so quickly between foci that much of the information required to populate the QOC was found to be missing. This again highlights the potential role of a reflective design process in helping to make these assumptions more explicit.

There was an apparent asymmetry with respect to the amount of discussion allocated to certain features over others. This asymmetry was especially acute with respect to *what* questions vs. *how* questions. Relatively little discussion was evoked by the identification of a new candidate entity for the system, while discussions of new processes more often resulted in long discussions. This seemed to lead in many cases to the inclusion in the design of system entities that were poorly defined and poorly understood outside the context of the processes in which they played a role. This is problematic in the context of object-oriented design, where the generation of a complete justification and description for a given entity can assist with the creation of more modular system objects with more well-defined semantics and behaviors.

2.4.2 Design Rationale for Technology Transfer: ATFP

The second case is an investigation into the use of DR as a facilitator of technology transfer. Since the Spring of 2002, we have been working with the United States Marine Corps on a decision model and cognitive support system to aid effective allocation of antiterrorism and force protection (ATFP) resources at Marine Corps installations. A central concern for the ATFP work is the migration or transfer of the technology across institutional boundaries and its adoption into local practices. In this particular case, technology developed in an academic partnership with a unit within the Marine Corps is to be transferred to other units both within the Marine Corps and to other services and government organizations. The work is ongoing and the report here is only a preliminary treatment.

The decision model and system developed for Marine Corps antiterrorism officers, facilities planners, public works officers, and military police provides support for asset prioritization, calculation of antiterrorism mitigation project utilities, resource allocation, and acts as a repository for organizational learning in the ATFP domain. Requirements have been gathered and refined through a series of briefings, informal and formal design reviews of the evolving prototype, and cognitive walkthroughs [22] with prospective users at Marine Corps installations. Over 100 Marine Corps officers and civilian personnel have reviewed the project, and over 30 have participated in focused cognitive walkthroughs.

In addition to the core decision model and cognitive support system that implements it, the project involved development of a range of knowledge resources to aid users working in the domain including a training module and explanation facility. The project's Website includes a scenario editor that captures details of real and envisioned interactions with the system in response to a range of decision making and planning problems collected in the field.

Discussion and Lessons Learned

We have found that a range of factors impact opportunities for successful adoption of the ATFP system at different installations. These include 'microscopic' issues such as domain terminology, which is unfamiliar to many planners facing ATFP problems for the first time, and 'macroscopic' issues such as whether the Department of Defense or Headquarters Marine Corps would mandate the use of a particular ATFP planning approach and supporting tools.

An initial finding from this work is that DR, in the form of scenarios of use and associated claims analyses [8] can act as boundary objects [25] to facilitate knowledge sharing, adoption decision-making, and technology evaluation across organizations. Boundary objects are "those objects that are plastic enough to be adaptable across multiple viewpoints, yet maintain continuity of identity" [25]. Central to the utilization of boundary objects as a theoretical orientation for technology transfer is Star's claim for the efficacy of boundary objects as touchstones for understanding among members of distributed and culturally diverse communities. According to Star, a 'good' or effective boundary object has many identities, definitions, and interpretations. One important insight is that the most effective boundary objects are those that are able to evoke and make explicit the largest quantity of tacit knowledge in a particular problem context [6]. In this way, the use of DR as boundary objects serves as the basis for the *active construction* of explanations for end users and other project stakeholders. In reviews and walkthroughs of the ATFP system, we witnessed cases where prospective users developed their understanding of the application by reflecting on scenarios supplied by previous users and how they were employed in development of a decision model, as exemplified in the walkthrough quote:

...if we had more of these [scenarios], *more well fleshed out and then these linked to these models, and someone could browse the scenarios and say, okay, that's sort of like my scenario, kind of like what I'm going to do here.*

We are actively exploring ways in which scenarios and other elements of the ATFP system DR can be most effectively captured and then packaged to facilitate explaining complex systems, and thereby fostering their adoption, and use. For example, we are exploring the use of a claims taxonomy tuned to the requirements of technology transfer as suggested in prior research. One such taxonomy focuses on relating each scenario to aspects of system *comprehensibility*, development organization *credibility*, and system adoption *cost*. The ultimate objective of this work is to provide prospective system adopters with means to understand how a particular system design relates to specific scenarios of use, and what this mapping entails for the technology adopting organization.

2.4.3 Design Rationale from Evaluations: PMLAV

The third and final case involves another system project from the Marine Corps domain. This project does not involve design per se, but rather an evaluation project in which DR concepts and representational tools have been used as focusing principles to guide the work and organize its results. As in the second case, techniques from scenario-based design and claims analysis were used, although adapted here to the task of evaluation of a complex, computer-supported cooperative work (CSCW) system that supports product lifecycle management (PLM).

Once again, the setting for the study is a unit of the United States Marine Corps, the office of the program manager, light armored vehicles (PM LAV). The PM LAV has implemented an integrated digital environment (IDE) to support the cooperative and collaborative work of both civilians and Marines in their use, maintenance and evolution of the LAV. The IDE is used by 70 PM LAV personnel as well as at Marine maintenance depots in the United States and in the field.

The PM LAV IDE includes communications (e-mail, videoconferencing), workflow, document management, project management, collaborative engineering, and performance reporting functionality. The PM LAV monitors a fleet of about 800 light armored vehicles deployed worldwide in a variety of configurations and tasked with a range of missions. The program manager is responsible for monitoring LAV health and field performance, developing enhancements to the vehicle, and directing vehicle maintenance. The IDE is designed to support this work with an integrated environment for communications and information management.

We interviewed PM LAV personnel across the organization from staff assistants to division chiefs with a range of responsibilities including engineering, logistics, and business operations. We used a semi-structured interview guide. The guide was designed to elicit scenarios and claims (DR tools) as the basic unit of analysis for the evaluation. An abbreviated version of the interview guide appears in Fig. 2.1.

---

1. **General questions: elicit roles, task goals, & setting**
   - Position, role, key tasks and priorities, collaborators, etc
2. **Questions related to current system use: scenarios & claims**
   - Describe scenarios of use with the IDE
   - How do these scenarios contribute to the PM LAV mission? (evaluative claims)
   - (follow-on questions, probes)
3. **Questions related to prospective system use**

Fig. 2.1. PM LAV IDE interview guide

The interviews were recorded, transcribed, and then coded. We were particularly interested in obtaining participant descriptions of their use scenarios and how they felt that IDE support for these scenarios contributed to their work and to the mission of the PM LAV.

Analysis of the interview transcripts yielded 43 unique scenarios. Twenty seven of these are scenarios describing actual, current use of the system, and 16 were scenarios envisioned by study participants. We identified 464 total claims in the transcripts, where claims were propositions made about the system's support for scenarios. Following the claims analysis technique, these propositions were assessed as either positive or negative. Individual scenarios were related to between 0 and 22 claims each, with a mean of 5.6. In addition, the method identified 223 claims that were disconnected from any one scenario but in general represented statements about the IDE system as a whole. After the scenarios and claims had been gathered, we went back to the PM LAV to validate our scenario-claim sets in focus groups. Results from this part of the study suggested that our scenarios and claims were relatively complete and fairly representative of PM LAV perceptions towards the system.

Discussion and Lessons Learned

The scenarios and claims we extracted from the study may be seen as a reverse engineering of the original DR. They represent in many ways the consequences of the original DR, and describe how the system is perceived by its users in use. They help explain how the system is performing and how it is perceived by users. At the same time, they serve as a blueprint for redesign of the system and, further, account for the use context that is impossible to predict at design time.

Among the interesting aggregate findings from the study was the extent to which the scenario-based technique was able to ground evaluation in situations where the system is heavily used and in situations where use is especially consequential in the daily work life of the study participants. Of the 74 discrete features of the IDE (identified by us at a relatively arbitrary level of granularity), scenario coverage identified only 19 of these as being all important or impactful to the organization's mission and priorities. This finding has important implications for requirements engineering, at least in this case, and suggests that the use of scenario-based design in the early stages of the project may have helped focus development time and money on the most important aspects of the system.

The technique was able to elicit evaluative claims spanning a range of topics including how the organization's technical infrastructure, the design of the IDE itself, psychological and social–psychological, and organizational factors were all implicated in either or both the success or failings of the system. In terms of the IDE design, for example, we identified a number of critical areas for redesign including areas where the system possessed insufficient functionality, problems with usability and ease of use, inflexible task support, performance and reliability issues, and problems with security and accessibility of the system. Because claims in each of these areas are linked to specific scenarios of use, they implicate particular system features and functionality and suggest how they can be improved through future development efforts.

One area where the evaluation technique failed was in helping to identify the contributions gained from implementation of the IDE within the organization. Costs of systems such as this are relatively easy to measure; just sum the invoices from the development contractors and system integrators (though this of course does not account for the true lifecycle costs of these systems). Effective techniques to measure the benefits of distributed, collaborative systems, however, remain elusive. One of the chief aims of the method as described here was to link perceptions of system benefits, in the form of claims, to the specific scenarios supported by the IDE. Of the 212 claims we identified as relating to the system's contributions, only 6% were truly measurable benefits, with 26% being what we classified as tangible but immeasurable benefits, and 68% intangible.

2.5 Challenges and Opportunities for Design Rationale as Explanation

A number of challenges and research opportunities emerge from consideration of the findings from these three studies. Results from the Venture-Query case study highlight the difficulties associated with capturing complete DR when design activities occur not only in formal meetings, but also in informal and individual forums. If completeness is a critical attribute of the DR for a system, such as when it is used to provide an explanatory knowledge base, then design knowledge capture is one of the most pressing challenges for research. Design is a ubiquitous activity and can happen as often in the mind of a single individual riding on the train as it does in more formal contexts where it is amenable to capture. The challenge of pervasive design capture raises many questions to occupy researchers.

Our experience on the VentureQuery project also suggests that adoption of a DR process, in addition to notations and supporting tools, may help ensure capture of a more complete design knowledge base. Process prescriptions for experienced designers are, however, notoriously difficult to enforce as they are seen as disempowering these creative individuals. Explorations into better ways of integrating DR techniques into the day-to-day work of designers may help ease this problem, as might better tool support for DR capture.

Our work with the Marine Corps on antiterrorism planning decision models and tools has suggested a role for DR, in the form of scenarios, claims, and related systems artifacts, as a vehicle to facilitate transfer of technology between organizations. This work is ongoing and our results are tentative but experiences with antiterrorism planners in the field suggests the potential utility of DR, in the form of scenarios and claims analyses, as explanatory transfer packages to help prospective system adopters evaluate new technologies. Questions have already emerged about the form such a package should take, and the kinds of DR that are most useful for technology adopters in different roles and contexts.

Our work with the Marine Corps PM LAV on complex, distributed system evaluation suggests that there may be valuable linkages to be developed between evaluation techniques and tools and those used for DR. Developing techniques to relate DR to evaluation, then forward to redesign and subsequent evaluation in a cycle of learning and artifact improvement may be one way to achieve a truly progressive systems design science. Still under-researched are the downstream consequences of design decisions made when a system is still an abstract model as unrealized in working software. Repositories of DR that provide a longitudinal view of design deliberations and their consequences may help us better understand the effectiveness of the different design methodologies and tools created to support the systems design process.

It is not expected that the cases presented here and the lessons learned from their analysis will apply to all settings in which DR and design capture are attempted. In particular, situations less contrived than the 'zoo' study reported in the first case, and less structured and formal than in the second and third, may exhibit very different characteristics and outcomes. Still, empirical studies of DR are lacking and it is hoped that these cases can contribute to the evolving base of experiences with DR in both controlled and field settings.

2.6 Conclusion

This chapter has described three cases of design rationale in use as explanations. The theory motivating this work is that access to DR by an expanded group of project stakeholders, to include end users, may have the potential to significantly increase the comprehensibility of systems tools. This potential may be greatest for users of sophisticated software applications in complex domains, especially those users who require or desire a deeper understanding of the contextual factors that guide and constrain the design process. DR techniques and tools may have the added benefit of facilitating a kind of *virtual participatory design* in which users are able to provide meaningful input to the evolution of their systems. For design rationale to make sense may depend on showing how the costs of capture can be recovered through new and innovative uses of these design knowledge stores. Focusing on DR as a means to facilitate explanation and other communication between development project stakeholders may represent one way to expose this value proposition.

Acknowledgments. This work was supported by the United States Marine Corps through the Marine Corps Research University. The chapter was substantially improved by three anonymous reviewers who commented on an earlier draft.

References

[1] Bar-Yam, Y (1997) Dynamics of complex systems, Addison-Wesley, Reading, MA

[2] Bowker G, Leigh-Star S (1994) Knowledge and infrastructure in international information management: Problems of classification and coding. In: Bud-Frierman L (ed) Information Acumen: The Understanding and Use of Knowledge in Modern Business, Routledge, London, pp. 187–216

[3] Brooks, FP (1987) No silver bullet: Essence and accidents of software engineering. IEEE Computer, 20(4): 10–19

[4] Buchanan, BG, Shortliffe, EH (1984) Rule-based expert systems: the MYCIN experiments of the Stanford Heuristic Programming Project. Addison-Wesley, Reading, MA

[5] Buckingham Shum S, MacLean A, Bellotti V, Hammond N (1997) Graphical argumentation and design cognition. Hum.–Comput. Interact., 12(3): 267–300

[6] Carlile PR (2002) A pragmatic view of knowledge and boundaries: Boundary objects in new product development. Org Science, 13(4): 442–455

[7] Carroll, JM (1995) Scenario-based design: Envisioning Work and Technology in System Development, Wiley, New York

[8] Carroll, JM (2000) Making Use: Scenario-Based Design of Human–Computer Interactions, MIT Press, Cambridge, MA

[9] Carroll, JM, Rosson MB (1992) Getting around the task-artifact cycle: How to make claims and design by scenario. ACM Trans. Inform. Sys., 10(2): 181–212

[10] Clancey WJ (1983) The epistemology of a rule-based expert system – A framework for explanation. Artificial Intelligence, 20: 215–251

[11] Clancey WJ (1987) Knowledge-Based Tutoring: The GUIDON Program, MIT Press, Cambridge, MA

[12] Dutoit, AH, McCall R, Mistrik I, Paech B (2006) Rationale Management in Software Engineering. In: Dutoit AH, McCall R, Mistrik I, Paech B (eds.) Rationale Management in Software Engineering, Springer, Berlin Heidelberg New York

[13] Graesser AC, Person N, Huber J (1992) Mechanisms that Generate Questions. In: Lauer TW, Peacock E, Graesser AC (eds.) Questions and Information Systems, Lawrence Erlbaum, Hillsdale, NJ, pp. 167–187

[14] Gruber T (1991) Learning why by being told what. IEEE Expert, 6(4): 65–74

[15] Gruber TR, Russell, DM (1996) Generative design rationale: Beyond the record and relay paradigm. In: Moran TP, Carroll JM (eds.) Design Rationale: Concepts, Techniques and Use. Lawrence Erlbaum, Mahwah, NJ, pp. 21–51

[16] Haynes SR (2000) Explanation in information systems: Can philosophy help? Paper presented at The Eighth European Conference on Information Systems (ECIS), July 3–5, 2000, Vienna, Austria

[17] MacLean A, Young RM, Bellotti VME, Moran, T (1996) Questions, Options, and Criteria: Elements of Design Space Analysis. In Moran TP, Carroll JM (eds) Design Rationale: Concepts, Techniques and Use, Lawrence Erlbaum, Mahwah, NJ, pp. 21–51

[18] MacLean A, McKerlie, D (1995) Design Space Analysis and Use-Representations. In: Carroll JM (ed.) Scenario-Based Design: Envisioning Work and Technology in System Development, Wiley, New York

[19] Mirel B (1998) Minimalism for complex tasks. In: Carroll JM (ed.) Minimalism beyond the Nurnberg Funnel, MIT Press, Cambridge, MA, pp. 179–218

[20] Moran TP, Carroll JM (1996) Design Rationale: Concepts, Techniques, and Use. Lawrence Erlbaum, Mahwah, NJ

[21] Norman DA (1986) Cognitive Engineering. In: Norman DA, Draper SW (eds) User Centered System Design: New Perspectives on Human–Computer Interaction. Lawrence Erlbaum, Hillsdale, NJ, pp. 31–61

[22] Polson PG, Lewis C, Rieman J, Wharton C (1992) Cognitive walkthroughs: A method for theory-based evaluation of user interfaces. Int. J. Man–Mach. Stud., 36: 741–773

[23] Schön DA (1983) The reflective practitioner: how professionals think in action. Basic Books, New York

[24] Shipman, FM, McCall, RJ (1996) Integrating Different Perspectives on Design Rationale: Supporting the Emergence of Design Rationale from Design Communication (PDF CSDL 96-001). College Station, TX: Center for the Study of Digital Libraries, Texas A&M University

[25] Star SL (1989) The Structure of Ill-Structured Solutions: Heterogeneous Problem-Solving, Boundary Objects and Distributed Artificial Intelligence. In: M. Huhns M, Gasser L (eds.) Distributed Artificial Intelligence, Vol. 2, Morgan Kauffmann, Menlo Park CA, pp. 37–54

[26] Swartout W, Paris C, Moore J (1991) Design for explainable expert systems. IEEE Expert (June): 58–64

[27] Swartout WR (1983) XPLAIN: A system for creating and explaining expert consulting programs. Artif. Intell., 21: 285–325

[28] Winograd T (1995) Forward. In: Newman WM, Lamming MG (eds.) Interactive System Design. Addison-Wesley, Reading, MA
[29] Ye Y, Fischer G (2002) Information Delivery in Support of Learning
Reusable Software Components on Demand. Paper presented at the International Conference on Intelligent User Interface (IUI), January 13–16,
2002

3 Effective Design Rationale: Understanding the Barriers

J. Horner, M.E. Atwood

Abstract: One goal of design rationale systems is to support designers by providing a means to record and communicate the argumentation and reasoning behind the design process. However, there are several inherent limitations to developing systems that effectively capture and utilize design rationale. The dynamic and contextual nature of design and our inability to exhaustively analyze all possible design issues results in cognitive, capture, retrieval, and usage limitations. In this chapter, we analyze these issues in terms of current perspectives in design theory, and describe the implications to design research. We discuss the barriers to effective design rationale in terms of three major goals: reflection, communication, and analysis of design processes. We then suggest alternate means to achieve these goals that can be used with or instead of design rationale systems.

Keywords: design rationale, design theory, information retrieval

3.1 Introduction

Design is a goal-oriented process aimed at solving problems, meeting needs, improving situations, or creating something new or useful [8]. Design rationale (DR) is the reasoning and argumentation that underlies the activities that take place during the design process. DR tools are intended to support various design activities. In upstream design activities, where vague requirements are translated into concrete system specifications, DR schemas can provide a framework with which one can carefully reflect upon design decisions. Structuring design arguments also provides a mechanism by which people with different goals can communicate their positions on design issues. People involved in maintenance or redesign activities can use the documentation produced to avoid spending time reconsidering decisions that have been previously considered. This record can also be an aid in building a cumulative base of design knowledge, which would be a useful learning tool to both students of design and practicing designers [25]. DR systems are primarily intended to support communication, reflection, and analysis in design. DR systems provide support at various phases of design, including conceptual design, detail design, implementation, and maintenance. And, DR is used in a variety of design domains. In some situations, DR is the appropriate tool for the task;

however, it may not be in other situations. In this chapter, we will discuss many of the challenges that have impeded the ability for DR to effectively support designers.

3.2 Design Perspectives and Rationale

DR systems are intended to support people in the design process by allowing designers to share, structure, and record their thought processes that drive the tangible actions of design. In order to understand how DR can aid in the design process, it is important to understand current perspectives in design theory. There is no universally accepted definition of design within the broader design community [2] so the following paragraphs will briefly describe some of the diverse views.

3.2.1 Symbolic Information Processing

Simon [26] viewed design as symbolic information processing and humans as goal-oriented information processors. He argues that design involves devising courses of action aimed at changing current situations into preferred ones. This broad view of design includes, as Simon states, "the core of all professional training." Design is viewed as a process of generating and navigating through a state-space. He argues that people do not, and cannot, consider all possible conditions, alternatives, and constraints, and therefore cannot design an optimal course of action. This cognitive limitation he termed *bounded rationality* [26]. Rather than exhaustively considering design issues, people choose satisfactory solutions based on the information available.

The argumentation structure of DR is argued to provide a natural framework in which designers can reflect on decisions. This structure can help focus the search for design alternatives, making cognitive processing more effective. Although designers cannot consider all possible alternatives, if rationale is recorded, maintainers will better be able to identify which ideas were deliberated upon. Reviewers who are working on different projects may identify important issues that they would not have otherwise considered. And, students and researchers could assess the impact of design decisions based on the outcome of a design project.

However, it is often impossible to identify causal relationships in design because of the subtle factors that can influence the effectiveness of design projects. Recording DR creates the opportunity for people to perform a post hoc analysis of design decisions. Designers are constrained by the amount of information they can process. Because of this, they may be hesitant to record decisions that could later be scrutinized by people with more information at their disposal.

3.2.2 Wicked Problems

Rittel and Weber [21] dissented from Simon's notion that design could be represented as a state-space, stating that planning problems are "wicked problems." They list several reasons why planning problems are wicked problems, including the lack of a definitive formulation, stopping rules, or definitive measures of success. They also argue that each problem is essentially unique in certain aspects, and state there is not an *enumerable* set of potential solutions. Moreover, discrepancies in wicked problems can be explained in many ways, and the choice of explanation determines the nature of the resolution. In other words, different people will look at a single problem in different ways, and the way the problem is represented determines how the solution will be derived. For this reason, design can be viewed as an argumentative process aimed at coming to collective understanding of how to explain a problem.

Issue-based information system (IBIS) was developed by Rittel as a means to structure this argumentation. In this sense, DR is intended to support collaborative design that involves designers with differing goals and perspectives. The structure afforded by DR provides a mechanism for designers to communicate their diverse thoughts with other designers working on the same task.

The primary benefit of DR from this perspective is that it can act as a collaborative communication tool. In fact, the unique nature of planning problems would present a potential barrier to the reuse of DR by students of designers and persons working on other projects. Still, the DR record could be used as a communication tool between initial designers and later designers or maintainers, who may have different views than the initial designers.

3.2.3 Situated Action

Schön [22] describes design as a reflective conversation with the environment, and suggests that designers reflect on what they are doing in the *action present*. The action present is a term used to describe a time when the effects of an action can still be influenced. This *reflection-in-action* allows people to design based on the feedback that is received during the design situation.

Schön notes that designers are most inclined to reflect on their activities when they receive unexpected feedback from the environment. Designers in familiar situations may not see a need to capture their rationale as they are routinely going though their design process, especially if it interrupts the efficiency of the process. During these breakdowns, DR can help designers reflect on what may have resulted in the problem. Tracking the associated DR would help to communicate issues to future designers who may run into a similar problem. However, the designer's cognitive energy will be focused on understanding the situation and resolving the problems when these breakdowns occur. It is therefore important that if DR is used to support reflection, the efforts in recording these aspects are minimal.

Incremental formalization [24] is the process of gradually translating informal rationale into formal notations. Incremental formalization allows designers to easily capture DR in the act of designing and later come back and formalize the information into a DR schema. Incremental formalization allows designers to both reflect in the act of designing and also communicate their rationale.

Systems that support a more efficient design process by making solutions easily apparent could reduce the amount of reflection involved in the design process. Therefore, it is useful to consider whether DR systems should support efficient identification of solutions or reflective understanding of the problem.

3.2.4 Patterns

Alexander [1] describes the utility of patterns in design, which can be thought of as common solutions that resolve conflicting tendencies. He describes successful patterns in the architectural and city planning domains as "timeless" solutions that resolve the forces in a given area.

Designers may not be satisfied to trust that a given solution will work in a context without understanding the underlying reasons. And, recognizing why a pattern successfully resolves conflicting forces in a given environment can help give early insight into the success or failure of a solution.

However, Alexander argues that patterns depend on stability, not purpose (p. 119). He argues this point by comparing the streets in Greek villages to cafés in Los Angeles. In Greek villages there are whitewashes outside every house to allow people to set up chairs and contribute to the street life, while the cafés in Los Angeles are indoors away from the sidewalk so the food does not get contaminated. Alexander argues that while both of these patterns have purpose, only the Greek villages are *alive* and self-sustaining. Villagers keep the whitewashes clean "because it is deeply connected to their own experience" (p. 120). The Los Angeles cafés are not *alive* because the pattern is forced by law. The pattern will change when the law is changed because people want to be outdoors on a spring day. Alexander's point is that the purpose of a solution is not as important is its stability because solutions that do not naturally resolve the conflicts will eventually fail.

This suggests that applying design patterns requires both a thorough understanding of the context and a set of "timeless" solutions that work in these contexts. In the architectural domain, it is possible to look back thousands of years and identify patterns that seem to fit into a given context. However, in software engineering, solutions have typically only been around for a few decades. And, because of the rapidly changing advances in technology, there are few solutions that can be considered stable.

3.2.5 Implications

A brief analysis of these diverse perspectives on design helps to clarify the theoretical underpinnings of potential DR benefits, and also illuminate several potential barriers that impede the effective utilization of rationale. Table 3.1 summarizes the benefits and barriers to using DR that can be inferred from each of the four previously described design perspectives.

Table 3.1. Theoretical implications

theory	positive implications	potential barriers
symbolic information processing	DR can focus cognitive energy and provide reviewers an opportunity to view what considerations were given the most attention.	additional issues increase the complexity of a design problem, and, DR allows for a post-hoc analysis of decisions by people with more information than initial designer
wicked problems	DR Structure support integration of issues by people with different perspectives.	wicked nature of planning problems present barriers to using DR at a different time or in a different project
situated action	DR can help designers reflect on what decisions contributed to a breakdown. And, Incremental formalization could support the goals of both reflection-in-action and communication	using DR to identify solutions could result in less reflection. And, intrusive DR capture can hinder reflection on problems as they arise
patterns	DR provides a mechanism for designers to understand the problem context.	because of the rapid advances in software engineering, there are few stable design patterns.

3.3 The Fundamental Barriers

DR systems are intended to help support reflection, communication, and analysis. However, there are numerous barriers that hinder the effective use of DR for these purposes. In this chapter, we classify these barriers into four categories:

- Cognitive limitations
- Capture limitations
- Retrieval limitations
- Usage limitations

3.3.1 Cognitive Limitations

People have a limited capacity to process information. This limitation can hinder the effectiveness of DR. Simon [26] states that our rationality is bounded and we cannot consider all possible alternatives. Therefore, people choose satisfactory rather than optimal solutions. Since we are bounded by the amount of information we can process, DR is necessarily incomplete.

What Was not Considered

It is important to recognize the potential for unintended consequences, especially in systems where the risks are high [27]. In these situations, designers may want to ensure that they have exhaustively covered the design space so as to minimize the risk for unanticipated effects. The key question in this type of query is "what are we missing?" DR is a potential solution to help designers identify issues that they may have otherwise left unconsidered. Systems could allow designers to search for similar projects or issues to identify issues that were considered in those projects.

In order to use DR to identify what is missing, there must be a mechanism to relate projects to other projects that are most similar. It is also important that there is a large enough base of rationale to ensure that there will be enough comparable design projects. And, it is necessary to represent the information so that the most pertinent missing information is easily identifiable.

Added Complexity

One mechanism to more exhaustively analyze the design space is to use collaboration in the design process [6]. However, in any collaborative design context, maintaining conceptual integrity is important to keep the design project focused [4]. More people are capable of considering more ideas, but this adds complexity and effort in keeping persons on the design team up to speed. It also increases the effort of integrating diverse perspectives.

Simon [26] also notes that we are unable to exhaustively consider all possible alternatives, so we choose options that are satisfactory. Even if DR can effectively elicit additional issues, designers will not be able to spend more time reflecting on each issue. Therefore, it is important that DR be used to help designers think about the right issues. In situations where there are different viewpoints as to which of several alternative solutions should be used, reflecting on the *why* aspects of design can help identify better solutions. However, in situations where solution ideas are still being formulated, it may be better be spend time thinking about what options are possible rather than why each option is appropriate.

Groupthink

One goal of DR is to support collaboration among designers. A problem with collaborative design is that when poor processes are followed, teams may quickly arrive at a poor solution and focus the rest of their energy on relatively insignificant issues. Janis [13] termed this phenomenon *groupthink*, and noted that highly cohesive teams working on complex designs under strict deadlines where it is important to arrive at a solution are most at risk to undergo this detrimental phenomenon.

If designers used DR to explicitly structure their conversation around the issues that are most important to decision-making, they would be less likely to make poor decisions. However, a tool alone will not necessarily result in better design processes. If DR tools are used to support reflection, how the tool can be used to support good design processes should be emphasized. It is important that tools support and enhance good work practices, but should not be expected to change poor practices.

3.3.2 Capture Limitations

There are two different situations in which DR may not be captured. In one case, the omission is unintentional. In the other, it is quite intentional. We consider both.

Capturing Rationale in Context

DR may be considered, but unintentionally not recorded by the capture process. There are several reasons why considerations could be unintentionally omitted from DR. If the DR capture takes place outside of the design process, it is possible that contextual cues may not be present, and designers may not recall what they deliberated upon, or designers may not be available at the time the rationale is captured.

For these reasons, it would appear that rationale should be captured in the context of design. However, it is not always possible or advantageous to capture rationale in the design context. Grudin [11] notes that in certain development environments, exploring design space can be detrimental because it diverts critical resources. Additionally, many design decisions are considered in informal situations, where capturing the rationale is infeasible [23]. Tracking the location of where the rationale was recorded, the persons present at the time of DR capture, their roles and expertise, and the environmental context of the capture can help reviewers infer why specific information was considered.

Tacit Knowledge

Tacit knowledge [20] is a term used to describe things that we know, but are not able to bring to consciousness. It is possible that DR may unintentionally be omitted because a designer may not be able to explicate their tacit knowledge. Designers may not be able or willing to spend the energy to articulate their thoughts into the DR system, especially when they reach breakdowns and are focusing on understanding and resolving the problem at hand. Conklin and Burgess-Yakemovic [6] state that designers focus should be on solving problems and not on capturing their decisions. During routine situations, designers react to problems as they arise without consciously thinking about them. Collaborative design can aid in eliciting tacit knowledge through the articulation of reasoning to others in the design. However, this elicitation is necessarily costly to the designers, and will only bring out ideas that are pertinent to the current design problem, which is not necessarily what someone reviewing the rationale will need.

Representation

DR may also be omitted because of inappropriate representations. Rationale capture tools can involve varying degrees of human involvement, but regardless of the technique, the type of information captured is dependent on the representation of the rationale. Lee and Lai [15] argue that design rationale inadequately captures domain expressiveness, resulting in people not being able to get the information they need out of DR. The Questions, Options, and Criteria notation was suggested by MacLean et al. [17] and was argued to better fit the natural discussions of design. Others have argued that DR should be focused around concrete problems to make deliberations more tangible [15].

More comprehensive representations allow for more rationale to be captured, but the added effort to capture the rationale can shift the cognitive effort from the design process. More flexible notations, such as free text, are more difficult to index and utilize. Less intrusive techniques, such as capturing rationale during meetings, can ease problems associated with interrupting the design process. But, these techniques are likely to capture lesser amounts of rationale because designers may not be present at these meetings or contextual clues may not be present.

Communication Through Omission

There are also situations where the designers may communicate information through omission. For example, a manager may ask anyone on the design team with experience in a particular programming language to contact her or him. In this situation, certain employees will communicate their inexperience with the programming language by not responding. However, it is entirely possible that certain individuals did not respond because of other reasons. People may also communicate their reasoning through silence when they disagree with a particular viewpoint, but do not want to appear confrontational. DR systems do not adequately capture this information. It may be useful to link rationale with the generating designer and method of capture.

Incentive

There are situations where designers feel it is advantageous not to record their rationale. Design environments are constrained by time, costs, and changing personnel [23]. Designers who are constrained by time will need to prioritize which deliberated upon information to articulate. Often design deliberations under strict deadlines only discuss specific matters that are viewed by the designer as highly significant at the time.

Sharing knowledge can be detrimental to designers, especially if the information they share could potentially be used against them. Designers may be hesitant to simply give away knowledge without knowing who will use it or how it will be used. Rewarding knowledge sharing is a challenging task that involves creating tangible rewards for intangible ideas. This is especially difficult considering that there is often no way to evaluate which ideas resulted in the success or failure of an artifact.

Moreover, the time spent exhaustively searching design space and recording DR may cause designers to miss windows of opportunity [11]. It is therefore important to lessen the cost to designers in capturing rationale. However, removing the cost of DR capture is not always possible. And, reducing the costs to designers often displaces it to the reviewers who then may not be able to utilize the rationale because it is incomplete or inaccurate.

Cost and Benefit

Complex design is normally a group activity, and tools to support designers can therefore be considered a type of groupware. Grudin [10] describes several problems involved in developing groupware. Specifically, one of the obstacles he discusses is of particular interest to DR systems. He contends that there should not be a disparity between who incurs the cost and who receives the benefit. If the focus of DR is placed only on minimizing the cost to designers, it can add significant costs to the reviewers. A major shortcoming in DR is the failure to minimize the cost to reviewers. Gruber and Russell [9] contend that DR must go beyond the record and replay paradigm, and collect data that can benefit reviewers, while also not being a burden on designers. But, it is also important that DR provide a net benefit to the design process. And, capturing incomplete rationale can harm the design process if reviewers make inaccurate inferences based on the rationale.

Privacy and Security

In certain contexts, there are privacy and security concerns with the DR. For instance, organizations may want to keep their rationale secure so that competing organizations cannot gain a competitive advantage. Similarly, there may be political repercussions or security breaches if policy makers make their rationale available to the public. For example, designers may not want to document all of their considerations because politically motivated information could be held against them. There are also situations where people working outside the specified work procedures may not want to document their work-arounds in fear that it will be detrimental to them. Designers may not want to capture rationale that could be viewed as detrimental to themselves or certain other people, and therefore will intentionally omit certain rationale. Additionally, individual designers may not want their design considerations to be available for post hoc scrutiny.

Therefore, it is important to give designers a sense of security, and implement privacy and security features into rationale tools.

3.3.3 Retrieval Limitations

Karsenty [14] evaluated design documents and found that DR questions were by far the most frequent questions during design evaluation meetings. However, only 41% of the DR questions were answered by the DR documentation. The reasoning for the discrepancy between the needed and captured DR is broken into several high level explanations, including analysts not capturing questions, options, or criteria, the inadequacy of the DR method, and the lack of understanding. Other literature has focused on several issues that contribute to this failure, including inappropriate representations [15, 17] the added workload required of designers [6, 12] exigent organizational constraints [23] and contextual differences between the design environment at the time when the rationale is captured and the time when it is needed [9].

Relevance

Initial designers and subsequent users of rationale may have different notions of what is relevant in a given design context. Wilson [29] describes relevance as a relationship between a user and a piece of information, and as independent of truth. Relevance is based on a user's situational under-standing of a concern. Moreover, he argues that situational relevance is an inherently indeterminate notion because of the changing, unsettled, and undecided character of our concerns. This suggests that the rationale constructed at design time may not be relevant to those reviewing the rationale at a later time in a different context. When rationale is exhaustively captured, there is an additional effort required to capture the information. And, when too little information is captured, the reviewers' questions remain unanswered.

Belkin [3] describes information retrieval as a type of communication whereby a user is investigating their state of knowledge with respect to a problem. Belkin contends that the success of the communication is dependent upon the extent to which the anomaly can be resolved based on the information provided, and thus is controlled by the recipient. This suggests that designers cannot recognize the relevance of rationale until a person queries it. And, reviewers may not be able to specify what informa-tion will be most useful, but rather will only recognize that they do not have the necessary knowledge to resolve a problem.

Indexing

A more structured representation can make it more difficult to capture design ideas, but can facilitate indexing and retrieval. One problem is that there is an inherent tradeoff between representational flexibility and ease of retrieval. Unstructured text is easier to record, but more difficult to structure in a database. One solution is to push the burden on to those who are receiving the benefit [10] which would be the retrievers in this case. However, if the potential users of the rationale find the system to be too effortful, it will go unused. Then, designers will not be inclined to spend time entering DR into a system that will not be used.

3.3.4   Usage Limitations

People reviewing DR have a goal and a task at hand which they hope the DR will support. Often, these people are also involved in designing, or resolving ill-defined problems. If this is the case, the reviewers may not know whether retrieved rationale is applicable to their current problem.

Uniqueness

Because design problems are unique, even rationale that successfully resolved one design problem may not be applicable to a different problem. In addition to the problem of accurately and exhaustively capturing rationale, recognizing the impact of rationale can be a difficult task.

Understanding rationale tied to one problem could help resolve similar problems in the future. However, design is contextual, and external factors often interact with multiple subproblems. Therefore, designers must consider the holistic affects of external factors. Reviewers of rationale are interested in understanding information to help them with their task-at-hand, and without understanding the context of those problems, utilization of the information becomes difficult. The inherent problem of identifying the impact of rationale across different design problems adds a net cost to utilizing rationale, decreasing the overall utility in the design process. These costs should be evaluated against the overall payoff of using the rationale.

Measuring Effectiveness

Norman [19] states that systems need to bridge the gulf of evaluation. The gulf of evaluation refers to the effort involved in identifying how well the expectations of a system have been met. Bridging the gulf of evaluation involves giving users feedback on whether their actions have moved them closer to achieving their goal. One problem with DR systems is that there is no absolute measure of effectiveness. A DR system can give users feedback to indicate that the information was stored, but this does not necessarily mean that the system was effective. An inherent problem in using DR to support temporally distributed designers is that the designers will not immediately know what rationale will be most useful. Because of the complex nature of design, it may never be possible to evaluate the impact of rationale.

3.4 Transcending the Barriers

We note that there are three primary goals of DR systems, which are reflection, communication, and analysis. The previously described cognitive, capture, retrieval, and usage limitations do not equally impact each goal. The impact of each barrier is influenced by many factors, including the goal of the system and the social system in which the system is used.

3.4.1 Reflection

Reflection is a goal of many DR systems, and supporting this goal involves transcending the barriers associated with communicating ideas while in the act of designing, using overly restrictive frameworks to structure thinking, and prioritizing what to reflect upon.

DR provides a framework that can be used to reflect upon the design process or resulting artifact. But DR can also distract from design activities if the emphasis of DR is on recording for other people, rather than supporting the current design activities. The problem with using DR as both a reflective tool and a communication tool is that these goals tend to conflict at times, especially if there is significant effort needed in the communication. In these cases, DR can distract from reflection. To move beyond these barriers, it is important that DR systems facilitate communication with little effort during the design process. DR systems should focus on supporting one primary goal. If the goal of a DR system is to support reflection, features that are used for documenting the rationale should be either eliminated or extremely nonintrusive.

Brown and Duguid [5] note caused context, background, history, common knowledge, and social resources to be ignored when envisioning solutions to problems. They note that "attending too closely to information overlooks the social context that helps people understand what that information might mean and why it matters" (p. 5). And, viewing problems in a less restricted view can offer "alternatives, breadth of vision, and choices" (p. 1).

Using DR schemas that are focused on specific aspects of arguments may overly focus thoughts on aspects that may not be the most vital to design deliberations. It is therefore important to prioritize what items to reflect upon. Sometimes it is more important to think about the *what, where, who,* or *when* aspects of design rather than the why [13, 31]. In these cases, it may be more appropriate to reflect on usage scenarios, design patterns, or project management constraints. Research into how to integrate DR with other reflective activities would help make DR systems more useful.

3.4.2 Communication

As a communication tool, DR systems provide both structure and availability. The degree of structure refers to the variation flexibility that a system allows. And, the availability refers to how many people have access to communications. DR systems range from requiring specific fields of information to be completed (e.g. questions, criteria, etc.) to having designers record their deliberations in free-form notation. In any case, the structure provides a framework within which designers can effectively focus their communication. Fischer [7] argues that much of the design work is done through evolutionary redesign, and long-term collaboration is essential. Long-term collaboration requires designers at one time to communicate with designer at another time. Written notes, letters, diagrams, photographs, electronic mail, and databases all record information that can later be reviewed. In Sect. 3.4.3, we will differentiate various modes of communication and suggest which may be appropriate in different situations.

Alternate Means of Communication

Communication can be classified based on its levels of structure and availability. Some communications are stored for extended periods of time and can be reviewed by anyone. Other communications take place informally between a limited number of people.

Informal conversations between designers occur through telephone calls, face-to-face conversations, before and after meetings, and through instant messaging tools. These communications are useful for designers because they can share ideas and gather feedback about what others think about the reasoning behind design decisions, while still having a certain degree of privacy and security.

These informal communications can also be captured for later review by integrating DR tools into web browsers, e-mail clients, phone systems, instant messaging tools, and meeting support tools. Communications can also be structured, yet remain unrecorded. Meetings may be following formal processes, and brainstorming strategies structure processes for identifying a wide range of alternatives.

Social communities offer another form of availability. Designers can share ideas within a social community, where other designers can freely share that information. Social communities in software engineering are composed of both Communities of Practice (CoP) and Communities of Interest (CoI) [28]. Communities of interest are heterogeneous social groups with different backgrounds and work activities all collaborating on a single problem. Fischer [7] notes that CoP more often deal with problems where the answers are known, and CoI are associated with ill-defined problems where there is no one right answer.

Muller and Carey [18] note that one difficulty in supporting designers through CoP is that designers are often the sole practitioners of their discipline within a multifunctional team. When designers are acting as sole practitioners, social communities may not be the appropriate outlet to make informal communications available.

Choosing a Mode of Communication

There are a number of factors that influence the amount of structure that should be used in communication.

When the primary goal of a DR system is to support reflection, using nonintrusive systems is more appropriate. And, it may not be advantageous to track preliminary and noncritical decisions that take place in design processes, even when the goal is to support temporal communication.

Structured communications may be useful for focusing arguments among designers with different goals. However, when privacy, security, or the risks of misinterpretation are important, steps should be taken to make the rationale less available. In these cases, it may be appropriate for DR systems to support multiple types of communication, whereby designers can choose what information to make available. Similarly, supporting both informal and formal representations of rationale are useful when structuring rationale could hinder the design process [24].

When the reason for structuring DR is to support later analysis, the information should be structured based on the analysts' needs. When the structuring is intended to provide a framework for communication, it is important to identify a structure that will best focus the communication.

3.4.3 Analysis

When DR is captured and structured, it can be utilized by those outside the design context to analyze artifacts and the influence of the decisions made in the process of designing the artifact. Effective use of DR as an analysis tool requires an accurate depiction of the design process.

Causal analysis in design is difficult, if not impossible, due to the wicked nature of design problems. The same process can lead to different results in different environments. Because of the complexity of design processes, the influence of decisions can never be completely known. DR can be used to identify factors that *could* have led to failures or successes; however, because of the complex nature of design, it is possible that the decisions may not have been very influential.

Therefore, any analysis of design processes should not place a heavy emphasis on the influence of the captured decisions. It is possible that the effects were caused by other factors. This barrier can be diminished by using additional tools and methods when analyzing design processes. DR is only one tool for analyzing design processes and artifacts and only shows a small part of the total activity. Other methods, such as ethnography, interviews, and quantitative analyses of a project's cost and measures of success can be used in conjunction to gain a fuller picture of the design process.

3.5 Conclusions

In this paper, we have looked at a number of barriers that impede DR as an effective tool for reflection, communication, and analysis. The barriers were discussed in terms of cognitive, capture, retrieval, and usage limitations. It is possible that the rationale was not considered, it was considered but either intentionally or unintentionally unrecorded, it could be recorded but not retrieved or it could be retrieved but not effectively applied.

One intent of DR is to transmit information from a designer working at one time and in one context to another designer working at another time and context; and, a second intent is to facilitate communication among designers working at the same time. The goal of research on DR is to improve the quality of designs. There are fundamental barriers to developing computer systems that support communication among designers working on design problems. Therefore, the focus of DR should be on identifying what tools are most appropriate for the task. Using less persistent modes of communication, putting a greater emphasis on supporting design processes rather than design tools, and creating systems that are optimized for a single purpose are necessary steps for improving design.

References

[1] Alexander C (1979) The Timeless Way of Building. Oxford University Press, Oxford

[2] Atwood ME, McCain KW, Williams JC (2002) How does the design community think about design? In: Symposium on Designing Interactive Systems, pp. 125–132

[3] Belkin N (1980) Anomalous states of knowledge as a basis for information retrieval. Can. J. Inform. Sci., 5: 133–143

[4] Brooks FP (1995) The Mythical Man–Month: Essays on Software Engineering. Addison-Wesley, Reading, MA

[5] Brown J, Duguid P (2000) The Social Life of Information. Harvard Business School Press

[6] Conklin J, Burgess-Yakemovic KC (1991) A process-oriented approach to design rationale. Hum.–Comput. Interact., 6(3–4): 357–391

[7] Fischer G. (2004) Social creativity: Turning barriers into opportunities for collaborative design. In: Proceeding from Participatory Design Conference, pp. 152–161

[8] Friedman K (2003) Theory construction in design research: criteria: approaches, and methods. Des. Stud. 24(6): 507–522

[9] Gruber T, Russell D (1996) Generative design rationale. Beyond the record and replay paradigm. In: Moran TP, Carroll JM (eds.) Design Rationale: Concepts, Techniques, and Use. Lawrence Erlbaum Associates, Mahwah NJ

[10] Grudin J (1994) Groupware and social dynamics: eight challenges for developers. Commun. ACM 37(1): 92–105

[11] Grudin J (1996) Evaluating opportunities for design capture. In: Moran TP, Carroll JM (eds.) Design Rationale: Concepts, Techniques, and Use. Erlbaum Associates, Mahwah NJ

[12] Herbsleb JD, Kuwana E (1993) Preserving knowledge in design projects: What designers need to know. In: Proceedings of Human Factors in Computing Systems, pp. 7–14

[13] Janis IL (1972) Victims of Group Think: A Psychological Study of Foreign Policy Decisions and Fiascos. Houghton-Mifflin, Boston MA

[14] Karsenty, L (1996) An empirical evaluation of design rationale documents. In: Proceedings of the SIGCHI Conference on Human Factors in Computing Systems, ACM, New York, pp. 150–156

[15] Lee J, Lai KY (1991) What's in design rationale? Human–Computer Interaction 6(3-4): 251–280

[16] Lewis C, Reiman J, Bell B (1996) Problem centered design for expressiveness and facility in a graphical programming system. In Moran TP, Carroll JM (eds.) Design Rationale: Concepts, Techniques, and Use. Lawrence Erlbaum Associates, Mahwah NJ, pp. 147–183

[17] MacLean A, Young RM, Bellotti VME, Moran TP (1991) Questions, options, and criteria: Elements of design space analysis. Hum.–Comput. Int. 6(3–4): 201–250

[18] Muller MJ, Carey K (2002) Design as a minority discipline in a software company: Towards requirements for a community of practice. In: Proceedings from CHI, ACM, New York, pp. 383–390

[19] Norman DA (1990) The Design of Everyday Things. Doubleday, New York

[20] Polanyi M (1966) The Tacit Dimension. Doubleday, New York

[21] Rittel H, Weber M (1984) Planning problems are wicked problems. In: Cross N (ed.), Developments in Design Methodology, Chichester. Wiley, New York, pp. 135–144

[22] Schön DA (1987) Educating the reflective practitioner: toward a new design for teaching and learning in the professions. Jossey-Bass.

[23] Sharrock W, Anderson R (1996) Synthesis organizational innovation and the articulation of design space. In: Moran TP, Carroll JM (eds.) Design rationale: Concepts, Techniques, and Use. Lawrence Erlbaum Associates, Mahwah NJ

[24] Shipman F, McCall R (1999) Incremental formalization with the hyperobject substrate, ACM Trans. Inform. Syst. 17: 199–227

[25] Buckingham Shum S, Hammond N (1994) Argumentation-based design rationale: What use at what cost? Int. J. Hum.–Comput. Stud. 40(4): 603–652

[26] Simon HA (1996) The sciences of the artificial, MIT Press, Cambridge MA

[27] Tenner E (1996) Why things bite back: technology and the revenge of unintended consequences. Vintage, New York

[28] Wenger E (2002) Cultivating communities of practice: A guide to managing knowledge. Harvard Business School Press, Cambridge MA

[29] Wilson P (1993) Situational relevance, Info Stor Retrieval, 9: 457–471

[30] Wolf C, Karat, J (1997) Capturing what is needed in multi-user system design: Observations from the design of three healthcare systems. In: Proceedings from DIS, ACM, New York, pp. 405–415

4   Rationale as a By-Product

K. Schneider

Abstract: Rationale is an asset in software engineering. Rationale is communicated during several project activities, like design or prototyping. Nevertheless, very little rationale is captured today. There seems to be an inherent tension between creating or externalizing rationale, and capturing it successfully. In this chapter, the "Rationale as a By-Product Approach" is defined through seven principles. Those principles were identified while building two applications. In both, tools were tailor-made to support capturing design rationale on the side while working on software project tasks as usual. The approach is best applied to project tasks that create or elicit a lot of rationale.

Keywords: capturing rationale, by-product, task-specific path, FOCUS

4.1 Introduction

Rationale is among the most important information a software project produces. It is important to know why a decision has been made and why one design or solution has been preferred over another. Later decisions are facilitated by knowing why earlier decisions have been made. During maintenance, documented rationale can save a large percentage of effort. Chapter 1 introduced many important aspects of when and how to use rationale.

However, capturing rationale is not straightforward. *The most productive* project phases in terms of decisions and concepts are the *least likely* to accommodate opportunities for documenting rationale. Exactly at the point in projects where most design decisions are made, documentation is often not a high priority. All available resources and time slots are devoted to the product but none is devoted to (or "wasted on") documentation or rationale.

Capturing "rationale as a by-product" takes those constraints into account. A number of principles describe the core of this approach. Selected human interactions are recorded in several modes in parallel: In addition to audio or video recording, specific "paths" are recorded and reused to index the large amount of audio/video data. A path is a time-indexed sequence of elements (e.g. code modules) visited during the human interaction. For example, the sequence of all modules explained by an expert is logged as one such path.

In Sect. 4.2, some situations are described in which rationale is built and communicated. The Rationale Paradox describes the phenomenon that usually none of the surfaced rationale gets captured where it occurs. Section 4.3 defines what is meant by the "Rationale as a By-Product Approach." There is a general definition and explanations of the principles that make up the approach. Related work is mentioned in this context. Two instantiations of the approach are introduced as examples: Sect. 4.4 addresses software prototypes, and Sect. 4.5 is devoted to risk management. The approach is discussed in Sect. 4.6. Section 4.7 concludes.

4.2 Origins of Rationale in Software Projects

As described in Chapt. 1, there are many uses for rationale in software projects. But where and when do different kinds of rationale surface? Where could they be captured?

4.2.1 Rationale Occurs when Decisions are Made

Visions, requirements, and reasons for them first appear in the earliest project phase. Communication in this phase is typically based on informal meetings, slide presentations, and oral discussions. After a while, more formal requirements engineering takes over.

Design decisions are mainly discussed by technical experts and architects during the design phase. Decisions are made by groups and by individuals. They are typically communicated through overview charts, architecture sketches, and oral explanations.

Prototypes are often used to decide between design alternatives. Different kinds of prototypes were differentiated by Lichter et al. [12]. The types of information provided by those prototypes have also been analyzed [16]. Prototypes spark insights that add to the rationale for technical decisions. Demonstration prototypes elicit customer requirements and rationale.

During the entire project, *requirements* are further negotiated, prioritized, and rearranged [1]. Some of these activities will require initial design proposals or prototypes. Reducing *project risks* is a constant task in project management. Identified risks may cause design decisions. Different stakeholders may disagree on requirements or risks – probably disagreeing on deeper assumptions and rationale as well. Compromises must be found that will be accompanied by rationale. Much of the above-mentioned rationale *resides in the heads of project participants*. Rationale is seldom documented.

Documenting rationale in a systematic way has long been an issue in software engineering. The Potts and Bruns model [15] was used by Lee [11] to describe rationale. The result resembles a specific kind of "semantic web" with qualified relationships, similar to ontologies [20]. However, a sophisticated (and maybe "intrusive") representation calls for effort, time, and resources to build and to maintain. This chapter advocates a very different approach. In analogy to agile methods in software engineering [2,3], light-weight approaches to rationale capturing were studied and adopted. *Light-weight* indicates a clear priority to save time and effort *from the perspective of bearers of rationale*. This reduction of effort is afforded by sophisticated preparation and tools: tailor-made recording software is used, and masses of data are recorded just to capture some of the above-mentioned valuable rationale. The trick is to pick the right occasion and the right indexing-mechanism ("paths") for each specific activity observed.

4.2.2 The Rationale Paradox

Since rationale is so essential for project success, one would expect it to be highly regarded and captured carefully. However, that is seldom the case, as Chap. 1 states in some detail and with reference to the literature. Due to its perplexing nature, I call this observation the "Rationale Paradox":

The Rationale Paradox:
When most rationale is created, chances to capture it are lowest.

This paradox is supported by a number of observations:

- Rationale is created when key decisions are made.
- During decision-making, participants are very attentive.
- Rationale is considered important and "evident" at the time when it is created. At that time, no one can imagine how it could ever be forgotten.
- Usually, further decisions are based on earlier ones, so there is pressure to continue fast in the project. New decisions overlay old rationale.
- Csikszentmihalyi [5] talks about the *flow state* in which knowledge and experience come together easily and knowledge workers seem to "flow" through their highly demanding work. During the flow state, knowledge workers are typically not willing to switch tasks and take care of rationale.

- Schön [19] and Fischer [7] discuss how practitioners need to be interrupted in their professional activities in order to become aware of the tacit (*internalized* [14]) expertise they currently apply, including experience and rationale. However, interrupting their flow (as in [19]) might endanger motivation and will slow down work. To avoid this, the team tends to focus on "essential constructive tasks" in the project – while capturing rationale is deferred.

When the project gets into a slower phase, rationale will already be partially forgotten (see above), so there is again little motivation to document it. Most software developers prefer doing what they consider "productive work" like designing or programming over documentation. They will rather make new decisions and continue designing or implementing than capturing rationale. As a consequence, rationale is least likely to be captured when it would be easiest to grab.

4.3 Rationale as a By-Product

Chapter 1 described many situations in which rationale can be beneficial in software projects. Section 4.2 indicated different situations in which rationale is communicated within a project. In many cases, there are only talks, telephone calls, or a few sketches in which the rationale is ever being made explicit. Usually, very little rationale is captured and documented. According to the above-mentioned Rationale Paradox, this is not an accident but an inevitability.

The approach presented in this paper is a generalization from several attempts we made at two different universities and a company to face the above-mentioned challenges of capturing rationale. The two applications stated below (FOCUS and Risk Analysis) are the most advanced implementations that incorporate the idea of "Rationale as a By-Product."

4.3.1 Definition of the By-Product Approach

The term *approach* refers to a set of guiding principles for someone to follow in order to achieve a certain goal.

The *By-Product Approach* is defined by two *goals* and *seven principles:*
  Goals
    (1) Capture rationale during specific tasks within software projects
    (2) Be as little intrusive as possible to the bearer of the rational

Principles

(1) Focus on a project task in which rationale is surfacing
(2) Capture rationale during that task (not as a separate activity)
(3) Put as little extra burden as possible on the bearer of the rationale
(but maybe on other people)
(4) Focus on recording during the original activity, defer indexing,
structuring etc. to a follow-up activity carried out by others.
(5) Use a computer for recording and for capturing additional task-
specific information for structuring
(6) Analyze recordings, search for patterns
(7) Encourage, but do not insist on further rationale management

All together, the principles shift effort away (1) from the time when
project tasks are being carried out and (2) from experts and bearers of
design rationale. Therefore, it may look from their perspective like the
rationale is really "captured as a by-product of doing normal work." This is
what counts. It justifies the name "By-Product Approach".

The style of describing a "method" or "approach" by a list of interconnected principles was successfully used by Beck in his widely known
description of eXtreme Programming [2].

The principles respond to the challenges mentioned in Sects. 4.1
and 4.2. They were inferred from observations and hypotheses in the
above-mentioned attempts to capture rationale. Like in Beck's description
of eXtreme Programming, principles are not fully comprehensible by reading their titles only. In the remainder of this section, each principle will be
explained with respect to the entire approach. Neither goals nor principles
may sound extremely new or innovative. The difference is in their details
and their combination.

For the purpose of the following discussion, a *learner role* is introduced.
A learner in this context is a person who will need to use a certain kind of
rationale in the future. Without support, a learner might simply talk to the
bearer of the rationale and search additional material to read. This is a
tedious task, as experts are often busy or not available. There may be a
larger group of learners sharing similar interests and information needs.
Instead of asking the same questions again and again, capturing rationale
and keeping it persistent will assist in distributing it. Moreover, by
focusing and supporting the teaching process the By-Product Approach is
intended to pay off even with only one learner involved.

The By-Product Approach can be applied to different situations and
activities in software engineering. It helps to identify rewarding activities
and to design specific computer support. To build those software features,

substantial technological preparation is required. It reduces effort during the capturing step so that rationale seems to be captured "as a by-product."

4.3.2 Principles and Related Work

Each of the principle is now explained. Reasons for each principle are provided. By referring to related work, the principles are further clarified.

Focus on a Project Task in which Rationale Surfaces

The approach uses an existing task to capture rationale, called the "focus task". This refers to a selected task or activity that is part of the usual software process – not one inserted for the favor or rationale capturing or rationale management. Many experiences in real projects support the Rationale Paradox: during interesting project phases, even the slightest additional "task" will not be accepted. Therefore, no additional task is inserted.

Section 4.2 mentions different kinds of decisions made during different project activities. Principle 1 requires focusing on *one* such focus task in which the desired type of rationale is created or discussed. Rationale is said to *surface* when it is discussed, documented or communicated, either in phone calls, meetings, or prototype demonstrations.

In the terminology of Chap. 1, the approach is concerned with descriptive rationale, and there is a clear commitment to avoid intrusions during that selected project task. Approaches like gIBIS [4] impose argumentation structures and extra tasks on project personnel. That is carefully avoided in the By-Product Approach.

Capture Rationale During that Task

It is important to capture rationale where it surfaces. Waiting to capture it later will probably fail: Much will be forgotten, and project pressure will force people to prefer project tasks over rationale management duties.

This principle may seem to contradict the previous one: what is the difference between inserting an extra rationale task (above) and capturing rationale *during* an existing task?

An important psychological issue is the need to schedule and carry out an additional task in the first case, while in the second case there may only be a small percentage of extra effort during the existing task, with no additional time slot needed. Of course, this principle by itself does not reduce the effort of capture, it just increases acceptance. However, the next principle calls for reduction of this extra effort as the *main optimization goal* – even at the cost of sophisticated preparation and lengthy follow-up work. Once again, this may not reduce overall effort, but it does reduce effort during the rationale-prone project task.

It has been argued (see Chap. 1) that IBIS captures rationale "on the fly" [13], just capturing the history of rationale as it occurs. While the By-Product Approach is descriptive in that same respect, it puts far more emphasis on low effort.

Put as Little Extra Burden as Possible on the Bearer of the Rationale

This principle makes a clear statement about the distribution of effort within the team. It is especially important that those who are the sources of rationale be spared the extra work of capturing it. This is contrary to many rationale capturing approaches that assume the experts will have to do most of the work (several mentioned in Chap. 1).

Grudin's seminal work [9] on "who is the beneficiary and who does the work?" reminds us to design work processes with the benefits and efforts of all stakeholders in mind. Grudin claims (originally in the field of CSCW) an approach will not be successful if some people are charged with extra work, while others receive all the benefits. Projected on capturing design rationale, the bearers of rationale will see little personal benefit in sharing or even documenting what they know. It is an old lesson from knowledge management that there may be incentives beyond money to create benefit. Demonstrating to experts the appreciation for their knowledge and help has often been a valuable benefit to them [6]. During our work with the two applications described later, the bearers of rationale recognized and appreciated our obvious attempts to save them time. Nevertheless, some effort needs to be invested for capturing and structuring. As a consequence, someone else has to do it, and at a later time. This differentiates the By-Product Approach from others that attempt to distribute the effort more "equally". However, benefits and potential contributions are not distributed equally, so why should efforts be? It is a conscious decision of this approach to let those people do most of rationale management work who benefit most from a well-structured base of rationale. Those who need the rationale are the ideal people to do that job.

Of course, there is a limit to all principles. When a learner has made an attempt to organize material, there should be the option for a feedback session. The expert could meet the learner and look through the results, as long as the expert is still available. The By-Product Approach and the tools developed to support each of its instantiations will support this feedback and provide a good basis for structuring and indexing (as explained later). When there is no time or opportunity for such a session, the By-Product

Approach will try to continue without: "raw" material in the form of paths can often be used since paths follow a well-known structure of products or work-processes. It is, in fact, not so raw. Skipping feedback will decrease the learning value, but not to zero (Principle 7).

Most of the extra work load for capturing rationale is shifted away from the focus project task, and most of the remaining rationale-related duties are assigned to learners or observers rather than bearers of rationale. Here is the capturing bottleneck.

As Chap. 1 points out, many approaches have shifted from intrusive to less-intrusive variants. We consider it important to distinguish the roles and balance effort, duties, and (potential) benefit, with a clear focus on relieving experts from any extra work.

Focus on Recording Rationale First

This principle is rather concrete compared to the first three principles. It resembles more a practice than a principle in Beck's terminology [2]. It describes one contribution to fulfill the first three principles: The main rationale-related activity is supposed to be recording, but recording of many different kinds (e.g. audio, video, event traces, paths, and structures used, see example cases).

According to Principles 2 and 3, recording devices and environment need to be set-up in a nonintrusive way. Recording must either be trivial, or the recording devices should be operated by a learner (beneficiary of rationale transfer, see Principle 3).

Use a Computer for Recording and for Capturing Additional Task-Specific Information for Structuring

This principle differentiates the approach from simple recording. While audio or video recording would not necessarily require a computer, this principle demands the recordings to be computerized (at least in the end). But there is more to this principle: the more one knows about the focus task at hand, the more additional information can be recorded *on the side*. There is often an internal structure associated with a task or a discussion. For example, the table of content of a document under discussion, the agenda of a meeting, or the file structure of a software project provide hooks and opportunities to refer to.

Since we know that the focus task is related to software engineering, and due to focusing on only *one* task, typical structures can be identified and used. Assume a meeting in which requirements are discussed with a customer. At some point, participants point to a requirement in a DOORS database, at another point they execute and comment a prototype. Time-stamped paths facilitate cross-referencing between DOORS document structures, code execution traces, and oral comments by the participants. What happened at the same time may be related. Analyses built upon the combined recordings will add value beyond simple replay, but will also require substantial up-front implementation work.

Natural language understanding, or any sophisticated form of artificial intelligent, is not the purpose. Time-stamped recordings are used as time-indexed paths through the discussion space. Given structures and paths provide an additional perspective on recorded rationale (e.g., code structure or DOORS-links).

There is a lot of similarity to approaches like domain-oriented design environments [8], but this principle is less general and more specific than DODEs. By stressing path and structures typical for the focus task at hand, the principle helps the user of the approach to narrow down on an issue.

Analyze Recordings, Search for Patterns

Additional paths and structures are captured while audio or video sources are recorded. For example, simple recordings can be replayed. In the end, there are several different recordings from *one* recorded session, e.g. a sequence of DOORS requirements discussed (sequence of Req.-IDs), specification structure (requirements within table of contents), and audio recording of discussion (time-indexed stream). All those parallel recordings are related through time stamps.

It is straightforward to link all recordings together for browsing, with an option to jump from one track of the record (audio, video, paths) to the other at common time-stamps. Looking at different perspectives (at the same recorded time) or following any of the paths creates an extended exploration space for learners. At the same time, the network of paths and structures is always associated with plain audio or video records that contextualize and explain things. One of the main values comes from guiding learners within a complex structure, such as a document or program.

We have also explored the opportunity to let a program search for suspicious or interesting patterns. In the FOCUS example, only a few trivial patterns were used, concerning hot spots (frequently executed or explained elements) and path deviations (when a method is executed but never explained) (issue explained but never executed).

Encourage, but do not Insist on Further Rationale Management

Most approaches about design rationale include capturing as well as index-ing and structuring. Raw data is considered unreadable and unsuited for learner use by some [13]. The task of abstracting and structuring raw data into more manageable rationale is indispensable.

According to this principle, the By-Product Approach is different. The recordings and paths and structural information usually add up to a large amount of data. A single Camtasia (screen video and audio) record of a one-hour meeting may easily be 100 MB large. However, there will be only a few of those essential meetings, and only a few recordings. This principle again represents a conscious and rather extreme decision: Do not care about a few Gigabytes of storage space, when they fit easily on a 2$-DVD. If no one takes the initiative to further extend or modify or transcribe recordings, the web of recorded "raw" data from one session might just be burnt on a DVD and represent a snapshot of the project history. If desired, it can always be loaded back into the computer and updated. It was our initial intention to keep the rationale alive over an extended period of time. During the experiments with the two case examples, we had to accept that this rarely happens. In most cases, the effort required for creating a snapshot is much less than the effort needed for continuous rationale management. This approach was shaped by observations in software projects and optimized from a pragmatic point of view. Continuing rationale management is certainly desirable from a methodological perspective.

From Principles to Practices

As with agile methods [2,3], principles are guidelines to follow. For each concrete instantiation of the approach, principles need to be turned into concrete, operational practices, techniques, or rules. In that sense, each of the principles explained earlier can be implemented quite differently.

The following two applications show different instantiations of the approach. First of all, the focus tasks are different (prototypes and risk management). Consequently, relevant rationale looks different and needs to be captured in a different way. The principles help to approach both cases.

4.4 Case 1: Capturing Rationale in Software Prototypes

FOCUS is a strategy and a family of tools to capture knowledge sparked by prototypes [16]. According to Lichter et al. [12], there are different kinds of prototypes that are built with different goals in mind.

The definitions of various types of prototypes are listed below, with respective rationale mentioned in parentheses.

- *Demonstrators* elicit requirements (and rationale for raising those requirements) from customers.
- *Prototypes proper* try out implementation ideas (soliciting design rationale) implementing the core functionality only.
- *Breadboard prototypes* try out single technical solutions in isolation. They produce insights in how to fulfill a requirement (and why!).
- *Pilot systems* start out as prototypes and slowly turn into product software (all kinds of rationale play a role during this full development that shares all aspects of other prototypes).

FOCUS was initially created to solve the specific problem of capturing knowledge from prototypes in a light-weight way [16]. Experience elicitation in software projects may follow a similar approach [17]. All those findings were compiled and generalized to the "Rationale as By-Product Approach," weaving in related other approaches like LIDs [17] or Collaborative Risk Management [18]. The different kinds of prototypes elicit different aspects of rationale (as differentiated in Sect. 4.2). In the terminology of Chap. 1, it is basically "supporting knowledge transfer" (Sect. 1.4.4) that is supported by FOCUS.

4.4.1 FOCUS Implementation of the Principles

Where Does Rationale Occur?
When one of the above types of prototypes is selected, a certain kind of information and rationale is sought. During prototype development, further rationale is created (*why to do it that way?*). During development, the flow state [5] may be reached, and an interruption will hamper the creation process. However, as soon as the prototype is presented to other people, developers will use this opportunity to talk about their findings and successes. Observers have a chance to ask questions. This is a good opportunity to capture and record rationale. We have experimented with separate tape recorders and with computer-based audio and on-screen video recording. FOCUS now uses the Camtasia commercial tool to record both a screen video and audio of the explanations given

(http://www.techsmith.com/). Demos often convey highly condensed information, far beyond "raw rationale".

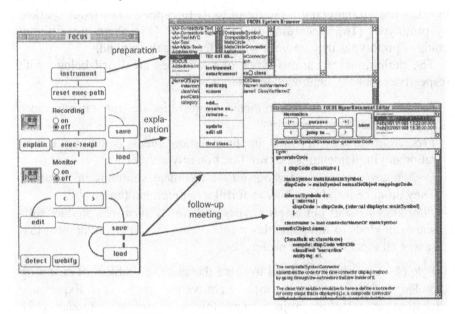

Fig. 4.1. From the FOCUS panel (*left*) commands are issued to control a code browser (*top*), code execution (not visible) and the rationale reader (*right*)

How to Shift Extra Effort Away from Experts?

There is very little extra effort from their perspective: The recording software is integrated in the FOCUS panel (see Fig. 4.1). Experts giving the demonstrations just follow the lines from top to bottom and press a few buttons, in order to start or stop recording.

A typical FOCUS use case follows the buttons in the FOCUS panel: (1) a learner or expert has marked the code to be discussed. After pushing the "instrument" button, all methods within that piece of code will be traced when executed. (2) A demo is started and recorded as both a Camtasia (video) file and as a sequence of executed methods (specific path). (3) The path may remote-control the code browser to guide follow-up explanations. In that case, method by method is displayed that was previously executed. During this second part of the demo, experts explain how the demoed features were implemented. (4) This explanation is again recorded via Camtasia into an "explanation path," which is a sequence of methods visited.

This original implementation was carried out in Smalltalk (Fig. 4.1). It is important to use an integrated environment that is used for writing, running, and explaining code. Smalltalk was such an environment. However, FOCUS as an instance of the By-Product Approach is not restricted to any single language. To demonstrate this, we recently completed an Eclipse/Java version of FOCUS (see Fig. 4.2). Eclipse is a widely used Java development platform. Four Eclipse plug-ins (integrated platform extensions) were implemented to allow instrumentation and tracing of selected methods, linking and replay of different recorded paths and videos in an integrated way.

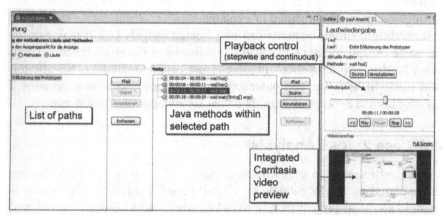

Fig. 4.2. Eclipse/Java version of FOCUS: On the *right* of the FOCUS window, there is a small Camtasia preview window (can be enlarged), buttons for stepwise replay of paths (method by method), and a slider for fast navigation. Of course, Camtasia videos with attached paths can also be replayed in continuous mode. Users may browse the entire web of paths and recordings at any point

In Fig. 4.2, a list of previously recorded paths provides access to the methods they consist of. From each recorded method, a learner can explore all paths that include that method.

Who will Benefit?

A prototype is created to answer questions about customer requirements or about technical options. Usually, only a small subset of developers is involved with prototyping, but their findings are used in a much larger team. Any person in that larger team who needs to learn about the prototype is an ideal candidate for transcribing or summarizing the audio record – if it is ever done.

What can be Captured During What Task?

That same computer that runs the demo, also executes Camtasia and path recording (see above). A main advantage is a perfect synchronization between explanations (audio), what is explained (video), and what part of the code is actually affected (path).

Additional Computer Recording or Analysis?

Prototype code is instrumented with tracing information. By running the code, a trace of executed (Smalltalk or Java) methods is created *as a by-product*. The sequence of executed methods is called an "execution path".

Recordings of explanations and screen video were synchronized with the execution paths and explanation paths through time stamps. The specific strength of FOCUS comes from its integration with the development platform, and code base. By being fully integrated, the code structure (inheritance, packages) is related to the execution and explanation paths through the methods executed or explained.

In addition, simple patterns can be detected by FOCUS. It may ask for rationale on "all methods that were explained but never executed." There is no "artificial intelligence" involved, just pattern matching. No attempt was made to have the computer explain a pattern. Explaining remains a task for human experts, as would be the case in a normal demonstration.

4.5 Case 2: Risk Analysis

In the next example, a very different task in software project management is supported by the "Rationale as a By-Product" approach. Risk management is a crucial project task to avoid running into foreseeable problems. For example, a subcontractor may have been unreliable in the past. Relying on this same contractor in a new project is a risk: it could cause a delay, and maybe contractual fees. Risk analysis is at the core of risk management. It deals with reasons and probabilities and consequences of risks. Since there is uncertainty involved, different stakeholders may use different reasoning (rationale) in assessing those risk parameters. In this phase, the Risk Analysis Tool comes into the picture.

Where does Rationale Occur?

During the discussion by stakeholders (project leader, experienced project staff), a lot of the previous experience made with the subcontractor or with other risks surfaces. Discussions elicit risk mitigation options.

How to Shift Extra Effort Away from Experts?

Usually, risk analysis is carried out in a regular project meeting as a separate topic. However, risks should be discussed frequently. When the project is running, risk analysis may only focus on the changes since the last meeting. Risk meetings are short, but they require that many stakeholders participate. A larger project might be distributed over different locations or buildings, causing traveling expenses.

We developed a Risk Analysis Tool that enables the team to save time by holding risk analysis meetings online. The tool offers a user interface displayed in Fig. 4.3. At the core, there is a chat facility (left) and a portfolio (right) on which risks are placed with respect to their probability and their impact. Numbered circles represent risks. They are described after the portfolio. Relative positions imply different priorities for mitigation. Portfolios are the typical tool for discussing risks during risk analysis [10].

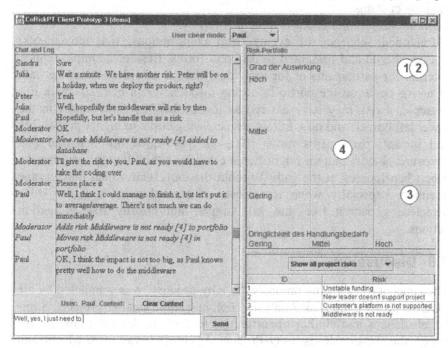

Fig. 4.3. Risk Analysis Tool. Integrates chat (*left*), portfolio (*right*), and recording control (*hidden*). Risks are represented by circles and listed below portfolio [18]

What can be Captured During What Task?

In the tool, an interactive risk portfolio is combined with a chat component. Both components are time-stamped and recorded. Since many comments refer to the same set of risks (on the portfolio), all chat contributions that mention a certain risk can be identified and cross-referenced. Of course, there could be a NetMeeting or Voice over IP component instead of the chat component. Nothing would change in principle as long as all relevant activities are recorded, time-stamped, and related. Again, the By-Product Approach can be implemented in several different ways. We used chat as the easiest option and because it can be easily demonstrated on paper and slides.

Who will Benefit?

Participants who would like to remember the meeting and the course of the discussion without taking notes. Future project members who would like to learn about earlier concerns and discussions on risks. New team members trying to understand the project better, are good candidates to summarize the recordings, if at all necessary. Project leader assistants could carry out those things as well, as they usually have to keep track of the project status.

Additional Computer Recording or Analysis?

Recorded sequence of events (chat contributions, risk movements) can be filtered and presented in different forms. Besides a simple replay, filtering for participants or for individual risks is afforded. Also, the path of a risk circle on the portfolio during discussion can be visualized. For example, a risk may have entered as low-probability, low-impact in the lower left corner, and now follow an increasing curve to higher probability and impact: participants move it up as they agree on increased risk exposure. Such a pattern might be detected by either the tool or a human user when looking at the path. Without the tool, such a path may escape attention, especially when it consists of several smaller shifts. Once detected, a pattern like this will trigger high-priority risk mitigation actions.

4.6 Discussion

The concept of capturing rationale "as a by-product" was stimulated by the FOCUS project, the Risk Analysis Tool, and some smaller projects. Similar challenges and similar opportunities lead to similar solutions. In this paper, the "Rationale as a By-Product Approach" was factored out and explicitly described. This approach provides guidance in setting-up tools to capture rationale by recording project tasks. The approach is pragmatic in taking constraints and observations from practice seriously – and accepting that some nice features will probably not be used a lot.

The two applications were developed in university and industry environments, respectively. They have been applied to different projects, and have demonstrated the *feasibility* of the approach: there were no fundamental breakdowns or objections, and some participants were delighted. However, we consider this anecdotal evidence and recommend empirical validation of future tools built according to the Rationale as a By-Product Approach. With our new Eclipse implementation of FOCUS, we plan to validate the approach with a series of increasingly rigid experiments. We are aware, however, that a full validation will take months or years: the tools will only unfold their full potential when the bearers of rationale are no longer available or cannot remember what was recorded. So far we have seen only short-term effects.

From developing and applying techniques like FOCUS [16], Risk Analysis Tool [18] or LIDs [17], the merit of the by-product approach becomes obvious: in all cases, there is almost no interruption of work. There is a low threshold for rationale bearers to use the techniques, as they require little or no extra work. There is always a form of recording "raw information" that contains valuable rationale. Mere recording and replay is already an important support for capturing rationale, but hardly deserves being called an "approach". But when computer tools are enriched with further recording features, and when the resulting web of paths is offered as guidance, a new level of support is reached. Indexing by time-stamps and task-specific paths are crucial means for fast retrieval. Pattern matching and advanced analysis and presentation facilities can add yet another step. The two cases give some concrete examples.

4.7 Conclusions

The approach presented in this paper focuses on the capturing and "saving" aspects of rationale management. By focusing on one essential project task, it is highly restricted and very specific. Due to that small focus, powerful recording mechanisms (e.g. executed program methods, risk movement events) can be identified and supported.

Care needs to be taken to reintroduce the rationale when it is needed later. It would go beyond the scope of this paper to discuss this aspect in depth, but the approach obviously facilitates presentation of rationale, too. Paths could be visualized, and they always should be used to browse the space of recorded material. In that respect, the approach typically leads to "Rationale Capturing" components that are tightly integrated with path-oriented "Rationale Retrieval" components (as defined in Chap. 1).

Capturing rationale "as a by-product" sounds easy, but requires sophisticated technological preparations. Rebuilding FOCUS within Eclipse, for example, consumed more than four persons–months of a highly skilled software developer. Obviously, there is no way to get rationale for free. This approach simply shifts all the effort into building a computer tool like FOCUS or the Risk Analysis Tool and away from the actual project task in which rationale surfaces.

"Rationale as a By-Product" is an approach for building tools and techniques that have a realistic chance of being accepted and successful in real projects.

References

[1]   Alexander IF, Stevens R (2002) Writing Better Requirements. Addison-Wesley, Reading, MA
[2]   Beck K (2000) Extreme Programming Explained. Addison-Wesley, Reading, MA
[3]   Cockburn A (2002) Agile software development. Addison-Wesley Reading, MA
[4]   Conklin J, Begeman ML (1988) gIBIS: A hypertext tool for exploratory policy discussion. ACM Trans. Off. Autom. Syst. 6(4): 303–331
[5]   Csikszentmihalyi M (1990) Flow: The Psychology of Optimal Experience. HarperPerennial, New York
[6]   Davenport TGP (2000) Knowledge management case book – Best practices. Publicis MCD, Wiley, München Berlin Heidelebrg New York, Germany, p. 260
[7]   Fischer G (1994) Turning breakdowns into opportunities for creativity. Knowledge-Based Syst.. 7(4): 221–232
[8]   Fischer G (1994) Domain-oriented design environments, Autom. Softw. Eng. 1(2): 177–203
[9]   Grudin J (1987) Social evaluation of the user interface: Who does the work and who gets the benefit. In: INTERACT'87. IFIP Conference on Human Computer Interaction. Stuttgart, Germany, pp. 805-811
[10] Kontio J (2001) Software engineering risk management – A method, improvement framework, and empirical evaluation. In: Department of Computer Science and Engineering. Helsinki University of Technology, p. 248
[11] Lee J (1991) Extending the Potts and Bruns model for recording design rationale. In: International Conference on Software Engineering, ICSE-13
[12] Lichter H, Schneider-Hufschmidt M, Züllighoven H (1993) Prototyping in industrial software projects – bridging the gap between theory and practice. In: International Conference on Software Engineering (ICSE-15), IEEE Computer Society Press, pp. 221–229
[13] MacLean A, Young RM, Bellotti VME, Moran T (1996) Questions, options and criteria. In: Moran TP, Carroll JM (eds.) Design Rationale: Concepts, Techniques and Use, Lawrence Erlbaum Associates, Mahwah, NJ, pp. 21–52 Moran T, Carroll J (1996) Design Rationale: Concepts, Techniques, and Use. Lawrence Erlbaum Associates, Mahwah, NJ
[14] Nonaka I, Hirotaka T (1995) The Knowledge-Creating Company. 17 ed. Oxford University Press, Oxford
[15] Potts C, Bruns G (1988) Recording the reasons for design decisions. In: International Conference on Software Engineering, ICSE-10
[16] Schneider K (1996) Prototypes as assets, not toys. Why and how to extract knowledge from prototypes. In: 18th International Conference on Software Engineering (ICSE-18) 1996. Berlin, Germany, pp. 522–531

[17] Schneider K (2000) LIDs: A light-weight approach to experience elicitation and reuse. In: Product Focused Software Process Improvement (PROFES 2000). Oulo, Finland, Springer, Berlin Heidelberg New York, pp. 407–424

[18] Schneider K (2001) Experience magnets – Attracting experiences, not just storing them. In: Conference on Product Focused Software Process Improvement PROFES 2001. Kaiserslautern, September 2001, pp. 126–140

[19] Schön DA (1983) The Reflective Practitioner: How Professionals Think in action. Basic Books, New York

[20] Van Heijst G, Schreiber AT, Wielinga BJ (1997) Using explicit ontologies in KBS development. Int. J. Hum.–Comput. Stud. 46 (2–3): 183–292

5 Hypermedia Support for Argumentation-Based Rationale: 15 Years on from gIBIS and QOC

S.J. Buckingham Shum, A.M. Selvin, M. Sierhuis,
J. Conklin, C.B. Haley, B. Nuseibeh

Abstract: Having developed, used and evaluated some of the early IBIS-based approaches to design rationale (DR) such as gIBIS and QOC in the late 1980s/mid-1990s, we describe the subsequent evolution of the argumentation-based paradigm through software support, and perspectives drawn from modeling and meeting facilitation. Particular attention is given to the challenge of negotiating the overheads of capturing this form of rationale. Our approach has maintained a strong emphasis on keeping the representational scheme as simple as possible to enable real time meeting mediation and capture, attending explicitly to the skills required to use the approach well, particularly for the sort of participatory, multistakeholder requirements analysis demanded by many design problems. However, we can then specialize the notation and the way in which the tool is used in the service of specific methodologies, supported by a customizable hypermedia environment, and interoperable with other software tools. After presenting this approach, called *Compendium*, we present examples to illustrate the capabilities for support security argumentation in requirements engineering, template driven modeling for document generation, and IBIS-based indexing of and navigation around video records of meetings.

Keywords: rationale capture, cognitive overhead, hypermedia, argumentation, compendium, IBIS, QOC

5.1 Introduction and Overview

Few would disagree with this book's opening chapter that the systematic management of design rationale (DR) is not yet common software engineering practice. By extension this applies to the particular flavor of DR with which we work, namely the IBIS/QOC approaches to creating graphical argumentation maps of design deliberation (reviewed in Chap. 1 and classed as "prescriptive, intrusive" in nature). It is the "intrusive" nature of such notations that represent an obstacle to adoption (we will unpack in more nuanced terms what this means), and which has led many to the conclusion that DR based around explicit, graphical argument maps is yet another failure of exciting research ideas to overcome the harsh realities of actual day-to-day practice.

This chapter argues that the story is more complicated but more hopeful. Since the late 1980s, through business and industrial case studies, detailed lab analysis, and continual design refinement, we have been reflecting on the set of interacting factors which together can "make or break" them in the heat of collaborative analysis, modeling and design. The *Compendium* technique and tool has matured to the point where a steering group (a subset of the authors) is coordinating the development of an open source Java hypermedia IBIS mapping tool, with an international user community spanning government, NGOs, education and business, documented case studies, and training courses and online resources. Clearly, there are no silver bullets, but progress has been made since the intense activity that led up to the first DR book in 1996, and the subsequent decline in activity as the challenges of truly embedding argumentation-based DR in work practices sank in. In particular, although quality software support is required, it turned out to be the human factors that required closer attention.

The objective of this chapter is to update the software engineering community on how and why the QOC [20, 21] and gIBIS approaches [10, 11] we helped to create originally, have subsequently evolved into the current Compendium approach and tool.

5.2 The Vision

Chapter 1 has already provided a broad summary of the rationale behind Horst Rittel's IBIS, and the ways on which software engineering DR researchers have appropriated and extended it, so we will not duplicate that review. What we can add by way of introduction is an amplification of the rationale behind "prescriptive, intrusive" approaches, whose goal is to support and improve design reasoning. A converging strand of research in the history of computing to augment intellectual work, Rittel's work converged with that of computing pioneers such as Vannevar Bush, Douglas Engelbart and John Seely Brown to forge an exciting vision of the power of cognitive, collaborative tools to both capture and augment design reasoning. The research community envisioned that hypertext groupware would make it easy to capture and structure the spectrum of informal and formal knowledge that goes into DR. Designers could capture their deliberations on the fly during design sessions. Visual networks of icons would be intuitive enough to realize the vision of participatory analysis amongst diverse stakeholders, who would not need to learn cryptic formal schemes in order to contribute tangibly to system requirements. Captured DR's might be reusable, or at least would contribute greatly to the process of maintaining and evolving that system over time by providing a skeletal group memory to help reconstruct what led to a decision.

We are simplifying a little for brevity (we review the roots to the field in more depth in [3]), but something close to the above vision was very much the driving energy in the decade from about 1986 in many leading computer science and HCI research groups. As will become clear, we consider many aspects of this exciting vision to merit continued pursuit, since providing traces of complex intellectual work has enormous potential. However, as we will elaborate in Sect. 5.3, great attention needs to be paid to the socio-technical skills required to successfully use such an approach, and there was naivety in some of the early assumptions. In particular, we had to solve "the DR capture problem."

5.3 The Design Rationale Capture Problem

The capture problem is the specter haunting all DR efforts (indeed, all knowledge management efforts attempting to meaningfully capture elements of human reasoning and discourse). How does one acquire quality input to a rationale management system, without disrupting the very process it is designed to support, or without having to employ dedicated scribes who do nothing but maintain rationale libraries?

The cost–benefit tradeoff is a slippery tightrope to walk, and has focused our energies on a "value now, value later" imperative. As Grudin [13] has pointed out, there cannot be a disparity between who invests effort in a groupware system, and who benefits. No designer can be expected to altruistically enter quality DR *solely* for the *possible benefit* of a *possibly unknown person* at an *unknown point in the future* for an *unknown task*. There must be immediate value. The difficulty, of course, is that it is not merely a "capture" problem, but "useful capture". One could minimize the capture effort and simply video record every design meeting, but this would not render a useful archive. Computationally tractable structure must be added by some means. Extracting useful content automatically from multimedia meeting records is an active research area, but very challenging. Later, we will report on the synergy of combining the richness of video-based DR with argumentation-oriented approaches, but let us first focus on the specific capture problem associated with the latter.

Very soon after "idea processing" visual hypertext systems such as NoteCards [14] and gIBIS [10] began to be used for structuring ideas, reports began to emerge of "cognitive overhead". A 1994 survey [3] found comparatively weak evidence regarding usability and utility compared to what might have been expected given the scale of system development efforts. A later survey echoed this, highlighting the pattern of failure in many kinds of interactive systems that assume the willingness of users to structure information [30]. The ray of hope that somehow we might find just the right balance of intuitive user interface, natural representation scheme, and fast computers began to dim, and many researchers moved on to other challenges.

Nonetheless, encouraged by the limited success of the gIBIS prototype in an industrial case study [11] that the problems stated earlier were surmountable, the early 1990s saw the launch by Conklin and colleagues of a commercial software tool that combined graphical hypertext, IBIS and groupware capabilities. The *QuestMap* Windows single user and groupware product made a mark in the hypertext and groupware communities, and even resulted in a few isolated cases of extended industrial-strength use [8]. However, this product ultimately succumbed to market pressures, and is no longer available. Much was learnt from this episode, in particular an appreciation of the value that can be added in design meetings *once people have learnt the meta-cognitive skills of using IBIS*, some of whom may then appreciate quality software support to overcome the limits of mapping on paper, whiteboards, or a generic drawing tool. Let us consider the nature of this skill in more detail.

5.4 Understanding Cognitive Overhead

We have studied the issue of "intrusiveness" (see Chap. 1) in depth via detailed, video-based analyses. Moreover, we are interested in characterizing not just the initial learning curve (which is what most people have focused on) but also the nature of highly skilled practice.

One study of beginners focused on software designers learning to use QOC (on paper), and provided a detailed account of how designers must learn to manage four interleaving cognitive tasks [2]: *unbundling* (identifying and separating constituent elements of ideas which have been 'bundled together' when they were initially expressed, but which from an argumentation perspective need to be teased apart), *classification* (deciding whether a contribution is a Question, Option, or Criterion), *naming* (labeling the new contribution succinctly but meaningfully), and *structuring* (linking in a new element to other ideas).

Should we be surprised that this feels like extra work? In introducing subsequent video analyses of these designers, Buckingham Shum et al. [4] argued that "On reflection, reports of cognitive overhead should not be surprising. The basis on which [concept mapping tools] work is that deeper understanding of a domain comes through the *discipline* of expressing knowledge within a structural framework, working to articulate important distinctions and relationships."

At this point, however, although Buckingham Shum had a lab-based account of when QOC seemed useful or obstructive, he had a poorly developed conception of how to turn that effort to the group's advantage. This was a "missing piece of the jigsaw" that some of the other authors of this chapter provided: Conklin from a facilitation perspective developed during the QuestMap/IBIS consulting period, and later, Selvin and Sierhuis from a collaborative modeling perspective [25]. Section 5.5 describes how these insights combine in our current understanding.

Beyond the initial learning curve for novices, we have recently begun to characterize the learning curve as one gains proficiency. What does it mean to become an expert in mapping IBIS structures to support problem solving and design cognition? Selvin [26] has characterized the kinds of skills that such a practitioner needs to possess, and more recently has begun to articulate, based on video analysis of Compendium in use in web-mediated meetings, the kinds of 'moves' that a mapper can make to assist the team in the problem solving, and the associated skills [27].

To summarize, DR that yields insight into the complex ideas and arguments that may lie behind a decision does not come "for free": effort must be invested at some point in the rationale management lifecycle.

5.5 Compendium

Compendium represents our current effort to take the raw conception of IBIS, and deliver it in a form where it can smoothly integrate in the 'matrix' of everyday tools and practices. Our technical objective is to provide a robust, open environment in the IBIS/argumentation-based DR paradigm, which can then be integrated with other DR paradigms and tools, such that services can be implemented over the extended-IBIS representational substrate.

Our approach to the capture problem is to invest rationale structuring effort primarily at the point of capture, validating it with the key stakeholders. This capturing process serves the stakeholders' needs to understand each other and know that their viewpoint has been heard. This co-evolves a shared picture of the problem, possible ways forward, and the rationale for deciding how to proceed. This is supported by a software tool which can further lower the data entry overhead: data already entered in other key tools can be imported, and data entered in the rationale tool can automatically populate other tools, or generate documentation.

There are three dimensions to understanding Compendium: (1) its functionality as a hypermedia concept mapping environment, (2) how it uses IBIS to support collaborative modeling of a problem using any conceptual framework, and (3) in the context of mapping ideas in real time during a meeting, the role of the person doing the mapping to facilitate the task at hand.

5.5.1 Hypermedia Concept Mapping

Compendium comes "preloaded" with node and link types for IBIS, derived from QuestMap's interpretation of the notation, for connecting key issues, possible responses to these, and relevant arguments. Figure 5.1 shows the default node types, which include additional nodes beyond IBIS for *Lists and Maps* (containers for nodes), *Decisions, Notes,* and *References* that can hyperlink to open a web page or other document.

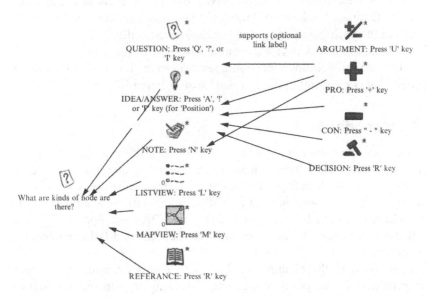

Fig. 5.1. IBIS plus additional node types rendered in Compendium. Any application document or website can be dropped in to create a hyperlink. Nodes can contain text content, and links can be labeled if desired

Figure 5.2 shows a DR extract from a project meeting, in which an issue is raised, two options explored, and one justified. Figure 5.3 shows the use of Compendium simply to record decisions (about metadata). While these might simply have been recorded in a word processor or slide tool, such tools do not support (i) the possibility of capturing important discussion/rationale if it arises, or (ii) the reuse of a decision in subsequent other contexts – see the links on the bottom node to its other appearances in the database. Users can also define their own custom modeling language, by building their own palettes of icons (called Stencils) and relational types (Linksets). This is not currently a full meta-modeling tool, however, in that constraints cannot be specified between nodes and links: any two nodes can be linked using any linktype.

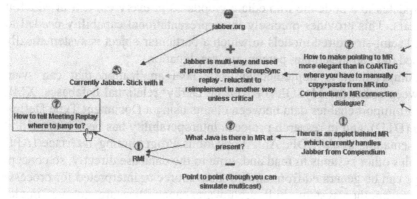

Fig. 5.2. Extract from a software design meeting, in which Compendium is used to map issues, options, arguments, the decision, and a relevant website. (This meeting was an Internet video conference, with Compendium viewed by participants via a desktop sharing application)

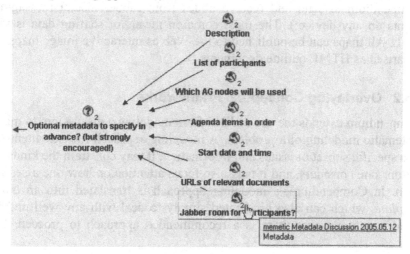

Fig. 5.3. Recording decisions (in this case without any significant rationale) in Compendium. Rolling the mouse over the digit on a node displays a link menu to other maps which contain the node

Compendium maps are not 'flat' drawings, but views onto a relational database that can be rendered in multiple formats. A given node (e.g., representing an idea, argument, entity, or document) can appear and be updated in multiple views. Since any application document or URL can be dragged and dropped into a map as a *Reference* node, so an external document can be linked into one or more discussions and tracked – that is, given one or more meaningful contexts where it plays a role. Corrections or updates to a node are immediately updated in every context in which it appears. This provides precisely the representational capability needed to build semi-structured models in which a particular object is systematically reused (e.g. an idea, plan, person, system, location).

Compendium is implemented as a Java application that can swap between either the MySQL[2] or Apache Derby[3] relational databases. XML export/import enables data between clients using a Document Type Definition (DTD), and in research projects, interoperability has been extended to the semantic web's RDF. An Applications Programming Interface (API) enables other systems to read and write to the database directly, so concept maps can be generated from another data source or interpreted for processing by another system. Full groupware capabilities are not yet implemented, although demand for this is growing. A shared database can be maintained either by using an MySQL server, or in experimental versions, through mirroring databases synchronously between two clients over the Internet, using the Jabber XML messaging protocol (which also enables Compendium to send and receive nodes from Jabber instant messaging clients on any device[4]). The most common means of sharing data is via XML. All maps can be published to the Web as interactive image maps or linearised as HTML outline documents.

5.5.2 Overlaying Conceptual Frameworks

Compendium extends the use of IBIS from modeling a discussion, to more systematic modeling of a problem. A modeling approach focuses attention on a specific subset of issues and information, it may constrain the kinds of options one considers, and it may also focus attention on how one assesses them. In Compendium, a modeling approach is translated into an *issue template*, which can also be created simply to deal with any well understood situation where there is a recommended approach to proceed, for

---

[2] See http://www.mysql.com.
[3] See http://db.apache.org/derby.
[4] See the CoAKTinG Project: www.aktors.org/coakting

instance, from best practice or a standard operating procedure. Figure 5.4 shows a template for modeling a business process, prior to its instantiation.

Templates were created to support structured modeling within the IBIS framework, which by definition moves the tool into the space of reasonably well-structured problems. These are much easier contexts in which a beginner can use Compendium, since they are provided with a representational scaffold for working through a set of predefined issues. Assuming the meeting has faith in the template, when its questions have been answered, the meeting can be confident that they have made some progress. A hallmark of the approach is, however, the ability to break from formal and prescribed representations into informal, ad hoc communication, incorporating both in the same view if that is helpful to the participants (e.g. "in this context we should really ask a different question..."). Hypertext nodes and links can thus be added either in accordance with templates or in an opportunistic fashion.

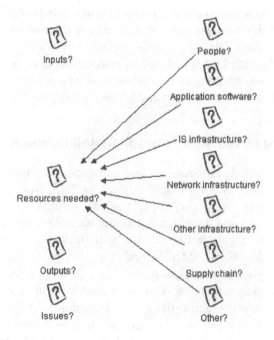

Fig. 5.4. An issue template that can be imported when required, linked to other views, and tagged with metadata. The issues raised are now stepped through, linking in answers and arguments as appropriate, and breaking out of the template if necessary to capture unexpected material, ideas or argumentation

A complement to issue templates are *tags* (metadata keywords) assigned to any concept (node) in the database to show connections through membership in a common category. Tags serve to specialize a node type with as many attributes as required for it to play multiple roles in different contexts. At the end of the session all of the nodes so marked can be harvested. In modeling, nodes sharing a tag are often tracked as a 'catalogue' of nodes stored for future reuse. Tags may reflect generic meeting processes (e.g. *Action-Jane*), or may be driven by an underlying methodology that Compendium is being used to support (e.g. *Data-Provider*). Alternatively, ad hoc tags can be created on the fly, to reflect the emergence of a new theme.

As reviewed in Chap. 1, it has long been recognized that DR cannot exist in a vacuum but must be connected to relevant design artifacts and views. This can be done by dropping an application document or Web URL into Compendium to create a hyperlinked Reference node, but tags provide a mechanism for deeper level connections. Since nodes may originate from other systems (written directly via the MySQL API or manually imported as XML) it is possible to use tags to mirror attributes of the domains which these external systems model. The world of IBIS is thus connected via the simple mechanisms of templates, tags and hyperlinks to any other relevant domain, from end-user scenarios and organizational processes, to software architecture and project management.

5.5.3 Meeting Facilitation Through Dialogue Mapping

Turning to the third element of the approach, *facilitation*, Dialogue Mapping[5] is a set of skills for mapping ideas as IBIS structures in order to support the analysis of wicked problems, as defined by Rittel.[6] It has turned out to be a critical development in argumentation-based DR, since it provides a way to negotiate the capture bottleneck: the structure required to construct useful DR is added in real time during the meeting, adding immediate value to the participants, but also creating a record. Mapping ideas in IBIS during a meeting is unquestionably an acquired ability, but equally, one that can be learnt (there is an international Compendium user community). This was the key oversight in early argumentation-based DR research, which experimented with small-scale demonstration examples,

---

[5] For an introductory account of how Dialogue Mapping is used during a meeting, see the fictional scenario at www.cognexus.org/dmepaper.htm.

[6] Churchman [7] appears to be the first person to have published the term 'wicked problem', in 1967, but in this brief editorial, he credits Rittel with the term.

and did not invest enough in what we now think of as hypermedia/IBIS "literacy". See Conklin [8] for a longer introduction to the craft skill involved in choreographing meetings and representational activities that we introduce later, and [9] for an extended resource.

The facilitation perspective places the Dialogue Mapper in a potentially very powerful role, quite the opposite of the lowly "DR scribe" whose role runs the risk of relegation to minute-taker or documenter. The mapper actively crafts structures on a shared display screen that both capture the meanings and ideas of the group and reflect back to it the larger implications of their thinking. There is a spectrum of how strongly discourse is mediated via this display (described in the DR continuum [3]). It may be used to periodically summarize and review "normal discussion" (e.g., at decision time), screens can be shown to reflect on progress, or the discussion and the map can "dance" – each shaping the other. It is hard to convey this in writing, but we contend that it exemplifies the kind of synergy between tools and sensemaking that was envisioned by the developers of early "idea processing"/DR hypertext systems.

To borrow a musical metaphor, there are several shifts in the "rhythm" or "timbre" of a meeting when Compendium is used well:

- *Beneficial slowing down.* A complaint sometimes heard when argumentation-based DR is first introduced to meetings, is that it disrupts the flow of the meeting [2,12]. When done appropriately, however, we find that it can be extremely beneficial to "disrupt" dysfunctional dynamics by focusing attention on a feature of the hypertext map. After a period of use, people become noticeably unhappy when their contributions are not mapped, because once captured on screen, they know that their view has been heard, correctly recorded, and will be harder to ignore when the map is assessed at decision time.
- *Depersonalization of conflict.* When ideas and concerns are mediated via a shared display, challenges to positions assume a more neutral, less personal tone. In situations where there are competing agendas, it helps participants clarify the nature of their disagreement (e.g., the definition of 'the problem'; understanding different criteria of "success"). We have seen Compendium defuse meetings which otherwise looked to be polarized, for instance, by surfacing the different connotations of a particular question. Recent work with Compendium has deployed specifically in conflict resolution and mediation [24].
- *Flexible rhythmic review.* To a surprising degree, collaborative knowledge work can be characterized as "group list processing." Whether the list is a set of requirements, budget items, or action items, a common activity is group review of a list of potentially complex elements. While

some items draw little comment, others can lead into deep discussions and even debate. A good mapper can establish a "call and response" rhythm with the group, creating a sense of shared purpose and momentum. When occasional elements lead to intense discussions about meaning, or spark disagreement among group members, the Compendium practitioner can open a new map and keep mapping or modeling the new conversation. With the new issues captured in the shared display, the group can return to the previous review task without losing momentum.

5.6 Reasoning Services and Verification

Referring back to Chap. 1's lists of requirements for future software engineering DR environments, in principle, Compendium's functionality could contribute to any software engineering activity and phase where issue-based deliberation or modeling is required. But our interest in collective sensemaking clearly has a particular orientation to the tasks listed under "supporting collaboration".

The evolution of Compendium from QuestMap and gIBIS has, however, opened the door technically and conceptually for integration with other software engineering tools and DR tools. Compendium does not come with any preprogrammed verification services that can perform structural checking (which could for instance be used to provide a DR service such as dependency management). Given the breadth of our user community, which goes beyond just software engineering and DR, our strategy has been twofold: (1) to create an open architecture (unlike QuestMap's) with a standard SQL database, XML DTD, and Java source code to enable other groups to access all levels of the system functionality and data; (2) to provide a visual user interface and generic issue-oriented representational substrate as described earlier (extended IBIS, a customizable visual language, tags, templates, node reuse, graphs, and lists) which can be appropriated to express many different kinds of design knowledge.

We have already shown (in the mission planning domain) that Compendium can be integrated with a tool that uses a more formal issue ontology and planning engine to reason about available options and constraints on issues [31]. We are now beginning to explore the requirements for a new layer over the generic environment, which would extend Compendium with services to support argumentation around the security of requirements specifications, a domain which provides the worked example described shortly.

5.7 Revisiting 'Intrusiveness'

After over 15 years' deployment in the field (gIBIS, QuestMap, Compendium), there is now a response to those who have argued that the need to be skilled in the use of IBIS is a fundamental weakness of the approach.

First, this has now been shown to be an effective strategy to negotiate the cost/benefit tradeoff associated with IBIS and its descendants: people *can* learn to do this, and can construct representations which their peers value both in the meeting, and afterwards. All of this evidence is from the field, often anecdotal from practitioners who are not interested in writing research papers, but experiences are beginning to be documented [6, 8, 23, 25, 27, 29]. Second, like any other complex artifact (whether a software tool, a physical tool, or a musical instrument), Compendium yields greater benefits with practice.

That being said, a DR approach is of no use if people cannot learn it in a reasonable period of time. The "facilitation" perspective has proven to be an important step forward in providing us with a language and orientation to describe to new users how personal and collective deliberation, a subset of which will be DR, can be captured. Two-day Dialogue Mapping training courses and on-line tutorials are available.[7] Experience to date suggests that novices can gain value from the tool as a personal concept mapping aid within days, while confident, effective use in meetings takes longer, although we have seen people use it effectively in meetings with minimal practice. Expert Compendium practitioners may be needed in contentious, unstructured contexts, but less experienced users can use the approach in more stable contexts by completing templates.

It is by no means the case that everyone who attends the two-day training course goes on to use the approach at work, but we are now supporting a sizeable online user community, with over 5,000 downloads of the application to date. Several consulting companies currently use Compendium to support clients in clarifying and integrating multistakeholder requirements in wicked problem contexts, and the approach is also in internal use within both commercial and nonprofit organizations.

---

[7] Compendium training: www.CompendiumInstitute.org/training/training.htm.

5.8 Examples of Compendium in Use

Compendium has been used on over 100 projects during the last 10 years[8] some of which are concerned with software and broader socio-technical systems design, though by no means all of them. Readers seeking empirical evidence of the approach's learnability and effectiveness from analyses of real world cases in the field can review [6, 8, 23, 25, 28, 29], while close video analysis is found in [27]. Pre-Compendium, video analysis of the QOC approach can be found in [2, 3, 4]; Conklin has reported on a large deployment of gIBIS [11] and a decade long deployment of QuestMap [8], Carr [5] has used QuestMap to teach legal argumentation, while Isenmann and Reuter have reflected on HyperIBIS [17] and Fischeret al. [12] on IBIS and PHI.

In this section, we present a small software engineering worked example that illustrates Compendium support for a particular form of argumentation in software engineering. We then extend this with two different examples to show first, the use of templates to drive organizational modeling and generate documentation, and secondly, the use of Compendium maps to index, navigate and query videos of meetings.

5.8.1 Security Satisfaction Arguments in Compendium

Satisfaction arguments [16] need to be constructed when analyzing the security needs of a system. One begins by representing the system using Jackson's problem frames [18], adds security requirements in the form of constraints [22], and then attempts to argue that the system satisfies the security requirements. These arguments are the satisfaction arguments.

In most cases, an initial argument will not be sufficiently convincing for one or more reasons:

1. The argument depends on properties of the system that are not currently known
2. The behavior of *domains* (the actors/components in the system) is not sufficiently understood
3. Domains required to satisfy the security requirements are not included in the system

To address the first two cases, the analyst might choose to go deeper into the system with the goal of better understanding the behavior and properties of the domains in the system. Unfortunately, this process can go

---

[8] Compendium case studies: www.CompendiumInstitute.org/library/library.htm.

on for a long time and, in the end, be inconclusive. At some point the analyst will decide to *trust* that the stated behavior and properties are as described. These decisions are called *trust assumptions* [15], and become an integral part of the satisfaction argument.

To support this kind of modeling, a new Compendium *Stencil* was created to provide a palette of Problem Frame modeling icons, specializations of the generic *Reference* node. If desired, a specific relational vocabulary (*Linkset*) can also be defined to provide labeled edges.

Consider a simple human resources personnel information display system. The proposed system has one requirement: *provide the HR data requested by a user*. Security goal analysis [1, 19, 24] results in one security requirement: *only to HR staff*. A problem diagram is constructed.

The attempt to construct a satisfaction argument that data is indeed provided only to HR staff shows that the analyst does not have sufficient information. One cannot answer the question *How do we know that "Users" consists of HR staff?* The problem information is not complete, and therefore the problem diagram must be changed. The choice made is to add authentication and authorization to the problem. The resulting problem diagram is shown in Fig. 5.5, and Fig. 5.6 the revised satisfaction argument.

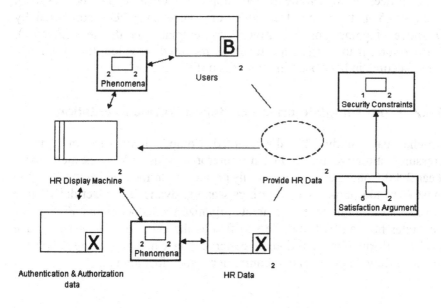

Fig. 5.5. Problem diagram with authentication

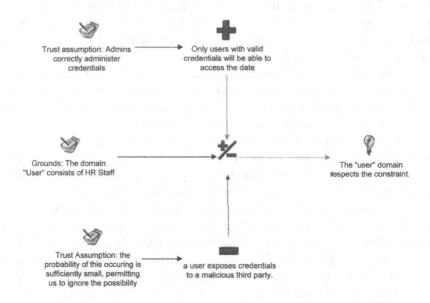

Fig. 5.6. Map of the satisfaction argument

The process by which the trust assumptions were agreed on is not shown in Figs. 5.5 and 5.6, but this could of course have been supported by Dialogue Mapping, possibly driven by a template (see the next example). Furthermore, if the design meeting was recorded on video, then the maps could become indices back into the video (third example).

5.8.2 From Template-driven Modeling To Documentation

Another case study [29] documented Compendium's use in a time-pressured initiative to conduct an enterprise-wide risk assessment for a Year 2000 Contingency Plan. In this project, as in many others, one of the most common purposes of meetings was to advance a project deliverable of some sort; in this case to generate organizational documents. Figure 5.7 illustrates how an IBIS map served first as the participatory user interface to elicit information from domain experts, after which it was then exported to a data flow diagram, and a requirements specification text.

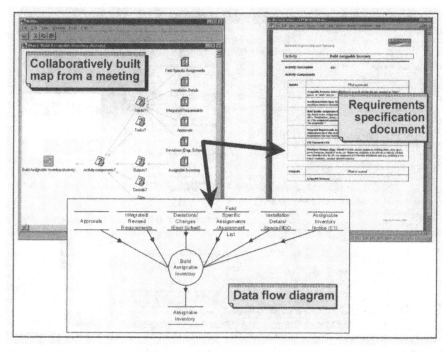

Fig. 5.7. Generating two alternative forms of documentation from a Compendium issue template

5.8.3 Rationale Management Via IBIS-Indexed Video

Our second extension to the worked example illustrates a recent dimension to meeting and rationale capture: Compendium integration with meeting videos. In the context of NASA mission planning [6], a multimedia Meeting Replay extension to Compendium was developed to assist the indexing and navigation of the meeting videos to assist one team's understanding of another's meetings, decisions, and rationale (Fig. 5.8).[9]

---

[9] Developed by the University of Southampton and the Open University as part of the *CoAKTinG* project: www.aktors.org/coakting.

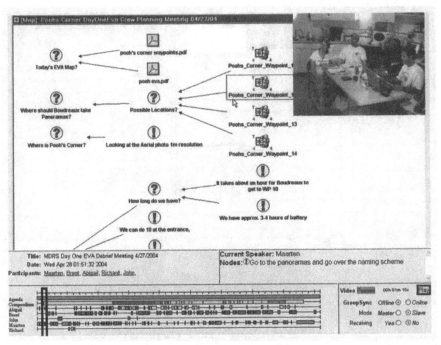

Fig. 5.8. Compendium-based Meeting Replay tool to help the science team on Earth recover the rationale behind the Mars crew's analysis and decisions

The upper region of Fig. 5.8 shows the video of the crew's meeting inset into the Compendium map they are building. The lower region contains summary information about the meeting: who was there, who was speaking, the agenda, and an overview of the current topic (derived from the Compendium map). Some of this information is presented as a timeline, providing a visual index for an RST member to navigate the video, jumping to relevant or interesting parts of the discussion by clicking on the timeline or moving the slider. As well as being able to navigate using the event streams at the footer, Compendium was extended to support conceptual navigation: thus, to see discussion prior to the recording of a particular *argument*, one can click on this node in the Compendium client and the replay jumps to the point in the meeting shortly before that node was created. Work is now under way to develop this infrastructure for wider use.[10]

---

[10]   The *Memetic* project: www.memetic-vre.net.

5.9 Lessons Learnt and Conclusions

In one sense, the whole of this chapter is an extended account of 'lessons learnt about the human factors of IBIS tools.' The vision of computational aids for design deliberation in the face of ill-structured, 'wicked' problems is an exciting one, but 'cool tools' alone cannot deliver this vision. The technologies of hypertext, digital video, and open standards for interoperability provide a powerful infrastructure, but to move from designers' fluid discussions to structured rationale representations, designers must become skilled with DR tools. Reluctance to persist long enough to gain some fluency with these new tools and their languages will result inevitably in the familiar complaints of intrusiveness. We have sought to show that the art and craft of DR – at least DR of this particular sort – is to know how to use the tools well enough that they are constructively disruptive, delivering immediate value to those using it, as well as supporting longer-term memory.

We recognize of course that there are representational limits to this particular paradigm, and organizational obstacles to the very idea of DR capture, as reviewed in Chap. 1. We have thus sought to assist in technical integration with other forms of rationale management tool. At this point, however, we do not yet have any examples to report, and welcome approaches from groups interested in collaboration.

In conclusion, as one would expect from the broad conception of "wicked problem," and the generic nature of IBIS as a representational scheme, Compendium is now finding application in many domains other than software engineering, but this is a virtuous circle: as the approach and infrastructure evolve to meet the challenges of new domains, they in turn provide new methodological insights (e.g., the nature of practitioner expertise; the disciplined use of templates) and practical functionality (e.g. data interoperability; modeling stencils; improved usability; document generation). Together these should assist the integration of argumentation-based rationale management with other forms of rationale, and the other tools of software engineering.

Acknowledgments. We are grateful to the book's editors and reviewers for feedback that has improved this chapter. The work reported has been funded by Verizon, NASA, The Open University, and public research grants from the UK Engineering and Physical Sciences Research Council (CoAKTinG Project) and Joint Information Systems Committee (Memetic Project), to whom we are indebted.

References

[1] Antón AI, Potts C (1998) The use of goals to surface requirements for evolving systems. In: Proceedings of the 20th International Conference on Software Engineering. Kyoto Japan, 19–25 April, pp. 157–166

[2] Buckingham Shum S (1996) Analyzing the usability of a design rationale notation. In: Moran TP, Carroll JM (eds.) Design Rationale: Concepts, Techniques, and Use. Lawrence Erlbaum Associates, Hillsdale, pp. 185–215

[3] Buckingham Shum S, Hammond N (1994) Argumentation-based design rationale: what use at what cost? Int. J. Hum.–Comput. Stud., 40(4), 603–652

[4] Buckingham Shum S, MacLean A, Bellotti V, Hammond N (1997) Graphical argumentation and design cognition. Hum.–Comput. Interact. 12(3), 267–300

[5] Carr C (2003) Using computer supported argument visualization to teach legal argumentation. In: Kirschner P, Buckingham Shum S, Carr C (eds.) Visualizing Argumentation: Software Tools for Collaborative and Educational Sense-making. Springer, London Berlin, Heidelberg New York

[6] Clancey WJ, Sierhuis M, Alena R, Berrios D, Dowding J, Graham JS, Tyree KS, Hirsh RL, Garry WB, Semple A, Buckingham Shum S, Shadbolt N, Rupert S (2005) Automating CapCom using mobile agents and robotic assistants. American Institute of Aeronautics and Astronautics 1st Space Exploration Conference, 31 January–1 February, Orlando, FL. Available from: AIAA Meeting Papers on CD-ROM

[7] Churchman, C (1967) Wicked problems (Guest Editorial), Manage. Sci., 4(14), 141–142

[8] Conklin J (2003) Dialog mapping: Reflections on an industrial strength case study. In: Kirschner P, Buckingham Shum S, Carr C (eds.) Visualizing Argumentation. Springer, London Berlin Heidelberg New York

[9] Conklin J (2005) Dialogue Mapping: Building Shared Understanding of Wicked Problems. Wiley, Chichester

[10] Conklin J, Begeman ML (1988) gIBIS: A hypertext tool for exploratory policy discussion. ACM Trans. Off. Inform. Syst., 4(6), 303–331

[11] Conklin J, Burgess Yakemovic KC (1991) A process-oriented approach to design rationale. Hum.–Comput. Interact., 6(3&4), 357–391

[12] Fischer G, Lemke AC, McCall R, Morch AI (1991) Making argumentation serve design. Hum.–Comput. Interact., 6(3&4), 393–419

[13] Grudin J (1996) Evaluating opportunities for design rationale capture. In: Moran TP, Carroll JM (eds.) Design Rationale: Concepts, Techniques, and use. Lawrence Erlbaum Associates, Hillsdale

[14] Halasz FG (1988) Reflections on Notecards: Seven issues for the next generation of hypermedia systems. Commun. ACM, 31, 836–852

[15] Haley CB, Laney RC, Moffett JD, Nuseibeh B (2004) The effect of trust assumptions on the elaboration of security requirements. In: Proceedings of the 12th International Requirements Engineering Conference, Kyoto, 6–10 September. IEEE Computer Society Press, pp. 102–111

[16] Haley CB, Laney RC, Nuseibeh B. (2005). Arguing security: Validating security requirements using structured argumentation, Department of Computing, The Open University, Milton Keynes, UK, Technical Report 2005/04

[17] Isenmann S, Reuter W (1997) IBIS – a convincing concept...but a lousy instrument? In: Proceedings of the Conference on Designing Interactive Systems: Processes, Practices, Methods, and Techniques. Amsterdam, pp. 163–172

[18] Jackson M (2001). Problem Frames. Addison Wesley, London

[19] van Lamsweerde A (2004) Elaborating security requirements by construction of intentional anti-models. In: Proceedings of the 26th International Conference on Software Engineering. Edinburgh, 26–28 May, pp. 148–157

[20] MacLean A, Young R, Bellotti V, Moran T (1991) Questions, options and criteria: Elements of design space analysis. Hum.–Comput. Interact., 6, 201–250

[21] MacLean A, Bellotti V, Shum S (1993), Developing the design space with design space analysis. In: Byerley PF, Barnard PJ, May J (eds.) Computers, communication and usability: design issues, research and methods for integrated services. Elsevier, Amsterdam, pp. 197–219

[22] Moffett JD, Haley CB, Nuseibeh B (2004) Core security requirements artifacts, Department of Computing, The Open University, Milton Keynes, UK, Technical Report 2004/23.

[23] Palus CJ, Horth DM, Pully ML, Selvin A (2003) Exploration for development: developing leadership by making shared sense of complex challenges. Consult. Psychol. J., 55 (1), 26–40

[24] Papadopolous N (2004) Conflict cartography: a methodology designed to support the efficient and effective resolution of complex, multi-stakeholder conflicts. ViewCraft LLC. Available from http://www.viewcraft.com/pdfs/ViewCraft_ConflictCartographyMarch04.pdf

[25] Selvin A (1999) Supporting collaborative analysis and design with hypertext functionality. J. Digit. Inform., 1(4). Available from http://jodi.ecs.soton.ac.uk/Articles/v01/i04/Selvin/

[26] Selvin A (2003) Fostering collective intelligence: Helping groups use visualized argumentation. In Kirschner P, Buckingham Shum S, Carr C (eds.) Visualizing argumentation: Software tools for collaborative and educational sense-making. Springer, London Berlin Heidelberg New York

[27] Selvin A (2004) Building collaborative knowledge representations in real time: An analysis of facilitative micro-actions. Departmental colloquium, Knowledge Media Institute, The Open University, UK. Available from http://stadium.open.ac.uk/stadia/preview.php?s=29&whichevent=494

[28] Selvin A, Sierhuis M (1999) Case studies of Project Compendium in different organizations. In: Workshop on Computer-Supported Collaborative Argumentation, Conference on Computer-Supported Collaborative Learning, Stanford, CA (12–15 Decemeber). Available from http://kmi.open.ac.uk/sbs/csca/cscl99

[29] Selvin A, Buckingham Shum S (2002) Rapid knowledge construction: a case study in corporate contingency planning using collaborative hypermedia. Knowl. Process Manage. 9(2), 119–128

[30] Shipman FM, Marshall CC (1999) Formality considered harmful: Experiences, emerging themes, and directions on the use of formal representations in interactive systems. Comput. Support. Cooperat. Work, 8(4), 333–352

[31] Tate A, Dalton J, Buckingham Shum S, Mancini C, Selvin A (2004) Co-OPR project experiment B report, Artificial Intelligence Applications Institute, Edinburgh University, UK. Available from: www.aiai.ed.ac.uk/project/coopr

Part 2
Rationale Management
for Requirements Engineering

A.H. Dutoit

This part focuses on rationale management approaches for supporting and understanding requirements engineering activities, such as eliciting application domain knowledge and end-user needs, formulating and structuring requirements into a coherent model, or negotiating the scope of the system. Historically, requirements engineering has been an early field of application of rationale approaches, as it exemplifies the concept of "wicked problems" as originally defined by Rittel and Weber [5]. For instance, let us examine three of the characteristics of wicked problems in the context of requirements engineering:

- *There is no definite formulation of a wicked problem.* End-user needs are usually not well understood until after requirements are formulated. Furthermore, requirements are reinterpreted and reformulated as development progresses [4].
- *Wicked problems have no objective stopping rule.* The stakeholders' understanding of user needs and of the system changes. Deploying the system impacts the way in which the user works, resulting in changed or new user needs. In other words, user needs are never completely addressed. Successful systems are upgraded and expanded until resources are depleted or stakeholders lose interest [6].
- *Solutions to wicked problems are not true-or-false but better-or-worse.* Stakeholders, such as the client, end users, application domain experts, and requirements engineers, have different perspectives on the system. Stakeholders have different frames of reference for evaluating requirements [2].

Looking at each of these characteristics, rationale approaches seem to offer much promise in supporting requirements engineering:

- *No definite formulation.* Requirements often embody system decisions, together with assumptions made by stakeholders about the system and the environment. Stakeholders capture the current state of their shared understanding by attaching rationale information to requirements, explaining how a requirement was surfaced, which user needs it addresses, and what other alternatives were considered.

Instead of viewing a requirement as a final, definite statement of how the system should perform, stakeholders accept that requirements will evolve and capture sufficient context to facilitate future changes.

- *No stopping rule.* As requirements decisions are revisited, captured rationale can provide context for reevaluating the decision. Reopening an issue and elaborating new alternatives then leverages off insights gained earlier. Examining new requirements in the light of the rationale of past releases can make it easier to identify which parts of the system should evolve (and which should remain untouched).
- *No true-or-false solutions.* Making rationale explicit makes stakeholders' criteria explicit. Discussing rationale creates opportunities for discovering misunderstandings, in particular in areas where terms are superficially similar, but have distinct meanings. Capturing rationale emphasizes the multiple frames in which requirements have to fit.

While rationale approaches in requirements engineering encounter the same obstacles in other domains (e.g., such as those discussed in depth in Part 1), requirements engineering provides particular opportunities for rationale approaches, including, for example, the relative high cost of requirements failures or the need for explicitly documented agreements in the presence of a contentious or distributed set of stakeholders.

This part includes five chapters, each proposing a rationale approach emphasizing one of the above characteristics of wicked problems.

Chapter 6, "A Hybrid Approach to Upstream Requirements: IBIS and Cognitive Mapping," by Rooksby, Sommerville, and Pidd, tackles the issue of problem formulation during the earliest phases of requirements. The proposed method, called Wisdom, is a hybrid between a cognitive mapping method (SODA [1]) for facilitating problem structuring, and dialog mapping techniques (IBIS [3]) for incrementally formalizing requirements and building consensus among stakeholders.

Chapter 7, "From DREAM to Reality: Specificities of Interactive Systems Development with respect to Rationale Management," by Lacaze, Palanque, Barboni, Bastide, and Navarre, tackles the problem of options exploration in the domain of interactive safety critical systems. In contrast to Chap. 6, stakeholders have already defined the scope of the system. Instead, their attention is on the details of interaction between the users and the system. To deal with the criteria from various stakeholders, a number of solutions are explored concurrently, making the management of their rationale challenging. The proposed approach provides a notation (TEAM) and a tool (DREAM) for capturing rationale and relating it with models from task analysis, software architecture, and prototypes.

Chapter 8, "The WinWin Approach: Using a Requirements Negotiation Tool for Rationale Capture and Use," by Boehm and Kitapci, tackles the problem of making explicit different stakeholders' frame of reference, on achieving an agreement on a set of user needs, and on maintaining this agreement throughout development. The proposed approach, centered on the EasyWinWin tool, supports the collaborative elicitation and reconciliation of mutually satisfactory Win conditions. The set of success critical stakeholders and their Win conditions are reidentified and reevaluated at the beginning of each development cycle.

The approaches described in Chaps. 6–8, while sharing common origins in the work of Rittel, cover a broad spectrum: Wisdom features a trained facilitator using a simple and responsive tool. DREAM features a sophisticated meta-model relating information from many different sources, focusing on the management of a large number of dependencies. WinWin includes prioritization and voting features for resolving conflicts in long lists of Win conditions.

The last two chapters in this part focus on our understanding of requirements engineering. Chapter 9, "Design Rationale in Exemplary Business Process Modeling," by Breitling, Kornstädt, and Sauer, examine the issue of understanding of a client's (current and future) business processes. They investigate an existing object-oriented method for modeling business processes (EBPM). They identify what rationale is already captured or can be inferred from existing models. They then discuss how such a method could be enhanced with rationale approaches.

Chapter 10, "Promoting and Supporting Requirements Engineering Creativity," by Nguyen and Swatman, tackles the issue of supporting creativity during requirements engineering. Creativity in requirements engineering is often acknowledged but seldom taken into account in current methods. This has often led to the misconception that requirements engineering is an incremental and orderly activity. Instead, focusing on encouraging creativity, this chapter proposes a hybrid approach, combining ad hoc and post hoc recording of rationale to support creative exploration and problem restructuring, respectively.

In summary, these five chapters propose a diverse set of rationale approaches. In evaluating their work with actual requirements engineering problems and case studies, they investigate many practical concerns that are typically encountered when using rationale approaches. More important, stepping back, looking at requirements engineering through rationale glasses, these chapters offer a fresh perspective, often challenging long-held assumptions about both requirements engineering and rationale management.

References

[1] Eden C, Ackermann F (2001) SODA - The principles. In: Rosenhead J, Mingers J (eds.) Rational analysis for a problematic world revisited, Wiley, Chichester

[2] Kotonya G, Sommerville I (2001) Requirements engineering. Processes and techniques, Wiley, Chichester.

[3] Kunz W, Rittel H (1970) Issues As Elements of Information Systems. PhD, University of California.

[4] Nguyen L, Swatman PA (2003) Managing the requirements engineering process. Require. Eng 8:55-68

[5] Rittel H, Weber M (1973) Dilemmas in a general theory of planning. Policy. Sci. 4: 155–169

[6] The Standish Group International, Inc. (1994) The CHAOS Report. http://www.standishgroup.com/chaos (accessed on 8/31/2005)

6 A Hybrid Approach to Upstream Requirements: IBIS and Cognitive Mapping

J. Rooksby, I. Sommerville, M. Pidd

Abstract: We address the problem of eliciting requirements for large-scale technical systems with multiple stakeholders, significant technological uncertainties and extended timescales. Our focus is on the early, 'upstream' stage where options and commitment are just beginning to emerge. Drawing both on problem structuring methods found in management science and on design rationale techniques found in software engineering, we have developed a hybrid process and accompanying software tool support to facilitate consensual problem definition. Negotiation occurs through a combination of informal group problem structuring (cognitive mapping) and incremental formalism (dialogue mapping with IBIS) of requirements. The process and tool have been successfully used in (1) strategy development for revision of a UK Government administrative system, and (2) the negotiation of a 25 year vision by stakeholders in a major technology company.

Keywords: design rationale; decision making; requirements engineering; IBIS; cognitive mapping

6.1 Introduction

Large-scale systems do not come into existence easily. Stakeholders rarely share a unique problem definition, and political, social, economic and environmental factors can have a significant and often dominant influence on the decisions made [16]. An initial obstacle is to get from an unstructured mess [17, 24] to a workable problem definition, and from that to an early set of requirements [19]. This is what we term the 'upstream' stage of requirements engineering.

Existing approaches to requirements engineering acknowledge that requirements stem from different stakeholders, from the operational environment, from the enterprise, and from the availability of new technologies. These approaches also acknowledge that the gestation period may be many years, in which time the staff involved, the available technologies, the organizations priorities and economic situation may change. Reconciling the requirements and implementing them is a crucial issue and is logically and technically difficult [16], is political [1] and is prone to points of crisis [22]; however, eliciting the requirements is often treated as if it were simple, if it is discussed at all. In fact, elicitation is often a highly fraught, conflictual undertaking requiring careful and intensive management by project managers and engineers.

In this chapter, we present a process and tool entitled Wisdom. The Wisdom process and tool addresses the primary obstacle in eliciting requirements: problem definition. This phase revolves around how to structure the problem or need which the system will answer. These early stages of requirements elicitation are primarily concerned with the high-level business or organizational requirements. Failure to get these right means that the more detailed requirements will not be aligned with the needs of the organization. At this early upstream stage, getting the right information (from multiple sources) is only part of the problem. Interacting around that information to structure it in ways that people will accept is also crucial. Conflicts are inevitable at this phase of negotiation [16]. The Wisdom process and tool negotiates these conflicts using a combination of formal and informal group processes supported by software. It also seeks to render this kind of negotiation accountable. Wisdom can therefore be characterized as a "prescriptive" and "intrusive" approach. By using the name Wisdom we are not attempting to specify what it means to be wise or receive wisdom, there being a diverse literature on this. Rather, the name is used to emphasize use of the process and tool to draw out existing organizational knowledge at the right time. We are concerned with how expansive rationale can be captured at the beginning of a project, and issues be explored without decisions necessarily being made.

In Sect. 6.2 of this chapter, we provide a description of the Wisdom process. In Sect. 6.3, we provide an account of the Wisdom tool, which is designed to support the process, with examples of usage in Sect. 6.4. Finally, in Sect. 6.5, we reflect on experiences with the system.

6.2 The Process

The Wisdom process is a hybrid of existing techniques from management science and software engineering. This section will begin by describing those techniques and then continue by explaining why Wisdom brings the two together and describing how this is done.

6.2.1 Background

Two problem-structuring techniques provide the background to Wisdom. The first is cognitive mapping, used in conjunction with the SODA (Strategic Options Development and Analysis) [12] approach to assisting strategic decision making. The second is dialogue mapping with IBIS. Cognitive mapping as a problem structuring technique has previously been introduced into requirements engineering [16]. The design rationale field, while not explicitly focused upon requirements engineering, has historical links to the problems faced: design rationale was originally proposed in the context of software system design as a means of presenting 'the design alternatives which were considered, the arguments for and against these alternatives and the reason why final design decisions were made' [21]. Dialogue mapping with IBIS is a particular technique useful for capturing and structuring design rationale.

Cognitive Mapping

The development and use of cognitive maps within management science owes much to the work of Eden. [12, 13]. An idea is represented in a cognitive map by a node and links between different nodes are intended to represent the relationship between the concepts [13]. These links are causal, in that "concept A" may lead to, or have implications for "concept B". This linking structures the concepts into a hierarchy showing the positive or negative cause and effect between individual concepts across the model (see Fig. 6.1). A complete model that represents the problem space comprises a series of interconnected maps.

Node types can be distinguished in the cognitive map by using different fonts and color coding for each goal, strategy, option and issue. Ad hoc coding of the concepts helps with visualizing or navigating the map, as well as analyzing it. The key to supporting decision making with cognitive maps lies in the SODA process of building maps collaboratively in workshops with groups sharing and negotiating problem issues.

An SODA workshop usually begins with a relatively free ranging brainstorm prompted by a question such as, "what are the issues facing the organization over the next x years?" These concepts are clustered and further developed by the group. Links are added between concepts and concepts color coded according to their type. This problem structuring helps build the big picture and identify key concepts. These key concepts are then ranked by voting to prioritize the issues on which to spend workshop time. The choice of activity at any particular point depends on what the facilitator considers most appropriate to the task.

During the course of a typical SODA workshop a group might cycle through several different brainstorming activities and elaborate various key issues through in-depth discussion. Goals, objectives, strategies, and options will be established before agreeing actions and a way forward.

Commitment to the action plan is achieved through developing shared understanding between participants through participation in the workshop process. Beginning problem definition in this way negotiates conflict upfront, rather than trying to resolve it after requirements have been articulated.

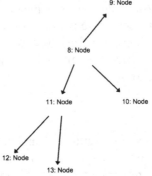

Fig. 6.1. Cognitive map

Dialogue Mapping

Here we discuss dialogue mapping, a facilitated form of argument visualization [7] that can be used as a means to capture design rationale. In dialogue mapping, maps of linked nodes similar to cognitive maps are produced, but with stronger semantics and a finer grain of detail. There are a number of different argument visualization approaches with supporting software tools [15]. Most of these have been inspired by the work of Rittel [25] who devised IBIS. Of these, the most expressive is DRL, implemented in SIBYL [18]. The expressive power of DRL stems from a rich polymorphic node type hierarchy and a set of typed relations that can be used to connect node instances. In contrast to DRL, QOC [20] is a much simpler notation which involves three node types: question, option, and criteria. Options can be evaluated in terms of criteria by linking instances of these node types using supports or challenges relationships. IBIS differs from the other design rationale notations in that it is not concerned with evaluating alternatives, but is geared towards the deliberation process. Conklin has further extended IBIS with regard to the process of using it in face-to-face meetings [8]. Buckingham Shum [5] provides a comprehensive introduction to the aims, uses and applications of the principal design rationale notations and presents the realities of using them.

The nodes of an IBIS map are labeled as questions, ideas or arguments (pros and cons). A map begins by asking a question around an issue that prompts for ideas. The pros and cons that are raised are added against each idea. The links are not causal rather nodes are connected by links with different semantic types. For example, ideas respond to questions and arguments support or object to these ideas (see Fig. 6.2). The IBIS notation ensures that the map represents the dialogue taking place in the group, rather than representing the decision space. The IBIS notation represents both the argument and provides a protocol for interacting. Questions are central to IBIS, particularly when there is disagreement or misunderstanding around an issue. The issue is transformed by the facilitator into a question, which is then explored as part of the map. This diffuses the personal issues that arise from adversarial discussion and supports collaborative enquiry of the "Yes, and ..." rather than "Yes, but ..." kind.

A session does not begin with a wide-ranging brainstorming activity, instead a question is posed that prompts for ideas (options) that directly address the problem. A map is built outwards from this, with parallel maps being added. This initial stage is less wide-ranging than SODA and risks elaborating a side issue in great depth before the true problem is identified [31]. It relies on the group self correcting itself to identify the real issues. It does however lend itself to fine-grained analysis of a specific issue and its structure makes it easier to maintain the map over time.

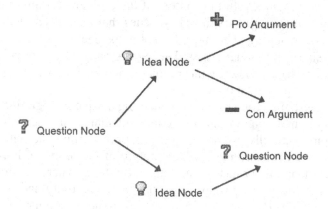

Fig. 6.2. Dialogue map

6.2.2 The Wisdom Process

Both cognitive mapping and dialogue mapping address different aspects of the problem of eliciting upstream requirements. While both techniques have been used in isolation by the management science and computing communities respectively, we are not aware of any work that has combined them. The value of the Wisdom process lies in capitalizing on the strengths of both cognitive mapping and dialogue mapping; we view the two techniques as complementary.

For typical systems engineering projects, the upstream requirements phase is essential to generate a sufficient level of understanding of the project. Furthermore, this understanding should be agreed and common to the many stakeholders who have an interest in the project. The Wisdom process is not a hard process leading to finalized requirements but aims to provide stakeholders with a common and agreed understanding with which they can proceed. Cognitive mapping is used in the initial phases of the Wisdom process. As reported earlier, cognitive mapping is fundamentally used with a group process to support procedural rationality. The result of cognitive mapping is agreement and commitment to a way forward that will likely have involved negotiation. Dialogue mapping is used in later phases of the Wisdom process. Dialogue mapping differs to cognitive mapping since its starting point is a relatively narrow issue. Dialogue mapping is more suited to situations where the key issues tend to be known and the focus is a more detailed analysis of these. In addition, argument visualization languages are more formal, being based on a type system with defined semantics. In the context of the problem definition phase, we use dialogue mapping to explore key issues that have been identified during cognitive mapping. The more formal maps enable rigorous discussion and analysis of individual issues. During the early phase, cognitive mapping gives a macro view of the problem, and in the later phase, design rationale maps provide a micro view.

We suggest that for systems engineering projects, cognitive mapping and dialogue mapping are not just complementary, but necessary. Cognitive mapping naturally promotes divergent brainstorming activities that are necessary to understand the systemic nature of the problem. Furthermore, cognitive mapping avoids groupthink, which is where a single issue becomes the focus of a group. This constrains creativity and impedes divergent thinking. Having identified the key issues, dialogue maps can be used to explore each issue in greater depth. A dialogue map explicitly captures the arguments that emerge for each issue. In essence, cognitive mapping is better at developing an understanding of the whole, while dialogue maps enable in-depth and detailed deliberation around particular issues. The benefit is twofold, not only is the rationale 'captured', but in the process of doing so that rationale is forced to be expansive and well articulated.

The effectiveness of a meeting is dependent on the skills of a neutral facilitator [9, 30]. A facilitator is not merely a passive agent who minutes a meeting. Rather the facilitator's objective is to foster procedural rationality, where stakeholders agree that sensible decisions have been made and commit to them. In practice, a facilitator ensures that a meeting remains focused, that the evolving cognitive map accurately reflects the ongoing discussion, that stakeholders get the opportunity to air their views and that the decision process is sensible. During the problem definition phase, such decisions will have an impact on the subsequent requirement definition phase. It is clearly important that where compromises have been made, affected stakeholders are aware of them and are willing to commit to them.

In developing the Wisdom process, we experimented with three methods of representation: QOC, DRL, and IBIS. With DRL, we found that its complex type hierarchy caused people without a background in computing difficult to use. QOC is a much simpler language, but similarly to DRL, is concerned with evaluating options to relatively well-understood problems. QOC is well suited to making long-term rationale explicit [11]. Since IBIS has been designed to support deliberation and discussion as opposed to evaluating particular design options, we have found it better suited the problem definition phase. Moreover, its simple and intuitive type system is easy to use by nontechnical personnel.

As final comments on the Wisdom process we will discuss preparation and final documentation. We recognize that stakeholders are likely to be represented by senior personnel from geographically distributed locations. These factors mean that organizing meetings is difficult and that they should be as productive as possible. We emphasize the benefit of holding face to face meetings at times such as the upstream stage where the 'what' and the 'why' must emerge. Distributed, facilitated meetings are possible but are still not as rich as face-to-face interactions [9]. Prior to meetings, we suggest a preparatory activity where all stakeholders are invited to provide initial input. Based on these inputs, a first-cut cognitive map is generated in terms of nodes but without links. This enables the facilitator to gain familiarity with the problem, in terms of issues, and to do initial work such as removing synonym issues. Furthermore, the preparatory activity allows meetings to be constructive more quickly than having to start from a blank sheet. Documentation from the problem definition phase is critical since it determines system requirements. Moreover, personnel who join a project can use the documentation to understand how and why requirements have been derived. The maps that result from the problem definition phase are the first of many documents that should be held in a project repository.

6.3 The Tool

We have developed a tool to support the wisdom process. We will begin this section with a background discussion of cognitive mapping and design rationale tools, and then continue with a discussion of the Wisdom tool.

6.3.1 Background

Cognitive mapping and dialogue mapping software exists (including Decision Explorer™, Questmap™ and Compendium™), and it is also true that whiteboards or sticky notes can be used to support the processes. So why develop a new piece of software? For a start, software is essential to manage the scale and complexity of data. For example, it is not uncommon for half-day workshops to generate 300 nodes. More importantly, during successive 'gathers' each participant may input several dozen ideas. The facilitator needs software to manage the flow of text that results from asynchronous and synchronous input. It is also important to store the data to make the rationale for decisions accessible at later stages of development. Given that the Wisdom process combines cognitive mapping and dialogue mapping, a software tool that allows users to work with both techniques is clearly required. Furthermore, for hybrid maps, the use of separate tools for each technique is unworkable. Although cognitive mapping and dialogue mapping software exists, no other tool readily supports both techniques.

6.3.2 The Wisdom Tool

The Wisdom tool (Figs. 6.3 and 6.4) supports facilitated meetings with functionality to create, edit, store, and browse cognitive maps, dialogue maps, and hybrid maps. Hybrid maps allow cognitive mapping and dialogue mapping activities to be intermixed where appropriate. For example, where a particular issue is being deliberated using IBIS, inclusion of cognitive mapping elements that relate to the holistic view may be desirable to clarify the context of the specific issue or to resolve uncertainty.

Based on formative evaluations, we have refined the tool in order to minimize its overhead in a facilitated session. A cumbersome tool is detrimental to the effectiveness of the facilitator. Indeed, this is consistent with our argument to use cognitive mapping as opposed to dialogue mapping in the early stages of problem definition since the overhead associated with using dialogue mapping may unduly constrain brainstorming work.

The tool does little more than support meetings and store maps from those meetings. Features associated with management of rationale over the duration of a project, or over a number of projects are deliberately left absent. We concentrated on producing a tool that runs at a consistently fast speed and offers nothing that is not core to the process. In particular, we concentrated on producing a streamlined user interface. Rather than include features for rationale management, we decided to create a facility to export maps to dedicated rationale management software.

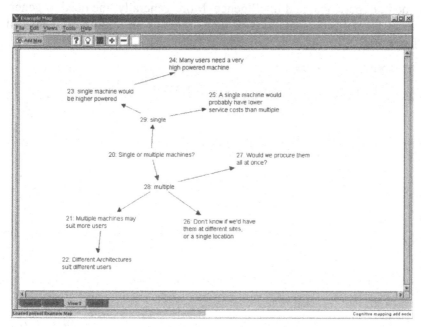

Fig. 6.3. Wisdom screen, cognitive map

To address premeeting preparation, the tool provides a distributed gather service. Initially, the facilitator uses this service to construct a questionnaire. The tool generates a web-based form which remote participants are then invited to complete. Based on the participants' responses, the tool generates a cognitive map. The facilitator uses this map to prepare for subsequent facilitated sessions. The same functionality can be used during meetings so that meeting participants can simultaneously build a cognitive map which the facilitator can structure "on the fly". For traceability, the tool stores maps and provides simple reporting facilities in addition to the graphical views.

We investigated whether we should provide support for the transition from cognitive to IBIS maps. For the latter, we considered building a set of heuristics that could be used. For example, one guideline involved finding cognitive mapping nodes which are tightly connected to others and make such nodes candidate IBIS questions. In this way, issues would be prioritized. However, based on experiments, it appears that active human involvement in this process is important to maintain a group's collective cognition of the problem. Furthermore, the transition requires human judgment, experience, and intelligence. More generally, the need to generate more formal representations of maps remains an important avenue of further work.

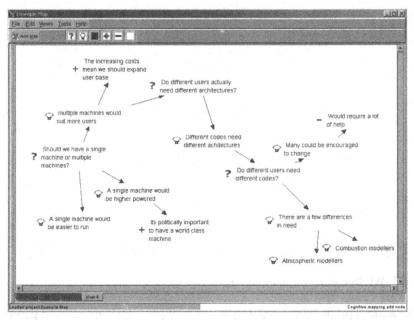

Fig. 6.4. Wisdom screen, dialogue map

6.4 Example

In Sect. 6.5 of this chapter, we will discuss real experiences of using Wisdom. As a result of the sensitivity of the information produced during those sessions we cannot publish the results in any detail and so will first use a scenario to illustrate the use of Wisdom. The scenario will concern upstream requirements in procurement of a high performance computing service.

Eliciting requirements for a national high performance computing (HPC) service is a complex procedure, encountering all of the problems a typical requirements engineering project might expect [26], including multiple stakeholders, extended timescales and limited resources. HPC procurement involves negotiation and agreement of multimillion pound, custom built machines. Different architectures suit different types of scientific computing and thus different stakeholders, and in addition different stakeholders will have different requirements for the services surrounding these machines including data visualization, acceptable queuing times and data security. Managing requirements is an intensive task, and in particular the upstream stage is complicated and difficult to get right. Bad decisions made at this point can have serious and costly repercussions later on. The upstream stage must address many issues, including how UK science might benefit from a new machine, which forms of science will be catered for, and whether the timing is right. The upstream stage will involve general discussions of possible technologies, but at this point should not involve decisions about them.

Using the Wisdom process to address these upstream issues, a workshop for senior stakeholders in national HPC would be convened. The stakeholders must include those with responsibility for the project, those with a good understanding of national scientific policy and practice, and with a good understanding of HPC. A few days prior to the workshop, the facilitator should gather information from participants via Wisdom's web-based gather facility. The facilitator will pose a very open question such as "What issues must the procurers of a new national HPC service address?" This will help to get stakeholders to start thinking about what they will discuss at the workshop. The facilitator will arrange the issues on a cognitive map to provide a starting point for the workshop. The workshop proper would begin with further brainstorming. In Fig. 6.3 we give an imagined cognitive map from such a brainstorming. The initial node on this map is node 20: "single or multiple machines?" This node will have been taken from a larger, more general map made earlier and is surrounded by issues that have arisen in response to it. The node has links to two other nodes: node 28 "multiple" and node 29 "single". Note that these two nodes have been put in later than some of the nodes they lead to. This has resulted from the facilitator reorganizing the map after a number of nodes have been added in response to node 20. Doing this reorganization makes the map easier to read, and also makes it easier to see that stakeholders are not fixated on, say, issues surrounding multiple machines.

At this point the facilitator will hold a discussion on what issues need to be focused on in the remainder of the workshop, and if necessary a vote. Later in the workshop, dialogue maps will begin with the issues selected. In Fig. 6.4 a dialogue map is begun with the question "should we have a single machine or multiple machines?" This question echoes the node discussed in the cognitive map. The facilitator has deliberately not divided the answers up into "single" and "multiple" here to avoid the stakeholders being pushed into conflict or to make a decision that would be too early at this point. Selected nodes from the cognitive map have been written up as ideas. The stakeholders are asked to focus more on the pros and cons of ideas here, and the idea "multiple machines would suit more users" is supported with the pro node "the increasing costs means we should expand the user base." By focusing on the issue, however, a stakeholder has begun to question its validity. The stakeholders have up to this point made the assumption that different scientists require different architectures, but the question is raised "Do users actually require different architectures?" and it transpires from this that different algorithms require different architectures and so the relationship between scientists' needs and their algorithms come into question. From discussions such as this, we believe that the problem becomes much better articulated and understood and the following steps in establishing requirements for, in this case a high performance computer, can be taken more competently.

6.5 Experience

This section will outline two uses of Wisdom and discuss the broad issues that arose. We discuss the revision of a UK Government administrative system, and negotiation of a 25-year vision for a military technology organization. The first took place as formative evaluation, with an early version of Wisdom, and a "friendly" client. The second took place with a completed version of Wisdom. We were fortunate in being able to use Wisdom in these major upstream requirements exercises, but with that comes the problem that we cannot reproduce the data from these exercises in print.

Substantive formative evaluation took place with a 'friendly' client undertaking a major project. A UK Government department was looking at wholesale revision of its administrative system and logistical support, and invited the Wisdom team to run a three-hour workshop with six of its employees. The client had devised an interim set of proposals and used the workshop to develop a strategy to take work forward. It was an ambiguous and complex problem with distributed stakeholders. Decisions made at that point would have a knock on effect for the remainder of the project. The client found the workshop useful, and proceeded using the strategy begun there. The workshop was a test case for Wisdom, in which we were able to get a good grasp of the divergence and convergence that the Wisdom process affords and to gain practical requirements for the software tool (such as the speeds it must allow node entry, appropriate font size and more) and to expose bugs.

Later, substantive evaluation took place with a planning project for a major military technology company. The client wished to hold a series of workshops to consider what they should be producing in 25-years time. Given the very long lead time for complex military systems, this meant that they were interested in developing high-level systems requirements now that could serve as a basis for technology assessment and conceptual system design. They had organized training in dialogue mapping for two of its employees, who became interested in Wisdom. The Wisdom team were invited to part run three workshops in collaboration with these two client employees. The Wisdom process and tool were used in two workshops and the Wisdom process and a commercially available tool in the third. Many high-ranking members of the client company were brought together, each with their own viewpoints, concerns and agendas. Wisdom is ideal for the upstream combination of ambiguous problem and multiple stakeholders. No decision or explicit consensus was sought as an outcome of the workshops but a map of the various issues.

The workshops were held with approximately 10–15 stakeholders attending plus a trainee facilitator from within the organization sharing the facilitator role with an experienced facilitator from the Wisdom team. In the first workshop, Wisdom was used to support a brainstorming session that produced 83 separate nodes. These were then discussed and reduced to 15 key issues. One of these issues, to give an example, was safety. Thus Wisdom was used to support an initial divergent phase and a following convergent activity. At this point the stakeholders wished to vote on the importance of each issue. This vote is not a part of the generic Wisdom process, but the process is flexible enough to allow for its inclusion. The importance ascribed to each issue was used to determine how long was spent discussing it. The Wisdom process was then continued with a dialogue mapping activity. The outcome of the workshop was an agreed map of the issues small enough to be printed on one side of A4 paper. The second workshop was dominated by brainstorming and clustering of ideas and by use of the Wisdom tool for cognitive mapping. Dialogue maps were used for the clustering of ideas. The third workshop was almost entirely composed of dialogue mapping, complementing the outcome of the second.

Our experience in the workshops was that the Wisdom process led to divergent followed by convergent group activity and that this was demonstrated to be particularly useful in relation to conflict. One issue that was raised by a participant was met be hostile groans by other participants and met with indifference by others. The issue was a cross cutting concern with potential relevance to much of the decisions to be made. The participant who raised it felt strongly about it. The facilitator was able to handle this by entering a divergent phase of mapping out the issue, covering why it might or might not be relevant, what the implications might be and attempts to recall precedents set for this issue in other planning situations and indeed legal issues related to it. This issue became accepted as having relevance, but as being of low priority. A very small IBIS map was produced around the issue.

The Wisdom process was used in all three of the workshops described earlier, however, the tool was not used throughout as the facilitator wished to use a commercially available tool for dialogue mapping. This was through no shortcoming of the Wisdom tool but because, as a product of a research project, the Wisdom tool cannot be given guaranteed support after the project is complete. This did not seem to adversely affect the workshop as the stakeholders did not seem to notice the change of software, although we question whether more hybrid maps might have been produced had we used the Wisdom tool throughout. The significant problem that arose for us was that when asked to comment on the effectiveness of the workshop, the workshop participants did not differentiate between Wisdom and the commercial tool. The comments made by participants at the end of the workshops were exclusively positive, but again were not simply attributable to Wisdom as the participants had rarely been in the same room together and so commented not just on how effective the Wisdom workshop was, but on how effective it is to have any sort of workshop in the first place.

6.6 Discussion

Evaluation and requirements engineering methodology do not always go hand in hand. Evaluation is very difficult in this situation; as we have discussed in the earlier section, comparison of a particular technique with another, or of one tool with another is often impossible in practice. Dix [10] points out that in situations such as this, evaluation can be methodologically unsound, and that rather than attempting to conform to some model of experimentation we must concentrate on qualitative insight. Research in this instance is investigation and exploration and not the construction of a product. Wisdom is not a product but a research project and our writing here is to communicate the insights from the research. We do not wish to persuade people to specifically use the Wisdom process and tool but to pick up upon the lessons learned and incorporate them into their own research or practice. It is true in much requirements engineering and design rationale research that the results presented are qualitative insights, and we believe that is no bad thing.

Given that the participants in our workshops were rarely in the same country, let alone the same room together, and that they had not used any visual argumentation in a facilitated requirements workshop before, they were unable to separate the value of Wisdom from the value of simply holding a workshop. Given that these were workshops to plan a 25-year vision, the outcomes and the connections of these outcomes to work done over the next quarter of a century are ambiguous. In this situation, we cannot make substantial claims about Wisdom being any more effective than alternative methods, but can conclude that Wisdom as a hybrid technique does work and is seen by participants to be better than no technique at all. This might be seen as a small claim, but it is a foundation for the legitimacy of the insights offered in this chapter.

We have focused on the early stage of requirements engineering, the upstream stage, where the "what" and "why" of a system must emerge. This is a stage where eliciting rather than managing rationale is required, and in conjunction with handling conflict, encouraging coverage of possibilities and formation of a team with ownership of the system. As a decision support tool, Wisdom is a tool for not making decisions, our notion being that it is too easy to rush into decisions without sufficient grounding. We put conflict up front, using early sessions that allow conflicting issues to be mapped out without forcing judgments to be made. We then seek to manage conflict, but not necessarily resolve it, by using a convergent technique that supports "yes...and" rather than "yes...but" argumentation.

A negotiation technique that has covered similar issues is WinWin [2, 3] whereby stakeholders iteratively negotiate shared "win" conditions for software and systems requirements. The WinWin technique is longitudinal and attempts to balance the discovering, negotiating, elaborating and prioritizing of objectives with things like maintaining a creative flow of ideas [4], and ensuring validity of the models produced [14]. Compendium [27, 29] is a method (with a suite of associated tools) for combining argumentation with knowledge management. It differs to Wisdom in that it does not address divergent cognitive mapping (although it has been put to other innovative uses [6,28]) and that it offers extensive facility for longitudinal knowledge management. At the time we compared the Wisdom tool to the Compendium tools we found the latter ran marginally too slow for our purposes.

Nguyen and Swatman [22] give an interesting account of the requirements engineering process as necessarily containing a number of crisis points where the problem space must be reconfigured. Our intention was to draw out conflict up front, but while doing that might be useful, it is probable that conflicts will always arise at points in a project. It is possible that a Wisdom style workshop would be appropriate for use at these various crisis points. We end with two broader points useful when thinking about what has been achieved in Wisdom and where future work may be needed. Law [17] makes the point that when representing complex situations we usually try to make the mess absent. He suggests rehabilitation of mess, or finding ways to know mess. Finally, making an interesting contrast to our intention to capture expansive rationale, Nietzsche has said "There is a great deal I do not want to know – wisdom sets bounds even to knowledge" [23,p. 73].

Acknowledgments. Adrian Mackenzie, Mark Westcombe, Ian Warren, and Victor Ochieng Onditi have made significant contributions to the work described in this chapter.

References

[1]   Bergman M, Leslie King J, Lyytinen K (2002) Large-scale requirements analysis revisited: The need for understanding the political ecology of requirements engineering. Requir. Eng. 7: 152–171

[2]   Boehm BW, Bose P, Horowitz, Lee MJ (1995) Software requirements negotiation and renegotiation aids: A theory W-based spiral approach. In: Proceedings of the 17th International Conference on Software Engineering (ICSE), ACM, New York, pp. 243–253

[3]   Boehm BW, Egyed A, Kwan J, Port D, Shah A, Madachy RJ (1998) Using the Win Win spiral model: A case study. IEEE Comput. 31(7): 33–44

[4]   Briggs RO, Grünbacher P (2002) EasyWinWin: Managing complexity in requirements negotiation with GSS. In: Proceedings of the Hawaii International Conference on System Sciences 2002, IEEE Computer Society, Los Alamitos, CA.

[5]   Buckingham Shum S (1996) Analysing the usability of a design rationale notation. In: Moran TP, Carroll JM (eds.) Design Rationale: Concepts, Techniques, and use, Lawrence Erlbaum Associates, Hillsdale, NJ pp. 185–215

[6]   Buckingham Shum S, De Roure D, Eisenstadt M, Shadbolt N (2002) CoAK-TinG: Collaborative advanced knowledge technologies in the grid. In: Proceedings of the Second Workshop on Advanced Collaborative Environments. Eleventh IEEE International Symposium on High Performance Distributed Computing. July 24–26, 2002, Edinburgh.

[7]   Conklin J (2003) Dialogue mapping: Reflections on an industrial strength case study. In: Kirschner P, Buckingham Shum S, Carr C (eds.) Visualizing argumentation. Software Tools for Collaborative and Educational Sensemaking. Springer, London Berlin Heidelberg New York, pp. 117–135

[8]   Conklin J, Selvin A, Buckingham Shum S, Sierhuis M (2001) Facilitated hypertext for collective sensemaking: 15 years on from gIBIS. In: Proceedings of ACM Hypertext 2001, Aarhus, Denmark, pp.123–124

[9]   Damian D, Eblerlein A, Shaw M, Gaines B (2003) An exploratory study of facilitation in distributed requirements engineering. Requir. Eng 8: 23-41

[10] Dix A (2005) Validity. In: Reflexive HCI: Towards a Critical Technical Practice, Workshop at CHI 2004, 26th April 2004, Vienna, Austria

[11] Dutoit A, Paech B (2002) Rationale-based use case specification. Requir. Eng. 7:3–19

[12] Eden C, Ackermann F (2001) SODA - The principles. In: Rosenhead J, Mingers J (eds.) Rational Analysis for a Problematic World Revisited, Wiley, Chichester

[13] Eden C, Ackermann F (1998) Making strategy: The Journey of Strategic Management. London, Sage Publications

[14] Halling M, Biffl S, Grünbacher P (2003) An economic approach for improving requirements negotiation models with inspection. Requir. Eng. 8:236–247

[15] Kirschner P, Buckingham Shum S, Carr C (eds) (2003) Visualizing argumentation. Software tools for collaborative and educational sense-making. Springer, London Berlin Heidelberg New York

[16] Kotonya G, Sommerville I (2001) Requirements engineering. Processes and techniques, Wiley, Chichester.

[17] Law J (2003) Making a mess of a method. Published by the Centre for Science Studies, Lancaster University, Lancaster LA1 4YN, UK. Available at http://www.comp.lancs.ac.uk/sociology/papers/law-making-a-mess-with-method.pdf

[18] Lee J, Lai KC (1991) What's in design rationale? Hum.–Comput. Interact. 6, 3&4: 251–280

[19] Mackenzie A, Pidd M, Rooksby J, Sommerville I, Warren I, Westcombe M (2006) *Wisdom*, decision support and paradigms of decision making. Eur. J. Operat. Res., 170, 1:156–171

[20] MacLean A, Bellotti T, Young R, Moran T (1991) Questions, options and criteria: Elements of design space analysis. Hum.–Comput. Interact. 6, 3&4: 201–250

[21] Monk S, Sommerville I, Pendaries JM, Durin B (1995) Supporting design rationale for system evolution. In: Schäfer W, Botella P (eds.) Proceedings of Software Engineering – ESEC'95, Springer, Berlin Heidelberg New York, pp. 307–323

[22] Nguyen L, Swatman PA (2003) Managing the requirements engineering process. Requir. Eng. 8:55–68

[23] Nietzsche N (1889/2004) Why I Am so Wise (Trans. Hollingdale RJ). Penguin Books, London

[24] Pidd M (2002) Tools for Thinking: Modelling in Management Science, 2nd ed.. Wiley, Chichester.

[25] Rittel HJ, Kunz W (1970) Issues as elements of information systems. Working paper 131, Institute of Urban and Regional Development, University of California at Berkeley.

[26] Rooksby J, Westcombe M, Pidd M, Sommerville I (2003) Managing stakeholder requirements in high performance computing procurement. In: Proc. of UK e-Science All Hands Meeting, Nottingham, 2–4 September, pp. 878–884

[27] Selvin A (2003) Fostering collective intelligence: Helping groups use visualized argumentation. In: Kirschner P, Buckingham Shum S, Carr C. (eds.) Visualizing Argumentation. Software Tools for Collaborative and Educational Sense-Making. Springer, London, pp.137–163

[28] Selvin A, Buckingham Shum S, Magellen Horth D, Palus C, Sierhuis M (2002) Knowledge art: Visual sensemaking using combined Compendium and Visual Explorer methodologies. Presented at The Art of Management and Organisation Conference, 3–6 September 2002, London.

[29] Selvin A, Buckingham Shum S, Sierhuis M, Conklin J, Zimmermann B, Palus C, Drath W, Horth D, Domingue J, Motta E, Li G (2001) Compendium: Making maps into knowledge events. Presented at Knowledge Technologies 2001, March 4–7, Austin TX.

[30] Viller S (1991) The group facilitator: A CSCW perspective. In: 2nd European Conference on Computer Supported Cooperative Work (ECSCW), Amsterdam, 25–27 September

[31] Westcombe M, Pidd M (2002) Problem solving dialogue: Cognitive mapping and IBIS. Working paper MS01/02. Management School, Lancaster University, UK

7 From DREAM to Reality: Specificities of Interactive Systems Development With Respect To Rationale Management

X. Lacaze, P. Palanque, E. Barboni, R. Bastide, D. Navarre

Abstract: This chapter presents a notation and a tool dedicated to the support of exploration of options and traceability of choices during the development process of interactive safety critical systems. The paper presents first the notation TEAM (Traceability, Exploration and Analysis Model) and its specificities with respect to other Design Rationale notations. Both the notation and the tools called DREAM (Design Rationale Environment for Argumentation and Modeling) are presented on a case study showing how they can support design of interaction techniques for Air Traffic Control work-stations.

Keywords: design rationale in software engineering; human computer interaction; case study; tool support; TEAM, DREAM, QOC

7.1 Introduction

Interactive systems construction requires customized development processes (with respect to main stream software engineering) [20] making more salient the implication of users throughout the various phases and especially during requirements elicitation and evaluation for which evaluation with users is critical. In the same way these development processes advocate the design of multiple solutions (in order to foster users' involvement) providing users with various kinds of prototypes (both low-fidelity and high-fidelity) [24]. The fact that several prototypes, either paper or software, are proposed and evaluated, increases the communication between designers and users and also increases usability of the system. However, this proliferation of options and solutions makes rationale management much more cumbersome.

In the field of safety critical interactive software, such as Air Traffic Control workstations or interactive cockpits, rationale management becomes more and more critical. Incidents/accidents investigation and certification prior to deployment are two main reasons for such an interest in the rationale for selected design options. Our approach focuses mainly on safety critical systems (see Sect. 1.6.1) to provide high-quality decisions.

Since 1990 we have been working in the field of formal description techniques for safety critical interactive distributed software. This work encompasses the definition of a formalism called Interactive Cooperative Objects based on High-level Petri nets and objects [3,4] specific extensions for distributed interactive systems [5, 6] and a CASE tool called PetShop [17, 18] for the edition, formal analysis and execution of the models.

Our notation and tools have been applied to several application domains such as satellite command and control workstations [22], Air Traffic Control workstation for en-route air traffic management [23], interactive military cockpits (RAFALE Aircraft) [7] or interactive civil aircraft cockpits (Airbus A380) [19].

Applying our research results to several domains has brought a new light on our work by showing that providing a reliable solution is not more valuable than providing the detailed rationale for that particular solution. Adding rationale behind decision improves the quality of interactive systems (see Sect. 1.4.3.). For approximately three years now, we have been working on a project for finding ways of providing the various participants throughout the development process of interactive safety critical software with notations and tools for the rationale management. The first version of the notation called TEAM (Traceability, Exploration and Analysis Mode) and its CASE tool (called DREAM for Design Rationale Environment for Argumentation and Modeling) are available on the web at the following address http://liihs.irit.fr/dream. They have been applied to several case studies and the aim of the chapter is to present those results in detail.

7.2 State of Art in Rationale Management for Interactive Systems

Since the seminal work from Toulmin [27] in the late 1950s, design management and argumentation have been the focus of many research activities.

Interactive systems design (and more broadly speaking the Human–Computer Interaction field) promotes a user-centered design approach [21] to interactive system engineering that involves users in various phases. For instance, task analysis and modeling provide support for capturing and representing user activities [9] while interacting with a system. Such information is then incorporated in many places in the design process as, for instance, in the design phases when the allocation of functions between the system and the users is defined, or later (in the evaluation phases) when the system is tested in order to check whether or not user activities are exhaustively supported by the system.

Our approach in design rationale is related to argumentation as defined in Sect. 1.3. The main notations related to this type of design rationale are IBIS (Issue-Based Information System) [12], see Sect. 1.3.1. and QOC (Questions, Options, Criteria) [14] see Sect. 1.3.2. These notations are able to capture argumentation and alternatives during the design process. These notations cannot store specific information related to interactive systems such as system modeling, task models, etc. Our proposal (detailed in Sect. 7.3) is to provide interactive systems designers with a notation for rationale management able to take into account specificities of interactive systems and more precisely safety critical ones. To this end, our approach focuses on Human–Computer Interaction concepts and how to integrate them. Besides, our approach is tool supported in order to address both scalability and cost/benefit concerns.

7.3 TEAM Notation

The TEAM (Traceability, Exploration and Analysis Mode) notation is based on QOC (as stated above introduced by MacLean [14]) and proposes several extensions in order to deal with the specificities of safety critical interactive systems and also to address some of the usability issues of QOC. The rationale for extending QOC is mainly based on its simplicity and readability that makes it understandable by most of the actors involved in interactive systems design such as graphic designers, developers, customers, certification authorities, etc. This easy to read and write notation, enhances collaboration between the participants as previously defined in Sect. 1.4.1. QOC was designed to support reuse [16] in order to improve the reusability of the models (see Sect. 1.4.2.).

7.3.1 Dealing with Usability (Criteria and Factors)

MacLean introduced the notion of criteria and criteria that are more general in order to gather criteria. Having the same name for two concepts makes diagrams fuzzy, thus we decided to define criteria that are more general into factors (which is a concept largely used in software engineering). We exploit the definition from McCall's work on factors from [15] and from other work [25] that defines a relationship between criteria and factors. The notion of criteria in QOC is thus defined by the following: (1)

quality factors correspond to requirements expressed by the clients and/or users; (2) quality criteria are elements that can be measured; (3) metrics: is the actual value of a couple option–criterion for a given scenario of use. Metrics values can be written on the connector between an option and a criterion. Metrics information must be considered as quantitative information and not as qualitative information. Additionally, previous work [13] we have done in the field explains how such values can be computed using performance evaluation techniques.

Buckingham Shum's [26] usability studies on QOC notation reveals that QOC users need to be able to compare the criteria related to an option (i.e., to express which one is more important for instance). To address this issue, our proposal is to associate a weight to criteria and to factors. Weights range from 1 (important) to 5 (optional). This extension allows users to capture more information in the models. However, Buckingham Shum warns that weight can make it possible for users to distort argumentation.

We propose to relate argument entities, previously defined by MacLean, to all elements of the models and not only to argue the evaluation put on the links option/criterion.

7.3.2 Integrating Task Analysis/Task Modeling Aspects

Task analysis and modeling [9] is also a critical element of user-centered design methods and thus critical for the engineering of safety critical interactive systems. A task model is a representation of user tasks often involving some form of interaction with a system influenced by its contextual environment. We propose extensions to QOC in order to deal explicitly with task models as well as with scenarios that correspond to execution paths in the task models. We add two new entities to the QOC notation namely task models and scenarios. A design option, dealing with the dialogue aspect (see Sect. 7.3.3), can propose a task model. From the task model we can extract relevant scenarios. A relevant scenario focuses on one of the metrics (introduced earlier) we want to measure on the interactive system. To this end, a scenario is related to a couple criterion–option and the metrics are directly stored on the edge between the option and the criterion.

7.3.3 Software Architecture Structuring of Rationale Management

Software architectures dedicated to interactive software have been proposed since the early 1980s and the most known ones are the Seeheim model [10] or the ARCH model [1,2]. The ARCH model is an extension of the Seeheim model. We chose the ARCH model because it proposes a generic view of an interactive system. The ARCH model breaks down an interactive system into five components: domain specific component, domain adaptor component, dialogue component, logical presentation component, and physical presentation component. We turn this model into a simple ARCH model within only three components. The first two components are dedicated to the noninteractive part of an interactive system and are thus merged in a component called *functional core*. As we are less concerned with implementation issues than design ones, we have decided to merge presentation components together in a component called *presentation component*. In our models, questions can be structured according to that architecture and thus related to one of the components: *functional core*, *dialogue*, and *presentation*. This relationship might not be defined and thus a question is not necessarily related to a component to capture, for instance, broader topics.

This structuring supports decomposition of problems adequately when dealing with interactive systems. In addition, it makes it possible for managing the argumentation at various levels of abstraction from higher-level phases such as specifications but also at lower level phases such as detailed design and implementation phases and this for any of these components.

7.3.4 Conclusion

All the extensions proposed are dedicated to the support of designers' activities such as structuring of models, editing of models and information retrieval from models. All the extensions supported by TEAM notation are summarized in the entity relationship diagram presented in Fig. 7.1. Additional extensions such as design choices for each node (i.e., questions, options, etc.) connection of arguments…are available in TEAM but have not been presented in the previous sections, as they are *standard* extensions in rationale management and not specific to interactive systems.

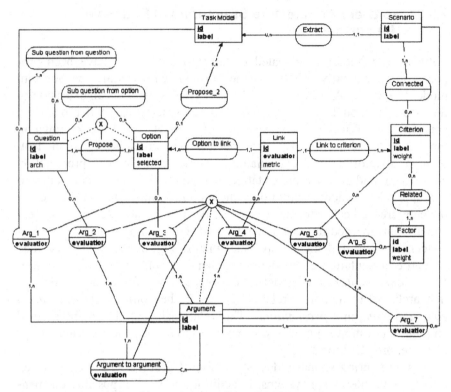

Fig. 7.1. Entity relationship model describing TEAM notation

Fig. 7.1 displays the entity relationship model of the TEAM notation. Rectangles represent entities; entity name is the first item in the box and the attributes describing the content of the entity below. Similarly, rounded rectangles represent relationships. Keys attributes are both bold and underlined while required attributes (at modeling time) are highlighted in bold. A cross in the circle highlights exclusions constraints between relationships.

7.4 DREAM Tool

The TEAM notation is supported by a tool and an environment called DREAM (Design Rationale Environment for Argumentation and Modeling) for the edition of models (taking into account all the elements of the notation presented above), the analysis of models (to check whether all the options have been argued, commented,…) and the exploitation of models (to allow for argumentation and traceability of the models throughout the project and to allow for reuse for further projects).

The DREAM tool also supports the management of teamwork and sessions thus supporting traceability of decisions according to the people that make them, but also according to the time when those decisions have been made. A session is made up of three elements: the model, the date, and the list of people involved in the construction of the model. Most of the time, a session corresponds to a meeting or an iteration in an UCD approach. DREAM tool does not address issues such as the capture problem defined in Sect. 1.7.2 because our first goal was to build a tool able to edit and store TEAM models. DREAM[11] is publicly available and can be downloaded on the following web page: http://liihs.irit.fr/dream/.

7.4.1 Overview and Principle

As can be seen in Fig. 7.2, the DREAM user interface is broken down into five frames. Frame 5 is the main editing zone where users can create, edit, modify and visualize models. Frame 1 displays the list of authors that contributed to the model. This list can be edited. Frame 2 contains the history of changes made to the model and displays all the sessions related to the current model. Selecting a session changes the display in frame 5 and replaces current model in that frame by the one stored in the selected session. Frame 3 presents a mini-map global view of the edited model displayed in frame 5; the red rectangle corresponds to the portion of the whole diagram that is displayed in frame 5. Modification of the displayed zone can be done using direct manipulation of the red rectangle in frame 3. Frame 4 presents another representation of the model; this tree like view is based on bifocal tree visualization techniques [8].

Edition of TEAM models can be done using direct manipulation of nodes and edges. A given node (let say criterion 3) can appear in several places in a model. In order to do so, the second occurrence of this node must be created by copying and pasting the first occurrence. These two occurrences of the same node are then linked i.e., one modification of one occurrence being automatically performed on the other instance. Node duplication reduces significantly the number of crossing edges in a model. It also makes the model more readable as all the criterion or options appear close to each question. User manages spatial arrangements in order to

---

[11] DREAM is fully based on model-view-controller architecture and develops in Java. Data are stored in XML (eXtensible Markup Language) files, according to a syntax described in a DTD (Document Type Definition).

make the model layout in a way that makes it easier to read. However, it increases significantly the complexity of some tasks such as, identifying all the options related to a given criterion if that criterion has been duplicated several times[12]. Frame 4 has been introduced in order to solve this problem. Indeed, manipulation in that frame allows users to select a given node to precisely check all its connected nodes. It is important to note that the spatial arrangement of the elements is free.

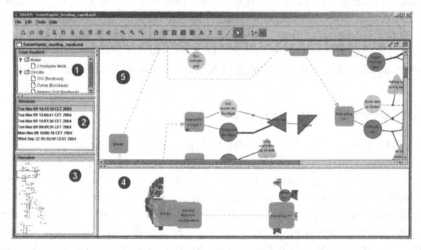

Fig. 7.2. User interface of DREAM

Performing a user-centered design approach on our tool, we have done some task analysis on users involved in rationale management. Two main tasks have been identified; first model creation and modification (called models edition); second model exploitation involving reading, printing, checking verification. The DREAM tool explicitly supports these two tasks (described in Sects. 7.4.2 and 7.4.3) providing users with highly interactive manipulation and visualization techniques.

The main advantages of the DREAM tool relative to the other tools, are a graphical representation and a direct manipulation of elements. It should also been noted that DREAM has not yet been tested by users, but it has been taught and used on a Masters in human computer interaction. The authors of the chapter have edited models presented in the following sections.

---

[12] Buckingham Shum's studies have shown that [11] paper-based use of QOC models is cumbersome. Indeed, users spend 52% of the time in renaming nodes when reusing criteria to keep consistency in the diagrams.

7.4.2 Models Edition

Users build models by creating and editing TEAM models elements such as questions, options, criteria, links, etc. A toolbar allowing the creation of elements is available at the top of the window. Once a node is created, the user sets its label. Model edition is made in the workspace (frame 5). The global view (frame 3) and workspace (frame 5) display models in a different scale in order to help users focus and work on a detailed question while remaining aware of contextual information i.e., where the currently edited zone is located in the whole diagram. DREAM embeds some constraints about edition, making it impossible to build models that are not compatible with the constraints described in the entity/relationship diagram of Fig. 7.1.

Each node has a graphical representation made up of two elements: a glyph (i.e., a shape) and a color. Questions are depicted as red rounded squares, options as orange discs, criteria as green triangles, factors as blue triangles, arguments as grey triangles, etc. When a decision has been made about an option, its appearance changes to an orange disc with a black bold line (see the option on the right-hand side of the black 5 in frame 5. Shape and color for criteria and factors change according to the weight assigned to them. A strong weight is represented by a brightness color and straight shape, whereas a weak weight is displayed by a pastel color and a fuzzy shape. Users can zoom-in and zoom-out models.

DREAM allows users to enter detailed information about a node using the edition window displayed in Fig. 7.3. Label information about a node (that will appear in the caption of the shape) is entered in area 1. A more detailed textual description about the node is edited in area 2. Area 3 provides a way to add external information about the node via attachments such as a web page, picture, video, text file, spreadsheet, Petri nets description, task model, etc. Area 4 relates the node to the components of the architectural model for interactive systems presented in Sect. 7.3.3.

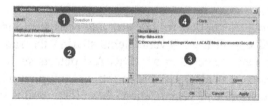

Fig. 7.3. Edition of detailed information for a node

As stated above, in order to support an iterative process, TEAM can store several versions/sessions of a model. Earlier sessions can be visualized, but not modified. Session management can be done by creating an empty new model or by copying current model to a new file. As TEAM notation is capable to store all versions, and then all decisions, refinements, back tracking in a model, it fully supports history management of the rationale.

7.4.3 Exploitation and Analysis of Models

TEAM offers several ways for users to extract information from models. One way is directly provided thanks to the graphical representation of the elements of TEAM, another one is offered by session history.

First of all, the graphical representation of models reveals several aspects of the diagram. Questions solved (i.e., presenting one and only one selected option) and questions still to be resolved are quickly identified by users. This is mainly due to the different appearance of these two types of options. Poorly argumented questions are also highlighted by the lack of criteria associated to their options. As we split design into four mains trends (related to architectural concerns) such as the dialogue part, functional core part, presentation part, and miscellaneous part, it is easy to detect which parts of the design have been the focus of a significant amount of work and which ones have not. The more the model contains resolved questions the more likely the model construction is close to be finished.

A lot of information can be extracted from sessions. Sessions offer a view of the diagram evolution: appearance of new branches, and disappearance of dead branches. New branches are the new questions, and dead branches are question not discussed anymore without having reached a consensus i.e., an option selected. Exploration of all sessions provides information about designers' backtracking, i.e., an option selected in one session and not selected anymore in following sessions. A regularly expanding part of a model clearly states that the question under consideration is important, gets a growing interest and raises hard to solve new problems.

DREAM provides support for constructing consistent models. All items of a duplicated option (i.e., several items sharing the same data) should have the same state: selected or not. DREAM detects such inconsistencies and notifies users. It is also possible to retrieve information (i.e., node) by query, by navigation, and visualization; these three points were defined in section 'Retrieval Components' in Chap 1.

DREAM provides three visualizations and two different representations of the same model. Bifocal tree representation (frame 4) modifies model representation into tree representation. Indeed, TEAM diagrams are not tree-like due to possible duplication of nodes. Leaves are factors and/or criteria. Criteria (respectively, factors) are duplicated for each relation with options (respectively, criteria). Arguments, task models and scenarios are not represented in the tree to prevent cyclic tree. A bifocal tree representation allows users to focus on a specific option without interference of other option evaluations. The bifocal tree visualization was built to support the reading activity and analyzing the importance of nodes for the design by looking (for instance) at their number of occurrence in the model.

Both representations are synchronized, a node selected in one of the view being also selected and displayed in the other views. Scalability issues (as defined in Sect. 1.7.2.) are also addressed by the bifocal tree visualization as this visualization technique has been explicitly design to handle large trees [8].

7.5 Case Study

This section presents the use of TEAM and DREAM on a case study. This case study comes from the Air Traffic Management domain and deals with interaction design issues on an Air Traffic Control workstation.

7.5.1 Context

The case study has been developed with colleagues at the CENA (French Centre for Studies on Air Traffic Management) and is based on an interactive application designed and developed by them. The context is the one of *approach* air traffic controllers i.e., controllers in charge of aircraft approaching an airport. Landing aircrafts are handed over to them by en-route air traffic controllers and they are supposed (after appropriately preparing the route of aircraft) to transfer them to the *tower* controllers in charge of take-off, landing and taxiing at the airport.

The approach air traffic controller can be in charge of a significant number of aircraft and might have to issue a lot of clearances[13] in a very short period of time. This activity is different from the one of the other types of controllers (such as enroute) for whom time scale is much longer.

---

[13] A clearance is the name given to the orders sent by the controller to the pilot. This can be modifying heading, flight level, speed, route,....

7.5.2 System Designed

The air traffic controller interaction on the application is the following: select a flight, choose a clearance, and valid or cancel the clearance.

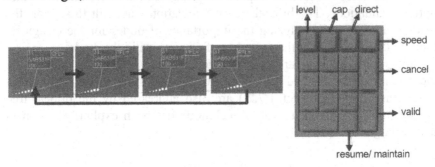

Fig. 7.4. *Left:* Cyclic access to level menu. *Right:* functions related to keys

Ten kinds of clearances are identified, only four buttons are available. Functions are classified by themes and statically associated to keys (see Fig. 7.4):

– Key "num lock" corresponds to level menu: CFL (Clearance Flight Level), TFL (Transfer Flight Level), PFL (Planned Fight Level), RFL (Requested Flight Level)
– Key "/" corresponds to direct menu
– Key "*" corresponds to cap menu (Cap, Right Cap, Left Cap)
– Key "-" corresponds to speed menu (Speed, Rate)

Fig. 7.4 (right) presents the four functions accessible sequentially via the "num lock" key. Menus are cyclic, for example to reach the PFL function users must press three times the (modulo four) "num lock" key.

The interactive system designed by CENA was mainly aimed at allowing air traffic controllers to issue clearances as rapidly as possible. Other (secondary) concerns were making the error rate as low as possible and avoiding syntactically incorrect clearances as much as possible. The current interactive application consists of a radar screen, a mouse and a keyboard. The radar screen displays all flights controlled by the air traffic controllers as well as incoming and outgoing flights. Each flight is graphically represented by a label (see Fig. 7.4, left), a set of dots representing the past five positions of the aircraft and speed vector (a straight line) providing information about both speed (line length) and direction (line direction). The flight label contains the following information flight id, plane id and altitude level.

7.5.3 Models

The design team at the CENA followed a user-centered design [20] and it-erative approach. After some information gathering, they implemented a first prototype. This version evolved during several meetings involving us-ers and designers. After each meeting minutes were prepared and distrib-uted. Those meetings, held on a regular basis, offered the opportunity for users to comment and practice the various prototypes. The process ended after the tenth meeting.

In order to validate the DREAM/TEAM approach we, the authors of the chapter, used the tool and the notation to model all the information contained in the minutes. The information gathered ranged from graphical design sketches (representing graphical appearance of objects), automata (describing the interaction technique) as well as decisions about the retained and discarded design options. A last report summarizing all the choices made during the meeting was also available and has been used by the CENA team as a set of requirements for the development of the final application. In order to trace the process we built diagrams starting from these ten reports and the summarizing report. We built a first diagram and this diagram evolved with information extracted from meetings in a chronological way. Only six sessions appear in the diagram as four ses-sions were not containing relevant information or ended prematurely. We then presented the models to the design team at the CENA to check if the models corresponded to the minutes. The design team validated the mod-els. The customers/users gave two strong requirements: data entries have to be fast and application had to be quickly implemented.

Due to space constraints, we do not present in this section the modeling process itself but we describe the output of the process. Task models and scenarios were not used in the design process by CENA and this is the rea-son why they do not appear in the diagram. Four criteria were identified and are duplicated (i.e., "rapid," "honesty,"[14] "user's automatism," and "ef-ficient quickly"). They are connected to most of the options. The resulting diagram is displayed on Fig. 7.5 and contains 203 nodes (41 questions, 55 options, 21 criteria, 6 factors, and 20 arguments). The point here is not to describe individually each node but to present salient information that pro-vides insights about the process, the notation and the tool. Fig. 7.5, left presents the entire diagram resulting from the modeling process while right hand side emphasizes five graphs extracted from the diagram and are discussed hereafter.

---

[14] Honesty means honesty of the system.

The five rectangles highlight one couple criterion/factor, see graph 4 on right side of the figure. This couple appears five times in the diagram. The criterion is "performance" meaning that performance can be assessed in several places in the diagram for several options. The factor is "rapid" and models a customer/user requirement that interaction is required to be fast. DREAM manages redundancy of information, if users modify factor "rapid" or criterion "performance," DREAM updates and provides an animated feedback on all entities.

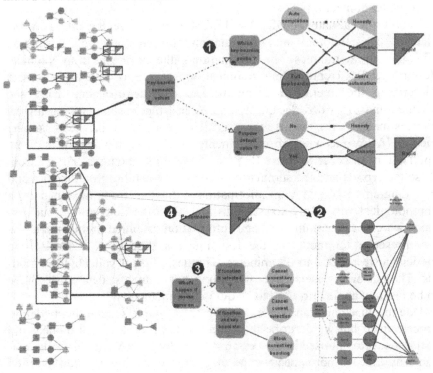

Fig. 7.5. Entire model of the case study and focus on relevant part of the model

Frame 1 shows a structured and argued section of the model. The first question (on the top) deals with keyboarding policy. Two solutions are available, one suggests an auto completion and the other one a full keyboarding (i.e., all the characters have to be fully typed in). Relevant criteria are honesty, performance (high weight), and user's automatism (i.e., that option that is the closer to users' habits). Performance criterion supports the auto completion option whereas honesty and user's automatism both support full keyboarding option. Even though performance has a strong weight, a choice has been made with respect to the all the criteria and thus designers chose the full keyboarding option. This discrepancy between the DR model and the choice can be easily seen in a TEAM diagram.

The second question deals with default values to be provided by the system when data or commands have to be entered. This question does not follow recommendations of the QOC notation as the options are only yes and no. The choice made by designers is to provide a default value and this choice is conformant with the model as it favors performance criterion. We can notice that the option "yes" produces the following two subquestions that deal with the content of the default value to be presented to the user. Due to space constraints, only the doted lines leading to these subquestions are represented.

Frame 2 is one of the most disputed points of the diagram and has been modified at each meeting. It deals with the syntax of each clearance (heading, speed, rate, TFL, PFL, RFL) and aims at defining how to represent authorized values. N represents a digit between one and nine and n a digit between zero and nine; for example, $Nnn5$ means that 5605 is a correct value, and 0125 is a wrong value. In the first session, designer proposed a different syntax for each clearance with no argumentation and only one option for each question. We believe that this is the main reason why users discussed strongly that point. As we can see, in the final session argumentation is still not present and no criteria have been provided.

Frame 3 deals with unexpected moves of the mouse. This question has been raised by an Air Traffic Controller during the second session. Designers broke down this issue into two different questions depending on when the mouse move occurs. If movement occurs when a function is selected, they propose to cancel the current input while if move occurs when an input has already been made, they propose to cancel the current selection or lock the current input (via the keyboard). As it can be easily seen in the diagram, no choice has been made by the designers. During the following sessions the question was not raised again. We believe that this point has been lost during the design process. The TEAM notation provides support for this issue by making explicit these unsolved dead branches.

Additionally, session management as provided by DREAM helps storing and retrieving information about design management. Discussed points can be modified at each step, modifications can be traced and the visual representation supports readers in identifying poorly/nicely argued points, solved issues and diagram evolution. Session management also provides information about backtrackings made during the design process (a choice made early in the design process and then cancelled later on).

In this case study we have shown that the TEAM notation was able to store all the information related to the design process. Factors were integrated easily and made the customer's requirements explicit. Impacts of user requirements appear in the entire diagram. Weights associated to criteria and factors help in understanding and reading the diagrams as well as in understanding choices made during the design process. Iterative process and meeting with users advocate the need for session management. The DREAM tool supports DR management activities by making impossible the edition of inconsistent diagrams.

7.6 Conclusion

This chapter has presented a notation (TEAM) and a tool (DREAM) dedicated to the engineering of interactive systems. Instead of focusing on the result of the development process i.e., the actual application, this approach focuses on the process itself and provides several means for improving it. The notation is anchored in HCI research and provides explicit links to architecture (Arch), user-centered development process (iterative prototyping), task analysis modeling and scenarios thus provides a generic framework for gathering these multiple information sources in a single model. The approach builds on existing work in the field of design rationale integrating successful aspects and providing solutions to the identified limitations. The approach has been applied to several case studies including interaction techniques design, graphics design, and to the software engineering side of interactive systems design. The work presented in this chapter aims at supporting activities currently under considered in the field of interactive systems design and engineering such as the certification phase of safety critical applications. If product certification (when the actual application is checked through by the certifiers) cannot be considered as feasible when large applications are concerned, process certification (when the design process itself is evaluated) can be highly facilitated by exploiting an approach like DREAM/TEAM. In order to improve the tool and to perceive clearly the benefits from the use of the tool, we plan to carry out user testing.

References

[1]   Bass L, Coutaz J (1991) In: Bass L, Coutaz J (eds.), Developing Software for the User Interface, Addison-Wesley, Reading, MA

[2]   Bass L, Little R, Pellegrino R, Reed S, Seacord R, Sheppard S, Szezur M (1991) The Arch Model: Seeheim Revisited. In: User Interface Developers' Workshop

[3]   Bastide R, Palanque P (1995) A Petri Net Based Environment for the Design of Event-Driven Interfaces. In: 16th International Conference on Application and Theory of Petri Nets (ATPN'95) Torino, Italy, 20–22 June 1995

[4]   Bastide R, Palanque P (1999) A Visual and Formal Glue between Application and Interaction. Int. J. Vis. Lang. Computing, 10(5):481–507

[5]   Bastide R, Sy O, Palanque P (1999) Formal Specification and Prototyping of CORBA servers. In: European Conference on Object Oriented Programming, ECOOP 99, 14–18 June 1999, Lisbon (Portugal), Lecture Notes in Computer Science Series, Springer, Berlin Heidelberg New York

[6]   Bastide R, Sy O, Palanque P, Navarre D (2000) Formal specification of CORBA services: experience and lessons learned. ACM Conference on Object-Oriented Programming, Systems, Languages, and Applications (OOPSLA 2000); Minneapolis, MA. ACM, New York

[7]   Bastide R, Navarre D, Palanque P, Schyn A, Dragicevic P (2004) A model-based approach for real-time embedded multimodal systems in military aircrafts. In: Sixth International Conference on Multimodal Interfaces (ICMI'04) October 14–15, 2004 Pennsylvania State University, PA

[8]   Cava RA, Luzzardi PRG, Freitas CMDS (2002) The bifocal tree: a technique for the visualization of hierarchical information structures. In: IHC 2002 – 5th Workshop On Human Factors In Computer Systems, Fortaleza

[9]   Diaper D, Stanton N (2003) The Handbook of Task Analysis for Human–Computer Interaction. Lawrence Erlbaum, Mahwah, NJ

[10] Green M (1985) Report on Dialogue Specification Tools. User Interface Management Systems. Springer, Berlin Heidelberg New York, pp. 9–20

[11] Horn RE (1998) Visual Language. Global communication for the 21st century. Macro VU USA. ISBN 189263709X

[12] Kunz W, Rittel H (1970) Issues as elements of information systems. PhD, University of California.

[13] Lacaze X, Palanque P, Navarre D, Bastide R (2002) Performance Evaluation as a Tool for Quantitative Assessment of Complexity of Interactive Systems. DSV-IS'02, 12–14 June 2002. Lecture Notes in Computer Science, no 2545, Springer, Berlin Heidelebrg New York, pp. 208–222

[14] MacLean A, Young RM, Bellotti VME, Moran TP (1996) Questions, Options, Criteria: Elements of design space analysis. In [25]

[15] McCall J, Richards P, Walters G (1977) Factors in Software Quality. Rome Air Development Center (RADC), RADC-TR-77-369, Vol. III, November

[16] McKerlie D, MacLean A (1994) Reasoning with design rationale: Practical experience with Design Space Analysis. Des. Stud.. 15:214–226

[17] Navarre D, Palanque P, Bastide R, Sy O (2001) A Model-Based Tool for Interactive Prototyping of Highly Interactive Applications. 12th IEEE, International Workshop on Rapid System Prototyping; Monterey (USA). IEEE, USA

[18] Navarre D, Palanque P, Bastide R (2003) A tool-supported design framework for safety critical interactive systems in interacting with computers, Interacting with Computers, 15(3):309—328

[19] Navarre D, Palanque P, Bastide R (2004) A Formal Description Technique for the Behavioural Description of Interactive Applications Compliant with ARINC 661 Specification. HCI-Aero'04 Toulouse, France, Septemeber 29–October 1

[20] Newman WM, Lamming MG (1995) Interactive System Design. Addison-Wesley, Reading, MA

[21] Norman DA, Draper SW (1986) User-Centred System Design: New Perspectives on Human–Computer Interaction. Lawrence Erlbaum Associates. Hillsdale

[22] Ould M, Palanque P, Schyn A, Bastide R, Navarre D, Rubio F (2004) Multimodal and 3D Graphic Man–Machine Interfaces to Improve Operations. In: Proceeding of the Eighth International Conference on Space Operations (SpaceOps 2004), May 17–21, Canada

[23] Palanque P, Paternò F, Bastide R (1997) Formal Specification for Designing User Interfaces of Air Traffic Control Applications (not available yet) In: Proceedings of the Second International Workshop on Formal Methods for Industrial Critical Systems, CESENA (Italy), July 4–5

[24] Rettig M (1994) Prototyping for tiny fingers. Commun. ACM 37(4):21–27

[25] Scapin DL, Bastien JMC (1997) Ergonomic criteria for evaluating the ergonomic quality of interactive systems. Behav. Inform. Technol., 6(4–5) 220–231

[26] Shum SJ (1991) Cognitive analysis of design rationale representation. PhD Thesis. York, UK: Department of Psychology, University of York

[27] Toulmin SE (1958) The Uses of Argument. Cambridge University

8 The WinWin Approach: Using a Requirements Negotiation Tool for Rationale Capture and Use

B. Boehm, H. Kitapci

Abstract: A highly cost-effective approach for rationale capture and management is to provide automated support, and capture the resulting artifacts of the process by which software and system requirements and solutions are negotiated. The WinWin process model, equilibrium model, and collaborative negotiation tool provide capabilities for capturing the artifacts. The MBASE software process model provides an approach for using and updating the rationale artifacts and process to keep it in a win-win state. Supporting requirements negotiation with attaching rationale can have a high impact on all phases of development by enabling much better context for change impact analysis as the increasingly frequent requirements changes arrive. The WinWin approach involves having a system's success-critical stakeholders participate in a negotiation process so they can converge on a mutually satisfactory or win-win set of requirements. The WinWin framework in essence captures stakeholder-oriented objectives, options and constraints in the form of a decision rationale.

Keywords: requirements negotiation; WinWin negotiation approach; rationale capture; Theory W; WinWin spiral model, EasyWinWin

8.1 Introduction

Negotiation techniques are critical success factor in improving the outcome of software projects. At the University of Southern California's Center for Software Engineering (USC-CSE), we have been developing a negotiation-based approach to software and system requirements engineering, architecture, development, and management. Our approach has three primary elements:

1. *Theory W*, a management theory and approach, which says that making winners of the system's key stakeholders is a necessary and sufficient condition for project success [2].
2. *The WinWin Spiral Model*, which extends the spiral software development model [1] by adding Theory W activities to the front of each cycle.
3. *EasyWinWin*, a collaborative groupware negotiation tool that makes it easier for distributed stakeholders to negotiate mutually satisfactory (win–win) system specifications.

Defining requirements is a complex and difficult process, and defects in the process often lead to costly project failures [16]. Requirements emerge in a highly collaborative, interactive, and interdisciplinary negotiation process that involves heterogeneous stakeholders. The EasyWinWin approach involves having a system's success-critical stakeholders participate in a negotiation process so they can converge on a mutually satisfactory (win–win) set of requirements.

Some difficulties within requirements engineering, e.g., determining a feasible and mutually satisfactory set of requirements, are eliminated by achieving a reconciliation of customer expectations with developer capabilities before firmly committing to a set of requirements. A hard to achieve customer's or user's win condition will conflict with the developer's win condition to minimize the risk of delivering an acceptable product within budget and schedule. Conflicting requirements must be identified and negotiated, relevant alternatives must be made explicit and it must be assured that the "right" decision is made. In the WinWin approach, this conflict is identified as an issue needing resolution before stakeholders commit on the agreements.

The overall WinWin negotiation approach is similar to other team approaches for software and system definition such as gIBIS [9], SIBYL [13], and REMAP [15]. Our primary distinguishing characteristic is the use of the stakeholder win–win relationship as the success criterion and organizing principle for the software and system definition process. Our negotiation guidelines are based on the Harvard Negotiation Project's techniques [11].

In this chapter, we first introduce the WinWin Spiral Model. Next, we identify the fundamental concepts of WinWin model and the use of Win-Win model in software development process. Then we introduce the EasyWinWin tool for converging stakeholders' interests to win–win agreements and the WinWin equilibrium state to test whether the negotiation process has converged. We provide an example of WinWin requirements negotiation results from our USC CS577 Software Engineering course projects. We then discuss how such results can serve as captured rationale for later user in avoiding mistakes in subsequent project decisions. We conclude with a discussion of using captured rationale to improve later decisions, related work, and future directions in requirements negotiation and rationale capture.

8.2   The Theory W and WinWin Spiral Model in Software Development Process

8.2.1   Theory W

The foundation for the WinWin approach is Theory W, a management theory similar to Theories X, Y, Z. Theory W's fundamental principle is that a necessary and sufficient condition for a successful enterprise is that the enterprise makes winners of all its success-critical stakeholders. It is well-matched to the problems of software project management. It holds that software project managers will be fully successful if and only if they make winners of all the other participants in the software process: superiors, subordinates, customers, users, maintainers, etc. This principle is particularly relevant in the software field, which is a highly people-intensive area whose products are often unfamiliar with user and management concerns.

Making everyone a winner may seem like an unachievable objective. Most situations tend to be zero–sum, win–lose situations. Nevertheless, win–win situations exist, and often they can be created by careful attention to people's interests and expectations. The best work on creating them has been done in the field of negotiation. The book *"Getting to Yes"* [11] is a classic in the area. Its primary thesis is that successful negotiations are not achieved by haggling from preset negotiation positions, but by following a four-step approach whose goal is basically to create a win–win situation for the negotiating parties (1) separate the people from the problem, (2) focus on interests, not positions, (3) invent options for mutual gain, (4) insist on using objective criteria.

The Theory W approach to software project management expands on these four steps to establish a set of win–win preconditions, and some further conditions for structuring the software process and the resulting software product.

8.2.2   WinWin Spiral Model

The original spiral model [1] uses a cyclic approach to develop increasingly detailed elaborations of a software system's definition, culminating in incremental releases of the system's operational capability. Each cycle involves four main activities:

– Elaborate the system or subsystem's product and process objectives, constraints, and alternatives
– Evaluate the alternatives with respect to the objectives and constraints. Identify and resolve major sources of product and process risk

- Elaborate the definition of the product and process
- Plan the next cycle, and update the life-cycle plan, including partition of the system into subsystems to be addressed in parallel cycles. This can include a plan to terminate the project if it is too risky or infeasible. Secure the management's commitment to proceed as planned

Since its creation, the spiral model has been extensively elaborated and successfully applied in numerous projects. However, some common difficulties led USC-CSE and its affiliate organizations to extend the model to the WinWin spiral model described in the following text.

WinWin Extensions: Negotiation Front End

One difficulty was determining where the elaborated objectives, constraints, and alternatives come from. The WinWin spiral model resolves this by adding three activities to the front of each spiral cycle, as Fig. 8.1 shows:

- Identify the system or subsystem's key stakeholders
- Identify the stakeholders' win conditions for the system or subsystem
- Negotiate win–win reconciliations of the stakeholders' win conditions

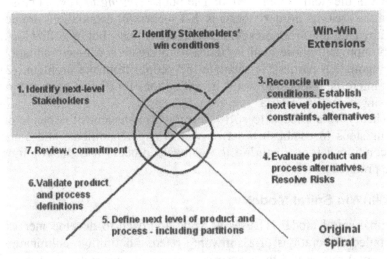

Fig. 8.1. The WinWin spiral model of software engineering includes front-end activities (*gray*) that show where objectives, constraints, and alternatives come from. This lets users more clearly identify the rationale involved in negotiating win conditions for the product

The new model adds front-end activities that show where objectives, constraints and alternatives come from. This lets stakeholders more clearly identify the rationale involved in negotiating win conditions for the product. A key aspect of the model is that it introduces economic, product quality, and risk considerations into the decision making steps and introduces tradeoff exploration into the process to address risks and conflicts.

Process Anchor Points

Another difficulty in applying the spiral model across an organization's various projects was that the organization has no common reference points for organizing its management procedures, cost and schedule estimates, and so on. This is because the cycles are risk driven, and each project has different risks. In attempting to work out this difficulty with USC-CSE's industry and government affiliates using our COCOMO II cost model [7], we found a set of three process milestones, or anchor points, which we could relate to both the completion of spiral cycles and to the organization's major decision milestones.

Over the years of developing electronic services applications for the USC Libraries, we have been evolving Model-Based Architecting and System/Software Engineering (MBASE). MBASE involves early reconciliation of a project's success models (correctness, business case, stakeholder winwin,...); product models (domain, requirements, architecture,...); process models (waterfall, evolutionary, spiral,...); and property models (performance, reliability,...). It extends the previous spiral model in two ways:

- Initiating each spiral cycle with a stakeholder win–win stage to determine a mutually satisfactory set of objectives, constraints, and alternatives for the system's next elaboration during the cycle.
- Orienting the spiral cycles to synchronize with a set of life cycle anchor points: Life Cycle Objectives (LCO), Life Cycle Architecture (LCA), and Initial Operational Capability (IOC)

The LCO version focuses on establishing a sound business case for the package. It need only show that there is at least one feasible architecture. The LCA version commits to a single choice of architecture and elaborates it to the point of covering all major sources of risk in the system's life cycle. The LCA is the most critical milestone in the software's life cycle. The IOC version focuses on a workable initial operational capability for the project including system preparation, training, use, and evolution support for user, administrators, and maintainers.

8.3   Fundamental WinWin Concepts

8.3.1 The WinWin Approach

The general win–win approach evolved more or less independently as an interpersonal-relations [17], success-management [10], and project-management [2] approach. We usually define it as "a set of principles, practices, and tools, which enable a set of interdependent stakeholders to work out a mutually satisfactory (win–win) set of shared commitments."

Interdependent stakeholders can be people or organizations. Their shared commitments can relate to information system requirements in particular (the WinWin groupware system's primary focus) or can cover most continuing relationships in work and life (for example, international diplomacy). Mutually satisfactory generally means that people do not get everything they want but can be reasonably assured of getting whatever it was to which they agreed. Shared commitments are not just good intentions but carefully defined conditions. If someone has a conditional commitment, he or she must make it explicit to ensure all stakeholders understand the condition as part of the agreement.

The WinWin approach is descriptive, in that the main purpose of the system is to negotiate a set of mutually satisfactory agreements that are foundations to requirements, constraints, and plans of the project.

The WinWin negotiation approach addresses some of the problems related with rationale capture. It reduces the work required to gather rationale by providing a well-defined structure and process to negotiate. In addition, the negotiation allows all success-critical stakeholders to participate the process where both recorders and users of the rationale are involved. The process also makes it easy to collect and share the rationale behind the decisions made. Stakeholders using the system simultaneously make rationale capture easier and faster. Rationale generated during negotiation is captured within EasyWinWin. The brainstorming statements are attached to the resulting win conditions to preserve the brainstorming rationale. Issues are attached to win conditions. The traceability links and the containment relations between elements are used to display the reasoning and knowledge behind the agreements. Moreover, the impact of changing decisions is traceable to the related elements.

Win–Lose Does Not Work

In requirements negotiation, nobody wants a lose–lose outcome. Win–lose might sound attractive to the party most likely to win, but it usually turns into a lose–lose situation. Table 8.1 shows three classic win-lose patterns among the three primary system stakeholders in which the loser's outcome usually turns the two "winners" into losers [6].

Table 8.1. Frequent software evelopment win–lose patterns

Proposed solution	Winner	Loser
quickly build a cheap, sloppy product	developer and customer	user
add lots of bells and whistles	developer and user	customer
drive too hard a bargain	customer and user	developer

As the table shows, building a quick and sloppy product might be a low-cost, near-term win for the software developer and customer, but the user (and maintainer) will lose in the long run. In addition, adding lots of marginally useful bells and whistles to a software product on a cost-plus contract might be a win for the developer and users, but it is a loss for the customer. Finally, "best and final offer" bidding wars that customers and users impose on competing developers generally lead to lowball winning bids, which place the selected developer in a losing position.

However, nobody really wins in these situations. Quick and sloppy products destroy a developer's reputation and have to be redone – inevitably at a higher cost to the customer. The bells and whistles either disappear or (worse) crowd out more essential product capabilities as the customer's budgets are exhausted. Inadequate lowball bids translate into inadequate products, which again incur increased customer costs and user delivery delays to reach adequacy.

Why WinWin Works

Builds Trust and Manages Expectations
If stakeholders consistently find other stakeholders asking about their needs and acting to understand and support them, they will end up trusting each other more. In addition, if they consistently find them balancing their needs with other stakeholders' needs, they will have more realistic expectations about getting everything they want. As they work together to negotiate their requirements, they give the project shape, and their merged visions become a system that all stakeholders can accept. If, on the other

hand, stakeholders do not negotiate together, there is little chance the resulting system will accommodate their needs, and the project will fail.

Helps Stakeholders Adapt to Changes in the Environment that Affect Requirements
Instead of rigorous requirements in ironbound contracts, doing business in Internet time requires stakeholders with a shared vision and the flexibility to quickly renegotiate a new solution once unforeseen problems or opportunities arise [3]. A WinWin approach builds a shared vision among stakeholders and provides the flexibility to adapt to change.

Helps Build Institutional Memory
The decisions, the why behind the what, that lead to a work result often vanish. By capturing and preserving stakeholder negotiations, WinWin supports long-term availability of the decision rationale and thus helps build institutional memory. Having more auditable decisions creates more detailed, accurate, and complete deliverables.

8.3.2 How Does the WinWin Negotiation Model Work

Key activities of WinWin negotiation model include (1) the identification of success-critical stakeholders; (2) the elicitation of the success-critical stakeholders' primary win conditions; (3) the negotiation of mutually satisfactory win-win situation packages (requirements, architectures, plans, critical components, etc.); and (4) value-based monitoring and control of a win-win equilibrium throughout the development process.

The WinWin negotiation model has four main conceptual artifacts: *Win condition*: capturing the desired objectives and constraints of the stakeholder; *Issue*: capturing the conflict between win conditions and their associated risks and uncertainties; *Option*: capturing a decision choice for resolving an issue; *Agreement*: capturing the agreed upon set of win conditions which satisfy stakeholder win conditions and/or capturing the agreed options for resolving issues.

The negotiation model guides success-critical stakeholders in elaborating mutually satisfactory agreements. Stakeholders express their goals as win conditions. If everyone concurs, the win conditions become agreements. When stakeholders do not concur, they identify their conflicted win conditions and register their conflicts as issues. In this case, stakeholders invent options for mutual gain and explore the option trade-offs. Options are iterated and turned into agreements when all stakeholders concur. It is important to notice that open, unresolved issues represent potential project risks or conflicts that need to be addressed. Additionally, a *domain taxonomy* is used to organize WinWin artifacts, and a glossary captures the domain's important *terms*. The stakeholders are in a WinWin equilibrium state when the agreements cover all of the win conditions and there are no outstanding issues (see Fig. 8.2). The negotiation proceeds until all of the stakeholders' win conditions are entered and the WinWin equilibrium state is achieved, or until the stakeholders agree that the project should be disbanded because some issues are irresolvable. In such situations, it is much preferable to determine this before rather than after developing the system.

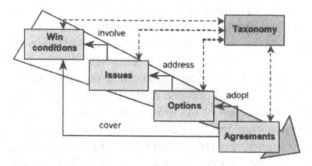

Fig. 8.2. The WinWin negotiation model

The WinWin negotiation model aims at coordinating decision-making activities made by various stakeholders in the software development process. It belongs to the category of supporting collaboration described in Sect. 1.4.1. It guides success-critical stakeholders through a process of eliciting, elaborating, prioritizing, and negotiating requirements. It also provides the support for future changes by keeping the traceability of the artifacts and their rationale.

The negotiation process supports the engineering and management activities of rationale capture. The artifacts and their rationale captured during requirements negotiation shapes the decision made through the software development. In addition, the artifacts provide additional information to check the project status and manage the project risks. The higher number of issues identified and resolved helps reduce risks early in a project and the chances of it derailing later.

The rationale capture during negotiation improves the communication between stakeholders and the quality of the products. Rationale on the negotiation results supports communication between all success-critical stakeholders.

8.4 Tool Support for WinWin Requirements Negotiation

EasyWinWin is a requirements negotiation methodology that combines the WinWin Spiral Model of Software Engineering from USC's Center for Software Engineering with state-of-the-art collaborative knowledge techniques and automation of a Group Support System (GSS) from GroupSystems.com. A GSS is a suite of software tools that can be used to create, sustain, and change patterns of group interaction in repeatable, predictable ways [14].

EasyWinWin helps a team of stakeholders to gain a better and more thorough understanding of the problem and supports cooperative learning about other's viewpoints. Moreover, it helps increase stakeholder involvement and interaction. EasyWinWin defines a set of activities guiding stakeholders through a process of gathering, elaborating, prioritizing, and negotiating requirements. The nominal purpose of the EasyWinWin methodology is to create an acceptable set of system requirements. Teams can use EasyWinWin throughout the development cycle to create a shared project vision, to develop high-levels requirements definition, to produce detailed requirements for features, functions, and properties, COTS acquisition and integration, COTS product enhancement, and to plan requirements for transitioning the system to the customer and user.

The negotiation model provides the capture, representation, and use of rationale. Rationale is captured during stakeholders' communication and negotiation in a structured way in which the relations between the artifacts are clear to the stakeholders. The tool provides the distribution of rationale feature for concurrent user. It is both easy to capture, modify, and review rationale during negotiation. It increases collaboration and coordination with group awareness, synchronous and asynchronous modes of communication, and support for trade-off analysis. Rationale used during and after negotiation to agree on the development artifacts. However, the tool doesn't provide support for rationale preservation and interfaces to legacy components currently because of the reason it is being used for requirements negotiation.

8.4.1 The Negotiation Process

The input to an EasyWinWin workshop is typically a mission statement outlining the high-level objectives of a project and another statement specifying the negotiation purpose, i.e., the objectives of a negotiation within a project. In each activity in this process the team adds details and increases precision. The EasyWinWin process is comprised of the following activities:

Review and expand negotiation topics. Stakeholders jointly refine and customize an outline of negotiation topics based on a taxonomy of software requirements. The shared outline helps to stimulate thinking, to organize negotiation results, and serves as a completeness checklist for negotiations.

Brainstorm stakeholder interests. Stakeholder share their goals, perspectives, views, background, and expectations by gathering statements about their vested interests.

Converge on win conditions. Stakeholders jointly craft a list of clearly stated, unambiguous win conditions by considering and discussing all ideas contributed in the brainstorming session.

Capture a glossary of terms. Stakeholders define and share the meaning of important terms of the project in a glossary.

Prioritize win conditions. Stakeholders prioritize the win conditions to define the scope of work and to gain focus.

Reveal issues and constraints. Stakeholders surface and understand issues.

Identify issues and options. Stakeholders surface the issues that arise due to constraints, risks, uncertainties, and conflicting win conditions. They propose options to resolve these issues.

Negotiate agreements. Stakeholders negotiate mutual commitments by considering win conditions that raised no issues and all proposed options.

8.4.2 The Negotiation Process Deliverables

The activities of the EasyWinWin process are summarized above and shown in Fig. 8.3 with related work products (for a more detailed description please refer to [8, 12]). The results of each activity in the process is a well-defined deliverable (1) negotiation topics organized in a domain taxonomy, (2) a glossary defining key project terms, (3) agreements providing the foundation for further plans, (4) open issues addressing constraints, conflicts, and known problems, as well as (5) further rationale showing the negotiation history (comments, win conditions, issues, options, etc.).

Major results of the negotiation process are a list of agreements and a list of unresolved issues (e.g., caused by stakeholder dissent), which have to be managed as potential projects risks. Agreements of success-critical stakeholders are input to the project contract and to refinement during requirements engineering activities. The WinWin tree shows how agreements and open issues can be traced back to stakeholder win conditions.

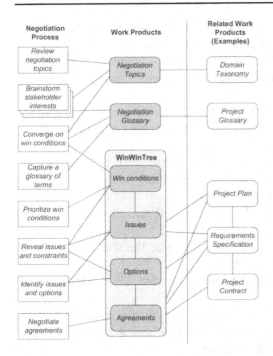

Fig. 8.3. EasyWinWin activities and work products with relationships to important work products in the software life-cycle

8.5   An Example – Using WinWin in Software Development

EasyWinWin has been used in more than 100 real-world projects in various domains (e.g., digital libraries, e-marketplace, and collaboration technology). By using the MBASE approach throughout the software development, we find that using a WinWin requirements negotiation approach helps stakeholders prioritize their requirements and capture the rationale for their decisions.

One of project from the real-world projects that we will use as an example is as follows:

"Information Services Division (ISD) would like to replace its current timecard and timesheet (paper) system with an electronic, web-based system to simplify data collection, to more accurately record hours worked for all its employees, and to provide personnel management tools for supervisors and directors."

The EasyWinWin workshop started with the team reviewing and expanding the negotiation topics based on domain taxonomy which helped organize the artifacts that emerge later in the process. Figure 8.4 shows part of the taxonomy for our project.

```
Project Requirements
        Budget and Schedule
                Tool Requirements
                ...
        Development Requirements
        Packaging Requirements
        ...
Capability Requirements
        ...
System Interface Requirements
        User Interface Requirements
        Communications Interface Requirements
        Other System Interface Requirements
Level of Service Requirements
        Dependability
        Interoperability
        Usability
        Performance
        Adaptability
        Reusability
Evolution Requirements
        Capability Evolution Requirements
        ...
```

Fig. 8.4. Part of the domain taxonomy

Then stakeholders brainstormed on the project and contributed their interests. Some examples are:

- The system must provide some benefit to the employees that are using it – such as providing them with their current vacation balance.
- System should have capability to correct errors on previous timecards.
- Hierarchical structures can provide several levels of access for different management groups.
- Some ISD constituents would prefer a card swipe or biometric clock-in/-out system connected to the network. Supervisors feel this will reduce clocking-in/-out for others.

The resulting collection of stakeholder statements and ideas provided a starting point and rationale for elaborating win conditions and defining important terms of the project domain. The brainstorming statements were attached to resulting win conditions to preserve brainstorming rationale.

After that, stakeholders voted on each win condition according to two criteria: *Business Importance* and *Ease of Implementation*. During this activity, developers typically focused on technical issues, while clients and users concentrated on the business relevance (see Fig. 8.5).

In the next step, stakeholders examined the results of the prioritization and identified issues and options in several iterations. During the revealing issues and constraints, the stakeholders modified the priorities according to the updated information they got. The WinWin equilibrium state holds when all win conditions are covered by agreements, and there are no outstanding issues. As soon as some stakeholder enters an issue and an associated conflicting win condition, the negotiation leaves the WinWin equilibrium state, and the stakeholders attempt to formulate options to resolve the issue. For example, if the conflicting win conditions are to have the system run on a Windows platform and a UNIX platform, an acceptable option might be to build the system to run on a Java Virtual Machine.

	Win Conditions	Business Importance	Ease of Implementation
1.	Application Capabilities		
1.1	W7 System should have the capability to generate reports required by th	8.80	
1.2	W8 System should have multiple levels of security	8.80	
1.3	W10 Rules governing vacation/sick time should be programmable into t	8.60	
1.4	W19 System shall be capable of validating input		7.80
1.5	W20 System shall be firewalled from outside of USC	8.80	
1.6	W30 Proof of concecpt should be able to support maximum of 30 users	8.00	
1.7	W24 System shall handle multiple users concurrently	8.20	
2.	Interfaces		
2.1	W12 System should support web-based and card swipe interfaces.	6.20	6.60
2.2	W17 User interface shall be able to support Internet Explorer and Netsc	8.40	8.60
2.3	W18 The output of the system shall be compatible with the Payroll accor		6.40
3.	Level of Service		
3.1	W2 System shall reduce time and effort required to process payroll hour	8.60	

Fig. 8.5. Some voting results of Win Conditions – *gray* as consensus, *black* as lack of consensus

The WinWin Tree has all the information gathered during the requirements negotiation: Unique numbers for artifacts that help tracing the artifacts through the software's life cycle, priorities for win conditions, stakeholders who identified issues and options, and the taxonomy elements those artifacts belong to. The WinWin Tree also captures the rationale for win conditions and how stakeholders reach an agreement by including all proposed options, whether adopted or not, all issues which eventually addressed and all win conditions (see Fig. 8.6).

The negotiation results, mainly agreements, become the foundations of requirements whereas the other artifacts are the rationale for further decisions made during the development life cycle such as major risks, iteration plans, etc. Agreements that cover the lower-priority win conditions become evolution requirements, providing the basis for architecting the system to easily drop them (if necessary to meet the schedule) or incorporate them in later increments. For example, "W12 [FGT] System should support web-based and/or card swipe interfaces. [Taxonomy 3.1]" belonged to User Interface Requirements during the negotiation. However, after the prioritization it is categorized as not important and very difficult to implement. An issue identified by the administrator as "I12 Supporting card swipe interfaces requires additional hardware purchase and integration [Administrator] [Taxonomy 3.1]". This issue occurred because of a budget limit for the project. So the stakeholders provided an option to have web-based user interface first, and left the card swipe interface as a technology evolution requirements. At the end there were two requirements (1) Web-based interface as interface requirements, (2) adding new input devices as magnetic card readers as an evolution requirement.

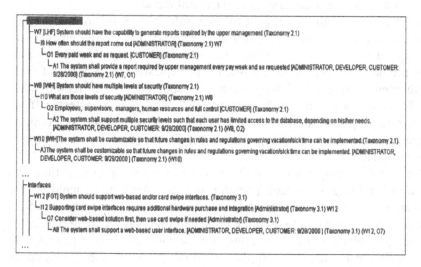

Fig. 8.6. A small part of WinWin Tree – initial capability and interface sections

The team using EasyWinWin is able to develop a broader and deeper set of results in a shorter time. An EasyWinWin negotiation results in a significantly higher number of artifacts compared to traditional paper or blackboard-based approaches: our experience to date shows that typical negotiations about system requirements with 10+ stakeholders result in 300+ brainstorming ideas, 100+ win conditions, 50+ issues, 50+ options, and 100+ agreements in less time than other traditional techniques. Even though, the teams had a similar educational background and basically the same win conditions, they came up with very different negotiation approaches and solutions.

The focus on consensus leads to a higher acceptance of decisions and to an increased mutual understanding among the involved parties. The evaluation of the WinWin model shows that the use of an issue model for negotiation support enhances trust and shared understanding among shareholders, even in the presence of uncertainties and changing requirements.

8.6 Using the Captured Rationale to Improve Later Decisions

Design rationale is documented in the WinWin artifacts to provide a corporate memory. Risks are explicitly addressed in WinWin to pinpoint possible breakdowns and propose early fixes. This makes it easier to increment and evolve requirements in the spiral model.

As the project unfolds, the WinWin results are useful in many ways. First and foremost it is the highest-level expression of requirements. All subsequent requirements specifications refer back to the WinWin results. This provides an answer to the often-asked questions, "Where did these requirements come from? Why were they adopted? Which requirements satisfy which needs of which stakeholders? Who will be affected if we change the specification?" The WinWin results provide a common reference point for organizing management procedures, cost estimates, schedules, etc.

An initial developer win condition was to save development time and money by reusing a research planning module. An issue entered by the maintainer indicated that module would be risky and expensive to maintain. An agreement to drop the win condition was recorded. Later, the project got behind schedule and the new developer manager proposed to recover by reusing the research planning module. Without the captured rationale, the project would have done this and caused major maintenance problems. With the captured rationale, the developers can check the status of the planning module and reject its use if it is still risky and expensive to maintain.

Thus, capturing the rationale behind the decisions generated by the WinWin negotiation enables the stakeholders to avoid mistaken decisions often associated with personnel turnover. This allows the designers to accommodate a much broader set of needs, and allows the stakeholders to negotiate trade-offs with one another based on well understood interest. WinWin also makes it far easier to modify requirements part-way through the project as new constraints are discovered because every requirement can be tied back to some set of win conditions, which in turn tied back to some set of stakeholders. For example, a budget cut would invalidate some previous agreements. Therefore, change management is necessary to accommodate changes in objectives, constraints, or alternatives. In addition, the rationale for previous requirements needs to be incorporated to help determine how to change requirements.

8.7 Related Work

Rationale capture models for software requirements and design decisions capture dependencies between multiple stakeholder objectives, issues, requirements, design, and trade-off options. IBIS addresses multistakeholder consideration by supporting relations among system objectives. Issues can be viewed as requirements that impact on design decisions. Conklin et al. [9] attempted to allow less disruption to the design process with a graphical tool, gIBIS, to record the rationale. Although IBIS structures support analysis of requirements interactions, no tools are provided for analyzing trade-offs, so the design decision may overlook optimal solutions. There is also no negotiation strategy embedded to reconcile different perspectives. The WinWin approach is specifically for recording architectural rationale. While both gIBIS and WinWin attempt to reduce the overhead in capturing rationale, they focus on particular elements that must still be formally documented during the discussions.

The WinWin approach is aimed to provide not as much structure as attempted in gIBIS, SIBYL, and REMAP, which have difficulties in scaling up to large systems. However, the Win–Win Spiral Process model and WinWin are also trying to provide stronger support for scalable shared ontologies and for collaboration objectives via the domain taxonomy and via the conceptual bases for collaboration and software development provided by Theory W and the Spiral Model. For example, the objective of achieving a win–win situation among stakeholders' win conditions provides a much more explicit answer to the question, "What are we trying to collaborate about?" than other conceptual frameworks for collaboration.

8.8 Future Directions

EasyWinWin helps smooth the transition from WinWin stakeholder agreements to requirements specifications. Mapping the WinWin domain taxonomy onto the table of contents of the requirements specification and requiring the use of the domain taxonomy as a checklist for developing WinWin agreements effectively focused stakeholder negotiations. But the result of a WinWin negotiation is typically not a complete, consistent, traceable, testable requirements specification. For example, stakeholders may become enthusiastic about proposed new capabilities and ratify idealistic agreements such as "anytime, anywhere" service. We are exploring how to automate parts of the requirements transition to make it even smoother. For rationale capture, further formatting and indexing capabilities need to be researched and experimented with to capture rejected as well as accepted win conditions and options. Also, some research capabilities are experimented with rationale capture such as audio or video clips are now becoming economically feasible to incorporate.

References

[1]   Boehm B (1988) A spiral model of software development and enhancement. Computer, 21(5): 61–72
[2]   Boehm B (1996) Anchoring the Software Process. IEEE Software, 13(4): 73-82
[3]   Boehm B (2000) Requirements That Handle IKIWISI, COTS, and Rapid Change. Computer, 33(7): 99-102
[4]   Boehm B, Bose P (1994) A Collaborative Spiral Software Process Model Based on Theory W. Proc. Int'l Conf. Software Process, IEEE CS Press, Los Alamitos, California, pp 59-68
[5]   Boehm B, Ross R (1989) Theory W software project management: Principles and examples. IEEE Trans. Softw. Eng., 15(7): 902–916
[6]   Boehm B, Bose P, Horowitz E, Lee MJ (1994) Software Requirements as Negotiated Win Conditions. In: Proceedings of the First International Conference on Requirements Engineering. IEEE Computer Society, Colorado Springs CO, pp. 74–83
[7]   Boehm B, Abts C, Brown AW, Chulani S, Clark BK, Horowitz E, Madachy R, Reifer D, Steece B (2000) Software Cost Estimation with COCOMO II. Prentice Hall, Upper Saddle River, NJ
[8]   Boehm B, Gruenbacher P, Briggs RO (2001) Developing Groupware for Requirements Negotiation: Lessons Learned. IEEE Softw., 18(3): 46–55
[9]   Conklin J, Begeman M (1988) gIBIS: A Hypertext Tool for Exploratory Policy Discussion. ACM Trans. Off. Inform. Syst., 6(3): 303–331
[10] Covey S (1990) The Seven Habits of Highly Effective People. Fireside Books, New York
[11] Fisher R, Ury W (1981) Getting To Yes. Houghton-Mifflin, Boston
[12] Gruenbacher P (2000) EasyWinWin OnLine: Moderator's Guidebook. GroupSystems.com and USC-CSE
[13] Lee J (1990) SIBYL: A Qualitative Decision Management System. In: Winston P and Shellard S (eds.) Artificial Intelligence at MIT; Expanding Frontiers, MIT Press, Cambridge, pp. 106–133
[14] Nunamaker J, Briggs R, Mittleman D, Vogel D, Balthazard P (1996) Lessons from a dozen years of group support systems research: A discussion of lab and field findings. J. Manage. Inform. Syst., 13(3):163–207
[15] Ramesh B, Dhar V (1992) Supporting Systems Development by Capturing Deliberations during Requirements Engineering. IEEE Trans. Softw. Eng. 18(6): 498–510
[16] The Standish Group (1995) CHAOS Report
[17] Waitley D (1985) The Double Win. Berkeley Books, New York

9   Design Rationale in Exemplary Business Process Modeling

H. Breitling, A. Kornstädt, J. Sauer

Abstract: Exemplary Business Process Modeling (EBPM) is an efficient approach to object-oriented software application design. With the help of EBPM, a substantial amount of information about business processes and work practice in the application domain can be gathered and connected to the design and usage model of the software system under scrutiny. Although EBPM was not originally conceived for this purpose, the experience which we share in this article suggests that EBPM should be a standard method for building a basis of knowledge from which design rationale can be gathered.

Keywords: design rationale in software engineering; exemplary business process modeling; cooperation scenario; scenario-based design; object orientation

9.1 Overview of Exemplary Business Process Modeling

The Exemplary Business Process Modeling (EBPM) approach is a scenario-based method that encompasses models and methodologies for the analysis and design of business processes and the software that supports them. It can be employed to model present as well as future processes.

EBPM was developed cooperatively at C1 WPS and Hamburg University in the context of the Tools and Materials approach and its application-oriented document types [19] – significantly influenced by Züllighoven. It was hedged when it occurred to us that neither texts nor standard UML diagrams alone are sufficient to discuss questions of work routine and software systems with users. Building on Krabbel's and Wetzel's Cooperation diagrams we added element after element and finally tool support on the basis of BOC's Adonis modeling tool.

The main benefit of EBPM is the comprehensibility of its models and its suitability for both software designers and domain experts. Therefore, it can be used in workshops and modeling sessions with participants from technically-oriented and domain-oriented groups. Its focus is on modeling exemplary, concrete scenarios without case differentiation.

Being exemplary instead of exhaustive and capturing knowledge about current and future business processes instead of decisions, EBPM is not a design rationale methodology. Instead, EBPM is a valuable auxiliary methodology on which methodologies that capture design rationale can foot. We have employed EBPM for several years to capture current and future processes in banking, insurance and logistics projects, often in the context of migrating between software systems. Depending on the cardinality of process groups under scrutiny, well over 100 EBPM models were furnished per project.

9.2 The EBPM Paradigm

We capture design rationale in order to provide a sound basis for deciding about how to design new or how to evolve existing software systems. To this end, we document decisions during the software development process together with problems, influencing variables, alternatives (also the discarded ones), arguments, and discussions. It has been shown that this information is extremely valuable when it comes to explain the system to new members of the development team [9].

A couple of methodologies for capturing design rationale have been developed (see [4][Chap. 1 in this book] for an introduction). In these interpretations of design rationale management, participants aim at recording *every* decision including its underlying decision base (*every* option (discarded or not), *every* influencing variable, and *every* discussion). These exhaustive forms of rationale management require substantial – sometimes prohibitive – investments of resources (see Sect. 1.5.1 for a discussion of the capture problem).

Experience from our projects suggests that in many cases it is not viable to manage design rationale information to that extent – especially when it comes to recording decisions which concern design alternatives that have been discarded and do not become a part of the shipped software product. Instead we follow suggestions brought forward by Dutoit and Paech [5] to closely integrate requirements engineering and capturing design rationale. Therefore, we aim at striking a balance between the need for – potentially quite costly – design rationale information and limiting ourselves to the information that we find to be essential when it comes to make design decisions.

But what rationale information is essential? We found that as in requirements engineering, the users' work context is the ultimate source for justifying the system's design. It is concepts and processes from that source that are responsible for the vast majority of requests for adding new or changing existing features. As EBPM was devised for capturing the users' work context complete with processes, work objects, and underlying concepts, it is ideally suited to form the basis for design rationale extraction, especially in the context of customized software development. It is these aspects of EBPM that we focus on in this contribution.

Regarding the categorization given in [4][Chap. 1 in this book], EBPM is a prescriptive approach in the sense that its models' basic structure is given by a meta model that has to be used and that guides the thinking of designers. EBPM aims to be less intrusive by granting the designers some flexibility in adopting this meta model for their specific needs.

9.2.1 EBPM as Scenario-Based Method

The term scenario was established in informatics at the latest at the beginning of the nineties. In [1] (pp. 46–47), Carroll describes them as follows:

- Scenarios are stories – about persons and their actions
- Scenarios are set in a specific context
- Scenarios contain agents or actors that have goals that they follow
- Scenarios have a plot; they consist of a sequence of actions and events
- The scenario's plot is supposed to be supported at least in part with the help of a software application

In EBPM, scenarios are represented graphically with

- Icons for actors, business objects and other artifacts
- Arrows for actions and
- Memo sheets for context information

See Fig. 9.1 for an example.

Scenarios are modeled in three layers with different model types: *Cooperation Scenarios* focus on the interaction between several actors, *Workplace Scenarios* focus on the actions that an individual actor carries out at his workplace alone and *IT Interaction Scenarios* describe the interaction of an individual actor with a single application system or a group of related systems. In every scenario type, the flow of action is clearly discernible.

Artifacts from these models can be associated with a *Model of Terms* that relates business terms with another and can give explanations for them in the form of a glossary. Different roles of actors can be described in a *model of roles*.

If a substantial number of cooperation scenarios needs to be modeled, *business use case diagrams* are added to provide a graphical overview.

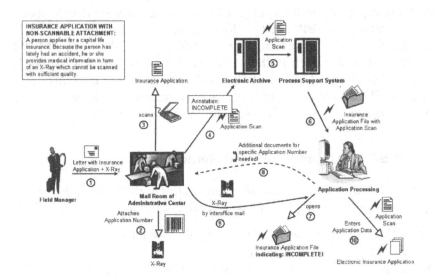

Fig. 9.1. Example cooperation scenario

A business process is typically modeled with EBPM in two to four related scenarios. As already said, scenarios depict one relevant, exemplary sequence of events without case differentiation. This greatly improves the comprehensibility of the models. If there are important variants, then these are depicted in scenarios of their own. Minor variants can be annotated in textual form with notes that are added to certain steps of scenarios.

9.2.2 Modeling Workshops

Sometimes we develop EBPM models with only one or two participants in direct interviews. Most often though, we hold modeling workshops with many participants from technically oriented and domain oriented groups.

The processes can be treated from different angles in these workshops. It has been constantly shown in our projects that the participants from different group can equally contribute their point of view and their knowledge. We have found that EBPM models are comprehensible for participants with different backgrounds and serve well as a common basis and design platform. This is mainly because the models capture domain specific actors and their action together with the related artifacts in a simple, graspable notation.

The models are created during the workshops. We often use a setting with a moderator who is in charge of the discussion and a modeler at a laptop connected to a video projector. The modeler immediately translates the contributions of the participants into EBPM models that are visible to everyone. This procedure shortens the feedback loop significantly.

9.2.3 Tool Support for EBPM

Even though the EBPM can be used with a flip chart, pen, and paper, software tool support is essential for its efficient use. A standard tool for graphical modeling (like MS Visio) can be used, but a specific software tool offers several advantages like stepwise visualization of scenarios, queries over a large quantity of models and navigation between models in a hypertext style. Such a tool enables the efficient, direct creation of models during modeling sessions.

We are using a tool that offers many more possibilities, e.g., the attachment of arbitrary files to all model elements or the automatic numbering of steps. This facilitates the modelers' work a lot and offers expanded possibilities. All models are filed in a centralized repository to promote coordination in the design team.

9.3 EBPM Models

In this section, we will present the main models of EBPM and their interconnections.

9.3.1 Cooperation Scenario

The starting point of EBPM is the Cooperation Scenario. Figure 9.2 shows the basic underlying meta model. A visual language is used to represent a specific cooperative work scenario. A fundamental part of the scenario is its background story, a short text that explicitly describes the story's context and states the domain-related assumptions made for the model. It needs to be reasonably strict in order to motivate the specific scenario and exclude alternative courses of action.

The story that is being told is divided into consecutive, numbered steps. Every step is performed by an actor. In a Cooperation Scenario step, an actor can basically do two things: either cooperate with another actor – by just communicating, or else transferring a work object to her or him for further processing – or inspect and/or modify a work object on her or his own. Each action type is visually represented by a different type of arrow.

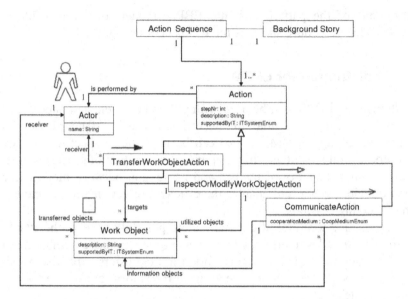

Fig. 9.2. Basic meta model of the Cooperation Scenario. For clarity, the corresponding EBPM symbols are located next to each box

Work objects are first level model elements of their own. A lightning bolt symbol indicates that the work object is not physically present but exits in an IT system only. The steps of the Cooperation Scenario are to be read in sequence according to the numbers on the action arrows. Thus, the Cooperation scenario is a story in pictures, resembling storyboards or comic strips. This is illustrated in Fig. 9.3 that starts showing step 1 only and then incrementally adds steps.

The steps of the Cooperation Scenario correspond to elementary sentences in natural language. For example, step 2 in Fig 9.3 reads as: "The Mail Room (team) uses a bar code sticker to attach an application number to the X-Ray". The actor performing the step takes the role of the subject, the action itself is represented as a verb, the involved other actor and the work objects become objects in the grammatical sense.

Also note that this closeness to natural language sentences requires that work objects are duplicated for every step. This means that there is not only one instance of a work object but it appears as many times as it is used in an action. For example, the scanned application form occurs several times in Figs. 9.1 and 9.3.

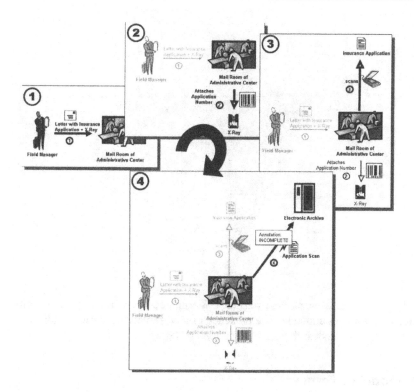

Fig. 9.3. The Cooperation Scenario as a story in pictures

9.3.2 Workplace Scenario

When a cooperation scenario becomes crowded with too many actions, they become less readable. Most of the time, not all actions have to deal with cooperation but take place at one individual actor's work place instead. In order to unclutter the cooperation scenarios, actions that are confined to one workplace only, can be "folded" into a Workplace Scenario that acts as a sub-model of the main Cooperation Scenario (see Fig. 9.4 for an example). A Cooperation Scenario references each of its Workplace Scenarios as one single step of the entire sequence. The Workplace Scenarios for a specific actor are visualized as numbered items over a desk symbol that is shown next to the actor. This way, Workplace Scenarios can be "stepped over" when examining the big picture of the Cooperation Scenario (see Fig. 9.4).

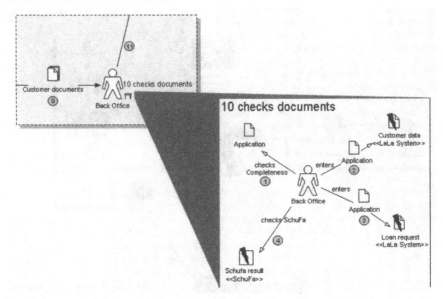

Fig. 9.4. Expanding a workplace step to a Workplace Scenario. Lightning bolts indicated electronic documents. The presence of a workplace scenario is indicated by the desk symbol next to the actor in the *top left* figure

9.3.3 Model of Terms

The Model of Terms contains the relevant terms for the domain concepts of one or more Cooperation as well as Workplace Scenarios and relates them to each other. The work objects in the scenario models are instances of the concepts in the Model of Terms.

The elements of the Model of Terms can be related via the "is-a" association, "is-part-of" association or a weak, untyped association type whose instances can be augmented with free text. Elements in the Model of Terms can be stereotyped as containers such as folders. Those are connected with other objects using the "contains"-association. Furthermore, there are IT-inspired stereotypes Tool and Service (see details given later).

Although the Model of Terms of EBPM can be a starting point for IT system design, it is important to emphasize that it cannot naively be mapped to a UML Class Model or to an ER model. It is strictly domain-oriented and does not define classes, class operations or the cardinality of relations. Consequently, transformation from the Model of Terms to UML's Class Model cannot be automated.

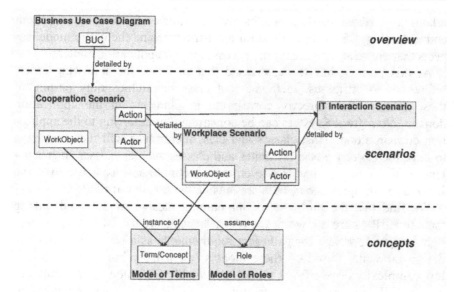

Fig. 9.5. Metamodel overview

9.3.4 Other Diagram Types

While the three diagram types discussed so far are invariably used when modeling business processes, diagrams of the following three types are only used when the specific need arises. We will not describe meta models for these types here, but show how they relate to others in Fig. 9.5.

- Models of Roles can be used in complex organizations to indicate which roles certain actors can take. It liberates modelers from using individual actors only.
- IT Interaction Scenarios depict one actor interacting with one or more IT systems. These scenarios resemble UML's sequence diagrams except that the communication shown is between the actor and the system, not inside a system
- Business Use Case Diagrams provide an overview of several Coopera-tion Scenarios. The Business Use Case bubbles in the diagram reference the Cooperation Scenario models

9.4 Capturing Design Rationale

In this section, we will elucidate how an application context captured with the various kinds of EBPM models can help software professionals to make rational design decisions about: the business object class model, the relational database model, tool features, candidates for services, the front end technology, the communication infrastructure and the usage model aspects that are related to the work processes in the application context.

At this point it has to be stressed that in all of the following cases, references to attributes, methods, and class hierarchies only pertain to those features that directly correspond to elements in the application domain. No software system can be constructed by referring to the application domain alone. Most classes and class hierarchies will therefore have to have technology-based attributes and classes such as classes for persistence and graphic display. However, these technological aspects only come into play in design stages which are outside the domain of EBPM.

We find that the problems of maintaining design models and linking them to EBPMs are not worth the effort. Instead, we use EBPMs as a mere light-weight approach for gathering requirements as a basis for extracting design rationale. Based on these models, we usually build prototypes of low complexity (PowerPoint mocks, executable GUI mocks, or prototypes with a GUI and very limited functionality) to discuss our understanding of the application domain and our solution approach with users. Based on these feedback cycles, we either modify EBPMs or refine our prototypes.

9.4.1 Business Object Class Model

The most straightforward way of deriving a design decision from an EBPM model is to take the *Models of Terms* as input for a class model of the application's business objects. These models comprise a wealth of information that corresponds to features of class models:

- Each work object in a *Model of Terms* is a good candidate for a *business object class*. This is in accordance with the underlying principle of object-oriented design – namely that objects in the system correspond to objects in the application domain. This principle of responsibility driven design (see [18]) follows the original purpose of the first object-oriented programming language "Simula" [3], namely simulation. Depending on the scope of a project, a certain number of work objects might not be considered parts of the application.
- A *business class's methods* can be derived from a work object's textual description as well as from the way it is referenced in Cooperation and Workplace Scenarios.
- For design purposes, it is highly useful to use the links in the opposite direction, namely to go from a *Model of Terms* to *Cooperation* or *Workplace Scenarios*, i.e., to find out in what way a work object is used in which scenarios.

- In conjunction with information taken from annotations, the way a work object is used – and thus its methods – can be taken from its usage in *Cooperation* and *Workplace Scenarios*.
- A *business class's attributes* can be derived from its methods and descriptive text plus from the aggregations indicated in *Models of Terms*. While aggregation information can be inferred directly just by looking at the aggregates relationship in a *Model of Terms*, finding attributes cannot be done visually but requires an examination of the methods (see above) and from the descriptive text: if there are methods that augment a work object in some way and others that query its status, then is obvious that there needs to be an attribute that holds that specific piece of information. Information about additional attributes or their type might be obtained from a format description stored in the annotations, e.g., whether an integer or a String is more appropriate to represent document IDs.
- A *business class's position in a class hierarchy* can be taken from its position in *is-a* relations in *Models of Terms*.

9.4.2 Relational Database Model

By exploiting the same features as in the section "Business object class model," elements of relational database model can be derived from EBPMs. Whereas strictly object-oriented features such as methods and class hierarchies cannot be transferred from EBPMs to a database model in a meaningful way, the other features can be derived analogous to those in Sect. 9.4.1:

- Each work object in a *Model of Terms* is a good candidate for an *entity* because these are the things that users work with. Even if it becomes obvious at later design stages that some work objects do not warrant introducing separate entities, using work objects as starting points for entities is a good idea.
- A *business class's attributes* can be derived from its methods and descriptive text plus from the aggregations indicated in *Models of Terms* (see above).
- While a *business class's position in a class hierarchy* cannot be directly transferred into a relational database model, it is a good indicator that the work objects are closely connected: they represent similar concepts on different levels of concreteness and feature at least some common attributes. This is an indicator that these work objects might be mapped to a single entity.

9.4.3 Tool Features

On a general level, every application can be regarded as a tool that allows users to accomplish a certain number of tasks with the help of an IT system. It is in accordance with this view to classify a calculator, a word processor or an ERP as tools. Nevertheless, in the context of modeling business processes, considering a whole ERP as a tool would be too coarse-grained. We therefore limit our definition too those tools which (1) typically have a main and sometimes some subwindows/dialogs and (2) which serve to view/manipulate business objects.

Using EBPM, the use of tools can be modeled explicitly or implicitly. Explicit modeling means that a tool appears as a specialized work object in *Cooperation Scenarios, Workplace Scenarios,* and *Models of Terms.* In this case a tool's features can be found by taking advantage of the link mechanism described in "Business object class model: Each link from a *Model of Terms* to *Cooperation* and *Workplace Scenarios* is followed and the accumulated ways of access are a tool's feature list. Implicit modeling means that a tool is not present yet but that there is high degree of similar access to a number of work objects. These similar ways of accessing a work object are indicative of potential tools.

Regardless of the way of modeling tools – which is usually a mixture of explicit and implicit modeling – other tool features can be gleaned from the EBPMs:

- *Tool modes* can be found be examining how tool use differs from user type to user type or from scenario to scenario. For example, some users might just use basic functionality while specialist users call upon similar functionality but require a higher degree of detail or additional kinds of information.
- A *tool's versatility* can be derived by looking at how many work object types are handled with a specific tool. Usage of just a single work object suggests a highly specialized tool while usage on many different work object types hints at a quite generic tool such as a browser or spreadsheet-like tool.

9.4.4 Candidates for Services

Identifying candidates for services requires that tools have already been found. On that basis, tools that make use of the same work object type in similar ways in several *Cooperation* and *Workplace Scenarios* indicate that the tools might be implemented by using the same service that provide access to business objects.

9.4.5 Workspace Types and Front End Technology

In general, (1) the number of tools employed, (2) their modes, and (3) their usage frequency provide important information about the workplace a user requires in a certain scenario. By looking at all scenarios that a user participates in, one can determine the degree of complexity, flexibility, and efficiency he or she requires. Based on those parameters, an informed choice of the appropriate front end technology, infrastructure, and usability-related criteria can be made. This naturally extends to the choice of general communication infrastructure including hardware: for example, employment of barcode scanners in a work process would receive attention in an EBPM Scenario.

However – as mentioned at the start of this section – we do not augment EBPMs to include explicit and detailed rationale information, e.g., "the front end technology for novice bank customers is an HTML 4.2 compliant web browser supporting JavaScript because most such customers are not willing to install new software on their home computers, do not have the skills to properly reconfigure their firewall, and access their bank account information sufficiently infrequently that they do not require more complex features of a graphical user interface." Instead, we rather make sure that the EBPMs contain every domain-oriented detail that the users deem important and base our decision thereon.

9.4.6 Difference Annotations

When designing a software system, the designers not only determine the behavior of an application but shape the future work processes. In most cases, these are bound to achieve the same effect (or a superset thereof) as the present ones, only faster and cheaper or with a higher quality.

Because of this, EBPM is often used to model the relevant existing processes of the application domain before beginning to design. These models show the actors doing their work as they do in the present, using today's artifacts and IT systems ("as-is" models). Based on these models, the future processes are designed with their respective future software support ("to-be" models). This helps to ensure that the old processes and the services they provide are not broken in transit to the future design.

For this purpose, the EBPM method offers an additional feature called *Difference Annotations*. Difference Annotations link specific actions in Cooperation Scenarios to actions in other Cooperation scenarios and are commented textually. In this way, new or different actions in to-be models can point to their present counterparts and describe relevant differences between present and future.

Difference Annotations can furthermore be used to compare several future scenarios. The creation of alternative EBPM scenario models is justified if they can support decisions on important design issues. For example, those scenarios can highlight different ways of distributing tasks in an organization or demonstrate the variety of possible usage models and their impact on the work process. A Difference Table as shown in Fig. 9.6 can be generated from the Difference annotations attached to a scenario.

action	referenced action	referenced scenario	comment
the Front Office is automatically informed that the contract is ready	the Back Office calls the Front Office to inform them that the contract is ready	application - minimal support	replacing a phone call by automation will speed things up, although detaching Front and Back Office a bit.

Fig. 9.6. One row of a Difference Table (schematic)

Difference Annotations are a simple and effective technique when examining the scenarios, whether to analyze the gap between current and future processes or to compare alternative scenarios. Sometimes we attach them while deriving a new scenario from a basic one. When analyzing retrospectively, we take printed versions of the models and compare them. First, we mark the differences with pen and paper, then, after evaluation, we attach them to the models in electronic form. This cannot be automated because it is all about finding the significant steps and interpreting them. When merging alternative scenarios, we recommend documenting the Difference Table together with the derived decisions in a protocol that is then attached to the "surviving" scenario.

9.4.7 Quantification

A second basis for deciding between different alternative scenarios is the quantification of EBPM scenarios. This is done very straightforward: the domain experts give rough estimates for how long actions take. Transportation and/or wait time is used when annotating transfers of work objects. Processing time is used when annotating inspections and modifications of work objects.

9.5 Relations to Other Approaches

There are other approaches in Requirements and Software Engineering as well as in economics that deal with the same issues as EBPM or have some overlap with it regarding the models and techniques that they use

EBPM's Cooperation Scenario is based on Krabbel's and Wetzel' Cooperation Pictures (cf. [10]). EBPM adds the strictly scenario-based approach and the comprehensive meta model. Another method that is remarkable for its visual representation and appropriateness for group work is PICTIVE (described in [11, 12]), which is rooted in Participatory Design. Contrary to EBPM, it does not provide a straightforward of deriving an object model.

Approaches sharing the scenario-based nature of EBPM come in a various formats, for example Jacobson's Use Cases (cf. [7]) and Rubin's and Goldberg's Object Behavior Analysis (described in [15]). These are more focused on the dialogue between user and software system than EBPM and less on the cooperative work process. They lack a visual representation for their scenarios and are therefore less suited for workshops with groups. Use Cases are superior to EBPM regarding variations and case differentiation when written as main success scenarios with extensions (cf. [2]).

Examples for more formal diagram techniques for processes are UML's Activity Diagram (see [8]) and the Event-Driven Process Chains of Scheer (see [16]). In contrast to EBPM, these can be used for a more formal specification of a process. On the other hand, they are not easily understandable for people without education in math or IT and therefore not well-suited for communication with users and domain experts. They are less object-oriented than EBPM because they do not focus on the domain objects and their usage (although there have been attempts to tackle this problem, see for example [17]). Furthermore, they are unable to "tell stories" like EBPM which can be applied even to cooperative work that consist to great extent of situated actions.

Concluding this section, we want to allude to approaches that deal with design rationale in a way that is potentially compatible to EBPM in the sense that only minor modifications would be necessary to fit them in. One of these approaches is Claims Analysis (see [1]) which augments scenarios that demonstrate specific design alternatives with claims that state expected advantages and disadvantages of those design decisions. Another one is Contribution Structures which adds to requirements explicit information about the persons contributing to them (cf. [6]). Yet another one is the Inquiry Cycle (see [13], [14]), a conceptual framework that recommends to incrementally refine scenarios and requirements documentation and attach information to them about the related discussions happening in the incremental process.

9.6 Conclusion

Exemplary Business Process Modeling (EBPM) is a lightweight yet highly useful basis for design rationale management. The three main factors that make EBPM so advantageous are:

1. *Its smooth integration with requirements engineering as suggested by Dutoit and Paech (see [5]).* As EBPM already provides all necessary means, there is no need to duplicate the relevant information in a design rationale management system.
2. *Its focus on just the most relevant scenarios.* Thus, a maximum of the daily work routine can be captured with optimal effort.
3. *Its focus on positive in formation.* While decisions against a certain alternative can still be derived by looking at the complement of the positive information, there is no need to keep, manage and update information about discarded alternatives.

EBPM has many qualities that can be traced to other approaches:

- It is scenario-based (like the Use Case approach and OBA)
- It models business processes (like UML Activity diagrams or EPCs)
- It analyzes cooperative work (like Cooperation Pictures)
- It is suitable for collaborative workshops (like PICTIVE)

EBPM is unique in its combination of those features. Its power lies in the immediate understandability of its models: all models are rendered graphically and are based on a simple meta model; the story-like structure of the scenarios makes it easy for domain and software experts alike to discuss domain-related matters in workshops. Models are usually very stable at the end of the first workshop. Based on these models, a substantial amount of design rationale can be derived (see Fig. 9.7).

In addition to the design-rationale-related advantages, the analysis of EBPMs can be employed to obtain rationale information for roll-out/migration planning (based on which application parts are used how intensively and on difference tables).

Rationale for ...	Provided by analysis of ...
business object classes/ ER entities	term or concept in *Model of Terms*
business object class methods	• Usage of work objects in *Scenarios* • glossary from *Model of Terms*
business object class attributes/ER attributes	• aggregations from Model of Terms • glossary from Model of Terms
business object class hierarchy/OR mapping	Hierarchy of Terms in *Model of Terms*
tools	• usage of work objects in *Scenarios* (explicitly modeled tools only) • glossary from *Model of Terms* (explicitly modeled tools only) • similar access to work objects in Scenarios • (implicit) • recurring sequences of work in Scenarios
tool modes	differences in usage for different Scenarios
tool versatility	number of work objects accessed (explicitly modeled tools only)
workplace types	• roles in *Model of Roles* • "work objects used from workplace
services	How different tools provide similar methods on work objects
endorsement of design decision	• difference tables for "as-is" and "to-be" models • difference tables for several "to-be" models • quantification information

Fig. 9.7. Rationale information provided by EBPM

References

[1] Caroll JM (2000) Making Use: Scenario-Based Design of Human–Computer Interaction. Cambridge: MIT

[2] Cockburn A (2000) Writing Effective Use Cases. Reading, MA: Addison-Wesley

[3] Dahl O-J, Nygaard K (1967) SIMULA - A language for Programming and Description of Discrete Event Systems, Oslo 3, Norway, Norwegian Computing Center, Forskningveien 1B, 5th ed.

[4] Dutoit AH, McCall R, Mistrík I, Paech B (2006) Rationale management in software engineering. Heidelberg Berlin New York: Springer

[5] Dutoit AH, Paech B (2000) Supporting evolution: Using rationale in use case driven software development. In: 6th Internaltional Workshop on Requirements Engineering for Software Quality (REFSQ'2000), Interlaken Switzerland, June

[6] Gotel O, Finkelstein A (1995) Contribution structures. In: Proceedings of the Second IEEE International Symposium on Requirements Engineering (RE '95), IEEE Computer Society, York UK, March 27–29, pp. 100–107

[7]   Jacobson I, Christerson M, Jonsson P, Overgaard G (1992) Object-Oriented Software Engineering: A Use Case Driven Approach. Reading, MA: Addison-Wesley

[8]   Jacobson I, Ericsson M, Jacobson A (1995) The Object Advantage: Business Process Reengineering with Object Technology. Reading, MA: Addison-Wesley

[9]   Karsenty L (1996) An Empirical Evaluation of Design Rationale Documents. In: Proc. of the SIGCHI conference on Human factors in computing systems, Vancouver, British Columbia, Canada, pp. 150–156

[10] Krabbel AM, Ratuski S, Wetzel I (1996) Requirements Analysis of Joint Task in Hospitals. In: B. Dahlbom et al. (ed.): IRIS 19 "The Future", Proceedings of the 19th Information Systems Research Seminar in Scandinavia, August 1996 at Lökeberg, Sweden. Gothenburg Studies in Informatics, Report 8, pp. 733–749

[11] Muller MJ (1991) PICTIVE – An exploration in participatory design. In Reaching through Technology: CHI'91 Conference Proceedings, pp. 225–231

[12] Muller M, Tudor L, Wildman D, White E, Root R, Dayton T, Carr R, Diekmann B, Dykstra-Erickson E (1995) Bifocal tools for scenarios and representations in participatory activities with users. In: J.M. Carroll (ed.): Scenario-Based Design. NY: Wiley

[13] Potts C, Bruns G (1988) Recording the reasons for design decisions. In: Proceedings of the 10th International Conference on Software Engineering. Los Alamitos, CA: IEEE Computer Society

[14] Potts C, Takahashi K, Anton A (1994) Inquiry-based scenario analysis of system requirements. IEEE Softw., 11(2):21–32, March

[15] Rubin KS, Goldberg A (1992) Object behavior analysis. Commun. ACM 35(9), 48–62

[16] Scheer A-W (2001) ARIS – Modellierungsmethoden, Metamodelle, Anwendungen.4. Auflage. Berlin Heideleberg New York: Springer-Verlag, 2001

[17] Scheer A-W, Nüttgens M, Zimmermann V (1997) Objektorientierte Ereignisgesteuerte Prozeßkette (oEPC) Methode und Anwendung. Veröffentlichungen des Instituts für Wirtschaftsinformatik, Heft 141, Saarbrücken URL: http://www.iwi.uni-sb.de/public/iwi-hefte.

[18] Wirfs-Brock R, Wilkerson B (1990) Designing Object-Oriented Software. Englewood Cliffs, NJ: Prentice Hall.

[19] Züllighoven H (2003) Object-Oriented Construction Handbook. San Fransisco: Morgan Kaufmann

10 Promoting and Supporting Requirements Engineering Creativity

L. Nguyen, P.A. Swatman

Abstract: Requirements Engineering (RE) is a commencing phase in the systems development life cycle and concerned with understanding and specifying the customer's requirements. RE has been recognized as a complex cognitive problem solving process which takes place in an unstructured and poorly understood problem context. A recent understanding describes the RE process as inherently creative, involving cycles of incremental building followed by insight-driven reconceptualization of the problem space. This chapter relates this new understanding to various creative process models described in the creativity and psychology of problem solving literature.

A review of current attempts to support problem solving in RE using various design rationale approaches suggests that their common major weakness lies in the lack of support for the creative and insight-driven problem solving process in RE. In addressing this weakness, the chapter suggests a new approach to promoting and supporting RE creativity using design rationale. The suggested approach involves the ad hoc recording of rationale to support the creative exploration complemented by a post hoc conceptual characterization of the problem space to support insight driven reconceptualization.

Keywords: RE process; problem solving; creativity; insight

10.1 Introduction

Creativity plays an increasingly significant role in the competitive and dynamic business world by enabling organizations to differentiate and innovate, to run more effective businesses, to attract customers and to compete with their rivals. In Requirements Engineering (RE), creativity manifests in professional activities such as exploring business domains, inventing and investigating ICT-enabled commercial opportunities and suggesting application requirements to support organization business strategies. Although creativity is required in RE, its study has recently emerged as an important trend in the domain. The fundamental question is: how do we support and promote creativity in RE?

As a problem solving process, RE involves intensive knowledge exploitation and decision making. There have been attempts to support this process in RE problem by capturing and accessing design rationale

(DR) – information about the deliberations behind the RE process – but previous work tends to focus on techniques and notations by which to structure and record an argument. The RE problem solving process to be supported by DR is assumed to be characteristically top-down and systematic. The intrinsic opportunism of (and associated creativity within) the RE process [6, 17, 34, 36,] has been largely ignored and thus the possibility of supporting creativity in RE using DR has not been fully explored.

In response, this chapter suggests a new approach to using DR with the potential to promote and support the inherently creative and insight-driven problem solving process in RE. The suggested approach involves the ad hoc recording of rationale to support creative exploration, complemented by a post hoc conceptual characterization of the problem space to support insight driven reconceptualization. The chapter also describes benefits and limitations of the suggested approach.

The structure of the chapter is as follows. Sect. 10.2 offers our critical observations of benefits and problems we face in using DR. Sect. 10.3 discusses the intrinsic nature of the problem we face in RE, reviews different perspectives on RE process, and describes a new understanding of the creative and insight-driven RE process. Sect. 10.4 describes creativity models and discusses RE creativity in this context. Sect. 10.5 proposes a new approach to using DR within RE to support and promote creativity. Sect. 10.6 provides a summary and conclusion.

10.2   Overview of Design Rationale

DR, in simple words, is information which represents and explains the reasoning behind the RE process. The notion of DR can be traced back to the philosopher Aristotle. The essence of Aristotelian logic lies in the deductive categorical syllogisms (premises and conclusions). Like Aristotelian logic, modern standard logic is also based on deductive rules or laws, such as Boolean algebra with propositional and predicate calculus, or hypothetico-deductivism with hypothesis proposal and testing, a widely adopted method in various scientific disciplines. While these traditional logical approaches exhibit advantages in their objectivity, they are often criticized by contemporary authors as being limited to well-defined deductive situations and as being less effective in inductive and social situations [56, 57].

Having criticized the deductive approaches as candid and insufficiently elaborate, philosopher Toulmin [56] develops a more sophisticated structure of argument by analogy with jurisprudence. The Toulmin model, represented in the graphical form, marks the first step in the area of modern "design rationale" and strongly influences subsequent DR notations.

Over the last three decades, DR has received an increasing attention in the research community. Various approaches, techniques and notations for the deliberations capturing and representing the deliberations behind the design process have been developed. DR research has been drawn from multiple fundamental sources: artificial intelligence, cognitive study and design research. They are classified as three strategies: ad hoc, post hoc, and psychology-oriented DR [14]. The two most popular strategies are ad hoc (process-oriented) and post hoc (structured-oriented). The psychology-oriented approach attempts to capture the psychological claims of usability in the artifact to suit the users' tasks rather than the deliberation of the designer during the RE process and will not be discussed in this chapter. This section focuses on presenting our conclusions drawn from a critical review of previous research into the two popular approaches to DR. Details about various DR notations, their descendants, techniques and tools can be found in Chap. 1 in this book. A more comprehensive review of previous DR research is available in [37].

10.2.1 Capturing the Design Process through Issue-Bases Information Systems (IBIS) and its Descendants

Early in 1970s, Rittel [reprinted in [44, p. 321]] coins the term *"wicked problem"* to refer to problems which are vague and open for interpretation, and have no stopping rule and no ultimate criteria for evaluation. In response to the challenge of wicked problems, Kunz and Rittel [25] propose and develop IBIS (Issue-Based Information System). IBIS offers a simple and intuitive notation: an Issue to be solved, a set of possible solutions (Positions) to solve it, a number of Arguments supporting or objecting the proposed Positions. It is used to record argumentative discussions as they occur. In this sense, IBIS supports the ad hoc approach to DR.

Since then, IBIS has been taken up in a wide range of applications and domains. Benefits and issues in applying IBIS have been reported [e.g., 4, 8, 43]. In our view, the previous research has focused limited to extending IBIS notations and the context of product development (software/requirements) rather then studying IBIS at the level of conceptual development of the problem. We offer two observations:

– IBIS DR rationale base could serve as a history of the design process.
– The flow of issues and the links between chosen Positions should reflect the psychology of problem solving process. The central activity supported by IBIS, i.e., the generation followed with the evaluation of

Issue, hints at an expectation of a systematic top-down development approach.

10.2.2 Representing Design Space Analysis with QOC

MacLean et al. [30] present an overview of the Design Space Analysis approach and propose the QOC notation to structure the design space analysis. Similarly to IBIS, the QOC notation consists of three core components: a design Question, its alternative solutions (Options) and a set of Criteria for the assessment of Options. The additional component Argument may be used to justify the assessment of Options against Criteria. In contrast to IBIS, QOC does not represent the historical record of the design process. QOC concentrates on the global logical design space, which can be retrospectively structured by the consideration of its alternatives. Therefore, QOC supports the post hoc approach to DR.

There are a growing number of intensive research projects into QOC. Research in QOC can be classified into the following main directions: developing the QOC representation and process [e.g., 29, 30, 49], studying QOC usefulness and usability [e.g., 22, 50, 51] and incorporating QOC within a specific design method [e.g., 21]. The QOC literature shows a common agreement that the strength of QOC is the promoted construction of highly abstract and reusable design knowledge and that the weakness of QOC is the additional time and effort required to construct a retrospective analysis. Two positions as when best to create QOC have emerged: using QOC to record the thought process during design [51, 53] *or* using QOC to retrospectively examine and structure the design space [22, 29, 30,]. Again, there was an assumption of a top down design process: "*QOC does not guide decomposition as clearly as some top down methods*" [53, p. 154]. But is the design process (especially in relation to RE) actually top-down and systematic in practice? We will return to this question in Sect. 10.3.

10.2.3 Overall Assessment

The effective and efficient creation and use of DR are still subjects of concern within the Software/RE communities. There are two possible extremes:

- *Having an evolving DR base* has advantages in providing a historical record of 'flying thoughts' while struggling with difficulties in managing and retrieving information from a large rationale base.
- *Capturing the deliberations in a purely post hoc manner* has advantages of producing highly abstract and global analyses of the design problem

while having difficulties of recognizing when to create rationale documents and requiring additional overhead effort to create them.

One way to address the above concerns is to study the evolution of the rationale information in relation to the evolution of design artifacts based on a deep understanding of the problem solving process in design.

10.3 Understanding the RE Process

10.3.1 What Kind of Problems do We Face in RE Problems?

The problems presenting in RE are ill-structured, complex, and rather domain specific. Ill-structuredness in RE is defined as the incomplete and ambiguous representation of problems, the multidisciplinary domains and knowledge, the nondeterministic approach to solving requirements problems and the open-ended nature of solutions [2, 7, 17;]. RE problems can be described as "wicked" in Rittel's [44] terms. Further, problems in RE are complex. Throughout the requirements development process, as the problem space is explored, requirements continue to be acquired, clarified, refined, and (re-)modeled by the RE. During this process, different facets of requirements problem are uncovered, leading to conflict identification and resolution. The problem space is evolving and involving many elements at different levels of abstraction. Carroll et al. [7] stated that "There is no problem tree representation for these problems" because requirements "are too complex; and there are many ways to 'solve' them" [7, p. 84]. Moreover, understanding and analyzing requirements often involves subjective interpretation and perception by different participants. RE problems are intrinsic to the client's business domains and their competitive positions and perspectives, and often require both the RE and the client to engage in mutual learning activities in order to understand and specify the client's requirements [e.g., 1, 5, 9, 20, 28].

The above factors are also inter-related. For example, the multidisciplinary domain of RE contributes to the ill-structuredness and complexity of the problem space. According to Batra and Davis [2, p. 87], requirements are constructed in a rather "open-ended" and "semantically rich problem space". Together, these factors contribute to the nondeterministic nature of the RE process. This leads to an interesting question: How do people do RE?

10.3.2 How do We Carry Out RE Tasks?

There are numerous methodologies and approaches to capturing, structuring and representing requirements (e.g., SSADM, UML, Z, and Object Z), and to managing the development process (e.g., Volere, SigSigma, and CMM). Throughout the literature, it is generally agreed:

- that the RE process is a knowledge intensive, problem solving and decision making process [18, 46].
- that RE requires creativity and heuristics as well as "standard" modeling techniques [18, 31, 36].

Interestingly, while most authors agree on the knowledge intensiveness and creativity in RE, the literature is limited in describing how the RE process happens and why requirements take a particular form. A 'classic' and especially "worrying" finding from an early survey [27] was that professionals find it hard to explain how they actually carry out their work. So how do professionals use their professional RE knowledge, skills and creativity during the RE process? More than a decade has passed. This question has not been clearly answered.

10.3.3 Two Emerging Perspectives of RE Process

Two perspectives on the RE process emerge – one which views the RE process as being essentially systematic and evolutionary and one which views it as being rather opportunistic and insight-driven.

There is common agreement within the RE community that the RE process is dynamic, evolutionary and involves continuous decisions. Through the textbooks, the RE process is often described as cyclic with each cycle consisting of elicitation, analysis and validation activities [e.g., 24, 26]. Robertson and Robertson [45] describe the RE process as an asynchronous network of activities which can be customized to specific applications. Alexander [1] acknowledges the collaboration between the users and developers and sees the RE process as consisting of four cycles of co-operative inquiry. Although the detailed description of the RE process vary from author to author, at a high level of abstraction, the requirements problem space is structured and refined in a generally cumulative mode.

Another school of thought in studying the RE process postulates the opportunistic nature of the RE process [e.g., 6, 17, 23, 58]. According to these authors, the RE process is not smoothly evolutionary; solutions to problems/subproblems are often insight-driven rather than being derived through a systematic evaluation of alternatives. As explained by Guindon [17], the ill-structuredness of the requirements problem is an important factor inducing the opportunistic behaviors of the designer. The human working memory is limited, so mental simulations of the overall solution could not be performed, only simulations of partial solutions. With partial solutions it is possible to keep in memory the subsolutions' values, calling others at a different (often lower) level of abstraction [16–18]. Guindon argues that the inferences of new information reduce the incompleteness and ambiguity of the problem and lead to opportunistic design process. In addition, the new inferred constraints may provide early insights critical in reducing the space of design possibilities and in discovering decomposition.

Later Khushalani and his colleagues describe the RE process as an unpredictable and adaptive exploration of problem areas, which is *"characterised by frequent discovery and/or adaptation of goals and activities, in response to changing circumstances"* [23, p. 13]. Carroll and Swatman [6] also suggest that requirements engineer's traversal of the problem space is by no means orderly during the RE process.

Previous studies (except [6]) focus primarily on the examination of designer's activities individually in the context of abstraction levels rather than provide a rich contextual analysis of the phenomenon. Consequently, they lack detailed examination of the dynamics of conceptual understanding and perception of the problem by the designer. Although Khushalani and his colleagues [23] profitably use QOC to represent and map cognitive concepts graphically, the study does not examine the impact of critical opportunistic decisions on the conceptual understanding of the designer.

Our action research [36] reveals the RE process as consisting of cycles of creative construction and insight-driven reconstruction of the problem space. This new understanding of the RE process will be used a basis for the new approach to DR proposed in this chapter.

10.3.4 Creative Structuring and Insight-Driven Reconceptualizing of the Problem Space

RE is inherently creative, involving cycles of extension and restructure of the requirements model, in contrast to the systematic and smoothly incremental process generally described in the literature. We illustrate the pattern of extension and restructure of the requirements model through our catastrophe-cycle RE process model (Fig. 10.1a).

The catastrophe-cycle RE process could be explained through the lens of three different types of complexity in the requirements model:

– Essential complexity represents the intrinsic understanding of the requirements problem gained and embedded in the requirements model.

This type of complexity grows over time towards "completeness". We can assume that our understanding of the problem must not be decreasing.

– Incidental complexity represents the complexity of representation rather than of substance in the model. In other words, it reflects the poor fit between the structure of the requirements model and the structure of the real world problem that the model attempts to mirror. Given an imperfect model structure, it becomes more difficult to fit new components into the model as it grows. Incidental complexity grows exponentially as the model evolves and decreases significantly when the model is restructured.

– Accidental complexity represents the hidden knowledge in the requirements model which becomes explicit only as a result of insight at the crisis points. After the model is restructured, the accidental complexity becomes a part of the essential complexity which continues to grow over

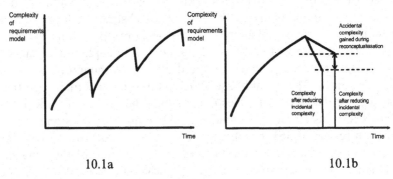

10.1a   10.1b

Fig. 10.1. The catastrophe-cycle RE process

The catastrophe-cycle RE process can be explained in more detail using the dynamics of these types of complexity. As time progresses, the requirements engineer continuously gathers information and details about the problem. Due to the complexity, ill-structured and context-based characteristics of the problem, the requirements engineer is actively engaged in an intensive exploration, searching, and learning process to explore and learn about the problem and its specific context. Therefore, the problem space is continually expanded with new directions being explored and revealed, possible solutions and constraints being investigated and structured. Working on a problem area often requires the problem solver to revisit previous solved and/or partially solved problem areas. This is consistent with the opportunistic characteristic of the design process described by Schön [48, p. 175]: "As you worked on a problem you are continually in the process of developing a path into it". This path significantly depends on the requirements engineer's perceptions, knowledge and interactions with the specific involved organizational context and people.

As the exploration and modeling of the problem space progresses, the complexity of the requirements model progressively increased. The construction a requirements model involves decision making activities, as a result of which, new components and their complex relationships are elaborated and added into the model. Therefore, the essential complexity of the requirements model increases, reflecting the increasing inherent understanding of the requirements problem by the requirements engineer. This is consistent with Guindon's description of RE as a knowledge discovery process [16]. The more complex the model becomes, the harder it becomes to add and fit new components to the growing model. The incidental complexity grows rapidly over time. This is also consistent with what is described as the increasing entropy in software engineering literature.

At some stage, a sudden unexpected flash of insight occurs, a new way of understanding and conceptualizing the problem suddenly becomes apparent. Insight is often referred to in many other human creative activities as "Eureka!" or the "Aha!" moments. The new understanding gained by insight, referred to as the accidental complexity, leads to a significant change in the problem space. The problem is reconceptualized and the model undergoes a major restructuring step. In addition, the incidental (and thus overall) complexity of the model significantly drops. This effect of reconceptualization insight can be illustrated as the dropping lines in Fig. 10.1b. After reconceptualization, the newly reconstructed model becomes the basis for further development cycles.

The above understanding reveals two essential characteristics of the RE process that it is a creative and insight-driven process – essentially, a design activity. During RE, the model undergoes a creative process of exploration and structuring of the problem space. At crisis point, as a result of insight the problem is reconceptualized and restructured. This often leads to the simplification of the model. This simplification should not be understood merely in terms of the reduction of the number of components of the model. Instead, the model had a new architecture reflecting a new perception of the problem by the requirements engineer. The RE process is, in essence, a design process. Gero [15, p. 435] offers a definition of design as "a purposeful, constrained, decision making, exploration, and learning activity". As Gero contends, this definition is an acceptable and sufficient to understand the creative design process. As described above, during RE, the requirements engineer continuously explores different problem areas and the problem context, searches for information and details, learns and makes decision to structure the requirements model. This learning process also involves occasional reconceptualization of the problem, subsequently major restructuring of the model, as a result of on-going conscious effort and unexpected insight. This understanding of the RE process can be comparable to Gero's conclusion after examining various creative design process models: "In design there is interest not only in synthesising solutions, even optimal solutions, but also in the novel and unexpected solution which as a consequence of its existence changes our expectations. this may require a change in structure, behavior or function—the essence of creative design [15, p. 448]."

Subsequently, this new understanding raises a new challenging question to the RE community: how to support the creative and insight-driven catastrophe cycle process in RE?

10.4   RE Creativity in Relation to Psychology of Problem Solving

Creativity is the subject of lively and frequently discussion in the literature of various disciplines, such as psychology of problem solving, design, creative performing arts, creative writing, and many other human endeavors and activities. Yet, it is still hard to define creativity in a precise and concise sentence for there appear to exist many forms and facets of creativity. In Sternberg's [52] handbook on creativity, creative outcome is described with the following qualities:

– *Novelty*. The outcome has to be new, original to a community. Boden [3] differentiates two levels of personal and historical creativity. This implies two creativity elements: the personal *ability* to produce something new and the social scope in perceiving/experiencing that something is novel.
– *Surprisingness*. The outcome often offers *unexpected* features which could be an *interesting* combination of existing ideas or the simplicity of a suggested solution.
– *Value*. The outcome should be *valuable* and *useful*, for example an appropriate solution to a problem. This quality implies a *process* of producing the value and an (often collective) *judgment* and *acceptance* of value.

In general, person, process, product, and context are essential components that form the basis for understanding creativity by many authors [e.g. 3, 11, 54, 55]. More recently, Plucker [42] described creativity as "the interplay between ability and process by which an individual or group produces an outcome or product that is both novel and useful as defined within some social context".

Interestingly, there is an implication that creativity in problem solving involves *individuals* engaged in a mental *process* to produce a valuable *outcome* (ideas, products, solutions) which will be subject to a reflective review by the creator and his/her peers. While these elements, as discussed above, all play their roles in DR as well as in RE, one has to wonder why creativity has been missing (or mysterious) in these disciplines?

10.4.1 Creativity Process Models

It is useful to briefly review existing creativity process models in the context of the catastrophe-cycle model.

Wallas' creativity model [59] has dominated 20th century creativity literature. Wallas describes the creativity process as consisting of four stages: preparation, incubation, illumination (insight), and the verification and expression of insight. This model was supported and further developed: in Hadamard's work, creativity involves an unconscious mental process and insight is seen as a breakthrough by unconscious ideas [19].

Gestalt psychology has been the dominant influence in the problem solving literature on the importance of problem restructuring and insight [e.g., 33, 39]. According to Gestalt psychologists, problem space restructuring is crucial in problem solving and reveals a new way of looking at the problem, often from a broader perspective. Restructuring is often associated with the occurrence of insight, a sudden, unpredictable flash of ideas which often involves a surprise and solves. However, how to trigger insight or make restructuring happen seem to remain an answered question: "A restructuring event has an involuntary character; it is experienced as something that 'happens', rather than as something the problem solver 'does'" [39, p. 69].

In the above classic creativity models, creativity while involving intentional mental effort by the problem solver (preparation phase), it is associated with insight and how insight happens is beyond control of the creator.

Modern creativity models attempt to move toward to a more structured approach to exercising creativity. Osborn–Parnes' Creative Problem Solving [13, 40], known as CPS, stresses the balance of analytical process and imagination through brainstorming:

– *Mess-Finding*. Looking for Objective and Goals
– *Data-Finding*. Gather data
– *Problem-Finding*. Clarify problems

- *Idea-Finding*. Generate ides
- *Solution-Finding*: Select and refine a solution
- *Acceptance-Finding*. Plan for actions to implement the solution

Based on a synthesis of classic and modern creativity models, Plsek [41] suggested a Directed Creativity Cycle consisting of sophisticated phases namely preparation, imagination, development and action, each phase consisting of sophisticated activities leading from one to the next phase.

In Systems Engineering, Cropley and Cropley [10] suggested a comprehensive creative process model. This model attempts to synthesize a Wallas-based model of creativity process, extended to include information, communication and validation phases, with other emotional psychological factors, such as interest, curiosity, determination, excitement, satisfaction, anticipation, pride, hope, and elation. These factors are associated with different systems engineering activities which happen in parallel with different phases of the creativity process model. It is interesting that this model offers new associations between (rather positive) emotions often reported in "artistic" forms of creativity (performance and visual art) and insight and problem solving activities and seeks ways through these associations to support creativity in systems engineering.

Having examined the above models, we make the following observations:

- Although these models are helpful in understanding how creativity could be supported, it is not clear how it happens. Interestingly, all models show a cyclic process of creativity. Although Gestalt psychologists do not state this explicitly, they recognize that unsuccessful attempts to solve the problem contribute to the occurrence of restructuring [39]. In RE, the catastrophe cycle process model supports Wallas and Gestalt theory of insight and restructuring in problem solving.
- While the modern creativity process models fail to describe the opportunistic behaviors of the problem solver in RE, they tend to structure and support the analytical conscious phases in the classic creativity models. These can be related to the preparation phase in Wallas's model, and Cropleys' information and communication phases [10]. In the RE catastrophe-cycle model, these phases happen during the creative and reflective structuring of the requirements model.

The above creativity process models, especially their links connecting different creativity phases, indicate some potential benefits of recording, capturing, and representing the ideas generated using DR. The following section will describe our new DR approach to supporting creativity in RE.

10.5   Using DR to Support Creative RE Process

Our synthesis of previous discussions in previous sections about the nature and characteristics of RE problems and problem solving process, ad hoc and post hoc approaches to DR, and dominant creativity models shows:

- The problem understanding and problem solving in RE are intertwined. RE is concerned with understanding and constructing the problem we are dealing with as well as suggesting and specifying the solution.
- The RE process is highly creative, involving an *interplay* between cognitive *ability* and problem solving *process* by which *an individual or group* of requirements engineers *produces* a *new* and *useful* understanding and representation of the requirements problem that is acceptable and agreeable within some socio-organizational *context* – i.e., the creativity elements in Plucker's [42] definition (see Sect. 10.4.1).
- The RE process can "best" be described as catastrophe-cyclic of exploring and uncovering of the problem space and structuring of the requirements model; and insight-driven reconceptualizing and restructuring of the model.

Therefore, there are two types of RE creativity activities:

- *Activities which are associated with the preparation and incubation phase in Wallas's model, and Cropley and Cropley's [10] information and communication phases.* In the catastrophe-cycle model, these phases usually happen during the creative and reflective structuring of the requirements model. Such activities include brainstorming, eliciting, generating, connecting and evaluating information and ideas, and communicating, maintaining, sharing, and accessing previous information and ideas. These creativity activities aim at supporting the building up of a requirements model – a generally evolutionary process as described in the dominant literature [e.g., 24, 26, 45]. This type of creativity could be supported with ad hoc DR.
- *Activities which are associated with recognizing, evaluating and implementing insight and restructuring in Wallas's and Gestalt psychology.* This is insight-driven reconceptualization and restructuring of the requirements model in the catastrophe cycle RE process model. Wallas model supporters and Gestalt psychologists agree on the *importance* and *unpredictability* of insight and restructuring. Modern creativity models tend to respond to former with the evaluation and implementation of well-structured and rationalized ideas. However, modern creativity models fail to actively address the *unpredictability* of insight and

restructuring. Post hoc DR could be used to evaluate and examine the restructured problem space.

Based on a synthesis of the above theoretical development and findings from a previous empirical investigation [36], we suggest an integrated approach to supporting RE creativity using both ad hoc and post hoc DR. IBIS and QOC are selected as representative notations of ad hoc and post hoc DR.

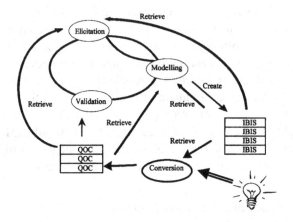

Fig. 10.2. Using DR to support creativity in RE

10.5.1 Using Ad Hoc Design Rationale to Support Creative Structuring of Requirements Model

IBIS arguments can be recorded during the RE meetings for various activities such as requirements analysis and modeling. The process of recoding and retrieving of IBIS issues can be described as follows:

– During the requirements analysis and modeling activities, brainstorming and divergent thinking sessions can be utilized to explore possibilities and generate ideas. IBIS arguments can be structured and recorded. Every time, a new IBIS Issue is recorded, an element Context can be added to describe a specific situation in which the Issue is raised (see Fig. 10.3 for an example of Context in an IBIS issue).
– During the elicitation of new requirements and further construction of the requirements model, related issues can be retrieved from the IBIS base to provide context for discussion and to avoid solving the same problem over again.

Therefore, the IBIS base describes the on-going evolutionary development of requirements, i.e., *how* the requirements develop over time.

Issue 3/97/GRANUL: Do we want to record/describe changes to the object Node?
Authors: RE1 and RE2
Context: As a solution to a previous Issue 2/97GRANUL, each object Decision keeps a reference to one or two objects Model and all objects Arguments shall keep references to a number of Node /Link involved in the Arguments.
?Position 1: Yes, we should be able to trace the evolution of a particular Node.
   AS: To support the understandability of whole the model in detail.
Subissue: How to implement this?
   ?Position 1: Keep only the final form of each Node and a history of changes in delta (s)
   a(n-1) = a(n) - delta (n-1,n)
      AS: implementation matter: save disk space...
      AO: this solution may get quite complicated and recursive with a network of different versions of Node.

Fig. 10.3. An extract of an IBIS issue

IBIS supports creativity activities in the following ways:

– IBIS encourages generation and discussion of "conscious" ideas which may otherwise be hidden in unconsciousness. Therefore, the construction of IBIS can be related to the Wallas's preparation phase.
– IBIS should be used in a flexible manner – issues with or without a full set of Positions or Arguments should be recorded to allow divergent thinking. Unsolves Issues should also be recorded.
– The IBIS base provides the requirements engineer with an accumulated knowledge of the problem space. This could be associated with the information phase [10] and Wallas's incubation phase.
– IBIS supports the communication between requirements engineers through enabling the sharing and debating of issues and possible solutions. Communication phase is suggested in Cropleys' model [10].

Two limitations of this approach include the locality of ad hoc arguments due to the lack of context in which the Issue element is explored difficulty in searching and managing the large IBIS base. To overcome former, we suggest extending the IBIS notation with a Context element. To overcome the latter, we suggest a supplementary use of post hoc QOC.

10.5.2 Using Design Rationale to Leverage Effects of Insight-Driven Reconceptualization in RE

QOC can be used as follows:

- QOC analyses can be constructed when the requirements model undergoes a major revision or restructuring. This often happens as a result of a reconceptualization insight. When this happens, relevant IBIS arguments can be retrieved from the IBIS base to support the construction of QOC. This can be also conducted at a critical point which requires the requirements engineer to review a broad problem area or a number of related problem areas.
- QOC analyses describe a holistic examination of the problem space at critical points during the RE project. This will assist the requirements engineers take advantage of insight to evaluate the insight, review the problem space and restructure the requirements model.
- The construction of a QOC analysis as a result of insight is often associated with a new conceptualization of the problem and thus requiring further elicitation and exploration of the problem in the new light. This QOC analysis can be a useful, historical source of information in subsequent elicitation activities.
- Later during the modeling and evaluation of the requirements model, QOC analyses can be retrieved to provide structured and systematic explanations of the problem space in order to resolve specific problems raised in new IBIS issues.

An example of a scenario of IBIS issues and QOC analysis can be found in Nguyen and Swatman [35].

QOC analyses describe the revolutionary development of requirements and *why* a requirement model takes a certain form it does. QOC supports creativity activities in the following ways:

- QOC assist the requirements engineer in evaluating insight and reconceptualize the problem by constructing an examination of the new problem space. Therefore, QOC assists the requirements engineer in gaining the accidental complexity of the problem at crux points.
- QOC provides the requirements engineer with an understanding of the current status of the requirements model. Therefore, QOC may be accessed during subsequent preparation and incubation phases when a specific local Issue is under consideration.

In order to effectively construct QOC, it is important to recognize insight events. Interestingly, insight events are often recognized by individuals, they may not be made available or receive sufficient attention by peers. The recognition, assessment and acceptance of new (out of the box) ideas may be affected by many factors such as personal traits, team composition and dynamics, and organizational culture [11, 12].

10.5.3 Discussion

In relation to catastrophe cycle model, IBIS would be useful in helping the problem solver explore the problem, build the model and highlight ideas hidden in unconsciousness. In addition, by laying out the arguments, requirements engineers are encouraged and supported to *reflect-in-action*. This is a concept introduced by Schön [47] to express that professionals continually think about their actions while they are working on a problem.

In addition, the structure-oriented QOC analysis helps the problem solver to step aside, synthesize conscious ideas and have a broad view of the problem. Therefore, this mechanism enables them to work at higher levels of abstraction and widen problem areas to allow unconscious ideas to emerge and break through at some point in time. When insight happens, QOC would be useful in gaining essential knowledge through more thoroughly and systematically articulating and evaluating insight. QOC assists the requirements engineer in *reflecting-on-action*, a concept introduced by Schön [47] to describe that professionals re-examine and reflect upon the whole process *at* a certain state in order to learn from their past actions.

In terms of overhead issues associated with applying both DR notations, the simplicity and ad hoc characteristics of the IBIS notation allow us to document the process nonintrusively while QOC could be used in taking advantage of insight and in interrogating and consolidating the IBIS base when needed. As discussed in Sect. 10.2.2, IBIS fails to enable an effective search and retrieval of the rationale knowledge from a large and fragmented rationale base largely due to its approach to progressively recording of local issues and their associated deliberations. In our proposed approach, the searching and retrieval of related IBIS issues are supported with supplementary QOC analyses. Required rationale information can be retrieved from a structured QOC base and newly created IBIS issues.

As stated in Sect. 1.2.3, the overhead associated with the construction of QOC analyses was due to the retrospective nature of the approach. A reason contributing to this problem was the unavailability of recorded process knowledge at time of QOC construction. In the proposed approach, the availability of process knowledge in the form of IBIS issues will help reduce the additional effort required to construct retrospective QOC analyses. Therefore, the complimentary approach to recording specific local IBIS issues and post hoc constructing QOC analyses will enable the effective capturing, structuring, and retrieving of rationale knowledge.

Although the proposed approach involves two notations, there are similarities in terms of their simplicity and structure of the argumentation components. Thus, the approach will be easy to learn and apply.

Moreover, the approach is grounded in a solid understanding of the creativity and insight-driven nature of the RE process. The suggested approach is descriptive, not prescriptive, therefore will:

- support purposeful creative activities required during the building of the requirements model using IBIS
- allow opportunistic insights to occur using flexible, ad hoc IBIS
- apply the post-hoc QOC to articulate and evaluate the reconceptualization insights and review the state of the requirements model

Hence, RE problem solving can be supported without significant interference to the process while allowing the flexibility needed for creative ideas to be generated and evaluated.

There is an interesting alternative attempt to integrate Wallas model within the RE process [32]. In their approach, divergent thinking techniques are applied during the Preparation, Incubation, and Illumination phases. Convergent thinking techniques are applied during the Illumination and Verification phases. The requirements model is revised after each Wallas cycle.

10.6   Summary and Conclusion

Based on a synthesis of a review of current research into DR, the intrinsic nature and creativity characteristics of the RE problem solving, specifically the catastrophe cyclic RE process and its relation to creativity models, we propose a new approach to supporting different creativity aspects in RE using different strategies to DR. Specifically, we suggest:

- Using ad hoc DR to capture and record the on the fly thoughts and ideas when exploring the problem space.
- Using post hoc DR to analyze, reconceptualize and restructure the problem space when insight occurs.

Future research will be conducted to further understand the nature and characteristics of the creative RE process and empirically evaluate the suggested DR approach to supporting this process. An observation laboratory facility called InSyL will be built in a near future at University of South Australia in collaborations with DSTO. The facility will enable researchers to observe "creative teamwork" in RE in various domains including military command and control groups. The facility will be built with:

- Video cameras and ambient microphones to capture and store audio-video records.
- Personal wireless microphones the output of which will run through a system called AuTM, designed by DSTO. This system will automatically create meeting transcripts. These transcripts can be semantically analyzed using Leximancer – a CASE tool software to assist in qualitative data analysis.
- eBeam system to capture the dynamics of artifact creation on whiteboards.

With the above laboratory utilities, we hope to capture rich and multifacet data on the RE creative team work in the form of intermediate diagrams and brainstorming documents, verbal and nonverbal expressions, interactions and communications, and insight flash moments, and emotion factors which may occur during the RE process. Benefits of using DR techniques in reaching shared understanding and improving RE team communication [30, 38] will be re-examined in the context of creativity and team dynamics. Expected research outcome is a deep understanding of the cognitive and creative aspects of RE problem solving and an evaluation of the suggested approach. CASE tools can be selected or built to support the construction, management and retrieval of rationale information and to support and promote RE creativity.

References

[1] Alexander I (1998) Requirements Engineering as a Co-operative Inquiry: A Framework, in Proceedings of Conference on European Industrial Requirements Engineering CEIRE '98. London, UK
[2] Batra D, Davis JG (1992) Conceptual data modelling in database design: similarities and differences between expert and novice designers. International Journal Man-Machine Studies. 37: pp. 83-101
[3] Boden MA (1991) *The Creative Mind: Myths and Mechanisms*: Basic Books
[4] Bruegge B, Dutoit AH (2000) *Object-Oriented Software Engineering.* Englewood Cliffs, NJ: Prentice Hall
[5] Carroll J, Swatman PA (1998) The Process of Deriving Requirements: Learning from Practice, in Proceedings of the Ninth Annual Australasian Conference on Information Systems. Sydney Australia
[6] Carroll J, Swatman PA (1999) Opportunism in the Requirements Engineering Process, School of Information Systems, Deakin University, Victoria, Australia
[7] Carroll JM, Thomas JC, Malhotra A (1979) *Clinical–experimental Analysis of Design Problem Solving.* Design Studies. 1(2): pp. 84-92

[8]   Conklin EJ, Yakemovic KB (1991) *A Process-Oriented Approach to Design Rationale.* Human–Computer Interaction. **6**: pp. 357-394

[9]   Coughlan J, Macredie RD (2002) Effective communication in requirements elicitation: A comparison of methodologies. Journal of Requirements Engineering. **7**(2): pp. 47–60

[10]   Cropley DH, Cropley AJ (2000) Creativity and Innovation in the Systems Engineering Process, in INCOSE 2000 Systems Engineering: A Decade of Progress and A New Century of Opportunity. USA

[11]   Csikszentmihalyi M (1997) Society, Culture, and Person: A System View of Creativity, in *The Nature of Creativity*, Sternberg RJ, (ed.), UK: Cambridge University. pp. 325–339

[12]   Cybulski J, Nguyen L, Thanasankit T, Lichtenstein S (2003) Understanding Problem Solving in Requirements Engineering: Debating Creativity with IS Practitioners, in Proceedings of Pacific Asia Conference on Information Systems PACIS'2003. Adelaide, Australia

[13]   Daupert D (2002) *The Osborne–Parnes Creative Problem Solving Process Manual.* Available at: http://www.ideastream.com/create/index.html

[14]   Dix A, Finlay J, Abowd G, Beale R (1993) *Human–Computer Interaction*, Cambridge: Prentice-Hall. pp. 180–190, chap. 5

[15]   Gero JS (1996) Creativity, emergence and evolution in design: concepts and framework. Knowledge-Based Systems. **9**(7): pp. 435–448

[16]   Guindon R (1989) *The Process of Knowledge Discovery in System Design*, in *Designing and Using Human-Computer Interfaces and Knowledge Based Systems*, Salvendy G, Smith MJ, (eds.), Elsevier Science: Amsterdam Netherlands. pp. 727–734

[17]   Guindon R (1990) Designing the Design Process: Exploiting Opportunistic Thoughts. International Human-Computer Interaction. **5**: pp. 305–344

[18]   Guindon R (1990) Knowledge Exploited by Experts during Software System Design. International Journal of Man–Machine Studies. **33**: pp. 279–304

[19]   Hadamard J (1954) *The Psychology of Invention in the Mathematical Field*, New York: Dover Publications

[20]   Jirotka M, Goguen J (1994) *Requirements Engineering: Social and Technical Issues*, London England: Academic Press Professional

[21]   Johnson CW (1996) *Literate specification: Using design rationale to support formal methods in the development of human–computer interfaces.* Human–Computer Interaction Journal. **11**(4): pp. 291–320

[22]   Jorgensen AH, Aboulafia A (1995) Perceptions of design rationale, in *Proceedings of the Human–Computer Interaction-INTERACT'95.* Norway: Chapman and Hall

[23]   Khushalani A, Smith R, Howard S (1994) What happens when designers don't play by the rules: Towards a model of opportunistic behaviour in design. Australian Journal of Information Systems. **1**(2): pp. 13–31

[24]   Kotonya G, Sommerville I (1998) *Requirements Engineering: Processes and Techniques*, UK.: Wiley, p. 294

[25] Kunz W, Rittel HWJ (1970) Issues as Elements of Information Systems, Studiengruppe für Systemforschung Heidelberg Germany and the Science of Design University of California Berkeley, Germany

[26] Loucopoulos P, Karakostas V (1995) *System Requirements Engineering*, New York USA: McGraw-Hill

[27] Lubars M, Potts C, Richter C (1993) A review of the state of the practice in requirements modelling, in *Proceedings of the IEEE International Symposium on Requirements Engineering: RE'93*. San Diego CA, USA: IEEE Computer Society

[28] Macaulay LA (1996) *Requirements Engineering*, Berlin Heidelebrg New York: Springer

[29] MacLean A, Bellotti V, Shum S (1993) Developing the Design Space with Design Space Analysis, in *Design Issues, Research and Methods for Integrated Services*, Byerley PF, Barnard PJ, May J, (eds.), Amsterdam Netherlands: Elsevier. pp. 197–219, chap. 2.4

[30] MacLean A, Young RM, Belloti V, Moran T (1991) *Question, Option, and Criteria: Elements of Design Space Analysis*. Human-Computer Interaction. **6**: pp. 201–250

[31] Maiden N, Gizikis A (2001) Where do Requirements Come from? IEEE Software. **18**(5): pp. 10–12

[32] Maiden N, Gizikis A, Robertson S (2004) Provoking creativity: imagine what your requirements could be like. Software IEEE. **21**(5): pp. 68–75

[33] Mayer RE (1992) *Thinking, Problem solving, Cognition*. 2nd ed., New York USA: W. H. Freeman

[34] Nguyen L, Carroll J, Swatman PA (2000) Supporting and Monitoring the Creativity of IS Personnel during the Requirements Engineering Process, in Proceedings of 33rd Hawaii International Conference on System Sciences HICSS-33. Maui, Hawaii

[35] Nguyen L, Swatman PA (2000) Complementary use of ad hoc and post hoc design rationale for creating and organising process knowledge, in *Proceedings of 33rd Hawaii International Conference on System Sciences HICSS-33*. Maui, Hawaii

[36] Nguyen L, Swatman PA (2003) Managing the requirements engineering process. Requirements Engineering. **8**(1): pp. 55-68

[37] Nguyen L, Swatman PA (2005) Promoting and supporting the creative and insight-driven RE process using design rationale, 2005/15, School of Computing and Information Science, University of South Australia, Adelaide

[38] Nguyen L, Swatman PA, Shanks G (1999) Using Design Explanation within Formal Object-Oriented Method. Requirements Engineering. **4**(3): pp. 152-164

[39] Ohlsson S (1984) I. Restructuring Revisited: Summary and Critique of the Gestalt Theory of Problem Solving. Scandinavian Journal of Psychology. **25**: pp. 65–78

[40] Osborn AF (1979) Applied Imagination: Principles and Procedures of Creative Problem-Solving. 3rd ed, USA: Charles Scribner's Sons

[41] Plsek PE (1997) *Directed Creativity Cycle*. Available at:
http://www.directedcreativity.com/pages/Cycle.html

[42] Plucker J (2003) *Creativity*: College of Arts and Sciences at Indiana University, USA. Available at:
http://www.homepages.indiana.edu/101703/text/dna.shtml

[43] Pries-Heje J (1993) Methods and Tools for Software Product Development Ph.D. Thesis series 4.93, English Summary, DASY Institut for Anvendt Datalogi og Systemvidenskab, Kobenhavn

[44] Rittel HWJ (1984) Second-generation design methods, in *Developments in Design Methodology*, N. Cross, (ed.) New York: Wiley ,pp. 317–327.

[45] Robertson, S. and Robertson J. (1999). *Mastering the Requirements Process*, London, UK: Addison-Wesley

[46] Robillard PN (1999) *The Role of Knowledge in Software Development.* Communication of the ACM. **42**(1): pp. 87–92

[47] Schön DA (1983) *The Reflective Practitioner: How Professionals Think in Action*, London England: Temple Smith

[48] Schön DA (1996) Reflective conversation with materials, in *Bringing Design to Software*, T. Winograd (ed.) USA: ACM.,pp. 171–184

[49] Shum SB (1993) QOC Design Rationale Retrieval: A Cognitive Task Analysis and Design Implication, Rank Xerox Research Centre Cambridge Laboratory, Cambridge CB2 1AB

[50] Shum SB (1996) *Analyzing the usability of a design rationale notation*, in *Design Rationale: Concepts, Techniques, and Use*, Morgan TP, Carroll JM (eds.), New Jersey USA: Lawrence Erlbaum. pp. 185–215, *chap. 6*

[51] Shum SB, Hammond N (1994) Argumentation-based design rationale: What use at what cost? Human–Computer Studies. **40**(4): 603–652

[52] Sternberg RJ (1997) *The Nature of Creativity*, UK: Cambridge University

[53] Sutcliffe A, Ryan M (1997) Assessing the Usability and Efficiency of Design Rationale, in *Proceeding of the Human–Computer Interaction-INTERACT'97*. Sydney Australia: Chapman and Hall

[54] Taylor CW (1997) Various approaches to and definitions of creativity, in *The Nature of Creativity: Contemporary Psychological Perspectives*, RJ Sternberg (ed.) Cambridge University: UK. pp. 99–121

[55] Torrance EP (1997) The nature of creativity as manifest in its testing, in *The Nature of Creativity: Contemporary Psychological Perspectives*, Sternberg RJ, (ed.) Cambridge University: UK. pp. 43–75

[56] Toulmin, SE (1958) *The Use of Arguments*, UK: Cambridge University

[57] Toulmin, SE (1972) *Human Understanding*, Princeton New Jersey USA: Princeton University

[58] Visser W (1992) *Designers' activities examined at three levels: organisation, strategies and problem-solving processes.* Knowledge-Based Systems. **5**(1): pp. 92–104

[59] Wallas G (1926) *The Art of Thought*, London England: Jonathan Cape.

Part 3
Design Rationale and Software Architecting

I. Mistrík

Design rationale as it applies to software architecture has become an established area of software engineering research. Design rationale can be defined as an expression of the relationships between a design product (in this case, an architecture), its purpose, the designer's (architect's) conceptualization and the contextual constraints on realizing the purpose [12]. It represents knowledge that provides the answers to questions about a particular design choice or the process followed to make that choice [8].

Software architecture is concerned with the study of the structure of software, including topologies, properties, constituent components and relationships and patterns of interaction and combination [7,14]. A modern definition of software architecture is given by Bass et al. in [2]: "The software architecture of a program or computing system is the structure or structures of the system, which comprise software elements, the externally visible properties of those elements, and the relationships among them".

The importance of relating design rationale and software architecting has been recognized by many researchers and practitioners [5,14,15]. Design rationale researchers have developed different representation schemas, capture methods, repository models, and use cases for recording design decisions. However, most approaches represent only arguments surrounding design decisions [11]; more work remains to be done in representing domain knowledge in terms that are understandable to the domain experts [9]. During the last 10 years it has been recognized that the quality requirements are heavily influenced by the architecture of the system [2,3] and capturing the relationship between architectural design decisions and quality attributes provides an important new role for rationale.

There are important issues that need further research:

- Architecture decisions are seldom documented in a rigorous and consistent manner. Meaningful explanations should include information explaining the context, reasoning, tradeoffs, criteria, and decision making that led to the selection of a particular design from various design options [3,6].
- Design rationale represents knowledge that provides the answers to questions about a particular design choice or the process followed to make that choice [8].

- If design rationale is not documented, knowledge concerning the domain analysis, design options evaluated, and decisions made are lost, and so is unavailable to support subsequent decisions in the development lifecycle [3,13].
- The IEEE 1471 Standard [10] and the SARA WG [12] identify design rationale as an important part of descriptions of software architecture and advocate capturing and maintaining rationale. There has been only one significant support mechanism for capturing and managing rationale about architectural decisions namely, the Views and Beyond [4]. However, there is neither sufficient support for all necessary architectural constructs nor conceptual guidance to develop a repository of architecture design knowledge and the experience of using it [1].
- By using design decisions as first class entities to build architecture, rationale management systems can be combined with software architecture, making architecture easier to use and communicate.

Chapters in this part of the book are reporting on advances on the issues mentioned above.

In particular, four chapters (Chaps. 11, 12, 14, 16) in this part deal with various aspects of relating design rationale and software architectures. Chap. 13 discusses design rationale in the context of the maintenance and evolution of a designed software product. It presents SEURAT, a system that supports entry and display of the rationale as well as inferences over the rationale. Chapter 15 argues that assumptions management is critical for evolving software, not only at the architectural level, but at all the levels of representation of the software and provides high-level recommendations on how this could be achieved. The architectural level is one of the first places in which assumptions management should be done.

Chapter 11 "A Framework for Supporting Architecture Knowledge and Rationale Management" by Muhammad Ali Babar, Ian Gorton, and Barbara Kitchenham proposes a framework for capturing and managing architecture design knowledge. This framework consists of techniques for capturing design knowledge, an approach to distilling design knowledge from patterns, and a data model to characterize the architecture knowledge domain. The data model not only provides guidelines as to what constitutes architecture rationale but can also be implemented to build a knowledge repository. Their approach to distilling architecture knowledge from patterns is one of the means of populating such a repository. The other objective of mining patterns is to capture and represent pattern-based design knowledge at an appropriate level of abstraction. The proposed template is an effective way of representing such knowledge. A design knowledge repository can provide a strong motivation for using and capturing rationale during architecture design or evaluation. The novelty of this approach resides in its ability to incorporate all three components into an integrated approach to capturing and managing architecture design knowledge.

Chapter 12 "Capturing and Using Rationale for Software Architecture" by Len Bass, Paul Clements, Robert Nord, and Judith Stafford presents an approach focused on software architecture rationale that allows stakeholders throughout the life of the system to determine why important design decisions were made, by tracing a design decision causally and as it relates to architectural structures. The architect needs some way to remember the conceptual path he or she has taken during the architecting process, as well as a way not to repeat dead-end design paths. Developers and maintainers can gain important insights from reading the architect's reasoning. Testers can design tests to validate the architect's precepts. Customers can examine the rationale to convince themselves that their business goals are being met by the design. Stakeholders in general can read the rationale to make sure their interests have been addressed.

Chapter 13 "Rationale-based Support for Software Maintenance" by Janet Burge and David Brown describes SEURAT (Software Engineering Using RATionale) which is a prototype system that provides both retrieval of and inferencing over, rationale. The main goal in developing SEURAT was to study uses of rationale during software maintenance. SEURAT checks for the likely completeness and consistency of design decisions by inferencing over the recorded rationale. The maintainer can also perform "what-if" inferencing by changing the priorities of rationale elements, assumptions and requirements to see the impact on the support for previous decisions. Entry and editing screens are provided for rationale capture. While SEURAT was designed for the maintenance phase, it could be used in other phases of development. Decisions made at the early stages of design, such as architecture, are the most risky to change. SEURAT supports software architecting in two ways: (1) it allows the software developer to record their rationale in an argumentation format that captures where selecting one alternative spawns additional decisions and (2) it performs inferencing over the rationale to check the impact on the system of changing those decisions further along in the development process.

Chapter 14 "The Role of Rationale in the Design of Product Line Architectures – A Case Study from Industry" by Jens Knodel and Dirk Muthig reports on an evaluation of alternative architectural concepts for a graphics component, which is a subsystem of an embedded system. The product line engineering aims at an efficient production of variants mainly enabled by large-scale and systematic reuse of artifacts throughout all development phases. A product line's central artifact is its architecture that defines fundamental concepts, abstractions, and mechanisms that hold for all products of an organization (if successful) for a long period of time. Therefore, key developers in organizations must fully agree on all decisions related to the definition of the product line architecture, as well as always reunderstand their rationales during architecture evolution. This chapter describes an industrial case of architecture evolution where one of the key mechanisms of an existing architecture was revisited as the potential subject of change.

Chapter 15 "Role and Impact of Assumptions in Software Engineering and its Products" by Meir (Manny) Lehman and J.C. Fernández-Ramil presents the Principle of Software Uncertainty and the reasoning underlying it. The principle states that the validity of the results of executing real-world software cannot be absolutely guaranteed. A key argument in the chapter is that every program used in the real-world reflects an unbounded set of assumptions about the environment where it operates. The environment is subject to change and assumptions may become invalid at any time. There have been software failures clearly due to "assumptions which became invalid". Examples include the software-related destruction of the Ariane 501 rocket and the failure to provide the expected results of experiments with a large particle accelerator. The chapter explains why assumptions are unbounded in number: it is impossible to record and monitor all the assumptions. However, in order to reduce the risk of software failure, software developers and maintainers should manage the assumptions they are conscious of. They will benefit from using techniques that support the systematic recording of assumptions that they reflect in the software as they make design and implementation decisions. Design rationale techniques can contribute to make explicit many implicit assumptions that are made during software design, and to systematically review the validity of these assumptions over time and releases, helping to reduce the risk of unanticipated software failure and its consequences.

Chapter 16 "Design Decisions: The Bridge between Rationale and Architecture" by Jan van der Ven, Anton Jansen, Jos Nijhuis, and Jan Bosch presents an approach in which the design decisions underlying software architectures are made explicit. Currently, the design decisions that drive the software architecture design remain implicit and are therefore easily lost and forgotten. This decreases the understandability of the architecture over time. Consequently, it is hard to make changes to the architecture when unknowledgeable about the underlying design decisions. Explicitly describing design decisions in software architecture design deals with these problems. In this new perspective, software architectures are seen as the result of the design decisions underlying them. The design decisions contain rationale, ranging from the issue(s) the decision tries to address to rationale explaining why certain alternative were (not) chosen. In this sense, design decisions act as a bridge between rationale and architecture.

As a first step, the Archium tool illustrates that designing architectures with design decisions is feasible. In Archium, a component and connector view of the system can be generated by creating a set of design decisions. The rationale is represented in the design decisions and is made traceable to the architecture. The authors envision that this close integration will help architects to represent the rationale of their decisions, making architectures easier to use and communicate.

References

[1]   Basili VR, Caldiera P (1995) Improving software quality reusing knowledge and experience. Sloan Management Review 37(1): 55–64

[2]   Bass L, Clements P, Kazman R (2003) Software architecture in practice, 2nd edition. Addison-Wesley, Reading, MA

[3]   Bosch J (2004) Software architecture: The next step. In: Proceedings of the European workshop on software architecture (EWSA 2004), May 21–22, pp. 194–199

[4]   Clements P, Bachmann F, Bass L, Garlan D, Ivers J, Little R, Nord R, Stafford J (2002) Documenting Software Architectures: Views and Beyond. Addison-Wesley, Reading, MA

[5]   Clements P, Kazman R, Klein M (2002) Evaluating Software Architectures: Methods and Case Studies. Addison-Wesley, Reading, MA

[6]   Curtis B, Krasner H, Iscoe N (1988) A field study of the software design process for large systems. Communications of the ACM 31(11): 1268–1287

[7]   Garlan D, Shaw M (1993) An Introduction to Software Architecture. Advances in Software Engineering and Knowledge Engineering 1. World Scientific Publishing, Singapore

[8]   Gruber T, Russell D (1991) Design knowledge and design rationale: A framework for representation, capture, and use. Technical Report KSL 90-45, Knowledge Laboratory, Stanford University

[9]   Hersleb JD, Kuwana E (1993) Preserving knowledge in design projects: What designers need to know. In: Proceedings of the SIGCHI conference on Human factors in computing systems, Amsterdam, pp. 7–14

[10] IEEE (2000) Recommended Practices for Architectural Description of Software-Intensive Systems. IEEE Standard No. 1471

[11] Moran TP, Carroll JM (1996) Overview of design rationale. In: Design Rationale: Concepts, Techniques, and Use, Moran TP, Carroll JM (eds) Lawrence Erlbaum Associates, pp. 1–19

[12] Obbink H et al (2001) Software architecture review and assessment. Technical Report SARA WG

[13] Pena-Mora F, Vadhavkar S (1977) Augmenting design patterns with design rationale. Artificial Intelligence for Engineering Design, Analysis and Manufacturing 11(2): 93–108

[14] Perry DE, Wolf AL (1992) Foundations for the study of software architecture. ACM SIGSOFT, Software Engineering Notes 17(4): 40–52
[15] Tyree J, Akerman A (2005) Architecture decisions: Demystifying architecture. IEEE Software 22(2): 19–27

11 A Framework for Supporting Architecture Knowledge and Rationale Management

M.A. Babar, I. Gorton, B. Kitchenham

Abstract: There is growing recognition of the importance of documenting and managing background knowledge about architecture design decisions. However, there is little guidance on the types of information that form Architecture Design Knowledge (ADK), how to make implicitly described ADK explicit, and how such knowledge can be documented to improve architecture processes. We propose a framework that provides a support mechanism to capture and manage ADK. We analyze different approaches to capturing tacit and implicit design knowledge describe a process of extracting ADK from patterns and an effective way of documenting it. We also present a data model to characterize architecture design primitives used or generated during architecture design and evaluation. This data model can be tailored to implement repositories of ADK. We complete this chapter with open issues that architecture research must confront in order to successfully transfer technology for capturing design rationale to the industry.

Keywords: software architecture; design rationale; knowledge management

11.1 Introduction

Many researchers and practitioners acknowledge the importance of capturing and maintaining knowledge underpinning architecture decisions [17, 42, 52]. However architecture/design decisions are seldom documented in a rigorous and consistent manner. Curtis et al. [19] and Bosch [12] suggest that a meaningful explanation should include information explaining the context, reasoning, tradeoffs, criteria, and decision making that led to the selection of a particular design from various design options. This type of knowledge is called *design rationale (DR)* [34, 43]. It represents knowledge that provides the answers to questions about a particular design choice or the process followed to make that choice [20, 24]. If it is not documented, knowledge concerning the domain analysis, patterns used, design options evaluated, and decisions made is lost, and so is unavailable to support subsequent decisions in development lifecycle [12, 41, 52].

Based on our experiences in designing and evaluating architectures for large-scale systems, we argue that lack of suitable techniques, tools, and guidance is one of the reasons that DR is not captured and managed. DR researchers have developed different methods, notations, and tools for recording design decisions, such as IBIS [32], Decision Representation

Language (DRL) [34], gIBIS [18], Questions, Options and Criteria (QOC) [35], and so on. However, these approaches only capture and represent the space or history of arguments surrounding the design decisions [15], rather than representing domain knowledge or system design in terms which are understandable by the domain experts [26]. Moreover, these approaches are not scaleable to large scale systems; nor do they ensure creation of re-usable assets, promote the use of DR, or improve the reuse of artifacts [25].

We propose a framework for managing DR to improve the quality of architecture process and artifacts. This framework consists of techniques for capturing DR, an approach to distill and document architectural information from patterns, and a data model to characterize architectural constructs, their attributes and relationships. These collectively comprise Architecture Design Knowledge (ADK) to support architecting process. The central objective of our research is to develop a generic framework for capturing architecture process knowledge (DR attached to artifacts) and provide mechanism to manage the captured knowledge to support architecture design decision making process.

In this chapter, like [20], we characterize DR as certain type of architecture knowledge developed and used during software development. We take the view that management of such knowledge can be greatly improved by considering the various tasks from a management perspective rather than computer science or artificial intelligence perspective [31]. Thus, our approach considers DR management tasks as Knowledge Management (KM) tasks and uses a KM task model described in [46] and used in [20, 31]. This model consists of two strategic and six operational tasks.

11.2 Background and Motivation

11.2.1 Design Rationale Approaches and Software Engineering

A DR is an explanation of how and why an artifact, or some part of it, is designed the way it is. DR represents knowledge about the reasoning justifying the resulting design. This includes how a structure satisfies functional and quality requirements, why certain structures are selected over alternatives, and what type of behavior is expected under different environmental conditions [24, 34]. Early research emphasizing the importance of DR in software design can be found in [40, 43]. Since then, the software engineering community has experimented with several DR approaches such as Issue-Based Information Systems (IBIS) [32], Questions, Options, and Criteria (QOC) [35], Procedural Hierarchy of Issues (PHI) [36], and

Decision Representation Language (DRL) [34]. All these approaches provide argumentation models, which use small numbers of node and link types to organize a hierarchy of questions posed to address issues. Alternatives, their rationales, and the final choice can be attached to the questions to document discussion paths [25].

Most of these approaches have been adopted or modified to capture rationale for software design decisions [33, 43] and requirements specifications [21, 47, 51]. Another approach [45] combine rationale and scenarios during requirements elicitation process to refine and review requirements. Dutoit and Paech [20] describe various tasks of rationale management in software engineering and their application. Heninnger developed an approach for supporting reuse-based software development by explicitly capturing and using past rationale [25]. Pena-Mora and Vadhavkar's DRIM [41] approach combines patterns and rationale to support reusable software development. Our approach has some similarities with the last three approaches. But, instead of attaching DR to patterns like the DRIM, we distill architectural information from patterns and represent it as a reusable ADK. We believe that rationale should be attached to design decisions, which apply patterns, rather than patterns themselves.

Software architecture (SA) researchers have also emphasized the need to document DR to maintain and evolve architectural artifacts and to avoid violating fundamental rules underpinning the original design decisions [8, 12]. The IEEE 1471 standard [27] identifies DR as an important part of SA description. However, there has not been any significant support mechanism for capturing and managing rationale for architecture decisions except the *Views and Beyond* (V&B) approach to document SA [17]. Though, the V&B approach recommends explicit documentation of rationale for design decisions, interface designs and the information that cuts across multiple views, it also has certain limitations mentioned later.

11.2.2 Relationship among Quality Attributes, Scenarios, and Patterns as Architecture Design Knowledge

A quality attribute is a nonfunctional requirement (NFR) of a software system, such as maintainability, performance and so forth. Scenarios have been found effective and useful for specifying quality attributes. That is why scenarios are widely used to design and evaluate SA. Scenarios are considered flexible as they can be used for systematically reasoning about, or evaluating, most quality attributes [2, 29]. A pattern is a known solution to a recurring problem in a particular context. Patterns provide a mechanism for documenting design knowledge [22]. The architecture of complex systems is usually designed by successively integrating different patterns, which may be described at different levels of abstraction. Each pattern supports or inhibits certain quality attributes [8, 14].

Patterns documentation also contains reasons for the use of a pattern for a certain class of problems. Relating quality attributes, scenarios, and patterns in this way forms architecturally significant knowledge, which may also have rationale about the relationships attached. Recently, there have been a few efforts to explicitly codify the relationships among quality attributes, scenarios, and patterns [9, 23]. These approaches identify and link scenarios, quality attributes, and patters from sources other than the patterns themselves. However, we have demonstrated that each pattern's documentation contains implicit description of the relationships among scenarios, quality attributes, and patterns [3].

Having reviewed various approaches to rationale management, we conclude that most of the efforts to introduce argumentation methods in software engineering have experienced very limited success. There are many reasons for this, for example, the need for extensive training, changes in thinking styles, focus on some tasks only, and lack of guidance on using past rationale [13, 25]. Generally, knowledge and rationale management support in the architecture domain is limited.

Obbink et al. [39] and the IEEE 1471 standard [27] advocate capturing and maintaining rationale but do not provide any support mechanism. V&B provides templates to capture knowledge about DR, which is documented along with the architecture description. However, there is no sufficient support mechanism to capture and manage knowledge and rationale about other architectural constructs such as scenarios, patterns and so on, and their relationships. Moreover, none of the existing approaches in the architecture domain help users to identify and define the main constructs and their properties and relationships involved in forming ADK. Nor do they provide sufficient conceptual guidance to develop a repository of ADK and experiences of using it [6].

The main object of this research is to develop a support mechanism for capturing and maintaining ADK to improve architecting process. To achieve this goal, the issues that we intend to address are to identify techniques that make the effort of capturing rationale worthwhile without heavily disrupting the design process, help utilize the large amount of architecturally significant information implicitly embedded in patterns, and to identify architectural constructs, their properties and relationship and put them into a framework that can be used to design and implement an organizational repository to store and retrieve ADK generated or used during architecting process. In Sect. 11.3, we propose a solution that incorporates techniques that complement each other and provide an integrated support framework for capturing and maintaining ADK.

11.3   Managing Architecture Design Knowledge

In this section, we present a framework for managing ADK . This framework comprises three components:

1. A means of capturing knowledge underlying decisions from architects as well as electronic sources such as annotations attached to artifacts.
2. A procedure for capturing architecture knowledge and associated rationale from patterns in order to explicate the relationships among scenarios, quality attributes, and patterns that is a form of reusable ADK.
3. A model for characterizing the main architectural constructs and their relationships that form ADK and rationale. This data model can be tailored and implemented to provide a repository for managing process knowledge, relating design knowledge to architecture artifacts or the reusable ADK extracted from patterns.

These three components complement each other to support the tasks of capturing ADK from different sources (such as architects, artifacts, and patterns), structuring and maintaining the captured ADK, which is presented in a format that is readily usable in making and assessing design decisions with an informed knowledge of the consequences of those decisions. The first two components are aimed at capturing ADK, while the third component represents architecture domain knowledge that can help develop a knowledge base to store, maintain, and retrieve the captured ADK. The balance of this chapter is heavily skewed towards the *pattern-mining* (3.1) and the data model (3.2)) components of the framework. However, we discuss briefly three approaches that are being used to capture DR, process knowledge, or experiences in software engineering:

1. Designers themselves can be required to document their DRs [4]. Knowledge can be captured during the design process or constructed after the fact [43]. In either case, the designer needs to be motivated to document the DR. In practice such motivation depends on appropriate rewards and explicitly demonstrated future benefits [25].
2. A knowledge engineer [50] or rationale maintainer [20] can be appointed to the task of capturing design knowledge from designers, meeting recordings, emails, memos, and design documentation. Industrial trials conclude that a KM tool and a knowledge engineer should be an integral part of software development process [50]. However, this

approach should be used with caution as the knowledge engineers may become a bottleneck [25].

3. ADK can be captured during architecting process. This is called *contextualised* knowledge. Designers are provided with appropriate tools so that knowledge can be encoded into the system as part of the knowledge creation process [25]. This is similar to the V&B approach, which provides templates to capture contextualized design knowledge [16].

We find the second and third approaches less disruptive and useful. We are also studying the architectural processes to integrate design knowledge capture practices in a manner that is not overly disruptive [25].

11.3.1 Mining Patterns for Architecture Knowledge

The idea of mining patterns for architecturally significant information was conceived as part of our efforts to improve SA evaluation. We found that software patterns are a valuable source of abstract scenarios, which can be distilled to support SA evaluation. We later found that each pattern's description is also a source of architecturally significant relationships that exist among scenarios, quality attributes, and patterns. We argued that such synergistic relationships form ADK that needs to be explicitly documented in a readily reusable format to support architecting process.

Our initial experiences of capturing architectural artifacts and relationships among them from patterns were encouraging. However, we found that being a manual procedure it relies heavily on the pattern miner's experience with different classes of patterns (such as architectural, design and platform specific) and with several formats of documenting patterns. In addition, the extracted information needs to be documented in a format that explicates the relationships among scenarios, quality attributes, and patterns as ADK along with the rationale for using a pattern. Thus, we have developed an approach to identify, capture and document architecturally significant information from patterns as ADK.

This approach consists of a process model, guidelines, and a template to identify, capture, and document architecturally significant information from patterns as architecturally significant reusable artifacts. We call this process "pattern-mining" and the extracted information "Architecturally Significant Information extracted from Patterns (ASIP)" [3]. The novelty of our approach resides in its ability to incorporate all the components into an integrated approach, which can be used to capture and populate ADK repository like [38] backed by an experience factory infrastructure [6] to grow organizational capabilities in architecting process.

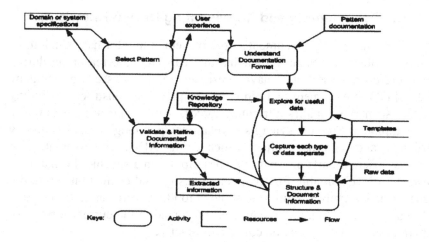

Fig. 11.1. Pattern-mining process model

11.3.1.1 The Pattern-Mining Process

The *pattern-mining* process is shown in Fig. 11.1. This manual process consists of following six steps:

1. Select a software pattern to be explored for architectural information
2. Understand the pattern documentation format to identify the variations that exist among different patterns' description styles
3. Explore different parts of the selected patterns to identify architectural information described in a pattern's documentation
4. Capture each type of information separately
5. Structure and document the extracted information
6. Validate and refine documented information based on domain knowledge and experience of using different patterns

Patterns are usually documented in a variation of format used in [22], which require the inclusion of problem, solution, and quality consequences parts. We have found that scenarios are mostly found in problem and solution sections. Forces can also be found in these sections. However, there are some pattern description styles that use separate sections for forces. The forces of a pattern describe the factors which can cause a problem if they interfere with one another. The pattern attempts to resolve clashes among those factors. Discussion of forces also captures necessary tradeoffs and justification for using that pattern, which is considered the DR of that pattern [23, 28]. The quality attributes (positively or negatively affected) are usually described at the end of a pattern's description.

11.3.1.2 Documenting and Representing Design Knowledge

The *ASIP* must also be documented and presented in a format, which turns it into architecture design knowledge that can facilitate reasoning during architecture process. We have designed and assessed a template (Table 11.1) to document and represent architectural constructs, including abstract scenarios, quality attributes, forces, tactics, and usage examples. This template makes the synergistic relationship among scenarios, quality attributes, and patterns explicit, which forms ADK. The template also presents different parts of a pattern's description in a succinct format at an abstraction level suitable for architecture design and evaluation. Since designers usually apply breadth first strategy to identify available solutions to a design problem [49], too much detail presented in the current formats of pattern documentation may be counter-productive [3].

Table 11.1 A template to document ADK extracted from patterns

Pattern Name: *Name of the pattern*		Pattern Type: *Architecture, design, or style*
Description		*A brief description of the pattern.*
Context		*The situation for which the pattern is recommended.*
Problem		*What types of problem the pattern is supposed to address?*
Suggested		*What is the solution suggested by the pattern to address the problem?*
Forces		*Factors affecting the problem and solution and pattern's justification.*
Tactics		*What tactics are used by the pattern to implement the solution?*
Affected Attributes	**Positively**	**Negatively**
	Attributes supported	*Attributes hindered*
Abstract scenarios	S	*A textual, system independent specification of a quality attribute.*
	S	
Example		*Some known examples of the usage of the pattern to solve the problems.*

Apart from providing a structured way of documenting the *ASIP*, the template also support the *pattern-mining* process by helping a pattern-miner (e.g., software architect) concentrate on the pieces of information that need to be extracted to populate the template. Moreover, the ADK presented in this template enables a user of the template to reason about the ramifications of the tactics being implemented by a particular pattern within the context of scenarios, quality attributes affected (positively or negatively), and usage examples, while considering the justification for using a certain pattern and tradeoffs needs to be made, information that forms rationale described by a pattern's forces.

The *ASIP* presented in Table 11.1 helps improve the scenario development task, select suitable reasoning frameworks and increase confidence in the capabilities of architecture to satisfy particular quality sensitive scenarios as a result of using certain patterns. For example, architects can identify suitable patterns by comparing the scenarios and quality attributes supported by different patterns with the ones required by the stakeholders. Moreover, the abstract scenarios extracted from patterns can be used to instigate stakeholders' thinking while developing quality sensitive scenarios or the abstract scenarios can be concretized to specify quality attributes for a particular system. We have found the template a promising way of capturing, using, and transferring ADK [3].

11.3.2 Modeling Architecture Knowledge and Rationale

We have developed a conceptual data model that identifies and defines the main architectural constructs and their relationships, which form ADK to support architecting process. A conceptual model is the first stage in the development of an automated system for storing DR which could help organizations to store and access ADK [30]. The DAta Model for Software Architecture Knowledge (DAMSAK) is a customizable model to characterize the data required to capture architecture knowledge and rationale.

Table 11.2 Sample data for various architectural constructs

Generic quality attribute	Flexibility/Scalability (ASR entity)
Abstract scenario	Application shall instantly notify changes to the interested clients (Scenario entity).
Abstract scenario	Application shall be able to handle simultaneous notification requests from increased number of clients (Scenario entity).
Architecture Decision	Event notification (Architecture Decision entity).
Design option 1	Publish scribe (Alternative entity).
Design option 2	Java RMI (Alternative entity).
Design Pattern	Publish on demand (Pattern entity).

We believe that the DAMSAK can help develop a repository of reusable ADK. To demonstrate the potential use of such a repository, we provide one example. One of the authors helped design an application which needed instantaneous event notification to unknown number of client tools (see [1] for details). The publish–scribe architecture pattern with a publish-on-demand design pattern was selected for this mechanism. However, the Java RMI was also considered, as it was decided it was not sufficiently scaleable for expected increase in the number of notification requests.

If there were a repository for ADK management, the architect or a knowledge engineer could have stored different architectural primitives as illustrated in Table 11.2. ADK can also be obtained from case studies such as described in [8, 17] or quality attribute sensitive design primitives reported in [7]. Thus, a ADK repository will be an organizational memory analogous to engineers' handbooks, which consolidate best knowledge [4].

Having access to a repository of generic ADK enables designers to use the accumulated "wisdom" in different projects. For example, instantiating abstract scenarios into concrete ones, contextualizing design decisions and others. The project specific data model will also have other entities to capture and consolidate ADK and rationale that is specific to a project. For example, design history, findings of SA evaluation, architectural views of interest to each type of stakeholders and others. A project specific repository system will be populated with the specialized versions of data drawn from the organizational repository, standard work products of the design process, logs of the deliberations and histories of documentation [4].

11.3.2.1 Model Development Process and Model Description

The conceptual data model of architecture knowledge consists of primitives or semantic elements, which characterize the constructs and terminology used in designing and communicating architecture artifacts. To develop DAMSAK presented in Fig. 11.2, we used several approaches to arrive at an appropriate set of architectural constructs, namely:

- We read several textbooks on software architecture (e.g. [8, 11, 14, 17, 22]) and analyzed their examples and case studies to support our exploration of relevant architectural constructs and their attributes.
- Our work on comparison and classification of SA evaluation methods [2] was an important means of identifying relevant literature.
- We reviewed a selected set of gray literature (such as PhD theses and technical reports) in software architecture (e.g. [7, 10, 39]) and standards for documenting architectures [27].
- We reviewed the literature in other engineering disciplines and Human–Computer Interaction (e.g. [18, 24, 34, 44, 48] to discover appropriate constructs, which describe DR.

Our next step was guided by using the Unified Modeling Language for database design [37]. We assessed the model by reference to the literature, in particular [27, 39], which provide reference models for describing and evaluating SA. Following is a brief description of the data model.

The **Stakeholder** entity characterizes those people who have any kind of interest in the architecture process or product [39] such as developers, testers, managers, evaluators, maintainers, and many more [17]. This entity helps keep track of the people who contribute to or consult a knowledge base. Such information can be used to design a recognition program to motivate people to contribute or use an architecture knowledge repository.

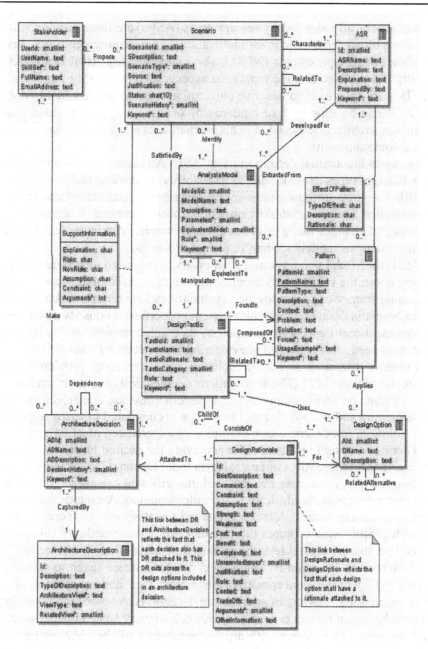

Fig. 11.2. Data model characterizing SA knowledge and rationale

Architecturally significant requirements (ASRs) are those requirements that have broad cross-functional implications. Such requirements are often Nonfunctional requirements (NFRs), also called Quality Attributes (QAs) [8, 39], but can also include functional aspects such as security functionality. This entity is used to describe and explain various aspects of an ASR. An ASR can be supported or hindered by one or more patterns used in a particular architecture decision. This is characterized by the *EffectOfPattern* association entity.

Scenario is a textual definition of an ASR. A scenario can be classified into different types of ASR such as availability, reliability, and modifiability [8]. A source attribute of a scenario describes whether the scenario has been elicited from a stakeholder or distilled from a pattern. A scenario has a history of changes made to it. An abstract scenario can help identify one or more analysis models to analyze design decisions.

Analysis Model is a reasoning framework that is used to systematically reason about the effect of different design tactics on required scenarios. A reasoning framework provides the vocabulary and analytical machinery for describing and deducing particular system properties. It consists of a set of independent and dependent parameters, their relationships and associated rules that need to be observed in evaluating the effects of a tactic [5].

Pattern characterizes known solution to a recurring problem in a particular context [22]. The term pattern denotes design pattern, architecture pattern, or architectural style. A pattern provides a mechanism for documenting and reusing design knowledge accumulated in terms of problem, solution, forces, and usage examples by experienced practitioners.

Tactic is a design mechanism for achieving the desired level of a QA by manipulating some aspect of an analysis model for that QA through design decisions [5]. A tactic may be classified into different categories of tactics, for example architectural, design, or implementation. A pattern may contain one or more tactics. A tactic is applied to satisfy one or more scenarios. This entity also captures the rationale for a tactic and any rules that should be observed to achieve the promised benefits of using that tactic.

Architecture Decision is a high-level design decision taken to satisfy a set of ASR. If we conceptualize the architecture design process as a decision making activity, an architecture decision is a choice among design options based on certain criteria [24]. A decision may have a history of the changes made to it along with any consequences of the changes on the other decisions. There may be interdependency between various decisions. For instance, an earlier decision may limit the options available or impose some constraints on the subsequent decisions. Any changes in a decision should consider the consequences for the dependency relationships.

Design option is a design decision that can be evaluated and selected to satisfy one or more functional or nonfunctional requirements [24]. Design decisions may be related to each other such that the selection of one design option requires the selection or rejection of another design option. A pattern may be used for one or more design options and a design option may apply one or more patterns. A design decision may use several tactics.

DR is the reason behind a design decision (architecture or option). DR consists of all the background information that may be used or generated during the decision making process. Such information is valuable to people who deal with the product of the decision making process [12, 24]. The DR associated with each design option records the required background knowledge essential to evaluate it with respect to other design options. The DR associated with an architecture decision cuts across all the design options selected for a particular architecture decision.

Effect of Pattern defines the effect (positive or negative) of a pattern on a particular ASR [14]. This entity captures the reason behind certain types of effect, information that forms the rationale. This is an association entity. There are a number of other association entities required to capture appropriate data: we show only the most important ones in Fig. 11.2.

Support information is an association entity that captures the background information to justify the choice of a specific architectural decision for a particular scenario. This background information includes explanation of the decision, risks considered, assumptions, and constraints. Such information is valuable for reusability of an architecture decision.

Architecture Description characterizes the data required to document an architecture according to certain standards or approaches (e.g. [16, 27]). An architecture description is usually organized into one or more views, which are models of architectural structures. Views can be categories into view types and architectural description should also capture the relationships among different views. The V&B [16] approach also emphasizes the need to capture information that cuts across several views. The view attribute of this entity is a complex attribute, which would be an entity in its own right in a fully normalized data model.

To the best of our knowledge, this data model represents a first systematic attempt to formally enumerate the architecture knowledge domain. There is always a tradeoff between the size and the representative ability of a data model as it is difficult to conceptualize a domain and tease it out to the level of entities, attributes, and relationships. Another source of difficulty in modeling architecture design knowledge is researchers and practitioners use different terms and describe architectures at various levels of abstractions. That is why we have developed a moderate size of data model that can be tailored or extended to various organizations' needs, e.g., to support the "*architecture decision description templates*" described in [52], to implement an architecture knowledge repository like [38], or to develop an architecture design decision support system. Moreover, this data model can be easily modified to cater the data needs of software architecture reviews, which help capture architecture DR.

11.3.3 Empirical Assessment

The three techniques to capture implicit and explicit design knowledge described in Sect. 3 have been empirically evaluated in research labs or industrial settings [4, 25, 50]. However, their effectiveness needs to be empirically assessed in SA domain with real projects, something which we plan to achieve in the next step on the project. As mentioned earlier, the conceptual data model has been assessed by reference to published literature as is evident from the citation for each entity. Moreover, this data model incorporates the concepts described in the meta-models of IEEE standards for architecture description [27], architecture review context conceptual model of SARA report [39]. Furthermore, it can capture most of the data recommended for V&B approach of documenting architecture [16]. However, we do not claim entity-to-entity mapping.

To assess the effectiveness of the different components of the *pattern-mining* approach and the usefulness of the *ASIP* in architecture design and evaluation, we have designed and implemented an empirical research program consisting of an observational study and two controlled experiments. The observational study was aimed at finding out the average amount of time taken for mining patterns, the effectiveness of the *pattern-mining* process, guidelines, template to support the process, and the perception of the participants of the usefulness of the *ASIP*. The controlled experiments were designed to assess the value of *ASIP* during design and evaluation activities. The results of the observation study support the view that the *pattern-mining* process is effective and that the information obtained is useful [3], all the 18 subjects that replied to our first questionnaire found the proposed process and guidelines helpful in mining information from patterns. And 22 of the 24 subjects replying to subsequent questionnaires found the extracted information in templates more useful than standard pattern information for performing architecting activities. Objective quantitative data gathered during controlled experiments are yet to be analyzed, and we are expecting that the findings of the controlled experiments will be available in the near future.

11.4 Conclusions and Open Issues

One of the general conclusions is that recording the rationale for architecture decisions is an intuitively appealing idea, which has enormous potential benefits. However, there is little guidance and no support mechanism for capturing and managing ADK. In this chapter, we contribute to the growing efforts of software architecture rationale management by proposing a framework of three components to support the management of ADK. We hope that both researchers and practitioners can experiment with the ideas presented in this chapter and provide us some insights to refine our approach. In particular, we look forward to seeing how the proposed data model can be applied in practice to develop an organizational repository, which can be populated with ADK by following the *"pattern-mining"* process.

Despite continuous efforts by researchers and practitioners, including ours, the architecture community has a long way to go before ADK capture becomes a widely accepted practice. As Conklin [18] mentioned, successful transfer of any technology of capturing rationale will need to answer the questions like: what is the cost of not capturing and managing ADK, who is responsible for capturing and maintaining it, what are the incentives for the designers to take extra burden of documenting DR, and what are the mechanisms in place to prevent rationale being used for firing or prosecuting architects if a decision turns out to be an error? These are some of the issues that we plan to explore in our future efforts

Acknowledgments. The first author wishes to thank Len Bass, Antony Tang, and Mark Staples for useful comments on various aspects of the data model. National ICT Australia is funded through the Australian Government's Backing Australia's Ability initiative, in part through the Australian Research Council.

References

[1]   Al-Naeem T, Gorton I, Ali-Babar M, Rabhi F, Benatallah B (2005) A quality-driven systematic approach for architecting distributed software applications. In: Proceedings of International Conference on Software Engineering, pp. 244–253
[2]   Ali-Babar M, Zhu L, Jeffery R (2004) A framework for classifying and comparing software architecture evaluation methods. In: Proceedings of Australian Software Engineering Conference, pp. 309–318

[3]   Ali-Babar M, Kitchenham B, Maheshwari P, Jeffery R (2005) Mining patterns for improving architecting activities – A research program and preliminary assessment. In: Proceedings of International Conference on Empirical Assessment in Software Engineering, 54–63

[4]   Arango G, Schoen E, Pettengill R (1993) A process for consolidating and reusing design knowledge. In: Proceedings of International Conference on Software Engineering, pp. 231–242

[5]   Bachmann F, Bass L, Klein M (2003) Deriving architectural tactics: A step toward methodical architectural design, Tech Report CMU/SEI-2003-TR-004, SEI, Carnegie Mellon University, USA

[6]   Basili VR, Caldiera G (1995) Improving software quality reusing knowledge and experience. Sloan Management Review 37(1): pp. 55–64

[7]   Bass L, Klein M, Bachmann F (2000) Quality attribute design primitives, Tech Report CMU/SEI-2000-TN-017, SEI, Carnegie Mellon University, USA

[8]   Bass L, Clements P, Kazman R (2003) Software Architecture in Practice. 2 ed. Addison–Wesley

[9]   Bass L., John B.E. (2003) Linking usability to software architecture patterns through general scenarios. Journal of Systems and Software 66(3): pp. 187–197

[10] Bengtsson P (2002) Architecture-level modifiability analysis Ph.D. Thesis Blekinge Institute of Technology, Sweden

[11] Bosch J (2000) Design and use of software architectures: Adopting and Evolving a Product-line Approach. Addison-Wesley

[12] Bosch J (2004) Software architecture: The next step. In: Proceedings of the European Workshop on Software Architecture, pp. 194–199

[13] Bratthall L, Johansson E, Regnell B (2000) Is a design rationale vital when predicting change impact? – A controlled experiment on software architecture evolution. In: Lecture Notes in Computer Science, F. Bomarius and M. Oivo (eds.) Springer, Berlin Heidelberg New York. pp. 126–139

[14] Buschmann F, Meunier R, Rohnert H, Sommerlad P, Stal M (1996) Pattern-oriented Software Architecture: A System of Patterns: Wiley, New York

[15] Carroll JM, Moran TP (1991) Introduction to the special issue on design rationale. Human–Computer Interaction 6: pp. 197–200

[16] Clements P, et al. (2002) Documenting software architectures: Views and Beyond: Addison-Wesley

[17] Clements P, Kazman R, Klein M (2002) Evaluating Software Architectures: Methods and Case Studies: Addison-Wesley

[18] Conklin J, Burgess-Yahkemovic KC (1991) A process-oriented approach to design rationale. Human–Computer Interaction 6(3–4): pp. 357–391

[19] Curtis B, Krasner H, Iscoe N (1988) A field study of the software design process for large systems. Communications of the ACM 31(11): pp. 1268–1287

[20] Dutoit AH, Paech B (2001) Rationale management in software engineering, in Handbook of Software Engineering and Knowledge Engineering, S. Change, (ed.): World Scientific Publishing, Singapore

[21] Dutoit AH, Paech B (2002) Rationale-based use case specification. Requirements Engineering 7(1): pp. 3–19

[22] Gamma E, Helm R, Johnson R, Vlissides J (1995) Design patterns-elements of reusable object-oriented software: Addison-Wesley, Reading, MA

[23] Gross D, Yu E (2000) From non-functional requirements to design through patterns. In: Proceedings of 6th International Workshop on Requirements Engineering Foundation for Software Quality

[24] Gruber T, Russell D (1991) Design knowledge and design rationale: A framework for representation, capture, and use, Tech Report KSL 90-45, Knowledge Laboratory, Stanford University, Stanford, USA

[25] Henninger S (2003) Tool support for experience-based software development methodologies. Advances in Computers 59: pp. 29–82

[26] Herbsleb JD, Kuwana E (1993) Preserving knowledge in design projects: What designers need to know. In: Proceedings of Human Factors in Computing Systems, 7–14

[27] IEEE (2000) Recommended practices for architecture description of software-intensive systems. IEEE Standard No. 1471

[28] John BE, Bass L, Sanchez-Segura MI, Adams RJ (2004) Bringing usability concerns to the design of software architecture. In: Proceedings of IFIP Working Conference on Engineering for Human–Computer Interaction, pp. 1–19

[29] Kazman R, Carriere SJ, Woods SG (2000) Toward a discipline of scenario-based architectural engineering. Annals of Software Engineering, 9(1–4): pp. 5–33

[30] Kitchenham BA, Hughes RT, Linkman SG (2001) Modeling software measurement data. IEEE Transactions on Software Engineering 27(9): pp. 788–804

[31] Kneuper R (2001) Supporting software processes using knowledge management, in Handbook of Software Engineering and Knowledge Engineering, S.K. Chang, (ed.). World Scientific Publishing, Singapore, pp. 579–606

[32] Kunz W, Rittel HWJ (1970) Issues as elements of information systems. W-P 131 Institute of Urban and Regional Development, University of California, Berkeley, USA

[33] Lee J (1991) Extending the Potts and Bruns model for recording design rationale. In: Proceedings of International Conference on Software Engineering, pp. 114–125

[34] Lee J, Lai KY (1991) What's in design rationale? Human–Computer Interaction 6(3–4): pp. 251–280

[35] MacLean A, Young RM, Bellotti VME, Moran TP (1991) Questions, options, and criteria: Elements of design space analysis. Human–Computer Interaction 6(3–4): pp. 201–250

[36] McCall R (1987) PHIBIS: Procedural hierarchical issue-based information systems. In: Proceedings of International Congress on Planning and Design Theory, pp. 17–22

[37] Naiburg EJ, Maksimchuk RA (2001) UML for database design: Addison-Wesley, Reading, MA

[38] Niemela E, Kalaoja J, Lago P (2005) Toward an architectural knowledge base for wireless service engineering. IEEE Transactions of Software Engineering 31(5): pp. 361–379

[39] Obbink H, et al. (2001) Software architecture review and assessment (SARA) report, Tech Report SARA W.G

[40] Parnas D, Clements P (1986) A rationale design process: How and why to fake it. IEEE Transactions of Software Engineering 12(2): pp. 251–257

[41] Pena-Mora F, Vadhavkar S (1997) Augmenting design patterns with design rationale. Artificial Intelligence for Engineering Design, Analysis and Manufacturing 11(2): pp. 93–108

[42] Perry DE, Wolf AL (1992) Foundations for the study of software architecture. ACM SIGSOFT, Software Engineering Notes 17(4): pp. 40–52

[43] Potts C, Burns G (1988) Recording the reasons for design decisions. In: Proceedings of International Conference on Software Engineering, pp. 418–427

[44] Potts C (1995) Supporting software design: Integrating design methods and design rationale. In: Design Rationale: Concepts, Techniques, and Use, J.M. Carroll (ed.). Lawrence Erlbaum Associates, Hillsdale, NJ. pp. 295–321

[45] Potts C (1999) Scenic: A strategy for inquiry-driven requirements determination. In: Proceedings of Symposium on Requirements Engineering, pp. 58–65

[46] Probst GJB (1998) Practical knowledge management: A model that works, in Prism. http://know.unige.ch/publications/Prismartikel.PDF, accessed on 1st July 2005

[47] Ramesh B, Dhar B (1992) Supporting systems development by capturing deliberations during requirements engineering. IEEE Transaction on Software Engineering 18(6): pp. 498–510

[48] Regli WC, Hu X, Atwood M, Sun W (2002) A survey of design rationale systems: Approaches, representation, capture and retrieval. Engineering with Computers 16: pp. 209–235

[49] Robillard PN (1999) The role of knowledge in software development. Communication of the ACM 42(1): pp. 87–92

[50] Skuce B (1995) Knowledge management in software design: A tool and a trial. Software Engineering Journal September: pp. 183–193

[51] Sutcliffe A (1995) Requirements rationales: Integrating approaches to requirement analysis. In: Proceedings of Symposium on Designing Interactive Systems, pp. 33–42

[52] Tyree J, Akerman A (2005) Architecture decisions: Demystifying architecture. IEEE Software 22(2): pp. 19–27

12 Capturing and Using Rationale for a Software Architecture

L. Bass, P. Clements, R.L. Nord, J. Stafford

Abstract: Documentation of design rationale acts as the collective memory for a system. A special case of design, and therefore of design rationale, is found by considering the set of design decisions that constitute a system's software architecture. This chapter discusses the special role of architecture in design and the kinds of rationale that are important to capture. We discuss capturing and structuring rationale using two different graphs (the causal graph and the structural graph) in order to facilitate its (possibly automated) recovery and use in question–answering later in the life cycle. The information collected in these structures can be used manually (especially in the case of documentation) or as the basis for an automatic search to determine the answers to common questions asked of architectural design rationale such as how a requirement has been satisfied and what are the implications of a proposed modification.

Keywords: software architecture; architectural design rationale; architectural tactic; architecture documentation; causal graph; structural graph

12.1 Introduction

The reason for maintaining design rationale is to allow stakeholders throughout the life of the system to determine why important design decisions were made, what those decisions were, and what alternatives were considered when making those decisions. Documentation of design rationale acts as the collective memory for the system; without knowledge of the reasoning behind decisions, decisions will be needlessly reconsidered and, in the future, unnecessary or incompatible decisions are likely to be made.

Our vision of design is one in which rationale management is an integral part of the design process. Tools to help manage design and related rationale inherently support such a process. We envision design tools that manage rationale as a side effect of design, rather than as a separate rationale management tool that is very intrusive.

A special case of design, and therefore of design rationale, is found by considering the set of design decisions that constitute a system's software architecture. This chapter discusses the special considerations that come into play for documenting the rationale of a software architecture. We begin in Sect. 12.2 by discussing the special role of architecture in design, why it is important, and the kinds of rationale that are particularly important to capture. We go on to discuss two main ways of organizing that rationale: *causally* and *structurally*. Section 12.3 shows how the organization of design rationale facilitates its use in answering questions later in the life cycle. Section 12.4 discusses a representation and guidelines for capturing design rationale. Section 12.5 illustrates the approach with an example of capturing and using design rationale. We conclude in Sect. 12.6.

Our approach is focused on software architecture rationale and thus its primary support of software engineering process areas (as distinguished by SPICE) is the process area of engineering. Secondary areas include operation and reuse, but only to the extent to which they support engineering.

12.2   Structuring Rationale

12.2.1 The Special Role of Software Architecture

A software architecture for a system is the structure or structures of the software, which comprise software elements, the externally visible properties of those elements, and the relationships among them [1]. Externally visible properties include both function (which we represent by responsibilities) [2] and quality attribute properties such as execution time, probability of a failure, and so forth. A system's software architecture represents a cohesive set of design decisions that shape the system and also shape the development project that produces the system. A system's software architecture permits or precludes many of the system's important quality attributes such as performance, security, reliability, and others. The architecture is the forum in which major design tradeoffs are engineered, requirements negotiated, and project and system resources are allocated. The architecture represents the earliest set of design decisions that begin to address how the system will meet its requirements. No system can be successful with the wrong software architecture. And, in many organizations, an architecture represents a significant capital investment that can be leveraged across an entire family of related systems.

In addition to the ways just described, an architecture is important because it represents a set of design decisions that are made early and that have far-reaching scope. These decisions are critical to get right because they will be extremely difficult to change later. We know from long experience that defects introduced early on can be orders of magnitude more expensive to correct than defects introduced much later.

12.2.2 What is an Architectural Design Decision?

An architectural design decision can be seen as a transformation from the state of the architecture prior to the design decision and the state of the architecture subsequent to the design decision.

This transformation can be a refinement of either the structural portions of the architecture or the responsibilities allocated to the various structural elements (such as dividing an element into sub-elements where the responsibilities in the subelements collectively satisfied the responsibilities in the original element), it can be a reallocation of responsibilities among structural elements (such as moving a responsibility from one element to another), it can be an aggregation of structural elements (such as combining two elements into one that provides a general set of responsibilities to satisfy the responsibilities in the original two elements), or it can be the change or addition of a property of one of the elements of the architecture. The transformation depicted in Fig. 12.1 shows that the known need for a connector between a client and the server of a compositional control dependence graph generator (CCDGG) system [3], which will be used as a running example in this chapter, has been refined to become a TCP/IP connector.

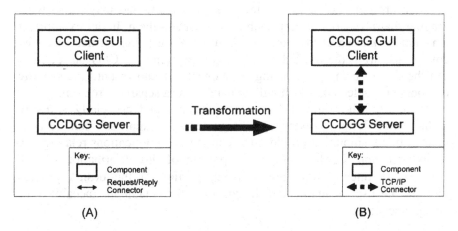

(A)   (B)

Fig. 12.1. Architectural transformation brought about by an architectural design decision

A common approach used for recording rationale is based on argumentation representations (as described in [4] [Chap. 1, Sect. 1.3 in this book]). Argumentation representations assume that the key element is the problem, i.e., the reason a decision is required. They then enumerate arguments for and against particular solutions to the problem and have a decision as the output. This approach captures the two key items for design rationale, what the decision is and why it was made, and sometimes the third key item, where it is manifested in the design, but context and implications are captured only insofar as they become a portion of the argument. For instance, referring to another decision made during the architecture development of the CCDGG introduced above, the architect was faced with the problem that a Control Flow Graph (CFG) builder is needed. This is discussed further in Sects. 12.4 and 12.5 but in brief, possible solutions include writing code in house or using a pre-existing component. Arguments for or against each of these revolve around costs and benefits of in house coding (benefit of optimized, custom solution vs. cost in terms of time and need for additional expertise); and the costs and benefits of using pre-existing components (benefit of reuse of specialized CFG expertise and coding effort vs. cost of likely need to adapt outputs).

The determination of the context and the implications of a design decision when solely recording argumentation depends both on the designers making context and implication an explicit portion of the arguments brought forward and being correct about the context and the implications of a design decision. This assumption is problematical, particularly with respect to the implications of a decision. Frequently, the implications of a decision are not known when the decision is made and may be so wide ranging that it is virtually impossible to document them. In our example, it may not be known at the time the arguments are being formed what the cost of acquiring the needed expertise for developing a CFG builder, nor can the cost of using pre-existing components be known until the specific component is selected, which will be handled as a separate problem.

Because of the particular nature of design, and especially software architectural design, however, the argumentation approach can be augmented in a fashion that provides the context and implications relating to a design decision. Furthermore, the capturing of this information can be done as an integral (and nonintrusive) portion of the design process through the use of augmented design tools that maintain traceability of design decisions.

12.2.3 A Causal Graph of Rationale

This notion of transformation leads to formulating a design as a sequence of decisions. This is true for any kind of design, not just software. For example, when drawing a picture, an early decision is the media to be used. The choice of pencil, crayon, oil or watercolor will influence the style of the picture. A subsequent choice is where to position the stylus for the initial segment. This choice will influence subsequent decisions as well.

Given a design as a sequence of decisions, these decisions can be ordered temporally. These decisions could be to provide properties to existing architectural elements (one interpretation of Fig. 12.1) or it could be to use a particular reusable component to implement the connector (another interpretation of Fig. 12.1). Each decision constrains some, although not necessarily all, subsequent decisions. Furthermore, each decision is constrained by some set, although not necessarily all, of the prior decisions.

Observe that this formulation includes evolution of existing systems as well as the initial design. Evolutionary decisions would be temporally positioned after all of the decisions that went into the original system although they would be constrained (most likely) by only a subset of the original decisions.

Any tool support for the design process can be augmented to capture the sequence of design decisions. Any change to the design represents a decision that is a portion of the causal graph. We see three levels of information that the tool would record:

1. *Just the decision.* This yields a temporal ordering of decisions. Gathering this information does not intrude on the design process at all.
2. *The decision together with its context.* That is, what prior decisions do this decision depends on. This yields more structure to the temporal order. Gathering this information is partially unobtrusive (the decisions that led to the decision element being modified area portion of the context) and partially obtrusive (design elements not being modified might have some influence on the current decision).
3. *The decision together with whatever information is appropriate.* Gathering this information is equivalent to the argumentation approach in obtrusiveness.

This gives us our first notion of a useful way to represent rationale: a *causal graph*. A causal view of design decisions is a directed acyclic graph where each node is a design decision, the parents of a node are those decisions that constrained it and the arcs represent the relation "constrained by". The fact that two nodes are children of the same parent reflects the fact that the decisions represented by the nodes are constrained by the parent but are independent and could have been made in any order. The fact that one node has two parents reflects that fact that constraints on that decision came from multiple sources.

Our assumption is that tools embedded in a design support environment support the creation of the causal graph. If the design is performed in a tool environment then every modification to the architecture is a design decision and can be placed in the causal graph in temporal order.

The causal graph is similar to the decision tree introduced by Parnas for representing program families [5]. Parnas's structure emphasizes the succession of program versions and variants (the nodes in the tree) that are created in response to design decisions (the arcs) in order to understand the relationships among members of a program family. Our causal graph, on the other hand, highlights the decisions, which are the nodes in our graph, in order to support traceability and to help one understand why a system is the way it is. Fig. 12.2 shows a part of the causal graph for the CCDGG starting at the decision to use a client–server approach.

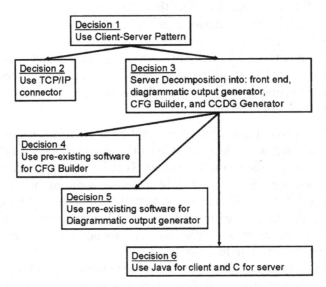

Fig. 12.2. Causal graph for CCDGG

12.2.4 A Structural Graph of Rationale

Architectural patterns (sometimes called styles) are a well-known approach for designing that are used to achieve specific quality attributes and, as such, imply rationale. Patterns represent known (partial) solutions to recurring design problems, where the problems are often couched in terms of quality attributes as well as desired functionality. For example, client–server is a well-known architectural pattern that is appropriate for use when it is desirable to decouple the provision of the service from the service itself. Using this pattern provides a basis for deploying the client on a different platform than the server. It also supports interoperability with services on legacy systems. A client–server approach is useful when the quality attributes of performance, scalability, and reliability are a concern. In our CCDGG example, the decision to apply the client–server pattern, which resulted in the architecture shown in Fig. 12.1A, was made in order to allow multiple, possibly geographically distributed, clients access to the CCDGG server. Catalogs of architectural patterns (e.g., [6]) can be consulted so that an architect does not have to reinvent known solutions to familiar problems.

While architectural patterns have proven extremely valuable, the number of different design problems confronting an architect is quite large. The number of patterns needed to do the job would lead to catalogs of unwieldy size. Instead, recent work has focused on architectural tactics [1]. These are the fine-grained design decisions that are the building blocks of patterns. Each quality attribute has associated with it a relatively small set of tactics. Applying an architectural tactic transforms a software architecture where the result of the transformation has a response measure for a quality attribute that has changed in a known direction. For example, Fig. 12.3 shows the available tactics that are related to performance. The response measure for performance involves the ability of the system to meet deadlines and to perform within the bounds of constraints imposed by available resources. Introducing any of the tactics for performance will improve the response measure the system exhibits in this area.

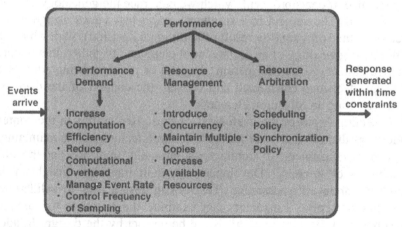

Fig. 12.3. Performance tactics

An architect's choice of patterns and tactics, then, represent specific and especially far-reaching design decisions that are taken to achieve quality attribute properties. They also suggest a way of regarding rationale that is different from the temporal view presented earlier: we are now discussing a structural graph of rationale. This graph maps to the set of architectural elements as they exist in the software. It captures the rationale that explains the origin of each architectural element in terms of the responsibilities (function and quality attributes) that it will have a hand in producing and the design decision alternatives considered and chosen to achieve them. Looking ahead, Fig. 12.6 shows a part of the structural graph for the CCDGG in the Primary Presentation portion of the document with annotations recorded in the Architecture Background.

Observe that only one structural graph exists at any point in time. Any modification to the structural graph will destroy the old version. The old version can be recovered either by consideration of the causal graph or by maintaining old versions of the structural graph through some version control mechanism. Also, notice that the structural graph can be reconstructed by traversing the causal graph. That is, the structural graph is a view of the current structure whereas the causal graph is a history of all of the decisions made to date.

12.3   How will Architectural Design Rationale be Used?

At this point we have identified two useful graphs to help one understand why a system is the way it is. The first is a causal graph that views design as a sequence of decisions, with which we can trace the genealogy of a design decision. The second is a structural graph that views design as the structure of the software (the result of applying a decision), with which we can trace the genealogy of an architectural element. Together, they record, for any architectural transformation, the goal or problem being addressed, the design decisions considered and chosen, the context of the decision, and the resulting architectural elements.

This section explores the usefulness of these two graphs in the context of questions that often arise of rationale for architecture. While maintainers are primary consumers of architectural rationale, they are not the only stakeholders of interest. Developers can gain important insights from reading the architect's reasoning. Testers can design tests to validate the architect's precepts. Customers can examine the rationale to convince themselves that their business goals are being met by the design. In addition, these stakeholders, and others, can read the rationale to make sure their interests have been addressed. But the stakeholder with perhaps the most vested interest in capturing the motivation and background for design decisions is the architect. In the maelstrom of developmental activities, the architect needs some way to remember the conceptual path he or she has taken, as well as a way not to repeat dead-end design paths.

Although the structural graph can be recreated by traversing the causal graph, the two graphs, in fact, serve different purposes as the Sects. 12.3.1 and 12.3.2. show.

Two common questions asked of architectural design rationale are (1) "How is requirement X satisfied?" and (2) "What are the implications of making modification Y?"

Of course, there are many other questions that design rationale could be used to answer, but in our experience these two are the most important.

12.3.1 Using Rationale to See How Requirements are Satisfied

Now let us reconsider the question of "How is requirement X satisfied?" we distinguish between functional requirements and quality attribute requirements. Functional requirements are initially mapped to a set of responsibilities. These responsibilities are transformed through design decisions. As long as traceability is maintained as the architecture is transformed, all of the decisions impacting a functional requirement can be enumerated and the final form of the responsibilities for implementing a functional requirement can be determined (they are the leaves of the directed acyclic graph that is the causal graph of design decisions).

Quality attribute requirements can be traced in a similar fashion. Each design decision (transformation) is the application of one or more architectural tactics. Each tactic that is applied is designed for the achievement of a particular quality attribute. Thus, the quality attribute specified by a particular quality attribute requirement can be used to determine which application of tactics is relevant to the achievement of that particular requirement. Again, it is the leaves that represent the decisions that are incorporated in the current state of the design.

Functional requirements are linked to a sequence of transformations of responsibilities to achieve those requirements. Quality attribute requirements are linked to a sequence of transformations determined by the tactics used to achieve that quality attribute. These assignments show up in both the causal graph and the structural graph of design decisions. The former records when a decision is constrained by prior decisions. The latter records the rationale associated with the creation of each architectural element.

12.3.2 Determining the Implications of a Modification

Now we turn our attention to the answering of the second common question that is asked of design rationale: "What are the implications of making modification Y?"

The implications of making a particular modification are frequently a cause for concern because of uncertainty of the side effects associated with any changes. A modification is made by locating portions of the system where the modification could be made, determining the potential side effects of making the modification in that location, and then implementing the modification. The determination of potential side effects of making a modification in a particular location can be bounded through our proposed method of structuring rationale.

Understanding the implications of making a modification is a matter of locating the decisions that are to be affected by a proposed change. The parents of those decisions are the context within which the decision was made (recall the decision to use TCP/IP described earlier); the children of those decisions are the decisions that will be affected by the proposed modification.

The use of a causal graph of design decisions enables understanding the direct consequences of making a particular modification. The decisions that are embodied in the portion of the system being modified have descendents in the temporal graph and the implications of an envisioned modification on those descendents can be analyzed.

It is the side effects of a modification that are a cause for concern. These side effects come about because of the manner in which particular responsibilities are packaged (and hence interact) with other responsibilities. For the analysis of potential side effects we turn to the second graph of rationale that we have identified: the one corresponding to element structure.

We can view architectural design as leading to the structure or structures of the software. The information captured during the series of transformation steps is organized structurally. This structural organization means that the determination of side effects is simplified, especially if the views chosen include dependency relations.

A side effect to a modification is caused by one of two phenomena. Either a modification to a responsibility in a module affects another responsibility in that module or a modification affects modules that are dependent on the originally modified module. In either case, the ability to track side effects of a modification can come from examining the appropriate view.

A module decomposition view will locate a responsibility in the context of other responsibilities. The decisions that led to this collocation may not have depended on each other so this information is not necessarily derivable from the temporal graph. The responsibilities collocated in the same module as the modified responsibility are the ones that might suffer side effects. Thus, the degree of isolation of a responsibility provides a means of identifying potential side effects.

Furthermore, the modules dependent in any fashion on the module being modified can be identified through the dependency relation. Not all of these modules will be affected by the modification but tracking the dependency relation scopes the possible side effects of a modification.

12.4   Capturing Rationale

12.4.1 How is Architecture and Rationale Documented?

We have seen that two basic graphs of rationale (causal and structural) will go a long way towards allowing us to answer the most common questions posed to architecture rationale. Ideally, there would be sophisticated tooling available to help an architect construct these graphs or even do so automatically. The fact is, no such tooling exists, and so we must examine the state of the practice today to see if we can derive the benefits of these two graphs from work likely to be carried out by a practicing architect.

Modern approaches to software architecture engineer it and document it as a set of views. A view is a representation of a set of system elements and relationships among them [7]. The current trend is not to prescribe a particular set of views, but rather to have the architect define the set of views that will be most relevant to the architecture's stakeholders. This is the approach prescribed by ANSI/IEEE-1471-2000 [8], the recommended best practice for documenting architectures of software-intensive systems.

The Software Engineering Institute's "views and beyond" approach to documentation [7] exemplifies this approach. It holds that documenting a software architecture is a matter of choosing and documenting the relevant views, and then documenting information that applies to all of the views (for example, how the views relate to each other). The V&B approach comes with a standard organization, or template, for a software architecture documentation package. This template, one version of which is summarized in Fig. 12.4, offers several places dedicated for capturing rationale behind architectural design decisions. In particular:

– Section 1 explains the structure and contents of the document. It includes an explanation – a rationale – for why a particular set of views was chosen, by framing the views as addressing the explicit concerns of a number of stakeholders.

- Section 2 provides a dedicated place for capturing rationale whose scope is the entire architecture. Dedicated subsections are provided to record the system's business goals, quality attribute goals that shape the architecture, the major architectural approaches – specifically, tactics and patterns – chosen to meet the quality attribute goals, and analysis results that provide an argument that the chosen approaches satisfy the stated goals.
- Section 3 contains the views of the architecture. Within each view, a subsection called "Architecture Background" is dedicated to providing rationale for the design decisions associated with that view. This section is a microcosm of the information found in Sect. 2: What are the business goals and quality attribute constraints that drive the selection of architectural approaches within the context of this view?
- Section 4 relates the views to each other by showing how the elements in one correspond to elements in another. In this way, a holistic view of the architecture emerges, showing how the views cooperatively work to serve the purposes of the system.
- Sections 5 and 6 are resources to help the reader find more information.

Templates such as the one in Fig. 12.4 make the architecture process much more effective. An architect always has a place to record a design decision, and the reasons behind it, as soon as the decision is made. The template provides a framework that helps gauge progress and the scope of remaining work. The architecture's stakeholders benefit because they can find specific information in predictable places, shortening their search time and avoiding frustration.

It is easy to see that a documentation template like the one in Fig. 12.4 is geared towards the structural graph of rationale – the rationale for the architectural structures and elements that appear in each view is documented alongside those structures and elements.

12.4.2 How Should an Architect Capture Rationale?

We suggest the following guidelines to architects for capturing rationale. First, there are five key items associated with a design decision:

1. What is it?
2. Why was it made?
3. Where is it manifested in the design?
4. What was the context for the decision? That is, what design decisions already in place led to it?
5. What are the implications of that decision?

1 Documentation Roadmap and Overview
1.1 Document Management and Configuration Control Information
1.2 Purpose and Scope of the Software Architecture Document
1.3 How the Software Architecture Document Is Organized
1.4 Stakeholder Representation
1.5 Explanation of Views Chosen
1.6 How a View is Documented
1.7 Relationship to Other Software Architecture Documents
1.8 Process for Updating this Software Architecture Document

2 Architecture Background
2.1 Problem Background
2.1.1 System Overview
2.1.2 Goals and Context
2.1.3 Significant Driving Requirements
2.2 Solution Background
2.2.1 Architectural Approaches
2.2.2 Causal graph
2.2.3 Analysis Results
2.2.4 Requirements Coverage
2.2.5 Summary of Changes in Current Version
2.3 Product Line Reuse Considerations

3 Views. Section 3 contains the set of views for the architecture.
Each view is documented using the following outline:
3.i View #i: <Insert view name> View
3.i.1 Primary Presentation
3.i.2 Element Catalog: elements, relations, interfaces, and behavior
3.i.3 Context Diagram
3.i.4 Variability Mechanisms
3.i.5 Architecture Background

4 Relations Among Views
4.1 General Relations Among Views
4.2 View-to-View Relations

5 Referenced Materials

6 Directory: Index, glossary, acronym list

Fig. 12.4. Summary of the V&B template with 2.2.2 (Causal graph) added

Obviously item #4 is grist for building the causal graph. Item #3 may be self-evident by the location of the rationale in the documentation package, but in any case this provides the structural graph information. It may also be desirable to add annotations so that additional information about the decision is recorded; for all decisions these five key items should be captured. In addition, the same five items should be recorded for alternatives considered but not chosen.

1. What is the alternative?
2. Why was it not made?
3. Where would it have been manifested in the design?
4. What would have been the context for the decision (i.e., what design decisions already in place would have led to it)?
5. What are the implications if that alternative had been chosen?

As an example, the following paragraph describes the rationale for deciding to use a pre-existing component to generate control flow graphs needed in a system that identifies dependencies among statements in source code. The parenthesized numbers indicate where each of the five pieces of rationale is communicated in the phrase:

Use pre-existing generator for control flow graph (CFG) (1). A decision needed to be made as to whether to develop the CFG builder in house or use readily available one (2). In response to the input of source code, the control flow graph generator produces control flow graphs, which are then used as input to the control dependence graph generator (3). The module decomposition of the server resulted in a CFG Builder module (4). Because control flow graphs are used as a base for many code analysis tools, the use of pre-existing control flow graph generator is advisable because availability of a high-quality pluggable component can be assumed, which will save development time. However, the use of a pre-existing CFG generator may require adjustment of the CCDA algorithm, which expects a specific form of CFG. (5)

Rules of thumb for capturing rationale include:

– Document those design decisions that either have far-reaching effect, or which the architect spent a significant amount of time or effort to resolve.
– Document the decision, the reason or goal behind it, and the context for making the decision.
– Explain rejected alternatives and why they were rejected, as well as the approaches that were chosen. This will prevent the same dead ends from being fruitlessly re-explored in the future.
– Analysis or formal review results often make excellent rationale, in that they illuminate goals and requirements driving the architecture and provide the connection between those constraints and the architectural decisions that satisfy them. See [9] [Chap. 11 in this book] for an elaboration of this concept.

The key to capturing the right rationale is to keep in mind the reason it is being written down – it will be used later to save time, effort, and consequently money because it will help people remember why the architecture is the way it is.

12.5   An Example of Capturing and Using Rationale

We now return to the example that we have been using to illustrate the concepts and show how the pieces fit together. Figures 12.5 and 12.6 show excerpts of the example using the software architecture template. The structural and causal graphs are threaded throughout.

2.1.2 Goals and Context
    Business goals
    –   Time to market...
    –   Maintain a quality reputation by providing robustness throughout the application...

2.1.3 Significant Driving Requirements
    Modifiability
    –   Addition of legacy software...
    Reliability
    –   Handles errors gracefully...

2.2 Solution Background

2.2.1 Architectural Approaches
    Client-server, pre-existing CFG generator...

2.2.2 Causal graph (pointer)

2.2.3 Analysis Results
    Analysis of cost/benefit of reusing CFG generator vs. new development shows better return on investment by using pre-existing software...

Fig. 12.5. Excerpts from the Architecture Background section of the template

Figure 12.5 shows excerpts from the Architecture Background section of the template. It makes the requirements and business goals explicit.

Figure 12.6 shows excerpts from the Views section of the template. A client-server C&C view is shown in Sect. 3.1. Decisions 1 and 2 from the causal graph (Fig. 12.2) are linked to this view. The tactic from Fig. 12.1 is documented as part of the rationale.

A decomposition of the server is shown in Sect. 3.2 showing the CFG Builder in the context of the parent (server) and siblings (front end, diagrammatic output generator, CCDG Generator). Decision 3 is linked to the entire view; decision 4 is linked to the CFG Builder element within the view. Structurally this decomposition view has as its context the client-server view.

We can now reconsider the original two questions in light of this example and how rationale is captured causally and structurally:

3   Views
3.1   View #1: CCDGG Client-server
         View
3.1.1   Primary Presentation

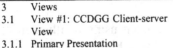

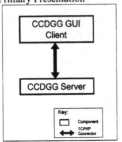

3.1.5   Architecture Background Decisions
        1 and 2 (Section 2.2.2) provide
        rationale in terms of sequence of
        design decisions that led to the final
        structure.

Transformation 1->2 (from Figure 12.1) provides rationale and analysis for the details
of moving from Decision 1 to Decision 2.
In addition to the change in structure recorded by the causal graph excerpt, the
transformation includes the design forces
(e.g., quality attributes) under consideration
and any analysis done to verify the transformation.

3.2   View #2: CCDGG Server Decom-
        position View

3.2.1   Primary Presentation

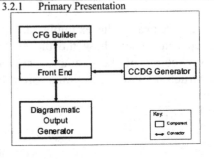

3.2.2   Element Catalog
        CFGBuilder_COMP: CFGBuilder
        (Decision 4: use pre-existing software)
        DOG_COMP:Diagrammatic Output
        Generator
        (Decision5: use pre-existing software)
        myFrontEnd:FrontEnd
        (Decision 6: to build constructed in C)
        myCCDGG:CCDG Generator
        (Decision 6: to build constructed in C)

3.2.3   Context Diagram
        CCDGG Server in the client-server view
        (Section 3.1.1)

3.2.5   Architecture Background
        Decisions 3 – 6 provide rationale
        Concerns addressed:
-       Correctness and performance require-
        ments of CFG builder and need for such
        tools is common so availability can be
        assumed
-       Superior graph layout tools exist
-       Costs of development vs. reuse
-       Staffing limitations and time constraints

Fig. 12.6 Excerpts from the Views section of the template

1. How is requirement X satisfied? The business goals of time to market
   and quality (implicit in the textual description: "high-quality pluggable
   component" and "save development time" and explicitly documented in
   the template in Sect. 2.1.2 Goals and Context) lead to quality attribute
   requirements of modifiability and reliability (explicitly documented in
   the template as Sect. 2.1.3 Significant Driving Requirements) which
   lead to the general architecture approaches (Sect. 2.2.1) and onto the
   specific approaches/design decisions in Sect. 3 (e.g., Decision 5 documented in Sect. 3.2).

2. What are the implications of making modification Y? To understand
   the implication of modifying the design to use pre-existing software for
   the CFG Builder presented in Sect. 3.2.1 we need to look at a more detailed behavioral description of the components of the server (Fig. 12.7).
   Since the CFG Builder is predefined and cannot be changed, the other
   design elements are constrained by its responsibilities and interface. For
   example, the responsibilities of the CCDG Generator need to be adjusted since it shares knowledge of control flow graphs (CFGs) with the
   CFG Builder.

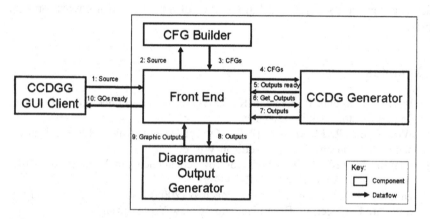

Fig. 12.7. Behavioral description of the server

12.6 Summary

In this chapter, we have described how design rationale for software architecture can be captured and how it can be used to answer the most common questions asked of design rationale. By exploiting two different
graphs (the causal graph and the structural graph) we have the information
necessary to determine how a requirement has been satisfied and what the
implications of a proposed modification. The information collected in
these structures can be used manually (especially in the case of documentation) or as the basis for an automatic search.

The process of capturing rationale improves design. The resulting
documentation is descriptive and used by system stakeholders for software
development life cycle activities including but not limited to design, such
as implementation and maintenance.

The approach is less intrusive to the extent which it considers rationale capture as a side effect of design and not as a separate activity. Some of the rationale is captured "for free" as part of good architecture documentation practices. Because the focus is on software architecture design, every decision does not need to be rationalized. The aim of the approach to be less intrusive will not be fully realized, though, without tool support.

Acknowledgments. This work is sponsored by the US Department of Defense. The Software Engineering Institute is a federally funded research and development center sponsored by the US Department of Defense. Len Bass was visiting NICTA and Ian Gorton for a portion of his work on this paper.

References

[1]   Bass L, Clements P, Kazman R (2003) Software Architecture in Practice, 2nd ed. Boston: Addison-Wesley
[2]   Wirfs-Brock R, McKean A (2002) Object Design: Roles, Responsibilities, and Collaborations. Boston: Addison-Wesley
[3]   Shevlin TP (2004) Composed control dependence graph generator. Tufts University Technical Report TR-2004-9
[4]   Dutoit AH, McCall R, Mistrik I, Paech B (2006) Rationale Management in Software Engineering. Berlin Heidelberg New York: Springer
[5]   Parnas DL (1976) On the design and development of program families. IEEE Transactions on Software Engineering 2(1): 1–9
[6]   Buschmann F, Meunier R, Rohnert H, Sommerlad P, Stal M (1996) Pattern-oriented software architecture: A system of patterns. Chichester: Wiley
[7]   Clements P, Bachmann F, Bass L, Garlan D, Ivers J, Little R, Nord R, Stafford J (2002) Documenting Software Architectures: Views and Beyond. Boston: Addison-Wesley
[8]   ANSI/IEEE 1471-2000 available at http://standards.ieee.org/reading/ieee/std_public/description/se/1471-2000_desc.html
[9]   Ali Babar M, Gorton I, Kitchenham BA (2006) A framework for supporting architecture knowledge and rationale management. In: Dutoit AH, McCall R, Mistrik I, Paech B (eds.) Rationale Management in Software Engineering. Berlin Heidelberg New York: Springer

13 Rationale-Based Support for Software Maintenance

J.E. Burge, D.C. Brown

Abstract: One of the many difficulties encountered while performing software maintenance is determining the impact of potential changes on what already exists. One way to address this difficulty is to give the maintainers access to the Design Rationale of the original system. This rationale would provide the intent behind the design and implementation decisions, as well as a history of design alternatives that have been considered. Unfortunately, this information is difficult and time consuming to capture and therefore is rarely available. Our approach to this problem is to look at how the rationale could be used. Rationale needs to be useful to provide incentive for its initial capture. We present SEURAT, a system that supports entry and display of the rationale as well as inferences over the rationale. It helps ensure that the reasoning given for modifications made during software maintenance is consistent with the designer's initial intent.

Keywords: design rationale; software maintenance; inference, argumentation

13.1 Introduction

Modifying working software that is currently in use is always a risky endeavor. It is very difficult to determine the impact of potential changes on what already exists. The problem gets even worse if the original developers of the software are not available or if the maintenance is turned over to an organization that did not initially design and build the software.

Some of these risks could be mitigated if the maintainers had access to the Design Rationale (DR) of the original system. DR documents the decision making process by capturing the intent behind the design and implementation decisions as well as a history of design alternatives that had been considered. The DR would include any assumptions made when developing the initial system and how they impacted the design. Assumptions can become invalid over time, which is a key reason for why software needs to continually evolve [19]. It is important to re-examine assumptions during maintenance to ensure that they still hold.

Unfortunately, most developers do not capture the rationale behind their decision-making. Recording rationale is seen as being time-consuming and disruptive. Documenting the decisions can impede the design process if decision recording is viewed as a separate process from constructing the artifact [14]. Developers are also reluctant to document their mistakes by keeping track of what they tried that did not work and are concerned about potential liability if a decision they record becomes responsible for a catastrophic failure of the system [9]. Another issue is that once the rationale is captured, will it be *used* and how, exactly, will it be *useful*?

We have chosen to address the use of and usefulness of rationale because the use of the rationale is what is ultimately needed to motivate its capture. Rationale has many potential uses throughout the software development cycle. At each stage of the process, it is useful to know the reasons behind the decisions made earlier. In addition, the act of recording the rationale can encourage developers to investigate alternative solutions and can support their selections with arguments. We feel that rationale is especially useful, however, during the maintenance phase. Rationale is valuable because even if the original developers of the system are available they may not remember all the details behind each decision made during a process that could span years. The usefulness, of course, is still bounded by what rationale has been captured and developers may still be reluctant to record all reasons for their decisions. We feel, however, that the value of the rationale outweighs its cost and that developing compelling uses for rationale is an important step towards motivating the developers to record it.

To investigate the uses of rationale, we have developed a prototype system, SEURAT (Software Engineering Using RATionale) [6], that provides both retrieval of, and inferencing over, rationale. The main focus has been on developing uses that support maintenance but SEURAT could be used during other development phases [12] as well. In this chapter, we will summarize our research into how rationale can be used to support software maintenance and how that can be done using the SEURAT system.

The remainder of the chapter is structured as follows: Sect. 13.2 describes related work, Sect. 13.3 describes how rationale can be used during several types of software maintenance, Sect. 13.4 describes the SEURAT system and how it represents, captures, presents, and inferences over the rationale, Sect. 13.5 summarizes the SEURAT evaluation, and Sect. 13.6 concludes the paper and describes future work.

13.2   Related Work

There has been significant work on capture, representation, and use of design rationale in the field of engineering design. Lee [18] has written an excellent survey of this work. The use of rationale for software development has been surveyed by Dutoit and Paech [11]. Potts and Bruns [25] created a model of generic elements in software design rationale that was then extended by Lee [17] to create Decision Representation Language (DRL), the basis of the RATSpeak representation used by SEURAT. Design Recommendation and Intent Model (DRIM) was used in a system to augment design patterns with design rationale [24]. This system is used to select design patterns based on the designers' intent and other constraints. WinWin [1] aims at coordinating decision-making activities made by various "stakeholders" in the software development process. Bose [2] defined ontology for the decision rationale needed to maintain the decision structure. The goal was to model the decision rationale in order to support decision maintenance by allowing the system to determine the impact of a change and propagate modification effects. Chung, et al. [10] developed an NFR Framework that uses nonfunctional requirements to drive the software design process, producing the design and its rationale.

There are also other systems that perform consistency checking. C–Re–CS [16] performs consistency checking on requirements and recommends a resolution strategy for detected exceptions. Reiss [26] has developed a constraint-based, semi-automatic maintenance support system that works on the code, abstracted code, design artifacts, or meta-data to assist with maintaining consistency between artifacts.

Lougher and Rodden [21] investigated maintenance rationale and built a system that attaches rationale to source code. Their approach differs from ours, however, in that they argue that maintenance rationale is very different from that captured during development and is not in the form of argumentation. Canfora et al. [7] also address maintenance rationale and break rationale into two parts: rationale in the large (rationale for higher level decisions in maintenance) and rationale in the small (rationale for change and testing). The focus on the rationale in the small is on *how* the change will be implemented but does not appear to focus on reasons behind implementation choices at a low level. They developed the Cooperative Maintenance Conceptual Model (CM^2) which is based on the QOC [22] argumentation format.

While the usefulness of rationale has not been studied in as much detail as the capture and representation, there have been some experiments performed. Field trials performed using itIBIS and gIBIS [9] indicated that capturing rationale was found to be useful during both requirements analysis and design, and that the process also helped with team communication by making meetings more productive. Karsenty [15] studied how DR could be used to evaluate a design. In this study, 50% of the designers' questions were about the rationale behind the design and 41% of those questions were answered using the recorded rationale. Bratthall et al. [3]

performed an experiment using rationale to assist in performing changes on two different systems. For one system, rationale was shown to be helpful in decreasing the time used to make the changes and improving the correctness of the changes but results were inconclusive for the second system.

13.3   Rationale for Software Maintenance

To determine how rationale can be used in software maintenance it is useful to look at what types of maintenance might be performed. There are a number of different classifications for types of software maintenance [8]. The three types that we address are corrective, adaptive (a combination of four of Chapin's types), and enhancive. We chose these types because they affect modifications to the source code.

Corrective maintenance involves correcting failures of the system [20]. Rationale can be useful in detecting the source of some types of failures. For example, if a failure occurs because an assumption is no longer valid, the rationale may, in some cases, help detect what parts of the design and code depend on the assumption being true. This would point out some places where changes are likely to be necessary. The rationale may also contain some possible alternatives that might be better candidates and, if selected, could fix the problem. It can also indicate if there are alternatives that should be avoided. Rationale can also be used proactively to find problems that may not have appeared yet – if a failure points to a decision made earlier it might be advisable to look at the reasons for making the decision and see if these reasons were important in other choices as well. This could indicate areas that might need changes to avoid future failures.

Adaptive maintenance involves making changes to the system that do not change the functionality seen by the customer. This is a combination of four of Chapin's types: groomative (improving elegance or security), preventive (improving maintainability), performance (improving performance), and adaptive (changing to account for different technology or resource use) [8]. The rationale can provide a guide to where improvements should be made. There are likely to be cases where decisions were made for reasons that are important in the short term but may require revision in the future. For example, a developer may choose the alternative that will be the fastest and easiest to code even though it may not be as desirable as other alternatives. The rationale can be used to look for decisions made for the sake of expediency and show what some of the better alternatives are so that the developers can consider those when updating the code.

Enhancive maintenance involves replacing, adding, or extending "customer-experienced functionality" [8]. It is important to ensure that the reasons used to make the enhancements are consistent with those used while developing the existing system. For example, if performance was important in the initial system, it should also be considered important when adding new functionality. It would be unfortunate if the new design choices resulted in significantly slower response time. Rationale can be used to check for any tradeoff violations that might be made by new additions to the system. A tradeoff violation would occur if there were system attributes where more of one meant less of another (such as flexibility versus development time) and the maintainer only considered one of the attributes when making a decision. Rationale can also be used to evaluate the strength of new design alternatives based on priorities set when the initial system was developed.

In all types of maintenance it is critical to "do no harm" to the working system. Rationale can be used to capture dependencies between the different alternatives considered. This would prevent developers from spending time implementing an alternative that is incompatible with earlier design choices.

13.4   The SEURAT System

We have developed the SEURAT system to support the use of rationale to assist with software maintenance. SEURAT presents the rationale to the maintainer and inferences over it to detect problems and inconsistencies within the rationale that may also indicate problems with the design. SEURAT also supports capture of rationale and fits into the RMS framework [12] by providing a Rationale Capture Component, a Rationale Retrieval Component, and a Rationale Representation Component (with the former two dependent on the latter). Our goal is to create a system that can be tightly integrated with existing development tools so that rationale capture and use can become a part of the development process, not something additional that is performed retrospectively after development is complete.

We have built the SEURAT system as a plug-in to the Eclipse Tool Platform (www.eclipse.org) so that it can be tightly integrated with an Interactive Development Environment (IDE). This allows us to connect the rationale with the code that it explains. This connection ensures that the software maintainers are aware of and use the rationale. The rationale is stored in relational database tables using MySQL.

SEURAT presents the relevant DR when it is needed and allows entry of new rationale for the modifications. The new DR will then be verified against the original DR to check for inconsistencies. There are two main types of checks that are made: structural inferences to ensure that the rationale is complete, for the decisions recorded, and evaluation, to ensure that the rationale is based on well-founded arguments. Of course, there is no way to ensure that all the designers' reasoning is recorded but SEURAT can check for omissions such as failing to select an alternative or selecting an alternative without any argumentation given.

Figure 13.1 shows SEURAT as part of the Eclipse Java IDE. SEURAT participates in the development environment in three ways: a Rationale Explorer (upper left pane), that shows a hierarchical view of the rationale and allows display and editing of it; a Rationale Task List (lower right pane), that shows a list of errors and warnings about the rationale; and Rationale Indicators that appear on the Java Package Explorer (lower left pane) and in the Java Editor (upper right pane), to show whether rationale is available for a specific Java element. The examples in this chapter come from a conference room scheduling system. Note that the screenshots are in color, making the icons much easier to distinguish on the actual SEURAT displays than when reproduced here in black and white.

This display design, which also reflects the architecture of the system, was chosen because it very closely parallels the Eclipse Java IDE. For example, the Rationale Explorer uses a tree view similar to that provided by the Java Package Explorer where items in the tree can be brought up in an editor by double-clicking on them. This tree format is also an appropriate one for showing the rationale argumentation and provides a high-level view of the rationale where the maintainer can choose how deep into the argumentation structure they want to go by "expanding" the rationale elements much like they would expand the view of Java files to show attributes and methods. The Rationale Task List was designed to be similar in appearance to the Tasks display provided by Eclipse. The Tasks display shows compilation errors and warnings about problems in the code while the Rationale Task List shows errors and warnings about problems in the rationale. The Java Editor used in SEURAT is the same as the one used in Eclipse. The Bookmark display is also the same except that SEURAT has added associations between alternatives in the rationale and elements in the code (files, classes, attributes, or methods) to the list. The maintainer can find the code mentioned in the bookmark by clicking on it and can find the rationale associated with code shown in the editor by moving their mouse cursor over the bookmark that indicates that rationale is present.

The software developer enters the rationale to be stored in SEURAT while the software system the rationale describes is being developed.

SEURAT supports this by providing rationale entry screens for each type of rationale element.

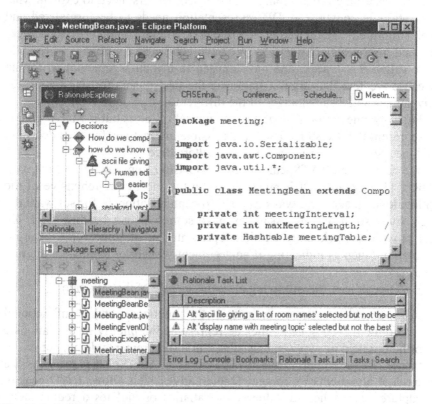

Fig. 13.1. SEURAT and Eclipse

SEURAT performs two main types of inferences over the rationale: syntactic inferences, which are concerned mostly with the structure (such as looking for missing relationships), and semantic inferences, which look at the content (such as evaluating the choices made). When problems are detected, they are displayed in two places: in the Rationale Explorer, as error and warning icons on the rationale, and on the Rationale Task List, which gives a more detailed explanation of what the problem is.

In the following sections, we will describe a subset of the capabilities provided by SEURAT and describe their use during software maintenance. The examples come from the rationale for a conference room scheduling system.

13.4.1 Representation

Before describing how rationale can be used, we first need to explain what our rationale contains. A DR representation needs to be formalized and well structured, as opposed to just free text, so that computer-based checking and inferences are possible. We have generated a rationale representation, called RATSpeak, and have chosen to use an argumentation format because we feel that argumentation is the best means for expressing the advantages and disadvantages of the different design options considered.

Each argumentation format has its own set of terms but the basic goal is to represent the decisions made, the possible alternatives for each decision, and the arguments for and against each alternative.

We have based RATSpeak on Lee's Decision Representation Language (DRL) [17] because DRL appeared to be the most comprehensive of the rationale languages and was designed to capture rationale for software design. Even so, it was necessary to make some changes because DRL did not provide a sufficiently explicit representation of some types of argumentation (such as indicating if an argument was for or against an alternative).

RATSpeak uses the following elements as part of the rationale:

- *Requirements* – these include both functional and nonfunctional requirements. They can either be represented explicitly in the rationale or be pointers to requirements stored in a requirements document or database. Requirements serve two purposes in RATSpeak. One is as the basis of arguments for or against alternatives. This allows RATSpeak to capture cases where an alternative satisfies or violates a requirement. The other purpose is so that the rationale for the requirements themselves can be captured.
- *Decision Problems* – these are the decisions that must be made as part of the development process.
- *Questions* – these are questions that need to be answered before the answer to the decision problem can be defined. A question can include the procedures or programs that need to be run or who should be asked to get the answer. Questions augment the argumentation by specifying the source of the information used to make the decisions (the procedure, program, or person).
- *Alternatives* – these are alternative solutions to the decision problems. Each alternative will have a status that indicates if it is accepted, rejected, or pending.
- *Arguments* – these are the arguments for and against the proposed alternatives. They can either refer to requirements (i.e., an alternative is good

or bad because of its relationship to a requirement), claims about the alternative, assumptions that are reasons for or against choosing an alternative, or relationships between alternatives (indicating dependencies or conflicts). Each argument is given an amount (how much the argument applies to the alternative, e.g., how flexible, how expensive) and an importance (how important the argument is to the overall system or to the specific decision).

- *Claims* – these are reasons why an alternative is good or bad. Each claim maps to an entry in an Argument Ontology of common arguments for or against software design decisions. Each claim also indicates what direction it is in for that argument. For example, a claim may state that a choice is NOT safe or that an alternative IS flexible. This allows claims to be stated as either positive or negative assertions. Claims also contain an importance, which can be inherited or overridden by the arguments referencing the claim.
- *Assumptions* – these are similar to claims except that it is not known if they are always true or whether they will continue to hold in the future. Assumptions do not map to items in the Argument Ontology.
- *Argument Ontology* – this is a hierarchy of common argument types that serve as types of claims that can be used in the system (e.g., Development Cost; Portability). These are used to provide the common vocabulary required for inferencing. Each ontology entry contains a default importance that can be overridden by claims that reference it. These arguments are tailored to the software development domain. A complete list of ontology entries can be found in Burge [4].
- *Background Knowledge* – this contains Tradeoffs and Co-Occurrence Relationships that give relationships between different arguments in the Argument Ontology. This is not the considered part of the argumentation but is used to check the rationale for any violations of these relationships.

Figure 13.2 shows the relationships between the different rationale entities.

RATSpeak provides the ability to express several different types of arguments for and against alternatives. One type of argument is that an alternative satisfies or violates a requirement. Other arguments refer to assumptions made or dependencies between alternatives. A fourth type of argument involves claims that an alternative supports or denies a Non-Functional Requirement (NFR). These NFRs, also known as "ilities" [13] or quality requirements, refer to overall qualities of the resulting system, as opposed to functional requirements, which refer to specific functionality. As we describe in [5], the distinction between functional and nonfunctional is often a matter of context. RATSpeak also allows NFRs to be represented as explicit requirements.

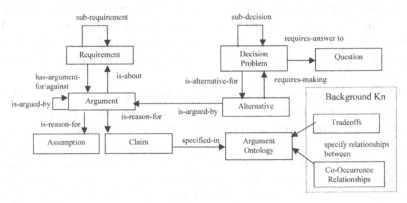

Fig. 13.2. Relationships between rationale entities

The RATSpeak representation describes the NFRs as part of the Argument Ontology. The Argument Ontology is a hierarchy of reasons for choosing one design alternative over another with abstract reasons at the root and increasingly detailed reasons towards the leaves. This is needed to provide a common vocabulary to support inferencing over the content of the rationale in addition to over its structure.

Figure 13.3 shows the top level of the Argument Ontology displayed in SEURAT.

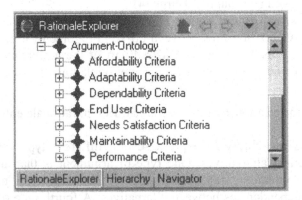

Fig. 13.3. Top level of argument ontology

Each of these criteria then has subcriteria at increasingly more detailed levels. As an example, Fig. 13.4 shows some of the subcriteria for Usability as displayed in SEURAT. The ontology terms are worded in terms of arguments: i.e., *<alternative>* is a good choice because it *<ontology entry>*, where *ontology entry* starts with a verb. The SEURAT system has been designed so that the user can easily extend this ontology to incorporate additional arguments that may be missing. With use, the ontology will continue to be augmented and will become more complete over time. It is possible to add deeper levels to the hierarchy but that will make it more time consuming for the developer to find the appropriate item when adding rationale.

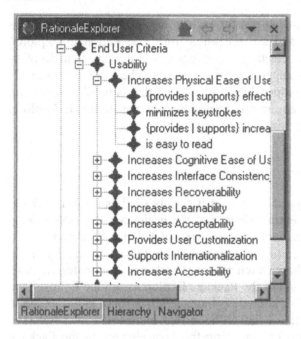

Fig. 13.4. Argument ontology for usability

Similar hierarchies have been developed for other high-level criteria in addition to Usability. One thing to note is that it is not a strict hierarchy – there are many cases where items contributing toward one criterion also apply to another. One example of this is the strong relationship between scalability and performance. Throughput and memory use, while primarily thought of as performance aspects, also impact the scalability of the system. In this case, and others that are similar, items will belong to more than one category.

13.4.2 Capture

The goal behind the development of SEURAT was to evaluate potential *uses* of rationale. While this shifted the focus away from capture, there still needed to be a way to capture rationale using SEURAT in order for it to become a complete system. SEURAT facilitates this by being tightly integrated with the IDE being used to write the code. The developer is more likely to be willing to record their rationale if they do not need to start an additional tool to do so.

Editing screens were developed for each of the different rationale items supported by SEURAT and are accessible from the Rationale Explorer. Each item is created by selecting a context-sensitive menu item from its parent. Capture is also supported by automatic checking for rationale completeness. If the developer does not enter all the required rationale for a decision there will be an error indicated both in the Rationale Explorer and in the Rationale Task List.

13.4.3 Presentation

Design Rationale is very useful even if it is only used as a form of documentation that provides extra insight into the designer's decision-making process [15]. SEURAT supports the viewing of DR by allowing the software developer to associate the rationale with the code and by using Rationale Indicators to show which pieces of code have rationale available. Figure 13.5 shows a portion of the Package Explorer from the Eclipse Java IDE where the presence of rationale is indicated by a small modification to the upper left-hand corner of the "J" icon that indicates a Java file. The associations are made by first selecting the Java element in the Package Explorer with the mouse, then selecting the alternative it implements in the Rationale Explorer, and then using a context-sensitive menu from the Rationale Explorer to indicate that the code and alternative are associated.

13.4.4 Inferencing

DR can provide even more useful information about the design and modifications made to the design if there is a way to perform inferences over it. Due to the nature of DR, the results may be in the form of warnings or information (as opposed to conclusions) that help the developer keep track of the development process and help the maintainer act carefully and consistently. This support for inferencing classifies SEURAT as a prescriptive, as well as descriptive [12], rationale system.

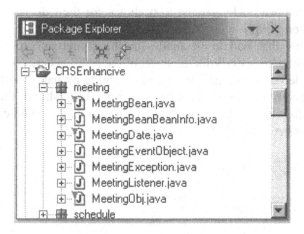

Fig. 13.5. Package explorer showing rationale associations

SEURAT supports four categories of inference: syntactic, semantic, queries, and historical. Syntactic inferences are those that are concerned mostly with the structure of the rationale. They look for information that is missing. Semantic inferences require looking into the content of the rationale to evaluate the consistency of the design reasoning. These inferences point out cases where less-supported decisions were made by evaluating each alternative based on the number and importance of the arguments for and against it. These are not logical inferences but calculations of the relative value of the alternatives. Rationale queries give the user the ability to ask questions about the rationale, and historical inferences use a history of rationale changes to help the user learn from past mistakes, rather than repeating them.

The following sections give a few examples of some of the SEURAT inferences. Each inference can have many uses but, for convenience, we have grouped them by the type of maintenance being performed.

Corrective Maintenance

As mentioned earlier, a common source of error in software is when an assumption that was true when the system was developed no longer holds. SEURAT provides the ability to capture these assumptions during development. When the assumption is no longer valid, the maintainer can disable the assumption. SEURAT then performs inferencing over all portions of the rationale that refer to the assumption and re-evaluates the affected alternatives. If the removal of the assumption means that there are selected alternatives that are no longer the best choice for their decision, the user will be informed of this.

One of the decisions that had to be made for the conference room scheduler system was how to specify the location of the room. There were two alternatives considered: combining the room and building names into a single string or specifying them separately. Figure 13.6 shows the Rationale Explorer after the assumption "customer normally combines room and building" has been disabled.

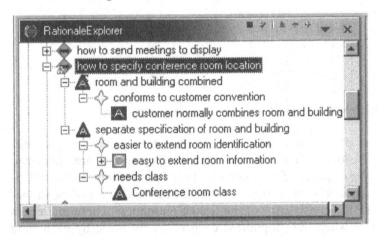

Fig. 13.6. Rationale explorer with disabled assumption

The assumption, denoted by an icon containing an "A," is changed to have a "D" in the upper right-hand corner showing it is disabled. When the decision is re-evaluated, a warning icon is shown because the selected alternative which combines them into one string (denoted by an "S" in the upper right-hand corner) is no longer the best supported (shown by the triangle icon with an exclamation point shown in the lower left-hand corner of the diamond shaped decision icon). The new warning is added to the bottom of the Rationale Task List shown in Fig. 13.7.

SEURAT also assists with corrective maintenance by providing access to any alternatives that have been either considered or implemented previously. This is useful both for pointing out what some possible corrections might be and to help make sure that a solution is not tried that was considered earlier and rejected. SEURAT also keeps track of dependencies between alternatives so that the user will be informed if they de-select an alternative on which another selected alternative depends.

For example, one response to the warning generated by the disabled assumption presented above would be to choose the other alternative, which separates out the specifications. This interacts with the alternative selected for the decision about how to represent the conference room. If the room and building need to be displayed separately then they need to be stored separately in a conference room class, not combined as a string. Since the string representation alternative is currently selected, choosing an alternative that depends on there being a class for the conference room will give an error. Figure 13.8 shows this error as indicated on the Rationale Explorer (by the square with a white "X" in the middle appearing at the lower left-hand corner of the diamond-shaped decision icon) while Fig. 13.9 shows the error in the Rationale Task List. The entire explanation is available in SEURAT by either scrolling or resizing the Rationale Task List window of the SEURAT display.

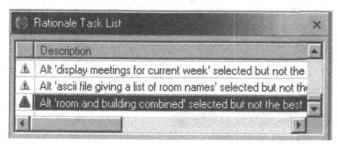

Fig. 13.7. Rationale task list with new warning

Adaptive Maintenance

SEURAT supports adaptive maintenance by providing an easy way to evaluate the impact of any of the arguments in the Argument Ontology on the design and implementation. This is done by allowing the maintainer to perform "what-if" inferencing to see what might happen if their design priorities change. In SEURAT, each claim or argument can inherit its importance from importance values that the developer stored in the Argument Ontology. Lowering the importance of an argument will point out decisions that should probably change if that argument is no longer an important design goal. Increasing the importance of an argument will point out decisions that need to change if the argument becomes a higher priority.

One argument that was used very frequently in the conference room scheduling system was the argument that choosing an alternative would reduce development time because it was easy to code. Changing the importance of that argument showed places in the system where there may have been better alternatives that were not chosen because they were perceived to be more difficult. One example was for a decision of how to display error messages. Figure 13.10 shows the Rationale Explorer with the rationale for that decision. The importance of "Reduces Development

Time" has been decreased and the decision now has a warning (indicated by a triangle icon with an exclamation point in it on the lower left-hand corner of the decision icon) because the alternative of displaying errors as a line of text on the main display is now not supported as well as the alternative to display them in a pop-up box. Figure 13.11 shows the warning displayed on the Rationale Task List.

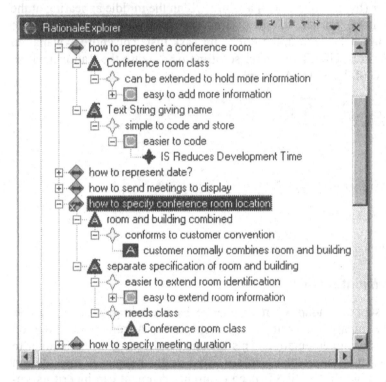

Fig. 13.8. Rationale explorer with decision error

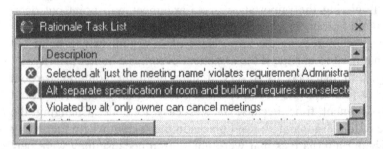

Fig. 13.9. Rationale task list explaining the error

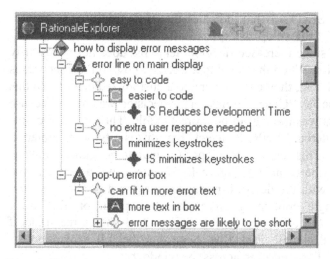

Fig. 13.10. Rationale explorer showing error message alternatives

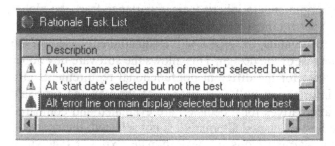

Fig. 13.11. Rationale task list with the warning

Enhancive Maintenance

The inferences mentioned earlier as supporting other maintenance types will also support enhancive maintenance. During enhancive maintenance it is important to ensure that the rationale for decisions made when extending functionality are consistent with the rationale for the initial version(s) of the system. One way to do this is to make use of the tradeoffs background knowledge stored in SEURAT. Tradeoffs are used to indicate that there are two characteristics of the software that oppose each other and should always appear on opposite sides of an argument. The elements in the trade-off are both items from the Argument Ontology described earlier. The new decisions made during enhancive maintenance should consider both sides of the tradeoff and be consistent with the designer's original intent.

An example of this in the meeting scheduler is the tradeoff between increased flexibility and reduced development time. The developer has added a tradeoff to SEURAT that indicates that if flexibility is increased, the amount of time to develop the system also increases. This is a non-symmetric tradeoff since increased development cost does not necessarily mean more flexibility. When the developer decided how to represent dates in the scheduling system, they chose to create a customized class to do this rather than using the Java Calendar class. This decision was made because the specialized class was thought to be more flexible. The cost of the new class was not considered. SEURAT detects that this is a tradeoff violation and warns the user. This lets the developer (or maintainer) know that the reasoning might not be complete. Figure 13.12 shows the rationale in the Rationale Explorer with the decision marked as having a problem (shown by the small triangle containing an exclamation point on the lower left-hand corner of the decision icon) and Fig. 13.13 shows the tradeoff explanation in the Rationale Task List. Note that the full explanation is available in SEURAT by scrolling across the window.

Another way that SEURAT can assist in checking decisions for consistency is by allowing arguments to inherit their importance from the global defaults stored in the Argument Ontology. If new decisions are made without overriding the defaults, SEURAT will evaluate them based on the same priorities as the rest of the design. This allows the software developer to define their priorities for the different nonfunctional requirements at a global level. This information will then propagate through the rationale when the different alternatives for a decision are evaluated and compared by SEURAT. If the best-evaluated alternative is not selected, the user will be informed both by warning icons in the Rationale Explorer (shown in Fig. 13.12) and warning descriptions in the Rationale Task List (shown in Fig. 13.13).

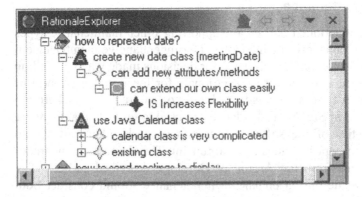

Fig. 13.12. Rationale for date representation

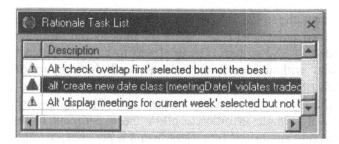

Fig. 13.13. Rationale task list with tradeoff violation

13.4.4 Rationale Retrieval

Both presentation of the rationale and inference over the rationale require that the system support efficient retrieval of the rationale elements. This is supported by storing the rationale in a MySQL database. The power of the relational database makes it possible for SEURAT to perform a number of different queries over the rationale. Several rationale queries, briefly mentioned in Sect. "Enhancive Maintenance", have been implemented in SEURAT. These include searching for entities of a particular type (requirement, decision, etc.); searching for requirements with a particular status (such as violated); searching for status messages that were overridden by the user so they could be re-enabled if necessary; and searching for claims and arguments where the default importance was overridden.

One interesting feature of SEURAT is the ability to look for common arguments occurring in the rationale. This can be valuable to the maintainers by giving them an overview of what the original developers thought was the most important criteria. The information can be shown for all alternatives or only for the selected ones.

13.5   SEURAT Evaluation

An initial evaluation was performed using SEURAT to assist with the three types of maintenance tasks described earlier: adaptive, corrective, and enhancive. Twenty subjects, a mixture of graduate students and industry professionals, were separated into control and experimental groups. The groups were divided in order to be balanced, based on their work experience and Java expertise. None of the subjects had used SEURAT before although some had attended research presentations describing the system. All were given a brief tutorial on how to use the system. The control group used the Eclipse IDE alone to perform the tasks while the experimental group used Eclipse with the SEURAT plug-in and rationale that had been recorded for the system. The goal was to compare subject performance with and without access to rationale and the support of SEURAT. In this case, the primary performance measure was the time required to complete the task, not the quality of the result. This is because the tasks were relatively simple in order to allow the experiment to be completed in a reasonable amount of time (less than 4 h per subject). The system being modified was the Conference Room Scheduling System described earlier. This was a Java program that had been originally written five years earlier as a meeting scheduler and had been adapted over the years to schedule meetings in multiple rooms. It had many characteristics of legacy code, such as using an obsolete version of Java and having been written by multiple developers.

Each subject was timed for each task with two times being measured: the time required to find the portion of the code that needed to be changed to complete the task and the time required to complete the task. The results were not statistically significant, suggesting that more experiments need to be performed, but the group using SEURAT did perform better on average than the control group. In addition, SEURAT helped nonexperts more than experts. We would expect this result to change when more challenging maintenance tasks are used. Figure 13.14 shows the average times for the delta (time to find change) and total time for each task.

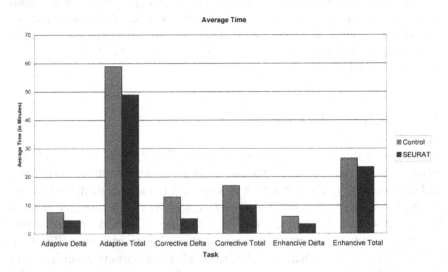

Fig. 13.14. Average times for each task

A survey asking the subjects who used SEURAT what they thought of it was also administered. These questions asked the subjects to give their opinion on a Likert scale where SA means Strongly Agree, A means Agree, U means Undecided, D means Disagree, and SD means Strongly Disagree. Figure 13.15 shows the summary of these results. The survey results indicated that the majority of the participants using SEURAT thought it was a useful tool and that it assisted them in performing the tasks given in the experiment.

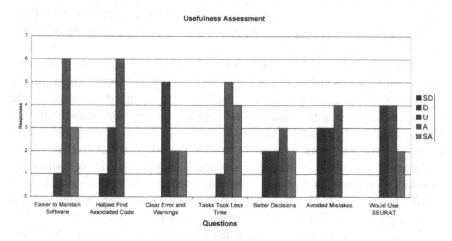

Fig. 13.15. SEURAT usefulness survey results

13.6 Conclusions and Recommendations

A way to help reduce the risk, and thereby the cost, of software maintenance is to give the maintainers insight into the intent behind the original design, i.e., the design rationale. This can be made even more useful if new changes can be checked to ensure that the reasoning behind new decisions is consistent with the original system. Conversely, if the goals of the system have changed, it would be useful if the maintainer could know how that would affect decisions made earlier.

To support DR use, we have developed the SEURAT system, which tightly integrates with an IDE to support the entry of, display of, and inferencing over the rationale. SEURAT allows the maintainer to take advantage of the knowledge captured during initial development to assist in maintenance changes, both by helping the maintainer figure out what needs to be changed and by verifying that new additions are consistent

294 J.E. Burge, D.C. Brown

with the designers original intent. This is helpful for all types of software maintenance.

One of the next steps planned for SEURAT is integration with additional tools used at different stages of the design process. These would include requirements tools, design tools, and possibly testing tools. This would allow us to continue to investigate the differences in the rationale generated and used at different stages in the development process. The goal is for SEURAT to be used during all stages of development by augmenting current development process and practice to support rationale capture and use. We also will address scalability concerns to transition SEURAT from a research prototype to a tool that can be used in full-scale software development.

We would also like to extend SEURAT to handle multiuser rationale. One thing that rationale can be very useful for is to capture the different viewpoints expressed by team members while making decisions [23]. It would be interesting to explore how capturing potentially conflicting information from different developers could be used in evaluating the design decisions. We also want to investigate systems that SEURAT could be interfaced with to assist in the capture process. Some possible sources of rationale are configuration management and problem reporting systems.

We feel that a system like SEURAT would be invaluable during software maintenance. The SEURAT system contributes a detailed, reusable list of reasons for making software decisions in the Argument Ontology. SEURAT then uses those reasons to support semantic inferencing to determine the impact of these decisions on the software system (and to promote consistency in the rationale). SEURAT also provides an integrated environment where rationale capture and use can be performed using the same tools that are used in development and maintenance. There are many benefits to having the design rationale available during maintenance but only with appropriate system support, such as that provided by SEURAT, can rationale live up to its full potential.

References

[1] Boehm B, Bose P (1994) A collaborative spiral software process model based on theory W. In: Proceedings of the International Conference on the Software Process, Reston, VA, pp. 59–68
[2] Bose P (1995) A model for decision maintenance in the WinWin Collaboration Framework. In: Proceedings of the Conference on Knowledge-based Software Engineering, Boston, MA, pp. 105–113
[3] Bratthall L, Johansson E, Regnell B (2000) Is a design rationale vital when predicting change impact? A controlled experiment on software architecture

evolution. In: Proceedings of the International Conference on Product Focused Software Process Improvement, Oulu, Finland, pp. 126–139

[4]   Burge JE (2005) Software Engineering Using design RATionale. Ph.D. thesis, Worcester Polytechnic Institute

[5]   Burge JE, Brown DC (2002) NFRs: fact or fiction? Technical Report WPI-CS-TR-02-01. Worcester Polytechnic Institute.

[6]   Burge JE, Brown DC (2004) An integrated approach for software design checking using rationale. In: Design Computing and Cognition '04, Gero J (ed). Kluwer Academic, Dordrecht, pp. 557–576

[7]   Canfora G, Casazza G, De Lucia A (2000) A Design rationale based environment for cooperative maintenance. International Journal of Software Engineering and Knowledge Engineering 10(5):627–645

[8]   Chapin N (2000) Software maintenance types – a fresh view. In: Proceedings of the International Conference on Software Maintenance, San Jose, CA, pp. 247–252

[9]   Conklin J, Burgess-Yakemovic K (1995) A process-oriented approach to design rationale. In: Design Rationale Concepts, Techniques, and Use, Moran T, Carroll J (eds.). Lawrence Erlbaum, Mahawah, NJ, pp. 293–428

[10] Chung L, Nixon BA, Yu E, Mylopoulos J (2000) Non-Functional Requirements in Software Engineering. Kluwer Academic, Dordrecht,

[11] Dutoit AH, Paech B (2001) Rationale management in software engineering. In: Handbook of Software Engineering and Knowledge Engineering, Chang SK (ed). World Scientific, Singapore, pp. 787–816

[12] Dutoit AH, McCall R, Mistrik I, Paech B (2006) Rationale management in software engineering: Concepts and Techniques. In: Rationale Management in Software Engineering, Dutoit AH, McCall R, Mistrik I, Paech B (eds.). Springer, Berlin Heidelberg New York, pp. 1–48

[13] Filman RE (1998) Achieving ilities. In: Proceedings of the Workshop on Compositional Software Architectures, Monterey CA

[14] Fischer G, Lemke A, McCall R, Morch A (1995) Making argumentation serve design. In: Design Rationale Concepts, Techniques, and Use, Moran T, Carroll J (eds.). Lawrence Erlbaum, Mahawah, NJ, pp. 267–294

[15] Karsenty L (1996) An empirical evaluation of design rationale documents. In: Proceedings of the Conference on Human Factors in Computing Systems. Vancouver, BC, pp. 150–156

[16] Klein M (1997) An exception handling approach to enhancing consistency, completeness and correctness in collaborative requirements capture. Concurrent Engineering Research and Applications 5(1):37–46

[17] Lee J (1991) Extending the Potts and Bruns model for recording design rationale. In: Proceedings of the International Conference on Software Engineering, Austin, TX, pp. 114–125

[18] Lee J (1997) Design rationale systems: understanding the issues. IEEE Expert 12(3): 78–85

[19] Lehman M (2003) Software evolution cause or effect? Stevens Award Lecture: International Conference on Software Maintenance, Amsterdam

[20] Lientz BP, Swanson EB (1988) Software Maintenance Management. Addison-Wesley, Reading, MA
[21] Lougher R, Rodden T (1993) Group support for the recording and sharing of maintenance rationale. Software Engineering Journal 8(6):295–306
[22] MacLean A, Young RM, Bellotti V, Moran TP (1995) Questions, Options and Criteria: Elements of Design Space Analysis In: Design Rationale Concepts, Techniques, and Use, Moran T, Carroll J (eds.). Lawrence Erlbaum, Mahawah NJ, pp. 201–251
[23] Peña-Mora F, Sriram D, Logcher R (1995) Design rationale for computer-supported conflict mitigation. ASCE Journal of Computing in Civil Engineering 9(1):57–72
[24] Peña-Mora F, Vadhavkar S (1996) Augmenting design patterns with design rationale. Artificial Intelligence for Engineering Design, Analysis and Manufacturing 11(2):93–108
[25] Potts C, Bruns G (1988) Recording the reasons for design decisions. In: Proceedings of the International Conference on Software Engineering. Singapore, pp. 418–427
[26] Reiss SP (2002) Constraining software evolution. In: Proceedings of the International Conference on Software Maintenance, Montreal, Que. Canada, pp. 162–171

14 The Role of Rationale in the Design of Product Line Architectures – A Case Study from Industry

J. Knodel, D. Muthig

Abstract: Product line engineering aims at an efficient production of variants mainly enabled by large-scale and systematic reuse of artifacts throughout all development phases. A product line's central artifact is its architecture that defines fundamental concepts, abstractions, and mechanisms that hold for all products of an organization (if successfully) for a long period of time. Therefore, key developers in organizations must fully agree on all decisions related to the definition of the product line architecture, as well as they must always reunderstand their rationales during architecture evolution. This chapter describes an industrial case of architecture evolution where one of the key mechanisms of an existing architecture was revisited as potential subject of change.

Keywords: architectural decisions; design; software architecture; product line architecture; product line engineering

14.1 Introduction

Nearly all organizations today develop and maintain more than a single product. Software organizations typically develop and maintain sets of similar products for different customers or market segments. This holds for organizations developing tailored systems individually for single customers, as well as for organizations developing products for mass markets. All products of an organization, however, are typically situated in the same application domain. Hence, these products share some common characteristics and thus can be viewed as a product line.

Product line engineering is the according development paradigm that differs significantly from traditional single system development. It aims at an efficient production of members of a product line mainly enabled by large-scale and systematic reuse of artifacts throughout all development phases (see [4] or [6] for definitions of software product line).

Product line engineering, thereby, analyzes the whole family of products rather than each product individually to systematically exploit commonality, proactively plan for variability and engineer variants efficiently. While performing these activities, the definition and design of the product line architecture is one of the most crucial activities. Since the architecture spans over the whole product line (including current products and envisioned or hypothetical products), the design decisions have a high strategic value and deep impact on the development organization. For this reason key decisions have to be well-founded and the rationales behind such decisions must be documented to be able to circumstantiate the decisions to the various stakeholders.

This chapter presents a real industrial case where an industry organization revisited one of the key mechanisms of an existing architecture while defining the product line architecture for its next generation of products. The evaluation of two alternative architectural concepts (i.e., a new candidate mechanism was identified to potentially replace a concept used in dozens of products of the previous generation), the common decision for one of the mechanisms, as well as the consistent documentation of the rationale was supported by an independent party, the Fraunhofer Institute for Experimental Software Engineering (IESE).

The approach followed during these activities is part of Fraunhofer PuLSE™ (Product Line Software and System Engineering, see Fig. 14.1)[15], which is presented in Sect. 14.2. Section 14.3 then describes the overall context by characterizing the analyzed TFT-panel product line – which is a main element in larger car radio and driver information systems product line – and, in particular, its Graphics component that is mainly impacted by the decision under consideration. Section 14.4 then presents details of the two alternative concepts, common design principles, and constraints on the decision. Finally, Sect. 14.5 concludes with experiences made and how the rationale approach additionally improved the quality of the product line architecture. Furthermore, impact and consequences of the decision are reflected with respect to both, concrete projects and the product line.

14.2 Approach

Fraunhofer's PuLSE method is a complete product line approach covering all life cycle phases and product line activities, as well as organizational issues or maturity models. Fig. 14.1 gives a complete overview of PuLSE components.

---

[15] PuLSE is a registered trademark of the Fraunhofer Institute for Experimental Software Engineering (IESE), Kaiserslautern, Germany (see [2] and [5]).

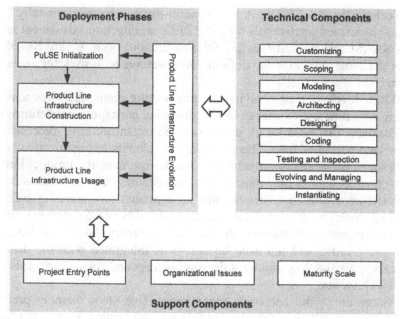

Fig. 14.1. PuLSE™ Overview

PuLSE-DSSA ("architecting") is one of its technical components covering all activities and aspects related to product line architectures (see [1]
for details). It is mainly concerned with the definition, evaluation, and evolution of product line architectures including the specification and execution of supporting reverse engineering activities. Overall, PuLSE-DSSA
follows an incremental approach (Fig. 14.2 depicts PuLSE-DSSA).

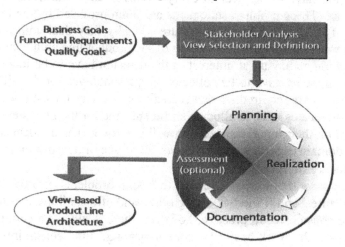

Fig. 14.2. PuLSE-DSSA

Technically, PuLSE-DSSA is a scenario-driven approach whereby "scenario" is defined consistently with the SEI's architecture assessment methods SAAM and ATAM (see [3] for a definition). That is, PuLSE-DSSA uses the same scenarios for defining architectures as it uses for assessing them.

While developing or evolving the architecture many decisions must be taken, which define or change the fundamental concepts, abstractions, and mechanisms that hold for all products of an organization (if successfully) for a long period of time. Therefore, key developers in organizations must fully agree on all decisions related to the definition of the product line architecture, as well as they must always reunderstand their rationales during architecture evolution. Consequently, an approach for managing architectural rationales is integrated into the general PuLSE-DSSA process, which is – consistently with the overall approach – scenario-based. Furthermore, it is prescriptive and intrusive because it is integrated with the decision process itself and thus improves decision makers and consequently also the final architecture.

Conceptually, the approach encompasses five steps, namely problem identification, criteria elicitation, evaluation and criteria assessment, decision making, and documentation:

- **Problem Identification**
  The first step is to identify, to understand and to learn about the problem that is linked to the decision. One the one hand one has to know the problem domain very well in order to be able to derive a sound decision, and on the other hand, the strategic goals that should be fostered by the decision have to be clear to everyone involved in the decision making process. These problem statements are often provided by the lead architect of the product line architecture. Usually they deal with crucial design problems in the development of the product line architecture. Other stakeholders having an interest in the decision have to be identified and their concerns have to be collected. Representatives for the different alternatives are required, so that each alternative has at least one advocate. The advocates have to allocate sufficient time for the next steps because based on their input, the decision will be drawn. The advocates are usually domain experts who promote or favor one of the solutions.
- **Criteria Elicitation**
  There are a lot of criteria related to design problems of product line architectures, and if there is enough time and effort, all these criteria have to be considered. In practice, however, there is always a certain project pressure, the work has to be done under tight time constraints, and the availability of experts and stakeholders is very limited. Therefore, it is

not efficient to assess all criteria. Some criteria have a higher priority than others, some cannot be influenced by the project management, developers or engineers, and again others are equivalent for all alternatives. For this reason, this step has the goal to elicit the important and determining criteria, which are based on the high-priority scenarios of PuLSE-DSSA. Usually those criteria divide the alternatives from each other. By eliciting these criteria, the effort for decision making is reduced, but nevertheless focused on the aspects that swing the decision. For each identified relevant criteria, one assessment table is created (see Table 14.1 for the template). Preceding the table, an explanation of the criteria is given, so that the meaning is recorded. The fill in of the table with content is done in the next two steps.

- **Evaluation and Criteria Assessment**

  Each advocate presents his favored solution to a moderator (the product line architect should participate here, but it is not mandatory) and explicitly addresses the criteria with pros and cons. The moderator records the arguments and the reasons why something is an advantage or a drawback. Furthermore, the moderator should actively participate by asking clarification questions. The same is done for other alternatives one after another. This results in filled criteria assessment tables, with the exception of the result cells.

- **Decision Making**

  The decision making step is conducted in a workshop where the product line architect and the advocates together discuss the arguments for the different alternatives. The goal of this joint workshop is to agree on the best alternatives with respect to the assessed criteria. The criteria are discussed stepwise so that obscurities are smoothed out and opposite views come to an understanding of all stakeholders. The result documents for each criterion, which of the alternatives is considered as best and for which reasons. In the end, the stakeholders agree on the best candidate based on the individual criteria. Furthermore, potential action items for future improvements for the selected alternatives can be identified by comparing it to other alternatives. The moderator summarizes the final decision and action items. Ideally, all involved stakeholders agree upon the decision.

- **Documentation**

  The documentation of the final decision and the aspects that led to it is an ongoing activity that accompanies all of the above steps. The final report contains the problem (i.e., why there was need to decide something), the alternatives (i.e., which solutions where considered for the decisions), the criteria (i.e., what was assessed, and what were the main drivers leading to the final decision), the arguments (i.e., what were the pros and cons of each alternative), and of course, the final decision, based on the important criteria (i.e., the selected solution), and derived action items (i.e., what has to be taken care of in future). The documentation can be used to inform other people of the organizational unit, and to put the decision on a firm footing, in case the higher management or other people challenge the decision made.

Table 14.1. Template for criteria assessment

	Alternative 1	Alternative 2
PRO	Alternative 1 – Pro Argument 1	Alternative 2 – Pro Argument 1
	Alternative 1 – Pro Argument 2	Alternative 2 – Pro Argument 2
CON	Alternative 1 – Con Argument 1	Alternative 2 – Con Argument 1
	Alternative 1 – Con Argument 2	Alternative 2 – Con Argument 2
→	Result and the derived decision based on the arguments	

The approach as described here usually has to be adapted slightly to the organization and the available resource constraints. Depending on the architectural design problem, the number of alternatives and elicited criteria can vary. The main goal is to consider only adequate alternatives (not everything is feasible or appropriate) and to select only criteria that are central to the decision (not everything is important or relevant).

14.3   The TFT-Panel Product Line

The case study was conducted in a larger context with the goal of the migration of an organization towards product line engineering. The activities were driven by the Fraunhofer Institute for Experimental Software Engineering (IESE) in cooperation with one of its industry partners. Product line concepts were introduced incrementally in pilot projects whereas one of the projects was concerned with the construction of the panels for 1-DIN navigation systems. 1-DIN navigation systems cover pure car radio products and navigation system products that provide route guidance solutions. Such a system supports different data mediums (e.g., CD, DVD,

HDD containing music data, voice data, video data, or navigation data) that constraint the features offered to the driver.

Fig. 14.3 depicts a sketch of the major components of a 1-DIN navigation system, which fits into the standard car radio slot of most vehicles. It is distinguished (physically and logically) between two embedded systems, the silver box and the panel, but both are closely related to each other. The silver box contains the CD or DVD drive, the navigation processor, and all other parts not related to the display. The panel has an integrated display for visualizing radio and navigation functionality. It consists of the display, different buttons and a physical interface to the silver box. Engineering panels deals not only with software, but also with aspects of hardware and mechanics.

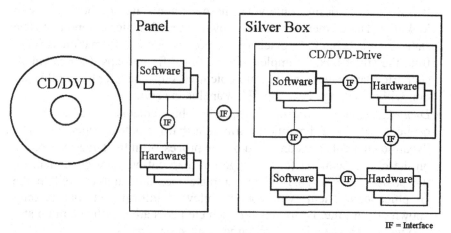

Fig. 14.3. Panel of the *1-DIN navigation system*

Most previous products of the company used monochrome panels only. For these monochrome panels, the complete information to visualize was provided by the silver box's processor. Such panels can be regarded as pure display facilities. On the contrary, the current development addresses a new type of panel, TFT-panels that become part of 1-DIN navigation systems. Such TFT-panels obtain some "intelligence" by having more computing power inside the panel. The larger context of the case study was to define a product line of TFT-panels that serves the current development and all upcoming car radio and navigation systems of the next years.

When developing the product line architecture for the TFT-panel product line, we reviewed the key concepts, mechanisms, and components of the existing monochrome panels, in order to decide, where reuse is possible and to identify the need of adaptation, and the need for the development of new components.

14.3.1 The Role of the Graphics Component

The Graphics component is one of the key components of the TFT-panel architecture. It is responsible for the communication between the silver box and the panel as well as for the composition and visualization of the correct output to the driver in the car. The interaction with the driver takes place via predefined masks. A mask is defined as a collection of graphical elements and positioning information (e.g., text fields, bitmaps, buttons, lists, labels). The graphical elements contributing to a mask are divided into two groups:

- *Static information relevant only for the Graphics component.* These elements are static and will not change once the system is in operation. It is decided at design time what these elements are and how they will look like. The elements are only known to the Graphics component. The static elements include placeholders for dynamic information coming from the silver box. Examples include fonts, fix bitmaps, fix text (in all supported languages), background pictures, etc. This graphical information will not change once the TFT-Panel is in service.
- *Dynamic sequence control information.* The elements related to the sequence control are dynamic information that is context dependent. The dynamic elements are computed by the processor in the silver box based on the current context (e.g., navigation map cut-outs are dependent on the position of the car). They complete the static masks held in the Graphics component with context relevant information that is only known at run time. Examples for such elements are headlines, radio station names, frequencies, town names, and street names.

14.3.2 Management and Transfer of Graphical Data

The main architectural driver for the Graphics component is the minimization of the data flow between panel and silver box. The communication interface is an SPI (Serial Peripheral Interface) protocol offering logical channels and encapsulating the hardware connection between the panel and the silver box.

Since the SPI bandwidth is limited, the amount of data transferred and the number of messages sent has to be kept as low as possible. This performance criterion was already the main architectural driver for the development of the Graphics component for the monochrome panels of previous products. Fig. 14.4 shows an example how the human—machine interaction (HMI is running in the silver box) communicates with the Graphics component (running in the panel) via the SPI interface. The messages received in the panel are parsed and decoded by the Graphics component, which then invokes basic painting functionality provided by a low-level Graphics API.

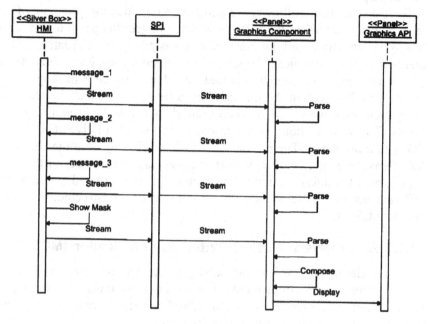

Fig. 14.4. Communication between Graphics component and Silver Box

When evaluating the existing architecture of monochrome panels for its reuse potential, the question arose whether the mechanisms applied for the Graphics components of monochrome panels (called Mask-Oriented Communication, MOC) can serve as well as a basis for the TFT-panel product line architecture. The suitability was questionable because of the required genericity of the Graphics component (i.e., to serve all variants of the product line), the uncertainty (i.e., to provide sufficient flexibility for anticipated changes), the changed technology (i.e., new type of panel, TFT instead of monochrome), and the increased computing power that enabled new features (i.e., a processor inside the panel to take over graphical drawing functionality). Some engineers of the company came up with an alternative mechanism for the Graphics component (called Framework-oriented Communication, FOC). Since this new mechanism was developed from scratch, no real project experiences were available, and the architects were doubtful about the reached maturity of the FOC mechanisms because only a first prototypical implementation existed at that moment. The project management became aware of the competing alternatives and demanded a justified decision, especially addressing the technical problems and product line aspects.

Both mechanisms followed the general communication principle of using a logical channel of the SPI protocol to connect the panel to the silver box. The data model of both mechanisms was practically the same, that is, identical sets of graphical elements were supported by both alternatives. The general mode of operation is that the silver box sends messages with parameters that contain the information to be displayed and the Graphics component then parses the messages and displays the right graphical elements. The next sections will introduce the two alternatives (MOC and FOC) in more detail. The mechanisms mainly differ in what messages are transferred (e.g., the content, format, the size, and the number of the messages), how the interpretation of these messages is addressed, and how the different masks visible to the driver are specified, constructed, managed, and maintained.

14.3.3 Alternative 1: Mask-Oriented Communication (MOC)

The first alternative, which was used for previous projects constructing monochrome panels, implements a mask-oriented transmission mechanism. The graphical elements are transferred one after another and then put together in the Graphics component of the panel.

Each message (e.g., ID_Tuner, ID_Frequenz "ffn") contributing to a mask is streamed directly over the SPI interface. The Graphics component then parses the messages and finally decodes the received information (i.e., selection of masks, references to bitmaps, replacement of dynamic information). Masks are composed in the panel's background until the message "ShowMask" is received by the Graphics component. The Graphics component then initiates displaying the graphical information by using services of the low-level Graphics API, which then triggers the display itself.

The masks are built with the help of a construction kit that consist of a row of graphical elements. Mask specifications are captured in header files that are shared between the HMI running in the silver box and the Graphics component running in the panel. Thus, the HMI can directly address all graphical elements of the masks. Data required by different products is configured via a tool that ensures consistency of data. The tool generates the header files, which typically have to be adjusted few by developers, and takes over consistency checks to ensure the match of the header files in the silver box and in the panel.

The MOC mechanism is realized in C and has been applied to several projects. The developers are experienced in applying this mechanism and know about the weaknesses and its pitfalls.

14.3.4 Alternative 2: Framework-Oriented Communication (FOC)

The FOC alternative follows the principle of object-oriented GUI frameworks as they are often implemented for desktop PCs. It is based on a model, view, controller pattern whereas the view resides on the panel and the controller on the silver box. The framework offers certain standard ways of constructing, modifying, manipulating, and managing graphical objects. The communication between silver box and panel takes places over abstract interfaces that are implemented by each graphical object.

In the FOC mechanism, a mask is decomposed into a hierarchy of structural elements. Terminals of the hierarchy are basic elements such as buttons, list boxes, text fields, text label used to represent concrete GUI objects, which are then combined with structural elements (e.g., columns, rows, widgets, buttons) to compose complex masks. Each of these objects is responsible for its own representation (a paint method invokes the respective functionality). Some masks require special extensions; these specialties are realized by inheritance from the most similar element. All graphical objects inherit from an abstract class and are positioned into a hierarchy relative to their direct parent.

Messages sent from the silver box to the panel are limited to the interfaces of the abstract classes. The parameter string contains the required information to display a mask, or to change the status of displayed graphical objects (e.g., scrolling, marking of an element). The realization of functionality is realized by the base elements (e.g., activation of a button within a button widget) from which other elements can inherit. The Graphics component takes over the serialization of graphical objects in order to ensure a smooth data exchange with the processor in the silver box.

Currently, there is no tool support for the construction of the masks, and no practical, real project experiences were available. The implementation of the FOC mechanism prototype was realized in the C++ programming language, and it adopted a lot of object-oriented principles.

14.4 Concept Assessment and Decision Making

We applied the concept assessment and decision making steps as described earlier to derive the decision whether to adapt the Mask-Oriented Communication or to extend the prototype of the FOC. IESE held the role of the moderator, while the advocates and the product line architect were part of the industry partner's development organization. The two alternative mechanisms were competing, each favored by different groups of developers. The concern of the product line architect was the question whether to reuse the "older" mask-oriented mechanism or to realize the "new" framework-oriented mechanism.

The impact of the decision to be made was regarded as critical by all stakeholders (including developers, architects, and project management) since the Graphics components of the TFT-panel product line is supposed to serve all upcoming variants of car radio and navigation system products in the future. The decision and the rationale leading to it have to be well understood and the key stakeholders have to fully agree on the decision made to pull together towards the success of the envisioned product line and its underlying architecture.

14.4.1 Assessment

In the criteria elicitation step, it became clear that the assessment criteria were threefold: technical constraints, general aspects, and product line related criteria. General aspects like available resources or time limitations were for both mechanisms the same, as well as some technical aspects like energy resource consumption or size of memory required on the TFT-panel. We left out these criteria and selected only relevant technical (e.g., SPI messages, tool support) and product line related aspects (e.g., support of new technologies, specialties and configurability, map processing, integration with car radio products).

One of the main criteria in favor for the FOC mechanism was the fitness towards very probable technology changes; the most likely are the introduction of touch screen functionality replacing mechanical buttons by on-screen soft buttons and the replacement of the SPI by another interface that enables faster communication between silver box and panel. The TFT-panel product line architecture has to be flexible toward these changes in underlying technologies. For instance, for the touch screen functionality, the Graphics component has to provide certain mechanisms to enable an input channel from the panel and to interpret the touch screen buttons pressed. Table 14.2 shows the arguments and the result of the assessment for the criterion "Fitness for New Technologies".

One of the main criteria for the MOC mechanism was the "Tool Support" criterion, as the excerpt in Table 14.3 shows.

Table 14.2. Assessment: Fitness for New Technologies

	Mask-Oriented Communication (MOC)	Framework-Oriented Communication (FOC)
P R O	replacement of the communication carrier: no rework is expected since transmissions are operating on a logical SPI channel	replacement of the communication carrier: no rework is expected since transmissions are operating on a logical SPI channel
		touch screen: direct mapping of buttons to graphical elements facilitates handling and resolution of touch screen events
	touch screen buttons: fixed button positions can be handled with a workaround	touch screen buttons: Position Change of buttons will require no rework in the silver box.
C O N	Touch screen: No support for touch screens events	touch screen: realization is not yet completely realized for this mechanism
	touch screen buttons: major rework in the silver box and the panel	touch screen buttons: some rework for in the panel
→	The FOC is the more future-proof mechanism since it already prepares the support of touch screen functionality.	

14.4.2 Results and Decision

We continued to evaluate both mechanisms in the same way for all criteria. The arguments (pro and con) for each criterion were recorded one after another, and the results were documented together with the rationales. Then all criteria were aggregated and put together to get the whole picture.

The result shows that the framework-oriented communication mechanism was rated overall as the better alternative in total. Furthermore, the FOC mechanism had higher ratings for the criteria with the highest priority. Those criteria were concerning product line related aspects (e.g., Fitness for New Technologies, Cross Organizational Product Line, Specialties and Configurability, Development Process Integration). Figure 14.5 depicts an overview on the assessed evaluation criteria. Overall, the FOC mechanism was evaluated to be more future-proof in this point than the already existing MOC. A side-effect was that all participants of the final workshop were able to understand each mechanism in detail, including advantages and drawbacks.

Table 14.3. Assessment: Tool support

	Mask-Oriented Communication (MOC)	Framework-Oriented Communication (FOC)
P R O	target group: HMI designers.	target group: developers.
	tool chain: Existing tools support simulation, header generation for masks, consistency checks	tool chain: existing tools support the simulation of panels
	experiences: applied in previous projects.	
C O N	tool state: development freeze in 1997, no experts are available, proprietary data format.	tool state: no tool support yet, high risk of new tool development (unclear impact on projects and organization).
	tool evolution: complex and costly tooling.	
→	although the tool support for the MOC mechanism has some weaknesses, it contributes significantly to the product development. Code generation and consistency checks support the management of a large number of product line variants.	

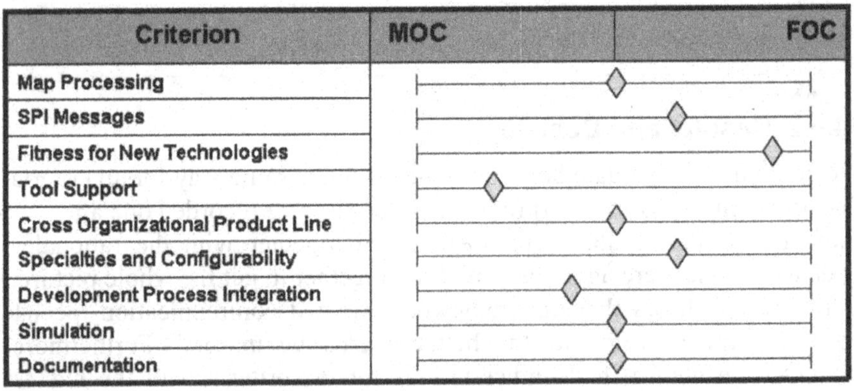

Fig. 14.5. Assessment results

Finally, all participants of the workshop (including both advocates and the product line architect) agreed on the framework-oriented communication mechanism as the solution to be implemented for the Graphics component of 1-DIN navigation systems with a TFT-panel. As shown in the for "Fitness for New Technologies" criterion, the advantages of the FOC mechanism outplay the MOC mechanism. In addition to the decision, some results of the workshop were identified as action items and improvements to the mechanism inspired by experiences with the other alternative.

The learning effects were gained by the common understanding of both mechanisms in detail. In particular, review dates were arranged to monitor the realization and implementation of the new mechanism. Tool support to comprise mask generation and consistency checks was identified as an important issue, and therefore development of tooling was scheduled. In addition to these product specific prerequisites, further architectural design goals for the TFT-panel product line have been documented. Both mechanisms were not yet adequate to address these architectural requirements. For instance, map processing features that generate the map within the panel and no longer in the silver box were not yet prepared, and the alignment of the overall development processes were an open issue with some impact on the TFT-panel product line. The rationales leading to the resulting Graphics component (and the reason for rejecting the other alternative) have been recorded. In case the decision is challenged by others developers or the higher management or other stakeholders not involved in the technical decision process, it can be defended based on the documentation. To retrace and understand the rationales for, and to be able to relate to the decision made, the criteria, the arguments and eventually the decision are documented. This enables as well a good start for new developers when learning about the product line architecture and its underlying concepts.

14.5 Conclusion

In the design of product line architecture the architects will face hard decision, where they are not immediately able to say one solution is more appropriate than the other. These decisions have a high impact and the consequences have to be covered not only by a single product, but the whole product line. When facing such a problem, it pays off to invest some effort and time to derive a sound, well-founded decision and to record the rationale and the reasons on which the decision is based on. Another benefit is the better understanding and the improvement of the quality of the selected solution gained in the workshop, where the alternatives are discussed in detail.

The approach we introduced here has not the goal to discuss all facets of the alternatives, but to focus only the key aspects that are of a high importance to the strategic goals of the product line and have a high architectural relevance. By reducing the evaluation criteria in this way, only limited effort is needed and the expert involvement can be reduced to a reasonable size.

One aspect in the introduction of product line engineering in the pilot project was to decide about the mechanism for the Graphics component. The two candidate mechanisms (MOC and FOC) were compared and assessed with respect to well-defined criteria. In examples, we highlighted the strengths and weaknesses of the two mechanisms, and the reasons for the decision were explained. The main reason for selecting the winning mechanism was its superior characteristic with respect to anticipated requirements of the envisioned product line. The common agreement (even the advocate of the other mechanism agreed on it) is a major gain for the next steps in the realization of the product line. A positive attitude toward the new mechanism was established and the stakeholders were highly motivated to start with the implementation. The explicit documentation of both mechanisms helped us to identify issues that must be addressed in the near future and topics that have to be addressed by the product line in a mid-term time frame.

The importance of rationale in product line architecture is critical since the product line architecture is the foundation for all derived variants. Next to putting the decision on a firm footing, the whole development team (and new members) can learn on the one hand about the design problem faced and the potential alternatives, and on the other hand about the reasons that lead to the decision made. By documenting it, the decision serves as well as justification in case the higher management or other architects challenge the decision at a later point in time. The approach helped to select the FOC mechanism and the experiences with this mechanism so far are very promising.

References

[1]   Bayer J, Forster T, Ganesan D, Girard J-F, John I, Knodel J, Kolb R, Muthig D (2004) Definition of Reference Architectures based on Existing Systems, Fraunhofer IESE Technical Report (IESE-Report 034.04/E), Kaiserslautern
[2]   Bayer J, Flege O, Knauber P, Laqua R, Muthig D, Schmid K, Widen T, DeBaud J-M (1999) PuLSE: A methodology to develop software product lines, in: Proceedings of the Fifth ACM SIGSOFT Symposium on Software Reusability (SSR'99), ACM, Los Angeles, CA, USA, May, pp. 122–131
[3]   Clements PC, Northrop L (2001) Software Product Lines: Practices and Patterns, SEI Series in Software Engineering, Addison-Wesley, Reading, MA, August
[4]   Clements P, Kazman R, Klein M (2002) Evaluating Software Architectures: Methods and Case Studies, Addison-Wesley, Reading, MA
[5]   PuLSE   (2005)   Product   Line   Software   Engineering http://www.iese.fraunhofer.de/PuLSE/, Fraunhofer IESE, Kaiserslautern
[6]   Weiss DM, Lai, CTR (1999) Software Product-Line Engineering: A Family-Based Software Development Process, Addison-Wesley, Reading, MA<AQ: Refs. [2,5] are not cited in text>

15 The Role and Impact of Assumptions in Software Engineering and its Products

M. M (Manny) Lehman, J. Fernández-Ramil

Abstract: This chapter presents the reasoning underlying a Principle of Software Uncertainty, first stated in 1989 and of primary significance in E-type software, that is, software operating in the real-world. The Principle states that the validity of the execution results of an E-type program cannot be absolutely predicted. This is so because every E-type program reflects an unbounded number of assumptions about the application it addresses, the domains in which it operates and so on. Invalidation of assumptions is one of the drivers of the need for continual software evolution and a major source of uncertainty. Techniques such as those devised by researchers in the Design Rationale field can help to mitigate such uncertainty by capturing, reviewing and generally managing assumptions embedded in the design and implementation of E-type programs.

Keywords: degradation of assumptions, E-type software, principle of software uncertainty, software evolution, SPE program classification

15.1 Introduction [16]

When computers first came into general use in the 1950s and 1960s it was assumed that, after correct implementation of a computer program, the outcome of execution in the real world that did not violate the limits set by their specification, would be absolutely predictable. However, the continual validity of the results of execution cannot be absolutely guaranteed. This is the inevitable consequence of the unbounded number of properties of E-type applications and of the real world in which such systems operate and the inevitability of changes in all of these. This fundamental observation has been termed the Principle of Software Uncertainty [14–17,21,23]. The uncertainty referred to is a consequence of assumptions made, explicitly or implicitly, that become invalid during the software process as a consequence of changes in the application or the real world [19]. The embedding of assumptions stems from a number of causes [19] when software is created, solved, or used. This chapter provides background and stresses the importance of their *management* by all those involved in these activities. This is a topic that researchers, in particular those looking into Rationale Management in Software Engineering, and all those involved with soft-

---

[16] The present chapter is a revised and updated version of an earlier paper [23].

ware, must take into account. This chapter refers to fundamental aspects of software, considers the reasons why assumptions are inevitable, and provides a justification for the Design Rationale field, discussing issues that, at best, are only addressed superficially, more often totally ignored.

Section 15.2 sets the scene with an overview of types of software. Section 15.3 discusses why assumptions, known and unknown, are inevitably reflected in E-type software which, as a consequence, is the most affected by uncertainty. Section 15.4 presents the Principle of Software Uncertainty. Section 15.5 provides examples of projects affected by invalid assumptions. In Section 15.6 practical recommendations and topics for further work are suggested. Section 15.7 concludes the paper.

15.2   SPE Classification Scheme and its Implications

In order to explain why assumption are inevitably reflected in software and to derive implications, this chapter briefly presents an *SPE program classification* scheme previously described and discussed, e.g., [11,12,20,28].

S-type programs (S for *specification*) implement solutions to problems that can be completely and unambiguously, possibly formally, specified so that, in principal at least, a program that addresses them can be proven correct with respect to the specification. Issues of programming elegance and efficiency are an orthogonal concern. These programs solve problems that are fully defined in a closed, abstract domain. S-type programs represent the domain extensively discussed in the Computer Science literature on formal methods, e.g., [5,8,30,32,34,35].

S-type programs stand in sharp contrast to those termed E (E for *evolutionary*). The type E addresses real-world computer applications and/or supports real-world activity. Once installed in their operational domains, they operate within and interact with them [12] and the results of execution depend on real-world properties. Such programs have become pervasive at all levels of human activity. Thus they are of universal interest. The type does present challenges in a number of areas. In the present discussion, the concern is the extent to which one can rely on their satisfactory behavior in execution. E-type software address applications that cannot, as required for demonstrations of absolute correctness, be completely and unambiguously specified though individual parts can be. Any formal specification of an E-type program would, at best, be only *partial*. Moreover, even where a partial specification is available, the proof of correctness would be incomplete because it could not address the unlimited properties of the real-world domain. However, correctness demonstration of even those parts of a program that can be fully and precisely specified is not likely to be the major interest to real-world users or other stakeholders, who, in any case, often hold multiple, sometimes inconsistent, viewpoints or requirements [7]. Some increase in confidence that the software as a whole will satisfy its stakeholders may result from a partial demonstration that parts of the program are correct with respect to their individual specification. The concern of stakeholders in general and users in particular will, however, in general be with the results of execution in the real-world. These are applied and assessed in the context of problems being solved or applications being pursued in the operational domain. What matters, is their validity and applicability and that of the consequential behavior when outputs are used. Its determination will depend, in part at least, on criteria for satisfactory execution. These will have been explicitly stated or may be considered intuitive in terms of what is required or desired. Such criteria are the ultimate determinant of software acceptability in the real-world.

In discussing uncertainty in software it is necessary to consider the obstacles to complete and unambiguous specification of real-world applications. Some arise from the fact that the domains involved are essentially unbounded in the number of their properties and that many of these are subject to change, some as a consequence of installation or use of the system. Moreover, when humans are involved in system operation, issues such as the unpredictability of individual human behavior also make formalization difficult or even impossible. Correctness, in the formal sense, is meaningless in the E-type context. One can merely consider how successful the system is in meeting its intended purpose. Conventionally, E-type program development is initiated by means of requirements elicitation, e.g., [27]. However, as will be seen, only parts of the statement of requirements, mathematical functions for example, can, at best, be fully and precisely described, defined and formalized. As remarked earlier, the criterion of correctness is replaced by concern for validity or acceptability of the results of execution in real-world application. If results are unsatisfactory in the context of the purpose for which the program was developed and executed, the system is likely to be sent back for modification. Whether the source of dissatisfaction originates in system conception, specification, software architecting (high level design), low level design and/or implementation is, in the context of the present discussion, not relevant.

Since the real-world and activities within it are dynamic, always changing, such changes are not confined to the period when the system is developed, accepted and first used. Similar choices and the need for action will arise throughout the system's active lifetime. The system must be continually evolved, adapted to a changing real-world and, in particular, to application and operational domain properties, needs and opportunities [10]. The changes may be the result of exogenous (e.g., [25]) or installation and usage changes, happenings that change the operational domain, the application implemented and/or the activity supported. As already stated *evolution is intrinsic to E-type systems and inevitable.* This is illustrated in Fig. 15.1 which presents a simplified, high level, view of the software evolution process as a *feedback system* [18]. In Fig. 15.1, the origin of an application is traced back to the activities of conceptualization, experimentation, and interaction between stakeholders which lead to the definition of an application and specification of software to address it. Moreover, precise definition of a problem requires bounding to establish its scope and limits. This, in itself introduces a whole series, in fact an unbounded number of assumptions, namely that each of the properties that lies outside the bounds is irrelevant at the required level of precision. Development of the software then starts. Though many different processes can be followed, for the sake of simplicity, Fig. 15.1 shows a sequential process. At the end of the first iteration the operational program is deployed in the application domain, effectively changing the domain (that output changes input is basic to the feedback concept). Exogenous changes can and will influence the domain (e.g., [25]). The cloud represented by a segmented line indicates the limits of the domain which are subject to variation over time. Domain changes are likely to trigger the need for program changes and so lead to program evolution indicated by the central circular arrow. A more detailed view would show the evolution process to be a multilevel, multiloop, multiagent feedback system, e.g., [1,11,18].

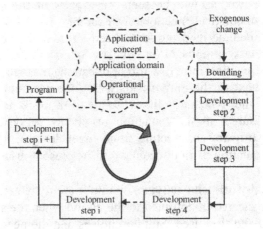

Fig. 15.1. Installation, operation and evolution

The original scheme included a third, type P (P for *problem*). For this type the program, the problem itself can be precisely defined. In theory a correct solution exists but circumstances prevent the development of a program that yields a correct solution. A chess playing program can be an example of this type. In theory, the program could calculate all possible future moves, from a given step in the game, and find out the next best move. However, computer memory and processing limitations would limit the number of moves forward a chess playing program could evaluate and how many moves could be evaluated at each stage. This represents a limit arising from an execution domain bound and suggests that such a program should be classified as of type E. In fact all P type programs may be classified as of type S or E. Hence the P type is redundant and was abandoned. However, recent work [4] has redefined type P and reinstated it in the classification scheme.

The S-type program concept is of help in clarifying the practical usefulness of concepts such as *complete specification, correctness,* and *verification.* Examples of programs of this type that are studied, and even used, in isolation are often described as toy programs. Their principal value is illustrative. However, a system component can often be completely and unambiguously specified, so be considered as of type S. The fact that its properties are mathematically verifiable, that the component can be shown to be correct with regards to a formal specification, indicates, to certain extent, the contribution it can make to overall system behavior. The more system components can and are formally described the greater their contribution to likely system satisfaction. However, the specification of the problem solved by such components, though complete and precise in themselves, must, as discussed further below, still reflect assumptions about the application and the domains within which they execute. Once integrated into its E-type host system, that component becomes part of the execution domain. Uncertainty in the validity of system behavior may then reflect back into component behavior. Hence, even if, in isolation, components are of type S, they acquire E-type properties once integrated into and executed within the E-type system and its domain.

The S-type property can make a contribution to achieving required validity of system behavior. It cannot guarantee the impact of that behavior in the encompassing domain. Nevertheless, it has a vital role to play in system building that will become ever more important as the use of components, COTS and reuse becomes more widespread. Knowledge of component properties and of assumptions made, explicitly or implicitly, during their conception, definition, architecting and design, implementation and testing, whether ab initio development for direct use, as a COTS offer, or development for in-house reuse, is vital for subsequent integration into a larger system. It has long been recognized that formal specification is a useful tool for recording, revealing, and understanding program behavior [30,32,34]. It would appear desirable for COTS, reuse and product-line units to be specified and processed as S-type programs even though they are to be used as bricks in E-type systems.

The S-type concept is also significant for other reasons. Development of elemental units for integration into a system is normally assigned to one individual, or to a small group. The activity they undertake generally involves assumptions, conscious or unconscious, that resolve on-the-spot issues that arise as the design, code and/or documentation is evolved. Adopted resolutions of issues will generally be based on time and space-local views of the problem and/or the solution being implemented and may well be at odds with the design or implementation of other parts of the system. Even when justified locally, the assumption(s) for such resolution will be reflected in the system and can become a future source of failure, a defect, changes in, for example, the application domain or other parts of the system. Assumptions are the seeds of uncertainty. In order to minimize this it has been suggested that, wherever possible, work assignments to individuals, whatever their function, should be of type S [12]. Application of the S-type program concept can simplify management of the potential conflicts, limit, and control the implanting of assumptions which arise when groups of people implement large systems, with individuals taking decisions under limited information and communication with other implementers and stakeholders. Basing work-assignments to individuals or small groups on a formal specification strictly limits their freedom of choice. It mitigates the risk of situations that force local decisions that are candidates for subsequent invalidation. Mitigates but does not remove, since unforeseen situations that arise later may again lead to local decision taking. Working practice should then, however, involve appropriate changes to the formal specification and, ideally, some form of assumption recording and their regular review [22].

Even S-type bricks, and software component technology, in general, have limitations. No matter how detailed the definition when an S-type task is assigned, issues demanding implementation-time decisions will still be identified by the implementer(s) during each step of development. In principle, they must be resolved by revision of the specification and/or other artifacts (e.g., design, documentation). However, explicit or implicit, conscious or unconscious adoption of assumptions by omission or commission will inevitably happen. Even if conscious they may remain unrecorded and are likely to be based on a limited view of the system as a whole and of its intended application. Above all, they may eventually be forgotten. Moreover, with the passage of time, and application and domain changes that are, generally, inevitable, some of these assumptions are likely to become invalid. Thus even S-type bricks carry seeds of uncertainty that can trigger invalid results. But, though it does not eliminate uncertainty, their use reduces the likelihood of failure, uncertainty at the lowest level of implementation, where sources of incorrect behavior are most difficult to identify. But overall the assumption issue is, as described in the Sect. 15.3, inescapable and a major source of E-type program uncertainty.

15.3   E-type Programs and the Role of Assumptions

The remainder of this chapter considers one aspect of the lifetime behavior of E-type software and applications. Underlying the phenomena to be considered is a view, Fig. 15.2, of the relationships between a program, its specification and the application it implements or supports. This view is a direct application of the mathematical concepts of *theory* and *models* in the software context [13,31,32].

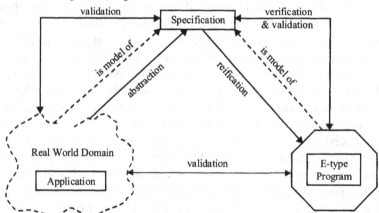

Fig. 15.2. The "Real-world/Specification/Program" relationship [13,20]

Though not indicated in the figure, a problem specification is also recognized by some as a theory of the application in its real-world operational domain [31] obtained, for example, by an abstraction process. It may, for example be presented as a statement of requirements, with formal parts where possible. Conversely, the real-world and the program are both models of that theory, that is, of the specification. Programs may be achieved by a *reification* process including successive refinement [35] or by other methods. Program elements formally specified should be verified and the program, in part and as a whole, validated against the specification and ultimately, against the application in its operational domain. This is intended to ensure that, within bounds set by the specification and to the extent to which the validation process covers the most likely states of the operational environment, the program will meet the purpose of the intended application. Validation is not a once-only activity. It must be repeated, in whole or part, whenever changes are subsequently made to the program to maintain the validity of the real-world/specification/program relationship.

The real-world per se and the bounded real-world operational subdomain have an unbounded number of properties. Since a statement of requirements and a program specification are, of necessity, finite an unbounded number of properties will have been excluded. Such exclusions will include properties that were unrecognized or assumed irrelevant with respect to the sought-for solution. Every exclusion implies one or more assumptions that, explicitly or implicitly, by omission or commission, knowingly or unknowingly become part of the specification. The conscious and unconscious bounding of the latter, of functional content and its detailed properties during the entire development process, determines to a great extent, the resultant unbounded assumption set. It will be up to the subsequent verification and validation processes to confirm the validity of the set of known assumptions in the context of the application and its operational domain. This cannot be done directly or completely, since, as already indicated, they are unbounded in number and mostly unknown.

The issue of assumptions does not arise only from the relationship between the specification and the intended application in its domain. The reification process also adds assumptions. This is exemplified, for example, by decisions taken to resolve issues not addressed in the specification which implies that, in generating the specification, they were overlooked or considered irrelevant. Moreover, the abstraction and reification processes are, generally, carried out independently and assumptions adopted in the two phases may well be incompatible. Real-world validation of the operational program is, therefore, necessary.

Figure 15.2 expresses the need for the program and the specification to be periodically (ideally continually) validated with respect to the real-world domain. A desirable complementary goal is to maintain the specification as a true abstraction of the real-world and the program. *Testing* over a wide range of input parameters and conditions is a common means for establishing the validity of the program. But the conclusions reached from tests are subject to Dijkstra's stricture [5], that "… testing can only demonstrate the presence of defects, not its absence". In a dynamic world, test results are, at most, valid at the time when the testing is undertaken or in relation to the future as then foreseen and taken into account during the design of the test. The overall validity of the assumption set relates to real-world properties at the time of validation.

Specification validation seeks to demonstrate that if precisely implemented, the system will satisfy the purpose of the application. Since the real-world is dynamic, periodic validation, in whole or in part ensures, inter alia, that, as far as possible, assumptions that have become invalid are fixed. Assumptions revealed by analysis failure or change analysis, must be included in the "known set" for subsequent validation.

As illustrated in Fig. 15.3, assumption relationships between the three entities, the specification, the application in its real-world domain and the program are mutual.

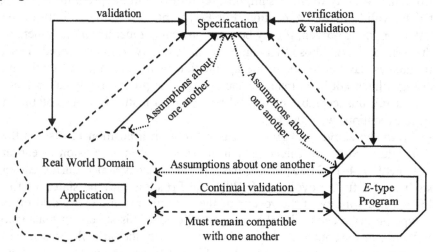

Fig. 15.3. The role of assumptions

The specification is necessarily based on assumptions about the application and its real-world operational domain because the latter are unbounded in the number of their properties and the specification is bounded. Moreover, in general, the application has potential for many more features than can be included on the basis of available budgets and the time available to the intended completion point. Hence, the specification also reflects assumptions about the application and implementation. Similarly, as they pursue their various responsibilities, system implementers will make interpretations and assumptions about the specification, particularly in its informally expressed parts. And, probably to a lesser extent, those responsible for developing the specification will make assumptions about the program, its content, performance and the system domain (human and hardware) in which it executes. *To the extent that assumptions are recognized and fully understood, attempts will be made to validate both individual assumptions and the mutual compatibility of the set. But those that have been adopted unconsciously or arise from omission cannot, in general be addressed.* Nor will validity bounds have been determined or even recognized. All these factors represent sources of assumptions reflected in the program and that may become invalid as the real-world changes.

15.4   A Principle of Software Uncertainty

Continual validity of the assumption set reflected in the program is essential for valid program execution. For E-type programs, the validity of the latter cannot be proven, if only because one cannot identify *all* members of that set. And even those that can be identified may become invalid. Thus, if changes have occurred in the application or the domain and rectifying changes have not been made in the system, the program may display unsuccessful, unacceptable or invalid behavior no matter how acceptable or valid executions were in the past.

Given the above background, we are now in a position to discuss the Principle of Software Uncertainty in its current form, a revision of earlier statements [14–17,21,23] on the basis of insights developed during earlier studies of software evolution [6,20]. The Principle may be stated as follows: "The validity of the results of the execution in the real-world of an E-type program cannot be absolutely predicted". This statement makes no reference to the source of the uncertainty. Clearly the possible presence of assumptions, known or implied, is sufficient to create uncertainty. There may be other uncertainty sources [19]. Additional remarks with regards to the interpretation of the Uncertainty Principle are provided in [19].

Use of the terms *acceptable/valid* and *unacceptable/invalid* in the statement is not intended to reflect individual or collective human judgment about the results of execution, though such judgment is certainly an issue, a possible source of uncertainty. The terms are intended to relate to the issue whether the results of execution fulfill the objective purpose of the program. The Principle is stated in terms of acceptability/validity rather than satisfaction to avoid any ambiguity which might arise from the mathematical meaning of *satisfy* [29] which, in the Computer Science context is used to address the relationship between a formal specification and a program which has been verified with respect to it.

Though not the only source, there are sound reasons to believe (see discussion in Sect. 15.3) that assumptions are the main underlying source of software uncertainty as reflected by the Principle of Software Uncertainty. Hence the latter indicates a need for assumption management. The original work and its extensions since indicates that the study of assumptions and how they may, or rather must, be determined, managed and controlled is vital to the future of a society that is becoming ever more dependant on software.

15.5   Examples of Invalidation of Assumptions

Given the reasoning that underlies its formulation it might be thought that the Principle is a curio of theoretical interest but of little practical value. Consider, for example, the statement that a real-world domain has an uncountable number of properties and cannot, therefore, be totally covered by an information base of finite capacity. The resultant incompleteness implies an uncountable number of assumptions that underlie use of the system and impact results achieved. The reader may well ask, "so what?" Clearly, the overwhelming majority of these assumptions are not relevant in the context of the software in use or contemplated. Neither do they have any impact on behavior or on the results of execution. It is, for example, quite safe to assume that one may ignore the existence of black holes in outer space when developing the vast majority of programs. It will certainly not lead to problems unless one is working in the area of cosmology or, perhaps, astronomy. On the other hand, after a painful search for the cause of errors during the commissioning of a particle accelerator at CERN, *a tacit assumption that one may ignore the influences of the moon for earth bound problems* has already been shown to be wrong when it was discovered that, as a result of the increased size of a new accelerator, an earlier assumption by default, the gravitational pull of the moon was a basic source of experimental error [3]. Another example: on June 4th 1996, the Ariane 5 rocket with a payload of four satellites and at a total cost of USD 500 million was destroyed by a remote command issued by the ground controller soon after being launched. This was the maiden flight (501) of the Ariane 5 rocket. The investigative board determined that an inadequate handling of an exception by the Inertial Reference System computer (SRI) software triggered the chain of events which eventually led to the rocket loss. Part of the software for Ariane 5 was reused from Ariane 4, the previous version of the launcher. *However, the two rocket versions have different requirements. Ariane 5 requirements were assumed to be correctly handled by the SRI software.* During ascension, one software module stopped computing meaningful results. This triggered an exception, which was not properly handled, leading to the shut-down of the SRI computers, the loss of rocket's ascension control and to a ground controller command to destroy it [26,28]. Many more examples [9,19] could be cited as examples of software or system failure ultimately due to the invalidation of reflected assumptions. The examples suggest that assumptions are of different types, but this is a matter for future research.

The conclusions that underlie the foregoing discussion were largely reached during the FEAST (Feedback, Evolution, And Software Technology) [6,24] studies. In particular, they revealed that continual evolution is inevitable for real-world applications. The empirical study [6] of a number of evolving E-type software have indirectly reinforced the reasoning that led to formulation of the Principle of Software Uncertainty as here stated. Unfortunately, sufficient relevant data, such as histories of fault reports relating to the industrial collaborators' systems, to permit even initial meaningful estimate of the degree of satisfaction or acceptability of stakeholders involved with the systems studied, were not available. It was, however, clear that continual change of portions of the software was present in all the systems observed, and that a portion of such changes addressed problems caused by invalidation of reflected assumptions.

15.6 Practical Approaches and Recommendations

The previous sections of this chapter have discussed why assumptions are inevitable and unbounded in number and the consequences of their presence: degradation of the assumption set reflected in software, in its widest sense, represents a major societal threat resulting from the ever wider, more penetrating and integrated use of software. The Principle provides a justification for the need of specific tools and technologies for rationale management in software engineering, including assumption recording, and, more generally, for uncertainty and risk management, particularly for long-lived critical software applications where the risks and penalties of assumption invalidation is the highest. There is room here for method and process research, development, and improvement, for finding out exactly how assumptions might be captured as part of the Design Rationale and how they might be used. Practical approaches are needed for assumption management and control. Despite its critical importance this topic has, with exceptions, e.g., [2,9,33], not been devoted the attention it deserves.

Future research needs to address how assumptions might be obtained and recorded, and assess how hard they might be to collect, and how such collection be facilitated

There follows a list of some recommendations [22] that, directly or indirectly, address implications of the above. Others practical measures are discussed elsewhere [19]:

a) when developing a computer software and associate systems, estimate and document the likelihood of change in the various areas of the application domains. Knowing which areas of the domain are likely to change, can simplify subsequent detection of assumptions that may have become invalid as a result of these changes

b) capture assumptions made during program development or change using appropriate techniques (see other chapters in this volume).

c) store appropriate information in a structured form, related possibly to the likelihood of change as in (a), so facilitating detection in a periodic review to identify any that have become invalid

d) to facilitate such review, assess the likelihood or expectation of change in various categories of catalogued assumptions

e) review the assumptions database by categories as identified in (c), and as reflected in the database structure, at intervals guided by the expectation or likelihood of change or as triggered by events as in (d)

f) develop and provide methods and tools to facilitate all of the above (see other chapters in this volume)

g) when possible, separate implementation and validation teams to improve questioning and control of assumptions

h) provide for ready access by the software development and maintenance teams to all appropriate domain specialists with in-depth knowledge and understanding of the application domain.

15.7   Final Remarks

Understanding the issues that lead to uncertainty is the essential first step in investigations seeking to produce means to overcome or at least minimize, the effects that result from errors in all these sources. These will arise both at creation time and as a consequence of changes in the domain that the system serves.

Provided the assumptions issue is recognized and acknowledged, solutions will be found to reduce the impact of uncertainty and of the consequences when failure to identify and resolve issues raised leads to system failure or erroneous results. The key issue is whether greater benefits are achieved by the use of a system with the uncertainties as outlined or by abandoning their use. There appears to be little doubt that in most instances the former will be the case. But the question must be asked whenever a new application is planned and developed so as to mitigate the risks by, for example, following the recommendations above indicated. Much work is required in this area.

Implicitly, the discussion has been exclusively in terms of programs, executable software and its documentation. More recently it has become clear both from theoretical considerations and from analysis of practical examples [6,9,19], that the phenomena identified are much more general, appear to apply to most areas of human endeavor. And within each area they apply to the *rationale* that underlies the structure and design of their constituent parts, the architectures, structures, and processes for example.

Acknowledgments. We are grateful to our colleagues and to the FEAST industrial collaborators for many useful discussions over the years. Financial support from the UK EPSRC through grants GR/K86008 (1996-8), GR/M44101 (1999–2001) and GR/S90782 (2004–2005) is gratefully acknowledged.

References[17]

[1] Belady LA, Lehman MM (1972) An introduction to program growth dynamics. In: Freiburger W (ed.) Statistical Computer Performance Evaluation, Academic, New York: 503–511

[2] Burge J, Brown DC (2003) Rationale support for maintenance of large scale systems. In: Proceedings of the Workshop on Evolution of Large-Scale Industrial Software Applications (ELISA), September 23, Amsterdam: 1–12 http://prog.vub.ac.be/FFSE/Workshops/ELISA-submissions <as of Jan. 2006>

[3] CERN Bulletin (1998) The Earth breathes on LEP and LHC, Bulletin 09/98; 23 February 1998, http://bulletin.cern.ch/9809/art1/Text_E.html <as of Jan. 2006>

[4] Cook S, Harrison R, Lehman MM, Wernick P (2006) Journal of Software Maintenance and Evolution: Research and Practice, 18(1): 1–35 lication

[5] Dijkstra EW (1972) The Humble Programmer. ACM Turing Award Lecture. Communications of the ACM, 15(10): 859–866

[6] FEAST/1 and 2: Feedback Evolution And Software Technology Projects (2001), http://www.doc.ic.ac.uk/~mml/feast/ <January 2006>

[7] Finkelstein A, Gabbay D, Hunter A, Kramer J, Nuseibeh B (1994). Inconsistency handling in multi-perspective specifications. IEEE Transactions on Software Engineering, 20(8): 569–578

---

[17] – An * indicates that the publication has been reprinted as a chapter in [20].

[8]   Hoare CAR (1971) Proof of a program: FIND. Communications of the ACM, 14(1): 39–45

[9]   Lago P, van Vliet H (2005) Explicit Assumption enrich Architectural Models. 27th International Conference on Software Engineering (ICSE), May 15–21, St Louis, MO: 206–214

[10] * Lehman MM (1974) Programs, Cities, Students – Limits to Growth. Imp. Col Inaug Lect Ser, 9, 1970–1974: 211–229. Also in: Gries D (ed) (1978) Programming Methodology, Springer, Berlin Heidelberg New York: 42–62

[11] * Lehman MM (1978) Laws of Program Evolution – Rules and Tools for Programming Management. Proc. Infotech State of the Art Conference, Why Software Projects Fail, April 9–11: 1V1–1V25

[12] * Lehman MM (1980) Program Life Cycles and Laws of Software Evolution, Proceedings of IEEE, Special Issue on Software. Engineering, September: 1060–1076

[13] Lehman MM (1984) A Further Model of Coherent Programming Process. In: Proceedings of Software Process Workshop, Egham, Surrey, 6–8 February, IEEE Cat. no. 84 CH 2044-6: 27–35

[14] Lehman MM (1989) Uncertainty in computer application and its control through the engineering of software, Journal of Software Maintenance: Research and Practice, 1(1): 3–27

[15] Lehman MM (1989) Software Engineering as the Control of Uncertainty in Computer Application. SEL Software Engineering Workshop, Goddard Space Centre, MD, 29 November published in 1990

[16] Lehman MM (1990) Uncertainty in Computer Application, Communications of the ACM, 33(5): 584–586

[17] Lehman MM (1990) Uncertainty in Computer Applications is Certain - Software Engineering as a Control. Proceedings of CompEuro 90, International Conference on Computer Systems and Software Engineering, Tel Aviv, May 7–9: 468–474

[18] Lehman MM (1994) Feedback in the software evolution process. Keynote Address. In: Proceedings of CSR Eleventh Annual Workshop on Software Evolution: Models and Metrics, Dublin, 7–9 September Also in: Information and Software Technology, special issue on Software Maintenance, 38(11), (1996): 681–686

[19] Lehman MM (2005) The role and impact of assumptions in software development, maintenance and evolution. In: Proceedings of International Conference on Software Maintenance (ICSM), Budapest, September

[20] Lehman MM, Belady LA (eds.) (1985) Program Evolution—Processes of Software Change. Academic Press, London. Available from http://w3.umh.ac.be/evol/ under "publications" <as of September 2005>

[21] Lehman MM, Ramil JF (2000) Towards a Theory of Software Evolution - And Its Practical Impact. Invited talk. Proc Intl Symp on the Principles of Softw Evolution ISPSE, Kanazawa, Japan, Nov 1–2: 2–11

[22] Lehman MM, Ramil JF (2001) Rules and tools of software evolution planning, management and control, Annals of Software Engineering, Special Issue on Software Management, 11(1): 15–44

[23] Lehman MM, Ramil JF (2002) Software uncertainty in general and in KBS applications in particular. Proceedings of the 9th International Conference on Information Processing and Management of Uncertainty in Knowledge-Based Systems, (IPMU), July 1–5, Annecy, France

[24] Lehman MM, Ramil JF (2002) An Overview of Some Lessons Learnt in FEAST. In: Proceedings Workshop on Empirical Studies of Software Maintenance (WESS), October 2nd, Montreal, Canada

[25] Nanda V, Madhavji A (2006) Case Study of Software Requirements Changes due to External Factors. In: Madhavji N, Fernández-Ramil J, Perry D (eds.): Software Evolution and Feedback – Theory and Practice, Wiley, New York, 2006

[26] Nuseibeh B (1997) Ariane 5 Who Dunnit?, IEEE Software, May/June: 15–16

[27] Nuseibeh B, Kramer J, Finkelstein A (1994) A framework for expressing the relationships between multiple views in requirements specification. IEEE Transactions on Software Engineering, 20(10): 760–773

[28] Pfleeger S (2001) Software Engineering – Theory and Practice. 2nd ed., Prentice-Hall, Englewood Cliffs, NJ

[29] The Compact Oxford English Dictionary (1989), 2nd micrographically reduced ed., Oxford University Press, Oxford

[30] Turski WM (1981) Specification as a Theory with Models in the Computer World and in the Real World. In: Henderson P (ed.): System Design. Infotech State of the Art Report, 9(6): 363–377

[31] Turski WM. (1981) Software Stability. In: Systems Architecture, Proceedings of ACM European Regional Conference, ICS 81: 107–116

[32] Turski WM, Maibaum TSE (1987) The Specification of Computer Programs. Addison-Wesley, Boston, MA

[33] Uchitel S, Yankelevich D (2000) Enhancing Architectural Mismatch Detection with Assumptions. In: Proceedings of the 7th IEEE International Conference on the Engineering of Computer Based Systems (ECBS), Scotland, UK

[34] Van Lamsweerde A (2000) Formal Specification: a Roadmap. In: Finkelstein A (ed.) The Future of Software Engineering. ICSE 2000, Limerick, Ireland, ACM Order N. 592000-1: 149–159

[35] Wirth N (1971) Program development by stepwise refinement. Communications of the ACM, 14(4): 221–227

16 Design Decisions: The Bridge between Rationale and Architecture

J.S. van der Ven, A.G. J. Jansen, J.A. G. Nijhuis, J. Bosch

Abstract: Software architecture can be seen as a decision making process; it involves making the right decisions at the right time. Typically, these design decisions are not explicitly represented in the artifacts describing the design. They reside in the minds of the designers and are therefore easily lost. Rationale management is often proposed as a solution, but lacks a close relationship with software architecture artifacts. Explicit modeling of design decisions in the software architecture bridges this gap, as it allows for a close integration of rationale management with software architecture. This improves the understandability of the software architecture. Consequently, the software architecture becomes easier to communicate, maintain, and evolve. Furthermore, it allows for analysis, improvement, and reuse of design decisions in the design process.

Keywords: software architecture; architectural design decisions

16.1 Introduction

Software design is currently seen as an iterative process. Often used phases in this process include: requirements discussions, requirements specification, software architecting, implementation, and testing. The Rationale Unified Process (RUP) is an example of an iterative design process split into several phases. In such an iterative design process, the software architecture has a vital role [19].

Architects describe the bare bones of the system by making high-level design decisions. Errors made in the design of the architecture generally have a huge impact on the final result. A lot of effort is spent on making the right design decisions in the initial design of the architecture. However, the argumentation underlying the architecture is usually not documented, because the focus is only on the results of the decisions (the architectural artifacts). Therefore the evaluated alternatives, made tradeoffs and rationale about the made decision remain in the heads of the designers. This tacit knowledge is easily lost. The lost architecture knowledge leads to evolution problems [8], increases the complexity of the design [5], and obstructs the reuse of design experience [14].

To solve the problem of lost architectural knowledge, often techniques for managing rationale are proposed. Experiments show that maintaining rationale in the architecture phase increases the understandability of the design [6]. However, creating and maintaining this rationale is very time-consuming. The connection to the architectural and design artifacts is usually very loose, making the rationale hard to use and keep up-to-date during the evolution of the system. Consequently, there seems to be a gap between rationale management and software architecture.

To bridge this gap, we unite rationale and architectural artifacts into the concept of a design decision, which couples rationale with software architecture. Design decisions are integrated with the software architecture design. By doing this, the rationale stays in the architecture, making it easier to understand, communicate, change, maintain, and evolve the design.

Section 16.2 of this chapter introduces software architectures. Section 16.3 discusses how rationale is used in software architectures. Section 16.4 introduces the concept of design decisions. Section 16.5 presents a concrete approach that uses this concept. After this, related and future work is discussed, followed by a summary, which concludes this chapter.

16.2 Software Architecture

This section focuses on the knowledge aspects of software architectures. In Sect. 16.2.1, the software architecture design process is discussed. Next, different ways are presented to describe software architectural knowledge in Sect. 16.2.2. Subsequently, the issue of knowledge vaporization in software architecture is discussed in Sect. 16.2.3.

16.2.1 The Software Architecture Design Process

A software architecture is based on the requirements for the system. Requirements define *what* the system should do, whereas the software architecture describes *how* this is achieved. Many software architecture design methods exist (e.g., [2] and [4]). They all use different methodologies for designing software architectures. However, they can all be summarized in the same abstract software architecture design process.

Figure 16.1 provides a view of this abstract software design process and its associated artifacts. The main input for a software architecture design process is the *requirements document*. During the *initial design* the *software architecture* is created, which satisfies (parts of) the requirements stated in the requirement document. After this initial design phase, the quality of the *software architecture* is *assessed*. When the quality of the architecture is not sufficient, it is modified (*architectural modification*).

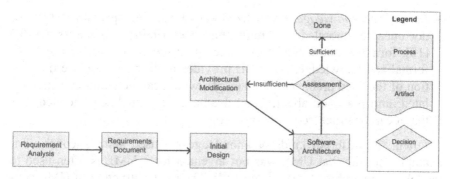

Fig. 16.1. An abstract view on the software architecture design process

Describing Software To modify the architecture, the architect can among others employ a number of tactics [2] or adopt one or more architectural styles or patterns [20] to improve the design. This is repeated, until the quality of the architecture is assessed sufficient.

16.2.2 Architectures

There is no general agreement of what a software architecture is and what it is not. This is mainly due to the fact that software architecture has many different aspects, which are either technically, process, organization, or business oriented [4]. Consequently, people perceive and express software architectures in many different ways.

Due to the many different notions of software architectures, a combination of different levels of knowledge is needed for its description. Roughly, the following three levels are usually discerned:

- *Tacit/implicit knowledge.* In many cases, (parts of) software architectures are not explicitly described or modeled, but remain as tacit information inside the head(s) of the designer(s). Making this implicit knowledge explicit is expensive, and some knowledge is not supposed to be written down, for example for political reasons. Consequently, (parts of) software architectures of many systems remain implicit.
- *Documented knowledge.* Documentation approaches provide guidelines on which aspects of the architecture should be documented and how this can be achieved. Typically, these approaches define multiple views on an architecture for different stakeholders [11]. Examples include: the Siemens four view [10], and the work of the Software Engineering Institute [7].

– *Formalized knowledge.* Formalized knowledge is a specialized form of documented knowledge. Architecture Description Languages (ADL) [18], formulas and calculations concerning the system are examples of formalized knowledge. An ADL provides a clear and concise description of the used architectural concepts, which can be communicated, related, and reasoned about. The advantage of formalized knowledge is that it can be processed by computers.

Often, the different kinds of knowledge are used simultaneously. For example, despite that UML was not invented for it UML is often used to model certain architectural concepts [7]. The model structure of UML contains formalized knowledge, which needs explanation in the form of documented knowledge. However, the use of the models is not unambiguous, and it is often found that UML is used in different ways. This implies the use of tacit knowledge to be able to understand and interpret the UML models in different contexts.

16.2.3 Problems in Software Architecture

There are several major problems with software architecture design [5,12,14]. These problems come from the large amount of tacit architectural knowledge. Currently, none of the existing approaches to describe software architectures (see Sect. 16.2.2) gives guidelines for describing the design decisions underlying the architecture. Consequently, design decisions only exist in the heads of the designers, which leads to the following problems:

– *Design decisions are cross cutting and intertwined.* Typical design decisions affect multiple parts of the design. However, these design decisions are not explicitly represented in the architecture. So, the associated architectural knowledge is fragmented across various parts of the design, making it hard to find and change the decisions.
– *Design rules and constraints are violated.* During the evolution of the system, designers can easily violate design rules and constraints arising from previously taken design decisions. Violations of these rules and constraints lead to architectural drift [19], and its associated problems (e.g. increased maintenance costs).
– *Obsolete design decisions are not removed.* When obsolete design decisions are not removed, the system has the tendency to erode more rapidly. In the current design practice removing design decisions is avoided, because of the effort needed, and the unexpected effects this removing can have on the system.

As a result of these problems, developed systems have a *high cost of change*, and they tend to *erode quickly*. Also, the *reusability* of the architectural artifacts is limited if design decision knowledge vaporizes into the design. These problems are caused by the focus in the software architecture design process on the resulting artifacts (e.g., components and connectors), instead of the decisions that lead to them. Clearly, design decisions currently lack a first-class representation in software architecture designs.

16.3   Rationale in Software Architecture

To tackle the problems described in the previous section, the use of rationale is often proposed. Rationale in the context of architectures describes and explains the used concepts, considered alternatives, and structures of systems [11]. This section describes the use of rationale in software architectures. First, an abstract rationale construction process is introduced in Sect. 16.3.1. Then, the reasons for rationale use in software architecture are described in Sect. 16.3.2. The section is concluded with a summary of problems for current rationale use in software architecture.

16.3.1 The Rationale Construction Process

A general process for creating rationale is visualized in Fig. 16.2. First, the problems are identified (*problem identification*) and described in a *problem statement*. Then, the problems are evaluated (*problems remaining*) one by one, and *solutions* are created (*create solutions*) for a problem. These *solutions* are evaluated and weighted for their suitability of solving the problem at hand (*decision making*). The best solution (for that situation) is chosen, and the choice is documented together with its rationale (*Choice + Rationale*). If new problems emerge from the decision made, they have to be written down and be solved within the same process.

This process is a generalized view from different rationale based approaches (like the ones described in Sect. 1.3). Take for example QOC, and the scenario described in [17]. The design of a scroll bar for a user interface is discussed. There are several questions (problems), like "Q1: How to display?" For this question, there are two options (solutions) described, "O1: permanent" and "O2: appearing". In the described example, the second option is considered as the best one, and selected. However, this option generated a new question (problem), "Q2: How to make it appear?". This new question needs to be solved in the same way. Other rationale management methods can be mapped on this process view too.

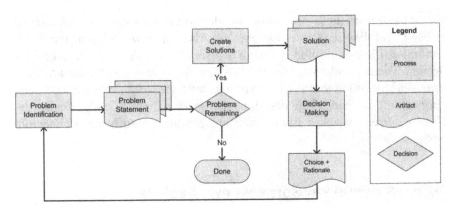

Fig. 16.2. An abstract view on the rationale management process

16.3.2 Reasons for Using Rationale in Software Architecture

As is discussed in Sect. 1.4, there are many reasons for using rationale in software projects. Here, the most important reasons are discussed, and related to the problems existing in software architecture.

– *Supporting reuse and change* (see Sect. 1.4.2). During the evolution of a system and its architecture, often the rules and constraints from previous decisions are violated. Rationale needs to be used to give the architects insight in previous decisions.
– *Improving quality* (see Sect. 1.4.3). As posed in the previous section, design decisions tend to get cross-cut and intertwined. Rationale based solutions are used to check consistency between decisions. This helps in managing the cross-cussing concerns.
– *Supporting knowledge transfer* (see Sect. 1.4.4). When using rationale for communication of the design. Transfer of knowledge can be done over two dimensions: location (different departments or companies across the world) and time (evolution, maintenance). Transferring knowledge is one of the most important goals of architecture.

16.3.3 Problems of Rationale Use in Software Architecture

As described in this section, rationale could be beneficial in architecture design. However, most methods developed for capturing rationale in architecture design suffer from the following problems:

- *Capture overhead.* Despite the attempt to automate the rationale capture process, both during and after the design, it is still a laborious process (see Sect. 1.5.1).
- For the designers, it is *hard to see the clear benefit* of documenting rationale about the architecture. Usually most of the rationale captured is not used by the designer itself, and therefore capturing rationale is generally seen as boring and useless work.
- The rationale typically *loses the context* in which it was created. When rationale is communicated in documented or formalized form, additional tacit information about the context is lost.
- There is *no clear connection from the architectural artifacts to the rationale.* Because the rationale and the architectural artifacts are usually kept separated, it is very hard to keep them synchronized. Especially when the system is evolving, the design artifacts are updated, while the rationale documentation tends to deteriorate.

As a consequence of these problems, rationale-based approaches are not often used in architecture design. However, as described in Sect. 16.2, there is a need for documenting the reasons behind the design. The following section describes an approach which couples rationale to architecture.

16.4   Design Decisions: The Bridge Between Rationale and Architecture

The problems from Sects. 16.2.3 and 16.3.3 can be addressed by the same solution. This is done by including rationale and architectural artifacts into one concept: the design decision. In the following section, the two processes from Sects. 16.2.1 and 16.3.1 are compared. In Sect. 16.4.2, design decisions are introduced by example and a definition is presented in Sect. 16.4.3. The last section discusses designing with design decisions.

16.4.1 Enriching Architecture with Rationale

The processes described in Sects. 16.2.1 and 16.3.1 have some clear resemblances. Problems (requirements) are handled by Solutions (software architectures/modifications), and the assessment determines if all the problems are solved adequately. The artifacts created in both processes tend to describe the same things (see Fig. 16.3). However, the software architecture design process focuses on the *results* of the decision process, while the rationale management focuses on the path to the decision.

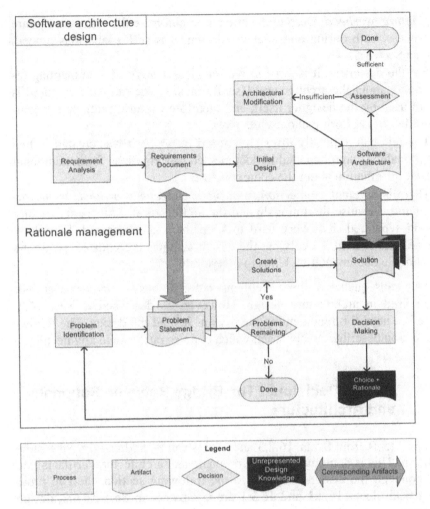

Fig. 16.3. Similarities between software architecture design process and the rationale management process

Some knowledge which is captured in the rationale management process is missing in the architecture design process (depicted as black boxes in Fig. 16.3). There are two artifacts which contain knowledge that is not available in the software architecture artifact: not selected solutions and choice + rationale. On the other hand, the results of the design process (the architecture and architectural modifications), are missing in the rationale management process.

The concept of first-class represented design decisions, composed of rationale, architectural modifications, and alternatives, is used to bring the two processes together. A software architecture design process no longer results in a static design description of a system, but in a set of design decisions leading up to the system. The design decisions reflect the rationale used for the decision making process, and form the natural bridge between rationale and the resulting architecture.

16.4.2 CD Player: A Design Decision Example

This section presents a simple case, which shows the impact of designing architecture with design decisions. The example is based on the design of a compact disc (CD) player. Changing customers' needs have made the software architecture of the CD player insufficient. Consequently, the architecture needs to evolve.

The software architecture of the CD player is presented in the top of Fig. 16.4, the current design. The design decisions leading to the current design are not shown in Fig. 16.4 and are instead represented as one design decision.

The CD players' architecture is visualized in a component and connector view [7]. The components are the principal computational elements that execute at run-time in the CD player. The connectors represent which component has a run-time pathway of interaction with another component.

Two functional additions to the software architecture are described. First, a software-update mechanism is added. This is used to update the CD player, to make easier to fix bugs and add new functionality in the future. Second, the Internet connection is used to download song information for the played CD, like song texts, additional artist information, etc.

As shown in Fig. 16.4, design decisions are taken to add the described functionality. The design decisions contain the rationale and the functional solution, represented as documentation and an architectural component and connector view. Note that the rationale in the picture is shortened very much because of space limitations. The added functionality is directly represented by two design decisions, *Updater* and *SongDatabase*.

The first idea for solving the Internet connectivity was to add a component which handled the communication to the Patcher. This idea was rejected, and another alternative was considered, to create a change to the Hardware Controller. This change enabled the Internet connectivity for the Internet song db too, and was considered better because it could reuse a lot of the functionality of the existing Hardware Controller. Note that the view on the current design shows a complete architecture, while it is also a set of design decisions. The resulting design (Fig. 16.5) is visualized with the two design decisions taken: the *Updater* and the *SongDatabase*.

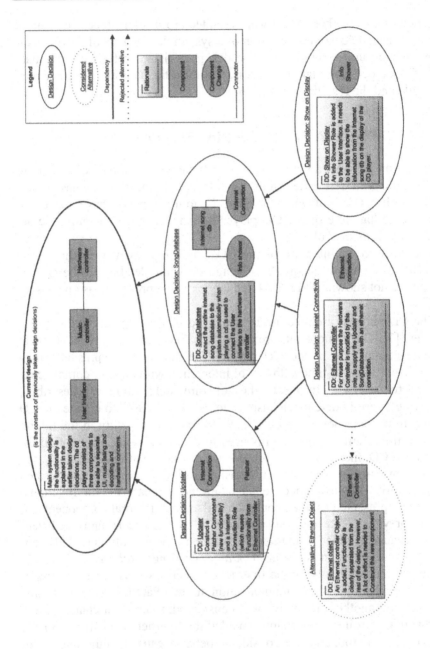

Fig. 16.4. The architecture of a CD player with extended functionality

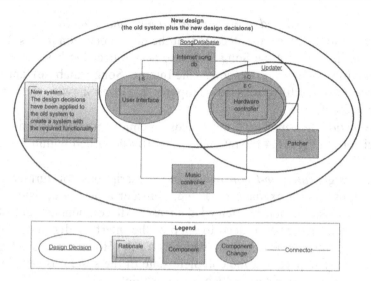

Fig. 16.5. The result of the design decisions of Fig. 16.4

16.4.3 Design Decisions

In the example of Sect. 16.4.2, the software architecture of the CD player is the set of design decisions leading to a particular design, as depicted in Fig. 16.4. In the classical notion of system design only the result depicted in Fig. 16.5 is visible while not capturing the design decisions leading up to a particular design.

Although the term architectural design decision is often used [2, 7, 10], a precise definition is hard to find. Therefore, we define an architectural design decision as:

"A description of the choice and considered alternatives that (partially) realize one or more requirements. Alternatives consist of a set of architectural additions, subtractions and modifications to the software architecture, the rationale, and the design rules, design constraints and additional requirements."

We detail this definition by describing the used elements:

– The *considered alternatives* are potential solutions to the requirement the design decision addresses. The *choice* is the decision part of an architectural design decision; it selects one of the considered alternatives. For example, Fig. 16.4 contains two considered alternatives for the connectivity design decisions. The Ethernet Object alternative is not selected. Instead, the Internet Connectivity is selected.

- The *architectural additions, subtractions, and modifications* are the changes to the given architecture that the design decision makes. For example, in Fig. 16.4 the Song Database design decision has one addition in the form of a new component (the Internet Song Database), and introduces two modifications to components (Info Shower and Internet Connection).
- The *rationale* represents the reasons behind an architectural design decision. In Fig. 16.4 the rationale is shortly described within the design decisions.
- The *design rules and constraints* are prescriptions for further design decisions. As an example of a rule, consider a design decision that is taken to use an object-oriented database. All components and objects that require persistence need to support the interface demanded by this database management system, which is a rule. However, this design decision may require that the complete state of the system is saved in this object-oriented database, which is a constraint.
- Timely fulfillment of *requirements* drives the design decision process. The requirements not only include the current requirements, but also include requirements expected in the future. They can either be explicit, e.g., mentioned in a requirements document, or implicit.
- A design decision may result in *additional requirements* to be satisfied by the architecture. Once a design decision is taken, new insights can lead to previous undiscovered requirements. For instance, the design decision to use the Internet as an interface to a system will cause security requirements like logins, secure transfer, etc.

The given *architecture* is a set of earlier made design decisions, which represent the architectural design at the moment the design decision is taken.

Architecture design decisions may be concerned with the application domain of the system, the architectural styles and patterns used in the system, COTS components and other infrastructure selections as well as other aspects described in classical architecture design. Consequently, architectural design decisions can have many different levels of abstraction. Furthermore, they involve a wide range of issues, from pure technical ones to organizational, business, political, and social ones.

16.4.4 Designing with Design Decisions

Existing design methods (e.g., [2,4]) describe ways in which alternatives are elicited and trade-offs are made. An architect designing with design decisions still uses these design methods. The main difference lies in the awareness of the architect, to explicitly capture the design decisions made and the associated design knowledge.

Section 16.2.3 presented key problems in software architecture. Designing with design decisions helps in handling these problems in the following way:

- *Design decisions are cross cutting and intertwined.* When designing with design decisions the architect explicitly defines design decisions, and the relationships between them. The architect is made aware of the cross cutting and intertwining of design decisions. In the short term, if the identified intertwining and cross cutting is not desirable, the involved design decisions can be reevaluated and alternative solutions can be considered before the design is further developed. In the long term, the architect can (re)learn which design decisions are closely intertwined with each other and what kind of problems are associated with this.
- *Design rules and constraints are violated.* Design decisions explicitly contain knowledge about the rules and constraints they impose on the architecture. Adequate tool support can make the architect aware about these rules and constraints and provide their associated rationale. This is mostly a long term benefit to the architect, as this knowledge is often forgotten and no longer available during evolution or maintenance of the system.
- *Obsolete design decisions are not removed.* In evolution and maintenance, explicit design decisions enable identification and removal of obsolete design decisions. The architect can predict the impact of the decision and the effort required for removal.

Designing with design decisions requires more effort from the architect, as the design decisions have to be documented along with their rationale. In traditional design, the architect forms the bridge between architecture and rationale. In designing with design decisions, this role is partially taken up by the design decisions.

Capturing the rationale of design decisions is a resource intensive process (see Sect. 1.5.1). To minimize the capture overhead, close integration between software architecture design, rationale, and design decisions is required. The following section presents an example of an approach that demonstrates this close integration.

3

16.5   Archium

Section 16.4 presented a general notion of architectural design decisions. In this section, a concrete example realization of this notion is presented: Archium [13]. First, the basic concepts of Archium are presented, after which this approach is illustrated with an example.

16.5.1 Basic Concepts of Archium

Archium is an extension of Java, consisting of a compiler and run-time platform. Archium consists of three different elements, which are integrated with each other. The first element is the architectural model, which formally defines the software architecture using ADL concepts [18]. Second, Archium incorporates a decision model, which models design decisions along with its rationale. Third, Archium includes a composition model, which describes how the different concepts are composed together.

The focus in this section is on the design decision model. For the composition and architectural model see [13]. The decision model (see Fig. 16.6) uses an issue-based approach [16]. The issues are problems, which the solutions of the architectural design decisions (partially) solve. The rationale part of the decision model focuses on *design decision rationale* and not *design rationale* in general (see section 'DRL' in Chap. 1).

Archium captures rationale in customizable rationale elements. They are described in natural text within the scope of a design decision. Rationale elements can explicitly refer to elements within this context, thereby creating a close relationship between rationale and design elements.

The motivation and cause elements provide rationale about the problem. The choice element chooses the right solution and makes a trade-off between the solutions. The choice results in an architectural modification.

To realize the chosen solution in an architectural design decision, the components and connectors of the architectural model can be altered. In this process, new elements might be required and existing elements of the design might be modified or removed. The architectural modification describes these changes, and thereby the history of the design. These architectural modifications are explicitly part of design decisions, which are first-class entities in Archium. This makes Archium capable of describing a software architecture as a set of design decisions [13].

Rationale acquisition (see Sect. 1.7.1) is a manual task in Archium. The approach tries to minimize the intrusiveness of the capturing process by letting the rationale elements of the design decisions be optional. The only intrusive factor is the identification and naming of design decisions.

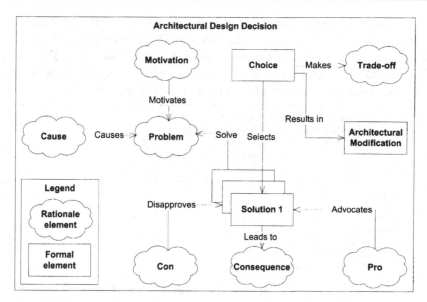

Fig. 16.6. The Archium design decision model

The rationale elements are to a certain extend similar to that of DRL [16] (see section 'DRL' in Chap. 1). The *Problem* element is comparable to a *Decision Problem* in DRL. A *Solution* solves a *Problem,* likewise *Alternatives* do in DRL. The *Motivation* element gives more rationale about the *Problem* and is comparable to a supportive *Claim* in DRL. A *Cause* can be seen as a special instance of a *Goal* in DRL. The *Consequence* element is like a DRL *Claim* about the expected impact of a *Solution.* The *Pro* and *Con* elements are comparable to supporting and denying DRL *Claim*s of a *Solution* (i.e., a DRL *Alternative*).

16.5.2 Example in Archium

An example of a design decision and the associated rationale in Archium is presented in Fig. 16.7. It describes the *Updater* design decision of Fig. 16.4. Rationale elements in Archium start with an @, which expresses rationale in natural text. In the rationale, any design element or requirement in the scope of the design decision can be referred to using square brackets (e.g., [iuc:patcher]). In this way, Archium allows architects to relate their rationale with their design in a natural way.

A design decision can contain multiple solutions. Each solution has a realization part, which contains programming code that realizes the solution. A realization can use other design decisions or change existing

components. In the *InternetUpdate solution* the realization contains the
InternetUpdateChange, which defines the Patcher component and the
component modifications for the *Internet Connection* (see Fig. 16.4).
The *IUCMapping* defines how the *InternetUpdateChange* is mapped onto
the current *design*, which is an argument of the design decision.

```
design decision Updater(CurrentDesign design) {
    @problem {# The CD player should be updatable.[R4] #}
    @motivation {# The system can have unexpected bugs or require
                    additional functionality once it is deployed. #}
    @cause {#Currently this functionality is not present in the [design],
               as the market did not require this functionality before. #}
    @context {# The original [design]. #}

    potential solutions {
      solution InternetUpdate {
        architectural entities {
          InternetUpdateChange iuc;
          IUCMapping iucMapping;
        }
      @description {# The system updates itself using a patch, which is downloaded from
                      the internet. #}
        realization {
          iuc = new InternetUpdateChange();
          iucMapping = new IUCMapping(design,iuc);
          return design composed with iuc using iucMapping;
        }
      @design rules {# When the [iuc:patcher] fails to update, the system needs to
                       revert back to the previous state. #}
      @design constraints {# #}
      @consequences {# The solution requires the system to have a [iuc:internetConnection]
                       to work. #}
        pros { @pro {# Distribution of new patches is cheap, easy, and fast #} }
        cons { @con {# The solution requires a connection to the internet to work. #} }
      }
      /* Other alternative solutions can be defined here */
      }
    choice {
      choice InternetUpdate;
      @tradeoff {# No economical other alternatives exist #}
      }
    }
```

Fig. 16.7. The updater design decision in Archium

To summarize, the architectural design decisions contain specific rationale
elements of the architecture, thereby not only describing how the architecture has become what it is, but also the reasons behind the architecture.
Consequently, design decisions can be used as a bridge between the software architecture and its rationale. The Archium environment shows that it
is feasible to create architectures with design decisions.

16.6   Related Work and Further Developments

This section describes related and future work. The related work focuses on software architecture, as the related work about rationale management is explained in more depth in previous chapters of this book. After this, Sect. 16.6.2 describes future work on design decisions.

16.6.1 Related Work

Software architecture design methods [2,4] focus on describing how the right design decisions can be made, as opposed to our approach which focuses on capturing these design decisions. Assessment methods, like ATAM [2], asses the quality attributes of a software architecture, and the outcome of such an assessment steers the direction of the design decision process.

Software documentation approaches [7,10] provide guidelines for the documentation of software architectures. However, these approaches do not explicitly capture the way to and the reasons behind the software architecture.

Architectural Description Languages (ADLs) [18] do not capture the road leading up to the design either. An exception is formed by the architectural change management tool Mae [9], which tracks changes of elements in an architectural model using a revision management system. However, this approach lacks the notion of design decisions and does not capture considered alternatives or rationale about the design.

Architectural styles and patterns [20] describe common (collections of) architectural design decisions, with known benefits and drawbacks. Tactics [2] are strategies for design decision making. They provide clues and hints about what kind of design decisions can help in certain situations. However, they do not provide a complete design decision perspective.

Currently, there is more attention in the software architecture community for the decisions behind the architectural design. Kruchten [14], stresses the importance of design decisions, and creates classifications of design decisions and the relationship between them. Tyree and Akerman [21] provide a first approach on documenting design decisions for software architectures. Both approaches model design decisions separately and do not integrate them with design. Closely related to this is the work of Lago [15], who models assumptions on which design decisions are often based, but not the design decisions themselves.

Integration of rationale with the design is also done in the design rationale field. With the SEURAT [3] system, rationale can be maintained in a

RationaleExplorer, which is loosely coupled to the source code. This rationale has to be added to the design tool, to let the rationale of the architecture and the implementation be maintained correctly. DRPG [1] couples rationale of well-known design patterns with elements in a Java implementation. Likewise SEURAT, DRPG also depends on the fact that the rationale of the design patterns is added to the system in advance.

16.6.2 Future Work

The notion of design decisions as first-class entities in a software architecture design raises a couple of research issues. Rationale capture is very expensive, so how can we determine which design decisions are economical worth capturing? So far, we have assumed that all the design decisions can be captured in practice this would often not be possible or feasible. How do we deal with the completeness and uncertainty of design decisions? How can we support addition, change, and removal of design decisions during evolution?

First, design decisions need to be adapted into commonly used design processes. Based on this, design decisions can be formalized and categorized. This will result in a thorough analysis of the types of design decisions. Also, dependencies need to be described between the requirements and design decisions, between the implementation and design decisions, and between design decisions among themselves.

Experiments by others have already proven that rationale management helps in improving maintenance tasks. Whether the desired effects outweigh the costs of rationale capturing is still largely unproven. The fact that most of the benefits of design decisions will be measurable after a longer period when maintenance and evolution takes place complicates the validation process. We are currently working on a case study which focuses on a sequence of architectural design decisions taken during evolution. Additional industrial studies in different domains are planned in the context of an ongoing industrial research project, which will address some of the aforementioned questions.

16.7 Summary

This chapter presented the position of rationale management in software architecture design. Rationale is widely accepted as an important part of the software architecture. However, no strict guidelines or methods exist to structure this rationale. This leaves the rationale management task in the hands of the individual software architect, which makes it hard to reuse and communicate this knowledge. Furthermore, rationale is typically kept separate from architectural artifacts. This makes it hard to see the benefit of rationale and maintaining it.

Giving design decisions a first-class representation in the architectural design creates the possibility to include problems, their solutions and the rationale of these decisions into one unified concept. This chapter described an approach in which decisions behind the architecture are seen as the new building blocks of the architecture. A first step is made by the Archium approach, which illustrated that designing an architecture with design decisions is possible. In the future, we think that rationale and architecture will be used together in design decision like concepts, bridging the gap between the rationale and the architecture.

Acknowledgments. This research has partially been sponsored by the Dutch Joint Academic and Commercial Quality Research and Development (Jacquard) program on Software Engineering Research via contract 638.001.406 GRIFFIN: a GRId For inFormatIoN about architectural knowledge.

References

[1] Baniassad ELA, Murphy GC, Schwanninger C (2003) Design pattern rationale graphs: Linking design to source. In: Proceedings of the 25th International Conference on Software Engineering (ICSE 2005), May 3–10, pp. 352–362

[2] Bass L, Clements P, Kazman R (2003) Software architecture in practice, 2nd edition. Addison-Wesley, Reading, MA

[3] Burge J, Brown DC (2004) An integrated approach for software design checking using rationale. In: Design Computing and Cognition '04, July 19–21, pp. 557–576

[4] Bosch J (2000) Design and use of software architectures. Addison-Wesley, Reading, MA

[5] Bosch J (2004) Software architecture: The next step. In: Proceedings of the first European Workshop on Software Architecture (EWSA 2004) LNCS 3047, May 21–22, pp. 194–199

[6] Bratthall L, Johansson E, Regnell B (2000) Is a design rationale vital when predicting change impact? – A controlled experiment on software architecture evolution. In: Proceedings of the Second International Conference on Product Focused Software Process Improvement (Profes 2000), June 20–22, pp. 126–139

[7] Clements P, Bachmann F, Bass L, Garlan D, Ivers J, Little R, Nord R, Stafford J (2002) Documenting software architectures: Views and beyond. Addison-Wesley, Reading, MA

[8] van Gurp J, Bosch J (2002) Design erosion: Problems and causes. Journal of Systems & Software 61(2): 105–119

[9] van der Hoek A, Mikic-Rakic M, Roshandel R, Medvidovic N (2001) Taming architectural evolution. In: Proceedings of the 8th European software engineering conference, September 10–14, pp. 1–10

[10] Hofmeister C, Nord R, Soni D (2000) Applied Software Architecture. Addison-Wesley, Reading, MA

[11] IEEE (2000) Recommended Practices for Architectural Description of Software-Intensive Systems. IEEE Standard No. 1471

[12] Jansen AGJ, Bosch J (2004) Evaluation of tool support for architectural evolution. In: Proceedings 19th IEEE International Conference Automated Software Engineering (ASE 2004), September 20–24, pp. 375–378

[13] Jansen AGJ, Bosch J (2005) Software architecture as a set of architectural design decisions. Accepted for the Fifth Working IEEE/IFIP Conference on Software Architecture (WICSA 5), November 6–9

[14] Kruchten P (2004) A taxonomy of architectural design decisions in software-intensive systems. In: Proceedings of the 2nd Groningen Workshop on Software Variability Management (SVM 2004), December 2–3, pp. 54–61

[15] Lago P, van Vliet H (2005) Explicit assumptions enrich architectural models. In: Proceedings of the 27th International Conference on Software engineering (ICSE 2005), May 15–21, pp. 206–214

[16] Lee J (1991) Extending the Potts and Bruns model for recording design rationale. In: Proceedings of the 13th International Conference on Software Engineering (ICSE 1991), May 13–17, pp. 114–125

[17] MacLean A, Young RM, Bellotti VME, Moran TP (1991) Questions, Options, and Criteria: Elements of design space analysis. Human–Computer Interaction 6(3&4): 201–250

[18] Medvidovic N, Taylor RN (2000) A classification and comparison framework for software architecture description languages. IEEE Transactions on Software Engineering, 26(1): 70–93

[19] Perry DE, Wolf AL (1992) Foundations for the study of software architecture. ACM SIGSOFT Software Engineering Notes 17(4): 40–52

[20] Shaw M, Garlan D (1996) Software architecture: perspectives on an emerging discipline. Prentice-Hall, Englewood Cliffs, NJ

[21] Tyree J, Akerman A (2005) Architecture decisions: Demystifying architecture. IEEE Software 22(2): 19–27

Part 4
Rationale for Organizing Bodies of Knowledge

B. Paech

The earlier parts have focused on the capture of rationale within a particular project or specific to a certain product. The rationale should be used within the same organization in this and subsequent projects. This part focuses on the rationale capturing general knowledge which can be reused universally. We call the former *project and product rationale (PPR for short)* and the latter *rationale for organizing bodies of knowledge (OBR for short)*. Capture and use are very different for these two kinds of rationale:

1. For OBR the capture problem is less relevant. First, OBR is captured from several projects and second there is more time to consolidate the knowledge. Typically, there will be extra effort allocated to building up OBR, e.g., within a general knowledge management effort in an organization. Another possibility, as exemplified in the following chapters, is that OBR is built in a research project or in a community effort.
2. The users of OBR are not only developers. Often OBR will be used in teaching or consulting. Teachers and consultants can be internal in an organization or external. This kind of rationale is often captured in text books and open repositories. So it is much easier for developers to access this rationale.

These two reasons explain the fact that OBR is much more widespread than PPR.

As mentioned in the editorial chapter, there are two kinds of OBR: *case-based OBR* supports the capture of individual experiences, comparing them with the actual experience. *Generalized OBR* aims at the consolidation of several individual cases. The chapters of this part focus on generalized OBR.

The most well-known examples of generalized OBR in the software engineering community are patterns for architecture, design, or implementation [3]. Patterns typically consist of a problem description, a recommended solution and the discussion of this solution. The problem description is often divided into a specific objective and a context which hinders the achievement of this objective. So, in contrast to a schema for capturing PPR such as QOC, patterns do not explicitly deal with several options for solving the problem. However, the discussion often alludes to alternatives. Furthermore, the criteria are mostly intertwined with the problem description. Thus, patterns typically focus on *how* to solve a problem, not so much on why this solution works.

Chapter 17 "Reusable Rationale Blocks: Improving Quality and Efficiency of Design Choices" by Wiebe Hordijk and Roel Wieringa presents an approach for capturing design knowledge focusing on the *why*. It introduces the notion of a reusable rationale block which relates several options and criteria important to solving a specific problem. The chapter demonstrates how such a reusable rationale block can be used beneficially in the design of a complex architecture. In particular, it supports a systematic and transparent process without much overhead. The chapter also provides detailed lessons learned e.g. on matching the actual problem to the OBR.

Another typical form of generalized OBR is process models. Process models mostly describe one particular solution only, namely a set of steps or practices to be followed during software engineering. The problems to be solved by the steps or practices are only implicitly mentioned. Similarly, the criteria are mostly implicit in the description. Alternatives are very rarely presented. Furthermore, process models are often very monolithic, requiring an all-or-nothing adaptation. This is true for heavy-weight processes such as the Rational Unified Process [4] as well as for light-weight process such as Extreme Programming [1]. These facts often hinder the introduction of new processes, as managers cannot take the risk of a whole new process and developers are not willing to give up all of their accustomed practices. It is therefore very important to provide support for a more piecewise introduction of new processes.

Chapter 18 "Defining Agile Patterns" by Teodora Bozheva and Maria Elisa Gallo proposes agile patterns as the basis for such a piecewise process change. Similar to the design patterns, agile patterns describe a particular practice to be applied to achieve a certain objective in a particular application scenario. Rationale is provided in terms of alternatives and details for their application. The patterns are collected from several agile methods. Patterns depending on each other are grouped together as they typically can only be introduced as a group. Thus, organizations can adapt groups of practices most suitable to their current situation.

This approach is most suitable for organizations which already know the strengths and weaknesses of their current process. It is, however, not trivial to identify these. In the 1990s several approaches for process assessments have been introduced, some are top-down others bottom-up [6]. The former start with a set of best practices such as CMM or SPICE and assess how well the current process reflects these practices [2,5]. The latter, such as GQM, start from current problems or improvement goals, analyze them in detail (in particular by gathering data) and define individual improvement steps to achieve the goal [7].

Chapter 19 "Capturing and Reusing Rationale Associated with Requirements Engineering Process Improvement: A Case Study" by Bhavani Palyagar and Debbie Richards shows how rationale can help to align such bottom-up process improvement to both, business goals and staff problems. On the one hand the rationale provides general justification why a certain process parameter is important for a certain business goal, on the other hand the rationale captures reasons for process problems and for prioritizing improvement actions. Thus, the former constitutes an OBR for generalized process improvement knowledge, while the latter helps to keep record of the improvement decisions. This is an interesting example of how (process improvement) project knowledge can be captured based on and intertwined with OBR, and how both help to improve the quality of process improvement. An industrial case study illustrates the details.

The final chapter, Chap. 20 "Using Patterns for Sharing Requirements Engineering Process Rationales" by Lars Hagge, Frank Houdek, Kathrin Lappe, and Barbara Paech, emphasizes yet another aspect of process OBR. Again it uses patterns to describe a solution for a process problem. In contrast to e.g., Chap. 18, it does not focus on activities, but on how patterns help to solve a particular *conflict* during requirements engineering. Due to the emphasis on conflict situations in addition to the usual context description, the patterns reveal two or more forces characterizing the conflict. The patterns have been collected by an industry working group. The emphasis on conflict situation reflects the industries' need of generalized OBR beyond the usual process models and practice collections. Very often in a real project the participants are well aware of the standard recommendations but cannot act according to them because there are too many forces to be taken care of. Of course, also one pattern cannot handle all aspects of such conflict situations. But the explicit forces help to analyze the conflict and to find a compatible group of patterns to alleviate the situation.

In summary, the four chapters show that despite many similarities there are many different ways of capturing and using OBR. It is encouraging to see how useful all of them have been in the industry.

References

[1] Beck K (2000) Extreme Programming Explained: Embrace Change. Addison-Wesley, Reading, MA

[2] CMM, http://www.sei.cmu.edu/cmm/

[3] Gamma E, Helm R, Johnson R, Vlissides J (1995) Design Patterns. Addison-Wesley, Reading, MA

[4] Kruchten PB (2000), The Rational Unified Process: An Introduction, Addison-Wesley, Reading, MA

[5] SPICE, http://www.sqi.gu.edu.au/spice/title.html

[6] Thomas M, McGarry F (1994) Top-Down vs. Bottom-Up Process Improvement. IEEE Software, July: 12–13

[7] van Solingen R, Berghout E (1999) The Goal-Question-Metric Method. Mc-Graw-Hill, New York

17 Reusable Rationale Blocks: Improving Quality and Efficiency of Design Choices

W. Hordijk*, R. Wieringa

Abstract: In the current practice of designing software for user organizations, as experienced by the authors, designers often produce design knowledge again and again for every decision: they reinvent the wheel. We want to improve the quality, predictability, and efficiency of the software design process by reusing design knowledge. Our proposed solution consists of Reusable Rationale Blocks (RRBs). An RRB is a schema and a notation to write down decision rationale. To manage RRBs, we introduce a generalized design space, that consists of a collection of RRBs. And to use RRBs, we define a process that can be added to any design process, as well as a set of heuristics to be used in applying this process. We illustrate our solution by a few examples taken from our own experience.

Keywords: architecture; design; rationale management; reuse; software process improvement

17.1 Introduction

This chapter proposes an improvement of the process of designing software for user organizations. It is based on our experience in designing enterprise information systems, but our solution is stated in general terms applicable to any software design process for user organizations.

17.1.1 Problem

In current practice the use and production of design knowledge by practitioners does not lead to a growth of design knowledge in the community of practitioners. Designers reinvent the wheel repeatedly [7] [see Chap 1, section "Organizing and Delivering Reusable Knowledge", in this book]. The same knowledge is produced again and again, and is not reused for later, similar decisions. This means that design takes more effort from the designers than needed. It also entails the risk of lower quality of results, and because

---
* Partially sponsored by Ordina BV.

knowledge is not reused, it makes the properties of the final product hard to predict, loading a lot of risk on the project.

17.1.2 Goal

As stated, the goal of our approach is to improve the quality [7] [Chap. 1, Sect. 1.4.3 in this book], predictability, and efficiency of the software design process by reusing design knowledge. We take a *generalized approach* to reuse [7] [Chap. 1, section "Organizing and Delivering Reusable Knowledge", in this book]. Decisions can be made more repeatable by reusing information used in them in later, similar decisions, and their quality can be improved by recording their impact on software quality. To achieve our goal of reuse, we provide a structure and a process for such reuse, and we produce and validate the design knowledge to be reused.

Before we proceed, we need to clarify this goal in a number of ways. First, our goal is not to provide a general knowledge management tool for reuse of design knowledge. We focus on reuse of decision rationale. This is knowledge about which options there are for a design decision, and how each option affects the relevant requirements. It is useful to reuse other knowledge too, but this is not what we do here.

Second, the application of our solution is in the areas of Engineering of systems and Acquisition of system components and infrastructural components [7] [Chap. 1, Sect. 1.6.6 in this book]. We do not rule out that the approach could be used in other process areas, but we have not looked at this.

Third, our experience is limited to Enterprise Information Systems (EISs), which are systems that serve administrative purposes in organizations and are used by people in those organizations. EISs typically store and use data, have some business logic, and one or more user interfaces. But the solutions that we come up with are stated in terms applicable to any software design problem.

Fourth, we only consider custom-built applications, as opposed to off-the-shelf software. These applications are of course built upon commercially available components.

Fifth, we focus on higher-level design decisions, and not on the lower-level decisions. The higher-level decisions cost more effort and represent more risks than lower-level decisions. Therefore, there is a higher demand for quality of higher-level decisions than there is for lower-level decisions. In our approach, we focus on the higher-level decisions. Also, these involve teams of people from different parts of an organization, and should be documented well for accountability and maintainability.

17.1.3 Solution Outline

Our proposed solution consists of four parts:

- Reusable Rationale Blocks (RRBs), a schema and a notation to write down decision rationale.
- A generalized design space, consisting of a collection of RRBs for EISs.
- A process description, where the use of RRBs is added to a standard design process. This description should enable you to add the use of RRBs to your own design process. The process also tells how to create RRBs.
- A set of heuristics to be used in applying the RRB process.

The RRBs are the core concepts of our approach. They are generalized pieces of decision rationale. Each of them contain one question, a set of solution options to the question, and an evaluation table where the options are compared to each other with respect to a set of requirements, called criteria. This is similar to the Questions–Options–Criteria (QOC) approach [13]. As criteria we use quality indicators, taken from the extended ISO 9126 quality model [16] because they are measurable and of interest to the customer. See "QOC" section for a comparison between QOC and our approach.

The generalized design space is a set of RRBs on a web site (http://quids.ewi.utwente.nl/). It is called a generalized design space because a regular design space is about a concrete system, while a generalized design space is about a class of systems. We will just write "design space" instead of "generalized design space". In addition to the decision rationale in the RRBs, the design space adds a "super/subproblem" structure, giving designers a minimum checklist of decisions they should have made before the design can be ready.

The process description is our idea of how RRBs should be used in practice, both in systems design and in research, but focusing on design. We do not prescribe a particular design process, but rather show how a design process can be extended to use RRBs. Our solution thus is prescriptive [7] [Chap. 1, section "Descriptive or Prescriptive" in this book].

Our solution is highly intrusive [7] [Chap. 1, section "Intrusiveness" in this book] on one hand, because the design process is changed. On the other hand, we argue that a good designer naturally documents the argumentation behind design decisions at the same time the decisions are made, and that doing this in our notation does not add extra effort. This is also proposed in [7] [Chap. 1, Sect. 1.5.2 in this book]. In our opinion, decisions should be first-class citizens of software architecture. Under those assumptions, our approach is nonintrusive. In other words, documenting rationale in such a way that it can be reused later, should not take more effort than just documenting the rationale.

17.1.4 Related Work

This section describes the differences between our solution and some alternative approaches from rationale management and architecture research.

Design Patterns

An important approach to the reuse of design knowledge is the use of patterns, which are descriptions of problems and corresponding solutions according to some format [1,6,8,9]. Design Patterns describe solutions in detail, which makes them ideal for teaching, knowledge management, and for describing *how* a system is structured. One problem with patterns is that they do not provide guidelines about how to choose among several patterns that all in different ways satisfy a set of requirements. As mentioned in [7] [Chap. 20 in this book], one pattern describes rationale for one solution instead of several ones. In the terminology of Lee and Lai [12], patterns contain *design rationale* (they tell us which problem a solution solves), but no *decision rationale* (they do not tell us how to choose among patterns). RRBs, on the other hand, describe alternatives and effects, but do not explain the options in great detail. They are meant for making and justifying design decisions. Ideally, the options in an RRB are described as patterns, or by references to known patterns, so that design rationale and explanation are in one place.

QOC

The Question–Options–Criteria approach was introduced [13] to illustrate and analyze the arguments that lead to design decisions about individual systems in a graphical way. Each option can score in only two ways on a criterion: good or bad. Our approach generalizes this to generic design problems and refines the scoring of options. Our design problems are QOC's Questions, our options are their Options, and our quality indicators are a refinement of their Criteria. We use the term "design problem" because we think that the term "question" is too broad.

We refined QOC by restricting ourselves to measurable quality indicators, and by ranking options on each quality indicator on more than two ranks. We felt we needed more ranks than two for codifying general design knowledge.

Another difference is in the goals of the methods. QOC is a descriptive method, aimed at describing the rationale of decisions. Our approach is prescriptive, aimed at improving design processes, for which we use rationale as a means to an end.

Attribute Driven Design

Attribute Driven Design (ADD) [5] is a field of research at the SEI. Their unit of research is the Design Primitive (also known as Architectural Mechanisms). An example of a design primitive is caching. Design primitives can be compared to our Solution Options, except that a Design Primitive is not linked to a Design Problem. Design primitives are problem-oriented: "The performance is too low, so we use caching to fix that." RRBs are choice-oriented: "Should we use caching or not?"

17.1.5 Structure of This Chapter

We start with a more thorough explanation of RRBs and the design space in Sect. 17.2. Then we show how to use RRBs in Sect. 17.3 about the RRB Process. In Sect. 17.4, we illustrate the process in three cases from a system design project in which one of the authors took part as an architect. In Sect. 17.5, we present the lessons learned from the cases, which make up the heuristics of our solution.

17.2   Reusable Rationale Blocks and the Design Space

This section first explains how design decisions and software quality are related, and then explains how such knowledge is documented in RRBs. We start our explanation with an example of an RRB, after which we show the general structure of RRBs. Then we proceed from individual RRBs to our design space.

17.2.1 Design Decisions and Software Quality

Central to our approach is the assumption that decisions taken during the design of a system partly define the quality that the system will have after implementation. The quality of a system falls apart in many quality attributes, which can be measured using quality indicators.

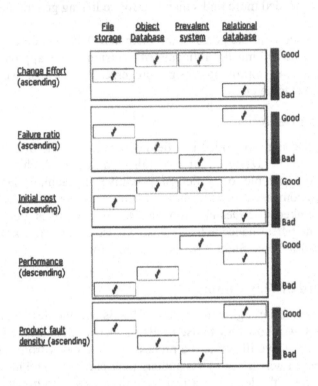

Fig. 17.1. Web site screen shot of Reusable Rationale Block "Data storage type." See http://quids.ewi.utwente.nl/. Prevalent systems are a new and experimental kind of systems that keep all data in memory; see http://www.prevayler.org/wiki. jsp for more information

17.2.2 RRB Example

Figure 17.1 shows (part of) the RRB of the design problem "data storage type". The leftmost column of the RRB shows the quality indicators that are affected by the solution options. The rows show how each solution option is ranked by each quality indicator. For example, the option "Relational database" scores best on the quality indicator "Failure ratio". This means that in a system where data are stored in a relational database, we expect the failure ratio will be lower than with other types of data storage. Note that a single column when taken out of the table does not have meaning: the RRB does not say that "Relational database" scores better on "Failure ratio" than it scores on "Initial cost".

The orderings in a row are partial. When two options have equal ranks for a quality indicator, such as Object databases and Prevalent systems for "Change effort", we do not say that those options are indifferent with respect to that indicator, but rather that they are indistinguishable. The statements we are making with respect to "Change effort" is that option 1 is worse than options 2 and 3, and option 4 is worse than all the other options.

Each row in the table is a hypothesis about the effects of options on the system's quality. In our design space, we motivate these hypotheses by reference to the literature [6,9,11], as well as our own experience.

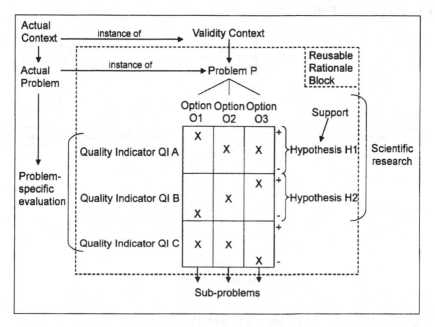

Fig. 17.2. Schematic representation of a Reusable Rationale Block in its environment. Some terminology is shortened because of space limitations

17.2.3 RRB General Structure

The general structure of a RRB is shown in Fig. 17.2. A design problem is described in conjunction with its available solution options and their effects. It occurs in the context of an earlier design problem, and provides the context for further design problems. In the RRB, we describe this in a general way, but in an actual piece of software we will encounter an actual design problem in an actual context. The RRB, on the other hand, only describes a generic problem, existing in a context described generically, called a validity context. The designer must relate the actual context to the validity context, and the actual problem to the generic design problem described in the design space. Then the designer can make his or her evaluation of the options based on knowledge of the actual problem in its actual context. This is shown at the left-hand side of Fig. 17.2. At the right-hand side, we show that every row in the table is a hypothesis that can be investigated by further empirical research. In future research, we will try to validate or refute some of the hypotheses in our design space empirically. The structure of a design problem with its context can be reused in other situations, provided the design problem and context match the specific situation.

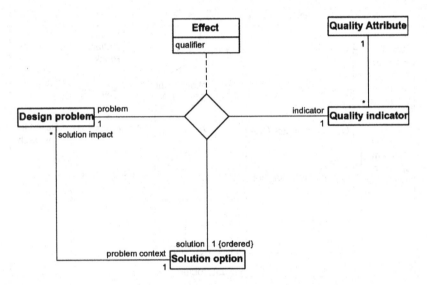

Fig. 17.3. UML static structure diagram of the design space

17.2.4 Design Space

As said earlier, an RRB contains knowledge about a particular problem in the design of systems, their solution options, and the relations between the problems and solutions. Whenever a design problem is present, the corresponding RRB documents its different options and their different effects on the system's quality attributes. This can be modeled as a ternary relation called *Effect* between a design problem, solution option and quality indicator (Fig. 17.3).

To link multiple RRBs together into a design space, a solution option can be the problem context for more detailed design problems. For example, after choosing the option "relational database" for the design problem "where should the data be stored," the design problem "what should the data model be?" is created, which also has a corresponding RRB in the design space. The design space therefore has the structure of a tree.

17.3 RRB Process

The RRB process is an approach to software design which uses decision rationale to improve design quality, predictability, and efficiency by reusing design knowledge. In this approach, rationale is a necessary component of the design, not a by-product for later use. Decisions are first-class citizens of the design world, at least as important as classes, components and subsystems. Since design is a decision-making activity, documenting decision rationale should be as natural to a good designer as documenting source code is to a good programmer.

In this section, we propose how to use RRBs in practice and in research. In Fig. 17.4 we show a process model consisting of the design cycle on the right-hand side, the research cycle on the left-hand side, and flows between them, making a double cycle.

The basic design cycle is shown on the far right of Fig. 17.4 [14]. In the *Problem analysis* phase, the designer develops an understanding of the problem, and identifies criteria by which the solution will be evaluated. Here the Design problem and the Quality indicators of Fig. 17.3 are generated. In the *Solution synthesis* phase, possible solution options are generated in some way. Sources for solution alternatives include the designer's experience, text books, and the Internet. The quality attributes of these alternatives are predicted next. This *property prediction* can be done for example by comparing solution alternatives to known existing systems, by modeling the solution, or by prototyping. Here the Effect relationships of Fig. 17.3 are established. The properties can be presented in the form of a rationale table such as in Fig. 17.1 or the tables in Sect. 17.4. Then the predicted properties are evaluated against criteria (*solution evaluation*). This leads to either a choice for one of the alternatives, or a decision to synthesize new solutions or analyze the problem more thoroughly.

We extended this basic design cycle with a *Problem matching* activity, in which the designer uses RRBs. *Problem matching* influences some of the other activities. In *Problem matching*, the designer tries to find an RRB which matches the actual problem at hand. This means that the actual problem can be regarded as an instance of the RRBs problem, and the context of the actual problem as an instance of the RRBs validity context. When a matching RRB is found, this makes the rest of the design cycle much easier. The RRBs *options* are input to the *Solution synthesis* activity, and the effects that the options have on quality indicators are input to *Property prediction*. When *Problem matching* does not yield a matching RRB, the regular design cycle activities are followed.

The designer must be aware that the RRB is more general than the actual problem, so in the actual problem, other options and effects may apply. That is why *Problem matching* does not replace the other activities.

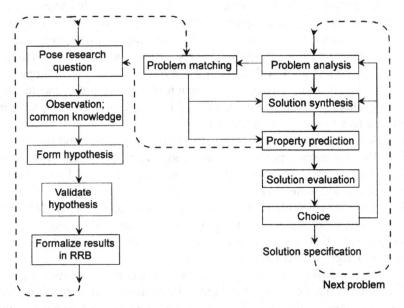

Fig. 17.4. Process diagram of the design cycle and research cycle linked together

On the far left of Fig. 17.4 we find the research cycle, assuming that the research hypotheses are stated in the form of RRBs. This research process can be used in an academic context to yield knowledge applicable to a class of problems, as well as in an organization that needs the knowledge to solve a particular problem.

Finally, Fig. 17.4 shows that the design cycle and research cycle are linked together. Note that the RRB process has many similarities with the more generic Experience Factory approach [3]. Our approach is more specific to design rationale. An RRB can be seen as a way to package experience, in the Experience Factory terminology.

17.4   Illustrations

To make the RRBs at http://quids.ewi.utwente.nl/ practically usable, we provided a Word template. Nothing more sophisticated is needed at this point in time. We use this template in the examples below. Note that in the Word template, we use pluses and minuses rather than vertical positioning of crosses to indicate ranking. This is convenient in Word, but it has the danger that designers may believe that it is meaningful to add and subtract pluses and minuses. We applied the current version of the design space in an industry project at a large Dutch government body. We investigated the application of the theory by using action research, a research method in which the researcher is actively involved in the activities that are being investigated [2,4]. To improve understandability of the examples, we simplify the system and the design decisions.

In these illustrations, all decisions are product choices. This is caused by the state of the project these examples have been taken from. We believe that other design decisions, like which pattern to use for a certain part of the software, can use the same process. To validate this is part of future research.

17.4.1 Setting

These cases took place in a large Dutch government body. The system under design (SuD) was an administrative system that supported one of the organization's most important primary processes. A distributed architecture had been chosen for the system, with a hub-and-spoke layout with one central node and 150 remote nodes, and asynchronous messaging as communication means between the nodes.

The rationale for choosing asynchronous messaging was that some of the communication channels between the nodes had too high latency for the system to perform well enough with synchronous communication. The hub-and-spoke layout was given by the geographical distribution of the end users. The organization had already chosen a programming language and an application server.

Up to this point, the architecture was given. These descriptions formed the context of subsequent design problems, and those are the subjects of the case studies in this section.

The team designing the system's architecture consisted of one project leader who was also a domain expert, one software architect who was also a domain expert, and one software architect (Hordijk). The team met weekly with the "architecture board," a group of representatives from the organization's IT infrastructure department, technological policy makers, and the application development team leader. The time frame of the design efforts was from November 2004 to April 2005, when implementation started.

17.4.2 Case Description Format

Each case presented below is described according to the following format.

– Introduction, describing the design problem that was solved in the case and the interest of the case to the chapter.
– Narrative, describing the events that happened in relation to the case in chronological order. The narrative consists of paragraphs named according to the steps in the design cycle, with an extra level for iterations in the first case. Each step can appear more than once because of the iterative nature of design.
– Lessons learned from the case.

17.4.3 Case 1: Message-Oriented Middleware

The most important decision for this system was which protocols and products to use for communication and message routing between the nodes of the system. For this decision, no matching RRB was found, so the regular design cycle was followed. We needed five iterations through the design cycle before arriving at a choice. We give no narrative here due to space limitations. The most important lessons learned are in Sect. 17.5.

17.4.4 Case 2: Remote Data Storage

This case illustrates how to use an RRB in an actual design decision, and that designers must still use their own knowledge and common sense when applying an RRB.

The next-most important design decision in our project was which kind of data storage to use for storing data on the remote nodes of the system. This decision limited the possible options for some other decisions, so it had to be answered first.

Problem analysis. Problem analysis for this decision raised interesting questions, which we answered in a meeting with domain experts. We needed to know what data were stored remotely and why. It turned out that two kinds of data were stored remotely. The first kind was data that was entered remotely, which was stored there for future reference but also sent to the central system. The second kind of data was entered in the central node, sent out to the remote nodes and stored there, in a cache, for faster reference. So all data in a remote data store either came out of, or would soon be sent to, the central database. This made reliability and backup facilities less important for the remote data stores.

Problem matching. After problem analysis, we found an RRB that matched our problem, shown in Fig. 17.1. Because this RRB was a bit limited and did not include any specific products, but only product types, we decided to generate extra options and quality indicators to be complete.

Problem analysis for criteria and Solution synthesis. Options and quality indicators for this decision were generated in one brainstorm meeting with the architecture board. The brainstorm added new options and quality indicators to the RRB in Fig. 17.1. The options "Object Database" and "Prevalent system" were intentionally left out, because they did not score well enough on "Product fault density," which is an indicator for Maturity. No matter how good these products may be, they were not yet widely in use, and our organization did not want to be a technological fore-runner. This ended the solution synthesis activity. The RRB was used further in property prediction.

Property prediction. The property prediction of the options in the RRB in Fig. 17.1 and our actual problem differ on some quality indicators. In the actual problem, three different RDBMS products were considered, with quite different quality indicator values. For example, we even regarded a particular RDBMS as less mature (indicated by scoring lower on product fault density) than file storage, while in the RRB, RDBMSs are considered more mature. Also, in the actual problem we added some quality indicators that were relevant in the specific context. This illustrates that an RRB contains generalized design knowledge, which should be tailored when used for actual problems. Still, RRBs are useful because they structure the decision and present an initial knowledge base to start from.

Table 17.1 Rationale for discarding the option Comma-separated files
Disk space usage was added as a criterium in the brain storm session

	Comma-separated files	XML files
failure ratio	−	+
initial cost	−	+
disk space usage	+	−

To make property prediction more efficient, we tried to reduce the number of options as quickly as possible. The option "comma-separated files" could be compared locally to the option "XML-files", as shown in Table 17.1. This shows that between the two, XML-files were better than comma-separated files, so we could discard comma-separated files. Likewise, the alternative RDBMS Product B was compared to Product A, and the only differences were that A had better Resource usage and B had better Performance. Resource usage was more important at the remote nodes and Product A would probably meet the minimum performance requirements, so Product B was discarded. Now we had four options left, and they were evaluated against all our criteria in Table 17.2. For this evaluation, we used the information in the RRB in Fig. 17.5, supplemented with product documentation and market knowledge.

Table 17.2 Rationale table for remote data storage type
The last three criteria were added in the brain storm session

	XML-files	RDMS "lite"	Open source RDBMS	RDBMS product A
change effort	++	−	−	+
failure ratio	−	+	+	++
initial cost	++	+/−	+	++
Performance	−	+	+	+
product fault density	+	+	−	++
maintenance effort	+/−	+	−	+
Installability	+	+	?	−
resource efficiency	++	+	+	−
vendor lock–in	++	−	+	−

Solution evaluation and Choice. The criteria Product fault density, Failure ratio and Initial cost were of high importance to the organization. Installability, Resource efficiency and Vendor lock-in were of minor importance. Therefore, RDBMS product A was chosen.

Lessons learned. This case illustrates how the knowledge contained in an RRB can be used in decision making. We learned the following lessons from it.

- It shows that matching the RRB to the actual problem is a difficult step, because many factors that influence which options are available, which quality indicators are important, and what effects the options have are involved. One should therefore take these factors into account and tailor the RRB to the problem at hand.
- The case also shows that designers should deal with the decision making process in an opportunistic way, cutting out options as early as possible when they can show that an option is inferior to another in small iterations of the design cycle. This opportunism saves time, but still preserves the accountability and reusability of the rationale.
- Another thing we learned from this case is that it was invaluable to have access to people who know the local infrastructure and the products that run on it. This local knowledge may continue to be more valuable than the general knowledge stored in RRBs.

17.4.5 Case 3: Central Data Storage

This case shows that application of the same RRB in different contexts can lead to different design decisions. Another important decision in our project was which kind of data storage to use at the central node of the system. For this decision, the rationale table constructed in the second case was reused. The quality indicators that were important for the central node were different from those at the remote nodes, which led to a choice for the same product but for different reasons.

Problem analysis. The quality indicators Maintenance effort, Installability, and Resource efficiency were less important for the central data store than for the remote ones, because it was only one node instead of 150 and central resources could easily be scaled up. Failure ratio and Product fault density, however, were far more important, because the central database double-served as a backup for the remote data stores. Also, some data was stored in the central database only.

Problem matching, Solution synthesis, and Property prediction. From the original RRB in Fig. 17.1, we saw that according to our quality indicators, an RDBMS was the only viable option. Because of Failure ratio and Product fault density, we only wanted to consider the RDBMS products that were already in use in the organization. Now we still had the two RDBMS products A and B that the organization already used as options. These were evaluated against each other in Table 17.3. Table 17.3 was derived from by removing the options that we could see were not viable and adding RDBMS product B back in. RDBMS A and B are evaluated against each other.

Table 17.3 Rationale table for central data storage product

	RDBMS product A	RDBMS product B
change effort	+	−
failure ratio	++	++
initial cost	++	+
performance	+	+
product fault density	++	++
vendor lock-in	−	−

Solution evaluation and Choice. This evaluation was presented to the architecture board, and RDBMS product A was chosen unanimously because everyone could easily see that the difference in initial cost and change effort made product A the better choice.

Lessons learned. This case shows that the same RRB applied to different design problems can yield the same result for different reasons. It did because the context of the actual problem was different. This case also shows that it is useful to reuse design knowledge, as the same knowledge in the RRB was used in two cases, and the rationale table from the previous case was reused in this one.

17.5   Discussion and Conclusions

17.5.1 Lessons Learned

Iterations through the design cycle do not always consist of sequences of steps through the entire cycle followed by a jump back to the start. Some iterations do, but others consist of backtracking to an earlier stage to get more information, and still others consist in jumping forward to later tasks before proceeding with the current one. In general, though, earlier iterations focus on earlier design tasks and later iterations focus on later tasks. This agrees with an observation made by Witte in a massive empirical survey of decision processes [15].

An existing RRB was used in case 2 and it was extended with quite some extra options and criteria. The results were fed back into the RRB and reused in case 3. With a less complex problem and most of the knowledge already there, this decision was comparably easy.

We have found many cases in which one problem affects another problem. In those cases, we keep the problems apart, and first decide on the affecting problem, and later on the affected problem. This "divide and conquer" tactic keeps the evaluation tables small and the decisions easy.

We have seen that RRBs give most of their input early in decision processes. They give the decision process a "quick start" by providing crude versions of the options and their effects for typical design problems. The current body of RRBs is not so useful later on in the decision process, when more detailed problem-specific knowledge is needed that is not yet codified in the RRBs. As indicated earlier, this is intentional, because the high-risk decisions are all made early in the design process.

It is more efficient to evaluate all the options to one decision at once than it is to add options after property prediction. In case 1, when we added a new option after the other options had been evaluated, we needed to re-evaluate all the options because in evaluation, all options are compared to each other.

17.5.2 Advantages and Disadvantages

Using the RRB process itself seems like nothing more than good design practice. However, recording all the decision rationale so explicitly as we did in our examples may incur high extra costs. In our cases, the use of the RRB process didn't incur extra costs, because explicit rationale was needed for the decision process anyway. In projects where there is no natural inclination to record rationale, our approach may be too intrusive to work.

Making use of the knowledge inside the RRBs certainly saves effort. Investing time to make this knowledge reusable for other projects in the same company is subject to the same sort of economical considerations as reusing software. For generating, harvesting and validating design knowledge beyond the scope of organizations, we see a role for the academia, and our future research will take part in it.

Acknowledgments. We thank Barbara Paech for her very constructive feedback on our early drafts and later versions, which have improved the quality of this chapter considerably. We thank the anonymous reviewers for their extensive feedback which has led to numerous further improvements.

References

[1] Alexander C, Ishikawa S, Silverstein M, King I, Angel S, Jacobson M, (1977) A Pattern Language: Towns, Buildings, Construction. Oxford University Press

[2] Avison D, Lau F, Myers M, Nielsen PA (1999) Action research. In: Communications of the ACM 42(1):94–97

[3] Basili VR, Caldiera G, Rombach HD (1994) Experience Factory. In: Marciniak JJ (ed.) Encyclopedia of Software Engineering. Wiley, vol. 1, pp. 528-532

[4] Baskerville RL (1999) Investigating Information Systems with Action Research (Tutorial). In: Communications of AIS 2, Article 19

[5] Bass L, Klein M, Bachmann F (2000) Quality attribute design primitives. Technical report, SEI, CMU/SEI-2000-TN-017

[6] Buschmann F, Meunier R, Rohnert H, Sommerlad P, Stal M (1996) Pattern-Oriented Software Architecture, volume 1: A System of Patterns. Wiley

[7] Dutoit AH, McCall R, Mistrik I, Paech B (2006) Rationale Management in Software Engineering. Berlin Heidelberg New York: Springer-Verlag

[8] Gamma E, Helm R, Johnson R, Vlissides J (1995) Design Patterns. Addison-Wesley, Reading, MA

[9] Fowler M, Rice D, Foemmel M, Hieatt E, Mee R, Stafford R (2002) Patterns of Enterprise Application Architecture. Addison-Wesley, Reading, MA

[10] Hofmeister C, Nord R, Soni D (1999) Applied Software Architecture. Addison-Wesley Object Technology Series

[11] Hohpe G, Woolf B (2003) Enterprise Integration Patterns: Designing, Building, and Deploying Messaging Solutions. Addison-Wesley, Reading, MA

[12] Lee J, Lai K (1996) What is design rationale? In: Moran TP, Carroll JM (eds) Design Rationale: Concepts, Techniques, and Use. Lawrence Erlbaum Associates, Mahwah, NJ, pp. 21–52

[13] MacLean A, Young RM, Bellotti VME, Moran TP (1996) Questions, options and criteria: Elements of design space analysis. In: Moran TP, Carroll JM (eds) Design Rationale – Concepts, Techniques, and Use (Computers, Cognition, and Work). Lawrence Erlbaum Associates, Mahwah, pp. 53–106

[14] Wieringa RJ (1996) Requirements Engineering: Frameworks for Understanding. Wiley, New York

[15] Witte E (1972) Field research on complex-decision-making processes–The phase theorem. In: International Studies of Management and Organization, Vol. 2, pp. 156–182

[16] Zeist B van, Hendriks P, Paulussen R, Trienekens J (1996) Quality of software products – experiences with a quality model. Kluwer Bedrijfsweten-schappen. Book in Dutch. Website contains all relevant information in English. See http://www.serc.nl/quint-book/index.htm.

18 Defining Agile Patterns

T. Bozheva, M.E. Gallo

Abstract: The variety of agile methods and their similarity could be a problem for software engineers to select a single or a number of methods and to properly utilize them in a project. An approach to resolving it is to provide concise and adjustable solutions of problems, recurring under certain circumstances, with justification of why and how to apply them. In this chapter we present an approach to acquiring and defining knowledge about agile software development in terms of patterns. We emphasize the rationale in the pattern structure. We discuss how the usage of the agile patterns contributes to organizing and delivering organizational knowledge and to improving the software processes in an organization. Early results from industrial trials are presented to demonstrate additional benefits, which an organizations gains from adopting the agile patterns. In the concluding part we define the directions for further research on the topic.

Keywords: agile methods; pattern; rationale representation; knowledge organization and delivery; software process improvement

18.1 Introduction

Software systems evolve from a large number of decisions taken over an extended period of time. Nowadays, there are plenty of methods, maturity models, and body-of-knowledge books explaining or providing guidelines on how to organize and perform software engineering and management activities. However, due to the continuous rush for improving business results, companies are usually interested in adopting methods which provide flexibility with respect to practice implementation and improvement.

Agile methods recognize that any project, team and organization have their unique peculiarities. Therefore, instead of trying to unify the approaches to developing software, these methods respond to the specific needs via business value-based prioritization, short feedback cycles, and quality-focused development. When appropriately applied, the agile practices bring a number of business benefits such as better project adaptability and reaction to changes, reduced production costs, improved product quality, and increased user satisfaction with the final solution. A good overview of the agile methods is provided in [10].

Different factors, however, determine the need and the success of implementing agile practices in an organization: team size, product criticality, project dynamism, personnel, and skills. In [3] Boehm and Turner define them as agile method home grounds. Although there are plenty of publications on the agile methods, the question how to combine single practices from different methods to define an organization's specific process and when such combinations are reasonable, still remains unclear. This might be the reason, for which lots of people find the agile methods rather unconvincing.

A pattern describes a solution to a recurring problem in such a way that the solution can be used multiple times without being done the same way twice. In general, a pattern has three essential elements: (1) problem – situations, in which the pattern is appropriate to be applied; (2) solution – activities which the pattern consists of; (3) consequences – results and trade-offs of applying the pattern. The solution is abstract enough to make it possible to apply it in different situations.

The usage of patterns for organizing reusable knowledge is not new in the software engineering field. Two widely known applications of it are described in [4] and [8]. Patterns provide a means for the organizations to build processes, which fully correspond to their project and organizational contexts; like building a house of Lego parts. From process improvement point of view, since each pattern addresses a specific problem, it can be easily tried out and adapted appropriately before being put in place in a project or in the whole organization.

Emphasizing rationale in a pattern that defines a software engineering activity facilitates the understanding of when and how to implement the pattern, and contributes to consistent rationale documentation and usage in an organization.

An agile pattern is a pattern, which is based on agile methods. This means that the solution to a problem uses practice(s) from one or several agile methods for software development. In addition an agile pattern includes rationale for applying the solution in a specific context. That is an agile pattern extends the classic pattern definition with providing guidelines on how to implement the pattern activities in different situations.

The agile patterns discussed herein are derived from the following agile methodologies eXtreme Programming (XP) [1,2], Scrum [14], Feature Driven Development (FDD) [12], Lean Development (LD) [13], Adaptive Software Development (ASD) [9], and Agile Modeling [1]. The work on the patterns definition has been initiated within the Framework of Agile Patterns project (S-OD03ES07), partially funded by the Basque Government. The main goal for the project was to contribute to the adoption of the agile methods by software intensive organizations by defining a framework of agile patterns, which can be easily deployed and adapted to the specific needs of an organization.

The results, which we present in this chapter, address two main issues:

- Defining agile patterns: derive and recover best practices from agile methods and emphasizing the rationale in the pattern structure;
- Using agile patterns for spreading knowledge through an organization and for software process improvement.

We present our motivation for defining the framework of agile patterns in Sect. 18.2. In Sect. 18.3 we discuss how we derive knowledge from the lightweight methods and how we structure it in the pattern template. Then we discuss the potential benefits from using the agile patterns from rationale management point of view (Sect. 18.4). In the final section we present open issues for further research.

18.2   Motivation for Defining Agile Patterns

There are a number of agile methods, which propose different approaches to software development and management. Although the individual practices can vary, all the methods propose maintaining good understanding of the project objectives, scope, and constraints among the team members, developing software in short, feature-driven, customer-relevant iterations, receiving constant feedback from the customer and the developers, and focusing on the delivery of business value.

Some agile approaches focus more heavily on project management and collaboration practices, e.g., LD, ASD, and Scrum. Others such as XP, FDD, and AM focus on software implementation practices (see Fig. 18.1).

Two main principles guided us when defining the Agile Patterns:

- *From software engineering point of view.* Provide benefits to the people involved in software development by defining a set of appropriate activities and alternatives of them in an agile manner, i.e., easy to understand and apply and flexible with respect to combining several patterns.
- *From knowledge management perspective.* Support the use of agile methods by providing rationale for implementing a pattern in terms of guidelines for selecting and executing appropriate activities, which address a specific problem. In this way, the rationale will be immediately available to the roles who execute the pattern at the time they need it.

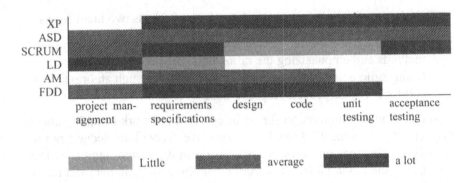

Fig. 18.1. Number of agile practices related to a software development process

We have focused on defining patterns related to:

- Software engineering practices
- Project management practices, and
- Practices related to customer involvement and collaboration

Software engineering and project management practices are the basic ones to be put in place to ensure effective, adaptive, and easy to implement software development process. Customer involvement and collaboration is one of the key factors for success of a software development project. Therefore, we have decided to start working on these three pattern categories first.

Each agile pattern addresses a very concrete issue, e.g., *Increase the feedback from the development team to the management (Development-FeedbackIncreaser)*. It describes activities to be performed to accomplish the issue, roles involved in executing the activities, and resulting products. Wherever possible, alternative activities are considered. The pattern also includes a piece of process rationale related to selecting an alternative solution to the addressed problem. The pattern structure is explained in the next section. The idea is to select patterns taking into account the characteristics of the work to be done and the context, in which it is going to be carried out, and to use them to organize and develop a project.

Several reasons made us decide to integrate rationale in the pattern structure:

- The patterns describe activities that are typically performed by software engineers and project managers who are accustomed to using well-structured information like pattern definitions.
- Using an already known and easy to read structure for rationale representation motivates rationale capturing and usage.
- As long as the rationale related to a specific problem is represented together with the approach to resolving the problem and the con-

text, in which the solution works, it is easier for the implementers to decide upon the activities they have to perform to address the problem.

- If several patterns are put together to form a process, the combination of the rationale related to each pattern will provide to a great extent the rationale for the whole process.

- The pattern descriptions are general enough to be used in different projects. Rationale captured in real-life projects carried out in an organization can be added into the pattern definitions. That is the patterns support sharing organizational knowledge across multiple projects.

In addition patterns could be used for representing rationale related to other types of activities, different from software engineering, e.g., contract management activities. In general, keeping organizational information consistent and in a common format supports its usage and maintenance.

18.3   Agile Pattern Definition Approach

A pattern describes a problem, which typically occurs under certain circumstances. It describes a basic approach to solve a problem providing opportunities to adapt the solution to the particular problem context. The three essential elements of a pattern are problem, solution and consequences.

18.3.1 Pattern Types

Three key terms take part in the agile methods descriptions: *practices, concepts,* and *principles. Practices* describe specific actions that are performed in the whole process of software development, e.g. create product backlog (SCRUM). *Concepts* describe the attributes of an item, e.g., a project plan. *Principles* are fundamental guidelines concerning software development activities, e.g., empower the team (LD).

Each practice can be described by pattern with the following attributes:

- *Intent.* A short description of what the objective is;
- *Origin.* Methodologies, from which the pattern originates;
- *Category to which the pattern belongs.* With respect to the type of issues addressed, the patterns are grouped in the following categories: *Project and Requirements Management, Design, Implementa-*

tion and Testing, Resource Management, Contract Management, and *Software Process Improvement.*
- *Application scenario.* Context, in which the pattern is appropriately applied
- *Roles.* People involved in carrying out the pattern and their responsibilities
- Main and alternative *Activities* that constitute the pattern. Activities can invoke other patterns
- *Tools* that support the pattern execution
- *Guidelines* for performing the activities including suggestions for making a decision about which alternative solution to choose and when

This structure is closest to the one used in [8]. Section 18.3.3 discusses in details the definition of practice patterns.

In the attempt to formalize the definitions of the *concepts* and the *principles*, we found out that the only difference from the *practice* definition by means of patterns is that the *concepts* and the *principles* do not include the Activities attribute. Therefore, we decided to handle *concepts* and *principles* as *practice* patterns, i.e., with nearly the same structure, but with different content.

ProjectPlan and *CollectiveCodeOwnership* are examples of a concept and a principle pattern, respectively. We include them here to illustrate the commonalities and the differences between the structures of the definitions of the three terms.

Concept Pattern: *ProjectPlan*

Intent: Serves as a focal point and quick reminder of the most important elements about the project.

Origin: ASD: Project Data Sheet
XP: Release plan
FDD: Development plan

Application
scenario: Project planning

Roles: Customer: makes business decision (scope, priorities, release planning)
Developers: make technical decisions (effort estimations, risks)
Project Leader: makes the planning

Definition: The Project Plan is one-page summary of the key information about the project. The Project Plan includes the following details:

- Project objectives statement
- Overall Architecture
- Major project milestones
- Core team members

The project objectives statement should be specific and short (25 words or less), and it should include important scope, schedule, and resource information.

Guidelines: In FDD the development plan consists of:

- Feature sets with completion dates
- Major feature sets with completion dates derived from the last completion date of their respective feature sets
- Chief Programmers assigned to feature sets
- The list of classes and the developers that own them

Principle pattern: *CollectiveCodeOwnership*

Intent: The code is collectively owned by the developers. Anyone can do changes to the code. The programmers use a coding standard standard to enforce a common style.

Origin: XP: Collective Code Ownership

Guidelines: Collective code ownership is more reliable than putting a single person in charge of watching specific pieces of code, especially because, if a person leaves a project at some time, the other project team members will know the code he has implemented and will be ready to continue his work.

18.3.2 Agile Patterns from Design Rationale Perspective

Let us consider the practice pattern definition structure as the most complete one.

Compared to the classic pattern definition (problem—solution—consequences), Intent and Application scenario correspond to the problem attribute. Activities match to solution. Some patterns provide alternative solutions to the same problem. This typically happens when the problem is addressed by more than one agile method and different solutions to it are proposed. Guidelines include hints for performing the activities and the consequences from them. The Guideline in the *CollectiveCodeOwnership* principle is an example of a consequence from applying a pattern.

A complete definition of an effective process for resolving a particular issue includes activities that address the problem, people with relevant skills and knowledge, and tools supporting the process implementation.

Therefore, to provide complete information about resolving a problem, we have added the Roles and Tools attributes.

To show how the rationale related to making a solution to a problem is included in the pattern itself, let us compare the agile pattern scheme with the Question–Option–Criteria (QOC) [6] [Chap. 1, Sect. 1.3 in this book] one for argumentative design rationale. Intent and Application scenario correspond to the QOC Question element. Activities match to the Options element. The Guidelines attribute of the agile pattern includes Criteria and Arguments for choosing an option. Wherever relevant, Guidelines also provide explanations about the relationship between Options and Criteria that is it includes the QOC Assessment element.

For instance, the *CodeImplementer* pattern, discussed in more details bellow, has intent "Implement code," which corresponds to the question "How do I implement code?" Two possible activities are defined for addressing the intent, namely apply the *FDDCoder* pattern or the *XPCoder* one. *FDDCoder* describes how to implement code following Feature Driven Development, while *XPCoder* explains how to do coding applying eXtreme Programming. These alternative activities match to the Options element of the QOC scheme.

Applying *XPCoder* requires a tool supporting test-driven-development to be used by the developers. That is the QOC assessment element "To use *XPCoder* you need a tool supporting test-driven development" is part of the Guidelines attribute of *CodeImplementer*.

Following the classification of design rationale approaches, made in [6] [Chap. 1, Sect. 1.2 in this book], the method we present herein can be characterized as prescriptive and less-intrusive. Although a predefined scheme for rationale representation is used, we categorize it as less-intrusive, because the scheme can be easily adapted to an organization's specific needs. Besides it is not required that all the pattern elements be defined at once. This scheme can be used for defining rationale from earlier to most elaborated stages.

18.3.3 Defining Agile Patterns: An Example

The patters, at the time of writing this book chapter, address software engineering activities from the Engineering, Management, and Reuse process areas from the SPICE process standard [15]. The patterns have been derived from the agile methods mentioned earlier.

Apart from the natural language description of the patterns, every category is graphically illustrated showing which patterns, concepts and principles it includes, and the relationships between them.

On the graphics the following symbols are used:

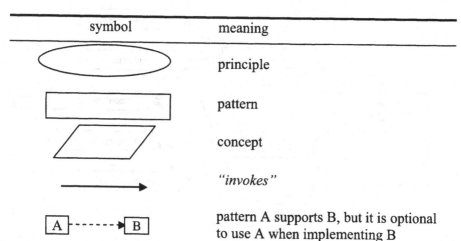

symbol	meaning
	principle
	pattern
	concept
	"invokes"
	pattern A supports B, but it is optional to use A when implementing B

Fig. 18.2. Symbols used in the pattern diagrams

As an example, Fig. 18.2 shows the diagram for the Implementation and Testing category.

We have studied the agile methods to determine to which phases of the software development process they are applicable. Since some methods consider the same issues (see Fig. 18.1), but provide different approaches to resolving them, the main difficulty was to identify the similarities and differences between the solutions and to decide when to use the activities proposed by each one of the methods. The granularity of the patterns was another debatable issue. We used our experience with the agile methodologies in defining the patterns content. However, we have realized that the decision-making criteria have to be explicitly specified and this is one direction of our future activities.

To define a pattern we grouped activities from different agile methods that had similar objectives and then we defined the pattern structure. Afterwards, we established the relationships among all the activities proposed in the different agile methods together with the reasons for selecting one over another activity, wherever alternatives were available. Then we identified which atomic practices formed a pattern, what alternatives were possible and for each alternative what made it feasible. We added the intent, the roles, the tools and the guidelines to the pattern structure as well.

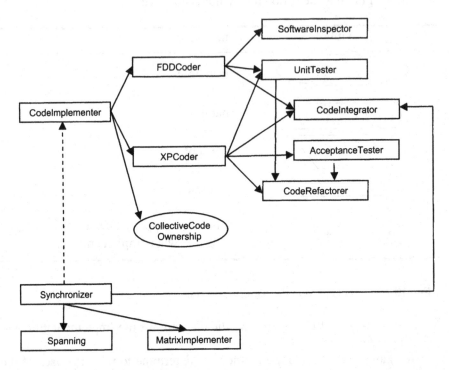

Fig. 18.3. Implementation and Testing category

The result was a group of patterns strongly related to each other. In this group there are patterns that invoke other patterns. This happens when a pattern contains a group of activities that can be used in other patterns as well. Therefore, one pattern can be shared across several other patterns. In the following example, we can see such relationships between patterns in the Implementation and Testing category.

Let us have a look at the *FDDCoder* and the *XPCoder* patterns.

Pattern: FDD Coder
   Intent: Implement defect-free code
   Origin: FDD: Build by feature
   Category: Implementation & Testing
   Application scenario: A developer implements a piece of code.
   Roles: Developers: write Unit Tests, implement and integrate the
       code;
       Customers write acceptance tests.
Activities
       1. Implement code for a feature.

    2. Apply *Unit Tester*.

    3. Apply *Code Integrator*.

    4. Run test cases and improve the code until all test cases pass. The cycle finishes when everything that could possibly break is tested. At the end of a feature implementation apply *Software Inspector*.

Tools: Reference to Testing supporting tools is provided in the original document.

Guidelines: No specific guidelines to the implementation of this pattern are defined yet.

Pattern: XP Coder

Intent: Implement defect-free software

Origin: XP: Coding

Category: Implementation & Testing

Application scenario: A developer implements a piece of a software product (a feature)

Roles: Developers: write Unit Tests, implement and integrate code; Customers write acceptance tests.

Activities

    1. Apply *Unit Tester* and implement code consecutively until a feature is implemented

    2. Apply *Code Integrator*.

    3. Apply *Unit Tester*.

    4. At the end of the day (or at the end of an iteration) apply *Acceptance Tester*.

    5. Apply *CodeRefactorer*.

Tools: Reference to tools supporting test-driven development is provided in the original document.

Guidelines:

1. Apply Pair Programming (Two developers, one keyboard) for higher quality, faster development, less defects and more fun during the implementation process

2. Apply *CollectiveCodeOwnership* to the code, i.e., all the team members may modify the whole code of the product.

3. Use a coding standard to ensure a common style of implementation and that everyone can read and understand any code in the system

4. Good names substitute comments

5. Express intention, not implementation

6. Use a coding standard to facilitate the modification of the code by any team member (XP: *collective code ownership*).

The underlined activities are patterns that are invoked by the *FDDCoder* and the *XPCoder* patterns. This means that to perform *XPCoder,* for instance, we need to perform the patterns *UnitTester, CodeIntegrator, AcceptanceTester,* and *CodeRefactorer.*

FDDCoder and *XPCoder* have two patterns in common: *UnitTester* and *CodeIntegrator.* However, in *FDDCoder UnitTester* and *CodeIntegrator* are performed after the implementation of the code, while in *XPCoder UnitTester* is the first practice to perform. In XP the developers first have to create a unit test framework to be able to define automated unit tests suites. All the tests must be created before the actual code that implements the test. The main reason for this is to keep writing code, which surely meets the software requirements and is always test-proven.

Figure 18.3 shows the relationships among the patterns that take part in the definitions of *FDDCoder*, the ones that take part in the *XPCoder* and the links between all the patterns and principles involved in the Implementation and Testing category. There are no concepts in this category.

The main pattern, **CodeImplementer,** defines the alternatives to develop the code: *FDDCoder* and *XPCoder.*

If *FDDCoder* is selected, then it invokes other patterns that include the activities needed to develop the code in the way FDD proposes. These patterns are *SoftwareInspector, UnitTester,* and *CodeIntegrator.* The complete group of activities included in these patterns tells us how to perform the Code following the FDD method.

If *X Coder* is selected, the patterns invoked are *UnitTester, CodeIntegrator, AcceptanceTester,* and *CodeRefactorer.*

CodeImplementer also invokes the *CollectiveCodeOwnership* principle. This means that for the development of the code, one important consideration to take into account is the ownership of the code.

There are other "invoke" relationships between patterns in this category: *Uni Tester* and *AcceptanceTester* invoke *CodeRefactorer.* This denotes that when implementing these patterns it is necessary to perform the activities included in *CodeRefactorer.*

Another pattern, *Synchronizer*, takes part in this category. It invokes *Spanning, Matrix Implementer,* and *CodeIntegrator* as different alternatives to perform the synchronization between codes, generated by several people. This means that *CodeIntegrator* is a pattern shared by several patterns in this category. The dotted arrow from *Synchronizer to CodeImplementer* shows that they are related, more precisely, *CodeImplementer* supports the implementation of *Synchronizer*, but *Synchronizer* does not explicitly invoke *CodeImplementer.*

A drawback of the diagrams, which we currently use, is that they do not explicitly show if some activities are alternative to each other or have to be executed collectively. In particular, in the Implementation and Testing category *FDDCoder* and *XPCoder* are alternative approaches (options) for implementing *CodeImplementer*. The same is true for *Spanning* and *MatrixImplementer* invoked by the *Synchronizer* pattern. However, this is clearly stated in the textual patterns definitions. For instance the *CodeImplementer* definition looks like this:

> **Pattern: CodeImplementer**
> **Intent:** Implement code
> **Origin:** FDD: Build by feature
>   XP: Coding
> **Category:** Implementation & Testing
> **Application scenario:** Developer implements a piece of code
> **Roles:** Developers
> **Activities**
>   Alternatives are:
>   o   *FDDCoder*
>   o   *XPCoder*
> **Tools:** see Guidelines.
> **Guidelines:**
> o   Applying *XPCoder* requires using a tool supporting test-driven development
> o   Automated tests can save hundred times the cost to create the tests themselves by finding and guarding against bugs. The practice of using automated tests shows that the harder it is to write a test, the more it is needed and the greater the savings will be.
> o   Consider applying the *CollectiveCodeOwnership* principle.
> o   Any place where several individuals are working on the same thing, a need for synchronization occurs. Refer to *Synchronizer* for putting together and maintaining code implemented by different developers.

18.4   Using the Agile Patterns

Nowadays lots of organizations face the need to adapt quickly to modifications requested by their customers, changes on the market or challenges from competitors. This happens in small as well as in large organizations, in disciplined certified (ISO 9001:2000, CMMI®[19]) companies as well as in ones that follow their internal development processes. Organizations that address these problems need to acquire, apply and extend the knowledge related to some or to all the aspects of software engineering and management.

The knowledge represented by means of the agile patterns addresses the key software development and process improvement activities. The patterns are easy to understand, neither require tool support for modifications, nor a special methodology to maintain them. They can be adjusted to the needs of each organization.

From design rationale point of view the main usage of the patterns is to facilitate the knowledge transfer, in particular the organization and delivery of reusable knowledge within an organization, as well as to support learning from the past and on-the-job training.

From software engineering perspective the activities that get most benefits from capturing rationale in terms of agile patterns are the engineering (from requirements elicitation to system testing) and the process improvement ones. Since the convenience of using patterns to define software engineering activities is obvious, later we are going to discuss only how the patterns support software process improvement.

These two viewpoints are completely aligned with the design rationale uses described in [6] [Chap. 1, Sect. 1.4 in this book] and are briefly discussed later.

At the time being a web repository of the agile patterns is being developed. It will provide possibilities for finding patterns and seeing their relationships with other patterns in the framework.

18.4.1 Supporting Knowledge Transfer

The agile patterns, at their current stage, are primarily focused on organizing knowledge about performing specific software engineering activities. The patterns are described in natural language and use a simple format. Therefore, it is very easy to maintain them and to add newly acquired knowledge.

The benefits for a company using the present state of the framework of agile patterns are that

---

[19] Capability Maturity Model Integrated, developed by Software Engineering Institute, Carnegie Mellon University, http://www.sei.cmu.edu.

- The framework structure can be easily adapted to reflect the way the software engineering activities are performed in the organization;
- The patterns can be enhanced with knowledge acquired by the software engineers in the company.

This increases the value of the framework for the organization since the knowledge presented in the patterns reflects the experience and the culture of the same organization. Moreover, the pieces of rationale, which the patterns include, typically address concerns how to approach a specific problem and what alternative solution to select when. That is, knowledge acquired by software engineers in the past is captured and available for delivery through the organization.

Improving the pattern scheme as to more explicitly define rationale related to a pattern problem, would additionally boost the know-how transfer within an organization.

Since the patterns focus on particular activities, it is easy to explain, understand and apply single ones of them. This significantly supports the on-the-job training of people. Besides, the application of the agile patterns implies lots of team work and collaboration that additionally facilitates the spreading of the available knowledge.

18.4.2 Supporting Process Improvement

People having experience with adoption of new approaches to software development know that the Big Bang style of implementation of new processes hides a number of potential drawbacks. Some of them are related to the risk that the new processes as a whole are only partially understood by the people who have to apply them due to the inherent complexity of the process architecture. At the same time difficulties are often faced when trying to split a process to smaller elements (steps) in order to focus on improving the performance of a particular element only. The agile patterns support the process improvement activities exactly by providing a means to pilot single process elements (patterns) before integrating them into an entire process.

Since the agile methods are all oriented towards rapid achievement of business goals, the successful implementation of the agile practices requires considering additional factors like personnel experience, organizational culture, and size and criticality of the projects, in which the practices are applied. That is, apart from the pure engineering activities to be performed, additional issues determine the successful application of the pattern in a specific context. The agile patterns include a wide spectrum of rationale issues related to the integration of a specific pattern in a process built of other patterns. For instance, the *CollectiveCodeOwnership* pattern implies that all the team members have access to and are allowed to modify the code of the product implemented by the team (organizational culture issue).

18.4.3 Industrial Usage

The definition of the agile patterns has been done on two steps: (1) define their structure and content based on study of the literature about the agile methodologies and (2) enrich them with practical experience gathered in trials of the agile methods and/or the agile patterns themselves. The second step can be considered as both piloting and continuous refinement of the patterns. It is not mandatory that the second step begins only when the first one is finished, because presenting an agile practice, known from the literature, by means of a pattern does not make much sense for the software engineers. However, when the description of the practice is complemented with rationale related to its implementation, it brings much more value.

We started piloting the patterns in parallel to defining them. Valuable input came from seven projects, which were focused on experimenting XP and Personal Software Process (PSP) practices in e-commerce and e-business application development. The trials were carried out within the *e*Xpert project (IST-2001-34488) [7], partially funded by the European Commission. They were performed by teams in different organizations, located in Spain, Germany, and Bulgaria. The main objectives for the trials were to study how the agile practices contribute to increasing the productivity and the efficiency of the software engineers, and to improving the quality of the products they develop[20].

From design rationale perspective, our main goal was to find out underlying principles that would help organizations to implement the agile patterns. The observations and the findings of the trials were used to refine the agile pattern definitions.

With respect to the patterns adoption the pilot projects in two of the companies showed that introduction of agile practices has to be made gradually. First, organizations have to select the process, whose agility they aim to increase. Then the patterns that could be used to improve

---

[20] For the sake of completeness, the results from the experiments are as follows: Productivity increased up to 73%. One company decreased its productivity; Schedule deviation reduced between 7% and 38%; Cost deviation decreased up to 31%. Only one company increased its cost deviation; Defect rates reduced between 10% and 83%.

activities from these processes have to be identified and piloted in order to be adjusted to the practices, which are currently in place in the organization. That is, the focus should be on a small set of activities and the patterns that affect them.

Three teams studied the communication between the development team and the customer (*FeedbackIncreaser*). In none of the teams the customer was on-site as recommended by XP. However, agreements were made that the customer would clarify developers' doubts and questions by means of regularly reviewing the current product status and providing feedback by email, phone or direct conversations. One of the teams tried the "developer-on-site" alternative, which consists of periodically sending a developer to the customer's office to demonstrate the product and collect feedback. All the developers recon that the improved communication with the customer had a positive feedback on the decisions made in the project with respect to what features to be implemented, how and when.

The rationale, acquired during the experiments, with respect to how to resolve specific problems, is documented in the patterns themselves. However, we realized that the approach of representing software engineering knowledge in terms of patterns will benefit significantly from improving the pattern structure as to better represent the design rationale related to the resolution of a particular problem. Yet, an important condition is that the patterns remain easy to maintain, use and adapt to organizational needs.

18.5 Conclusions

Formalizing knowledge is a costly process. Aiming at achieving a perfect formalization is perhaps not worth, because software development, as any other intensive human activity, is evolving. Therefore the focus should be on providing an easy to customize and simple to apply solutions like the framework of patterns. Then define criteria for making decisions on how to adapt a pattern to a particular context, why to choose a practice over another one, an option over another possibility, and so on. Enriching the framework with worst apart from best practices is also considered useful. However, it is most probable to be performed only for the internal needs of the organization.

The main directions of future work on the subject include improving the structure of the patterns to better organize different types of rationale associated with the problem, which a pattern addresses; investigating approaches for adopting the framework of agile patterns; studying the benefits an organization gains due to capturing rationale in terms of patterns and exploiting it.

References

[1]   Ambler S, Jeffries R (2002) Agile Modeling: Effective Practices for Extreme Programming and the Unified Process. New York: Wiley,
[2]   Beck K (2000) Extreme Programming Explained: Embrace Change. Reading, MA: Addison-Wesley,
[3]   Boehm B, Turner R (2003) Balancing Agility and Discipline: A Guide for the Perplexed. Addison -Wesley, Reading, MA
[4]   Coplien J, Douglas C. Schmidt (1995) Pattern Languages of Program Design. Addison-Wesley, Reading, MA
[5]   Dutoit A, Paech B (2002) Rationale Management in Software Engineering, Handbook of Software Engineering and Knowledge Engineering. World Scientific, Singapore
[6]   Dutoit AH, McCall R, Mistrík I, Paech B (2006) Rationale management in software engineering. Berlin Heidelberg New York: Springer-Verlag
[7]   eXpert project. http://www.esi.es/Expert
[8]   Gamma E, et al (1995) Design Patterns. Reading, MA: Addison-Wesley
[9]   Highsmith JA (2000) Adaptive Software Development: A Collaborative Approach to Managing Complex Systems. Dorset House Publishing
[10] http://www.agilealliance.org/
[11] http://www.dsdm.org
[12] Palmer S, Felsing J (2002) A Practical Guide to Feature-Driven Development, Englewood Cliffs, NJ: Prentice Hall
[13] Poppendieck M, Poppendieck T (2003) Lean Software Development: An Agile Toolkit for Software Development Managers. Reading, MA: Addison-Wesley
[14] Schwaber K, Beedle M (2002) Agile Software development with Scrum. Ambler SW (2002) Agile Modelling. New York: Wiley
[15] SPICE process standard. http://www.sqi.gu.edu.au/spice/

19 Capturing and Reusing Rationale Associated with Requirements Engineering Process Improvement: A Case Study

B. Palyagar, D. Richards

Abstract: Requirements Engineering is a process for determining stakeholder needs during the development of a software system. Requirements Engineering process quality influences the quality of the software produced due to its critical role in the Software Development Life Cycle. To ensure that software quality is continually being improved, it is thus important to ensure continuous Requirements Engineering process improvement. This involves identifying the poor quality requirements and the process problems that cause them, prioritizing the process problems for elimination and improving the process by eliminating the causes. All of these activities are driven by rationale based on numerous organizational factors such as business goals. We attempt to standardize a method for Requirements Engineering process improvement rationale capture and reuse through a strategy as demonstrated in our case study. The methodology presented here is a product of testing our metrics-driven process improvement framework in large software organizations.

Keywords: rationale capture; rationale reuse; requirements engineering; process improvement; quality measures

19.1 Introduction

Improving the Software Development Life Cycle (SDLC) process is becoming an increasingly accountable (defined as explanation of benefits of improvement against improvement costs) exercise in organizations [1, 6, 12]. Requirements Engineering (RE) is the initial phase of the SDLC that provides inputs to subsequent phases like design, development, testing and maintenance, and hence is the most frequently visited phase of the SDLC [31]. Since all SDLC staff will be affected by the quality of what is produced in the RE phase, it is important to establish a common understanding of any problems in the existing RE process, the impact of such problems, the plans to overcome the problems, and the costs and risks involved in the transition to an improved process.

An RE process in an organization can change over a period of time. The changes usually are RE Process Improvements (REPI) that are applied to circumvent the existing problems. Two noticeable problems of

RE processes are that they fail to produce an increased number of high quality requirements (defined as those requirements that reflect the exact needs of the stakeholder, and are complete, consistent and unambiguous [5]) per unit cost [18]; and RE processes of large software organizations are too complex and effort intensive to comply with [17]. Poor quality requirements that invariably do not reflect the exact needs of the stakeholder, when designed and developed, cause requirement defects in software.

REPI involves a number of decisions that can affect a role, a person or a task in the SDLC. In a metrics-based REPI, decisions involve balancing costs against proposed benefits. RE process changes can affect various SDLC issues such as estimation methods, activities, roles and responsibilities, automation, and various artifacts of the SDLC [19]. Further, REPI is a Process and Quality (P&Q) exercise that is usually the responsibility of a vertical group outside of the project group, whose perception of the RE problems may differ to those of the project team and customers. Thus, it is important to capture rationale associated with REPI decisions so that all involved can appreciate what is wrong with the RE process and how it can be made more effective and efficient. Capture also facilitates reuse.

RE in large organizations is usually identified as a continuous exercise within a Key Process Area (KPA). Continuous REPI is facilitated by using the rationale associated with historical REPI for comparison of the current process with its predecessors, and sometimes to rollback REPI decisions to one or more previous states. Further, REPI rationale can be reused for other SDLC process improvement such as improving the effectiveness of testing.

Despite these potential benefits, we observed in our case study that REPI recording of rationale is not very common in industry. When REPI occurs, instead of well-structured rationale, unstructured partial information at best is presented as the justification. Such justifications can be common even in quality certified companies. For instance, in Six Sigma companies that follow Define, Measure, Analyze, Improve, and Control (DMAIC) [20], unstructured justifications for actions can be made explicit in every phase. Because of their specificity and incompleteness, such justifications are not reusable. Further, unstructured justifications are used more as tools for selling the REPI ideas rather than reusing them as fundamental reasons behind decisions. They can be classified as "descriptive rationale" in nature, thus limiting their use for training as described in [7] [Chap. 1, Sect. 1.2 in this book]. Descriptive rationale does not alter the way process users think about what the process should really do. Similarly, quality standards such as Capability Maturity Model (CMM) [21] and Software Process Improvement and Capability dEtermination (SPICE) [9] do not prescribe or enforce rationale recording. Although, these standards act as important references for continuous REPI, unstructured justifications for REPI or mere adherence to quality standards may not provide solid grounding for future improvement decisions. REPI needs a "prescriptive approach" of rationale recording so that improvement reasoning evolves with time thus influencing significant and continuous REPI as described in [7] [Chap. 1, Sect. 1.2 in this book]. The reuse of rationale recorded using a prescriptive approach influences the way process users think in every REPI cycle. This method can radically influence REPI decisions, thus promoting the capture of rationale behind such radical decisions.

The objective of this chapter is to establish the significance of capturing the rationale associated with REPI decisions using a structured approach, starting with strategic outcomes and developing into detailed process related issues. This approach facilitates simple and easy capture of rationale, and provides selective and access-easy reuse of rationale for continuous REPI.

Section 19.2 introduces the notion of rationale related to REPI. Section 19.3 considers the challenges associated with REPI rationale. Our methodology to REPI rationale capture and a case study snapshot following the methodology are given in Sects. 19.4 and 19.5, respectively. Section 19.6 closes this chapter with our conclusions.

19.2   REPI Rationale

REPI rationale is defined as the fundamental reasons behind REPI decisions [25]. Research suggests that rationale usually is not a decision making mechanism, but is a mechanism by which decisions are influenced by improving the grounding of decisions [22]. Well-structured rationale assists RE process users to better comprehend the needs and benefits related to REPI and provide feedback such that eventually REPI rationale is transformed into reusable knowledge [29]. Our study indicated that rationale persistence among the SDLC staff increases conformance to the process, and feedback provided by rationale users will assist continuous REPI.

REPI rationale management is a mechanism by which RE process owners (usually P&Q staff or Project Management (PM) staff who take ownership of the process and improve it or retire it) capture the decisions involved in an RE process transition from the current state to the new state. An RE process transition usually involves [1, 3, 6, 12, 23, 24]:

– Defining precisely the problem with the current RE process
– Understanding the root cause(s) of the problem

- Establishing key metrics to monitor process performance
- Describing the solution with clarity against the defined problem
- Setting process transition goals
- Defining a strategy to achieve process transition goals
- Defining various process stakeholders and their privileges in RE
- Assigning clear roles and responsibilities
- Describing the interaction amongst the stakeholders
- Evaluating new technology, if any, associated with the transition
- Managing risks with respect to the process transition
- Transitioning to the new improved process
- Monitoring, and perhaps correcting, the improved process rollout
- User training of the new process
- Well established feedback mechanisms for further improvements

Most of the above steps need explicit rationale to justify the actions. While some may argue that recording rationale requires too much effort to learn and to do, we argue that:

1. REPI rationale has potential value as it is part of the Intellectual Property (IP) of an organization. Persistence of rationale facilitates transfer of an individual's process improvement knowledge into the organization's IP [29]. This allows avoidance of past expensive mistakes in REPI as described in [7] [Chap. 1, Sect. 1.4 in this book].
2. Rationale management supports collaboration by promoting coordination amongst RE staff, customer, and other SDLC staff by exposing differing points of view. Such differences, can become a knowledge source of various options useful for continuous REPI as described in [7] [Chap. 1, Sect. 1.4 in this book].
3. Currently, rationale recording is considered useful only until the decision has been made, which leads to the present state of affairs where there is no formal or semi-formal representation of argumentation. Our strategy supports feedback on the rationale after the decision is made and effective use of feedback for the next REPI cycle supporting the changes. Maximizing rationale reuse can maximize benefits of rationale.
4. Rationale management can support consistency of decisions leading to improved quality of REPI decisions. Consistency can be achieved only with explicitness of rationale as described in [7] [Chap. 1, Sect. 1.4 in this book]. Further, rationale management can influence correctness of the decisions positively.
5. Effort and complexity can be minimized and reuse maximized by using the practitioner's terminology and structuring rationale according to common industry dimensions and parameters.

Rationale management in requirements and system design is common in the SDLC [2, 15, 32]. With design rationale the emphasis is on simplicity, resting largely on the three node types Question, Option, and Criterion (QOC) [15, 25]. Another rationale recording method is Issues-Based Information Systems (IBIS) and is used to record ideas and relationships during design discussion as it unfolds. Existing rationale mechanisms are more suitable to system design that are focused on raising a number of questions or issues and providing answers to those questions using a reference for justification [2, 8, 15, 25].

REPI rationale management is relatively new compared to the role of rationale in requirements and system design. In contrast with requirements and design rationale, REPI rationale is not directly linked with the product or tangible artifacts such as a System/Software Requirements Specification (SRS) or Design Document. Instead, REPI is concerned with the process by which the requirements were developed and trapping failures early in the SDLC where the greatest benefit can be achieved [26]. Therefore, rationale management based on Failure Mode Effects Analysis (FMEA) [14], and applying improvements based on measured deficiency is more appropriate for REPI. Thus, we are using QOC largely based on FMEA.

Absence of REPI rationale can prevent an improvement decision from taking effect as intended. Complementing the uses of rationale described in [7] [Chap. 1, Sect. 1.4 in this book], our study indicated that poor rationale management contributed to the following situations:

1. *Incorrect decisions.* The SDLC staff attributed the poor quality requirements to perceived process problems rather than actual reasons.
2. *Resistance to change.* Lack of knowledge of the objectives and potential benefits of the improved RE process, led to resistance to change.
3. *Poor conformance to the improved process.* Lack of knowledge amongst users resulted in poor process conformance.
4. *Using inconsistent versions of the RE process.* The SDLC staff could not differentiate between the improved RE process and the previous version of it, because the improvement had not been made explicit.
5. *Poor perceptions of accountability of RE.* Without rationale and supporting metrics, senior managers could not see how REPI would produce high quality requirements.
6. *Poor planning of improvement beyond the current rollout.* P&Q staff could not plan for future rollouts, even though there was an opportunity. This further affected organizational learning.
7. *Poor knowledge reuse.* Process users did not reuse the knowledge of *why* behind the decisions and *how* such decisions were translated into

practice. This forced every process improvement cycle to be a "new" exercise that reinvented the wheel.

The above observations clearly suggested the need for RE process users to actively participate in REPI by understanding the rationale, providing feedback and participating in pilot REPI exercises and actual new process rollout.

19.3   Challenges Associated with REPI Rationale Capture and Reuse

In large projects, rationale plays a significant role in providing a justification for the involved costs [17]. Two major issues in REPI rationale management are: how to represent the rationale? and how to retrieve the rationale (for instance, browse, view, filter)? These two REPI rationale management issues raise the following challenges similar to those described in [7] [Chap. 1, Sects. 1.1 and 1.5 in this book]:

1. A group of people may be involved in an REPI exercise; but the decided REPI may not represent the consensus.
2. Some issues related to REPI may be tacitly, rather than explicitly, defined. Capture of tacit rationale is costly and its reuse is difficult especially in the absence of the staff that participated in earlier REPI.
3. Rationale involved in REPI can be voluminous and it may be difficult to record all of it. Further, effective reuse of voluminous rationale requires selective access.
4. Rationale to be categorized into two forms – one justifying the REPI costs against organizational benefits, and the other justifying REPI against day-to-day problems faced by the SDLC staff.
5. Finally, [6, 17, 18] have found that it is difficult to identify whether the organization's REPI mandate is synchronized against the business goals.

REPI rationale management should align with the activities of RE practitioners that involve customers, teams, schedules, costs, and budgets [28]. Inappropriate terminology and overly complex notations will result in an impractical, costly and untenable approach. REPI can be made less complex by employing a structured step-by-step approach of rationale capturing.

19.4   Capturing Rationale: A Tested Method

This section presents a methodology that is used to capture rationale for REPI. The method presented here has been tested in a large multinational software organization described in the Sect. 19.5. The rationale management method we define is based on the REPI framework that we have developed [17]. The framework uses a cause–effect decision matrix to examine and measure an RE process. If the process is found to be deficient, it is improved by identifying the needed improvement on the measured deficiency [17, 18]. The components of the REPI framework are RE process measurement, determining the strategic outcomes, identifying RE process gaps (defined as the difference between desired and actual processes), prioritizing and eliminating them, and rolling out a new and improved RE process. Identifying rationale capture points in the context of REPI's components forms a first step towards rationale capture and reuse. By making the rationale capture explicit in the framework, we can explore the possibility of applying this methodology to other REPI research frameworks such as good practice and risk-based REPI approaches [23, 27].

19.4.1 Positioning Rationale in REPI Framework

To provide a manageable structure to facilitate rationale reuse, it is important to position the rationale capture points. Figure 19.1 indicates the relationship between REPI and rationale.

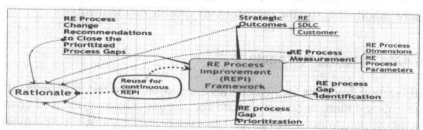

Fig. 19.1. REPI framework with horizontal lines representing its components. Dotted lines with arrows indicate the rationale capture points and reuse

Strategic outcomes shown in Fig. 19.1 are usually related to the way projects are managed, and include goals such as reduced software development cycle time due to reduced requirements defects and early detection of them, reduced rework due to removal of duplicate and erroneous requirements and enhanced customer satisfaction as errors are removed before reaching the customer [23]. Failures in one or more strategic outcomes will provide the justification for initiating REPI. For example, the strategic outcomes may identify the need to determine and record the percentage of severe requirement defects delivered to customer, schedule and cost overruns, and the amount of rework. This set of (annotated) failure data can be seen to provide a rationale to identify RE as a KPA for improvement. This rationale also helps to determine the urgency and importance of a particular REPI activity against the rest. Rationale behind RE process measurement scales are RE process effectiveness and efficiency applied against various process dimensions commonly employed by practitioners [18]. The REPI framework described here identifies the process gaps against the process dimensions, and prioritizes the process gaps based on urgency, importance and costs associated with process gap elimination in order to improve the RE process. The REPI framework will reuse the rationale captured for continuous REPI.

The rationale capture points shown in Fig. 19.1 provide the following information:

1. Strategic outcomes and how they are determined
2. Process metrics for measurement and how they are determined
3. Reasons behind identifying a process gap
4. Reasons behind prioritizing a process gap for elimination
5. How various recommendations, when implemented, will eliminate one or more RE process gaps

The general guidelines for rationale capture in the following sections can be modified to suit the organizations specific requirements.

19.4.2 Capturing Rationale

This section describes the methodology to capture rationale at various capture points. Often, organizations are focused on achieving reduced costs, optimized schedules, and enhanced customer satisfaction while improving their RE processes [12, 24, 28]. In the following section, we describe the rationale associated with determining the strategic outcomes and what benefit they bring to the organization. This forms a body of knowledge that can be reused across all projects in the organization as described in [7] [Chap. 1, Sect. 1.4 in this book]. Following this, we describe the need for measurement based on process dimensions and parameters, and the associated rationale. We then describe the rationale associated in identifying and classifying RE process gaps that influence poor quality requirements and provide recommendations and associated rationale for closing the RE process gaps. Examples of each of these capture points are provided in the case study snapshot in Sect. 19.5.

Rationale Associated with Strategic Outcomes

Since REPI is an accountable exercise, organizations usually set a list of strategic outcomes expected of REPI. The example provided in the case study snapshot (see Table 19.1) groups outcomes under RE, SDLC, and Customer. We observed in our study that the rationale options for strategic outcomes are: reduced defects leakage to customers; reduced rework in SDLC; and reduced SDLC time leading to cost savings. We have developed a formula that shows the relationships between these rationale options and how they can be used to determine strategic outcomes, however, we are bound to keep this formula confidential.

Rationale Associated with Process Dimensions

Irrespective of the strategy adopted by an organization, process dimensions are required to allow measurement of RE processes. Dimensions are required to assess an RE process while RE is active. Dimensions can prevent wrong decisions being made in a hurry towards the end of the SDLC (such as, cancellation of defects during release, in an effort to close them rather than fix them). Usually RE is examined and improved based on its subphases such as elicitation, analysis, validation, documentation, and management [11, 13, 31]. Each of the subphases are examined to see the input is transformed to the expected output [11, 13]. This approach deprives us of examining all options available for improvement. Further, we argue that these relate more closely to RE tasks and not to other dimensions such as estimations, artifacts produced by RE, automation, and roles [19]. Process dimensions provide two advantages. First, practitioners usually work in terms of schedules, tasks, artifacts that are created at the end of some milestones, disciplines, and roles. Second, categorizing process gaps under dimensions makes examination, prioritization, and elimination more manageable thus providing a structure for recording and reusing rationale. However, all of the process dimensions mentioned above may not be applicable to one organization. Therefore, we suggest that organizations tailor their process dimensions with rationale such that reuse of rationale will assist REPI. The example given in the case study snapshot (see Table 19.2) provides some suggested dimensions.

Rationale Associated with Process Parameters

Process dimensions are broad in nature and a further classification within the process dimensions is required irrespective of the strategic outcome used. Some examples of parameters against each of the dimensions are represented in Table 19.3. By doing this, various options of parameters are considered and argued as to why a parameter is an important subject. Further, parameters are required to attribute requirement defects to RE process problems. In the absence of this, a requirement defect can be mistaken for a coding problem that may be resolved using expensive methods such as iterative code review.

Rationale Associated with Identifying a Process Gap

We observe the RE process against the dimensions and parameters and determine various process gaps that cause poor quality requirements. Such observations without rationale do not convey a purpose. We can determine the process gaps by examining the intermediate causes that effect RE, Risk Management (RM) (because poor RM affects RE process effectiveness), and Change Management (CM) (because poor CM affects RE process efficiency) problems, and basic causes that influence the intermediate causes [17, 18]. When justifications of observations are recorded in the form of rationale, it is possible to answer the first question in REPI: "What is wrong with our RE processes?"

Rationale Associated with Prioritizing Process Gaps

Process gaps can be prioritized for elimination based on a quantitative approach that is common to cause–effect matrices wherein the priority is determined based on how many problems a cause is influencing [10]. However, this does not guarantee the best results always, since elimination of numbers of insignificant process problems may not lead to noticeable improvements. We argue that a qualitative approach will maximize returns on REPI. Therefore, we use strategic outcomes to prioritize the process gaps for elimination to guide REPI.

Rationale Associated with Process Improvement Recommendations

A list of recommendations in the form of direct negatives pinpointed against the prioritized process gaps is drawn up against the process gaps identified to improve the process. Section 19.5 provides examples of some recommendations. The recommendations, together with associated rationale will constitute answers to the second question in REPI: "How can we make RE processes more effective and efficient?"

In the following section, we present a case study snapshot that uses this rationale capture method.

19.5   A Snapshot of a Case Study

This section provides examples of the methodology in the previous section in the context of a case study we have conducted. Interested readers may contact the authors for a copy of the complete case study. The case study comprises a body of knowledge as to *why* REPI is needed and project and product rationale as to *how* REPI was captured. Both integrate to form reusable rationale for REPI.

19.5.1 Description of the Case Study

Z1[21] is a quality certified organization, wherein RE was a part of the quality program. Z1's RE process is well defined. The purpose of Z1's RE process is to establish complete and consistent requirements. The workproducts and various activities of the RE process are already established. Z1's RE process focuses on the requirements review process for validating and verifying requirements. Various documentation templates assist process users to comply with the RE process.

This study was initiated to establish industry-based evidence for the REPI framework we proposed [17]. The agreed goal of this study was in three phases: Assessment, Piloting REPI, and Continuous REPI.

The initial phase of the case study investigated whether senior management were aware of a problem with the RE process. Based on analysis of the data obtained through questionnaires, we concluded that an RE problem existed. Once this was established, we examined the RE process against the process dimensions and parameters. This examination involved participating in specification reviews, one-to-one interviews with SDLC and P&Q staff and various SDLC documentation that directly or indirectly related to RE and various metrics related to RE. To establish the correctness of the observations, we administered a very detailed questionnaire to the SDLC staff. There was consensus from the survey participants that inclusion of REPI rationale was important. Some respondents indicated a willingness to participate in future REPI, but only if the rationale

---

[21] De-identified for reasons of confidentiality

associated with the proposed changes were provided. In general, analysis of the questionnaire data confirmed what we had observed as part of the RE team.

The main sources of information used in this case study are Z1's business plans, process, and project specific SDLC information. The results presented are a subset of the data collected but serve to demonstrate the practical application of the steps given in Sect. 19.4.

19.5.2 Rationale Associated with Determining Strategic Outcomes for Z1

Applying the description in "Rationale Associated with Identifying a Process Gap," the strategic outcomes for Z1 are shown in Table 19.1. These were calculated using the cost savings formula mentioned before to allow finding and fixing of requirement defects during RE rather than later.

Table 19.1. Strategic outcome with rationale for Z1 with Benefit index of 1 = Reduced Costs, 2 = Optimized schedules and 3 = Enhanced customer satisfaction

	strategy	arguments to establish the strategy	benefits
RE	increased number of good quality requirements [18]	cost and schedule overruns are noticed by Z1's customers; therefore, it is important and urgent to reduce costs and schedule overruns	1, 2, 3
SDLC	improved CM, with customers commitment to changes [17, 18]	customers are introducing changes that in effect are additional features and functionality that were not initially agreed to, without committing to additional costs, time and material; this is important and urgent to the success of the project	1, 2
Customer	severe defects should be resolved before they leak through to the customer [16, 30, 32]	defects found by customers are expensive to fix; this can create unpaid work, therefore losses to Z1	1, 2, 3

19.5.3 Rationale Associated with Process Dimensions and Process Parameters for Z1

The various process dimensions we established to ensure that the RE process is assessed during RE rather than later are shown in Table 19.2. Process parameters established against the above process dimensions are indicated in Table 19.3. Process parameters help prevent requirement defects being mistaken for other defects.

Table 19.2. Some proposed RE process dimensions and associated rationale

dimension	arguments to establish dimensions
(A) time and effort	this is an important dimension that determines how RE is arranged over time and staffed
(B) RE artifacts	various deliverables like observations, data, information, effects, or results, in the form of documents or otherwise resulting from the process usage are important to determine during REPI
(C) RE activities	this is an important dimension to determine what activities produce which artifacts, or at the very least effect significant changes to an artifact
(D) disciplines & automation	automation is an important dimension for REPI as technology and tools are needed to support RE
(E) roles	identification of various roles and the differences between them is an important dimension in REPI

Table 19.3. Some process parameters for Z1 and associated rationale for the dimensions (#) in Table 19.2

#	parameter	arguments to establish parameters
A	appropriateness of allocated RE budget	this is required to determine if RE budget is explicit and sufficient
	consumption of RE budget	under-consumption of RE budget can result in the overall SDLC cost overruns; public domain data indicates RE effort as 13%-15% of the total SDLC effort [4]
B	establishing a set of artifacts	this will make sure that RE is not prematurely exited
	establishing change control on artifacts templates	change control is important to make sure that unpaid rework does not get into SDLC
	modeling information in SRS	models visually represent the customers needs, and the SDLC staff's understanding of those needs
C	formal identification of RE milestones	milestones are required to identify that a particular activity is due to complete
	identification of dependencies between activities	unidentified dependencies results in deadlock situations while two or more parties wait for each others deliverables, and go into indefinite wait state
D	identification of automation needs	automation is essential for RE where methods, such as manual traceability establishment and change management become too tedious
E	identification of roles in RE	it is important to identify roles of the SDLC staff in RE, particularly the role of the customers
	setting up privileges	this is an important parameter since certain activities should be limited only to certain roles

19.5.4 Rationale Associated with Identifying Process Gaps

Even though the RE process in Z1 is well-defined, some observations pointed to RE process gaps that influence poor quality requirements. An exhaustive list of low-level process gaps mapped against process dimensions and parameters were identified which converged to some high-level process gaps in our decision matrix [17, 18]. See Table 19.4 for examples.

Table 19.4. Low-level process gaps mapped against dimensions and parameters

#	parameter	low-level process gap identified
A	appropriateness of allocated RE budget	RE budget was not explicitly established in Z1, posing various risks associated with cost and effort
B	establishing change control on artifacts templates	template users edited templates to suit their projects without formalizing them. Inconsistencies in templates confused some SDLC staff forcing them to reinvent existing templates
C	identification of dependencies between activities	critical paths were not established in WBS
D	identification of automation needs	no automatic tools were used to track requirements
E	setting up privileges	most staff established their own definitions of "good quality requirement" even though their role was just to use the definition established by P&Q

19.5.5 Process Gap Prioritization and Recommendations

Using a cause–effect matrix, the low level gaps in Z1 converged to a smaller number of high level process gaps (PG)s. Direct negatives of process gaps form the recommendations to represent the criteria and options. The priority is established based on the organization's strategic outcomes.

Process Gap (PG)1 with associated rationale. RE's relationship to CM was not well-defined. *Criteria*: this increased the risks of penalty of accepting changes without the customer's commitment to those changes in terms of increased costs and enhanced schedules. Further, it was difficult to differentiate changes that influenced schedules from those that did not. *Options*: have a common CM for entire SDLC and take all changes through CM, *or* have a separate CM within RE to handle all requirements changes. *Priority*: low.

Process Gap (PG)2 with associated rationale. Various sub-phases of RE were not distinctive giving an impression that RE was an ad hoc collection of activities. *Criteria*: this led to inaccuracies in judgment related to an issue raised out of a review that demanded one or more iterations. *Options*: to require each RE subphase to output an identified PM artifact, or have a milestone-based approach wherein a milestone not necessarily produced an artifact, but marked the successful completion of an activity. *Priority*: medium.

Process Gap (PG)3 with associated rationale. Clearly, the definition of "Good quality requirements" was not tied to the process. *Criteria*: the checklist that was made available on Z1's intranet characterized a good quality requirement, but was not in consistent use as part of the RE process. Further, the level of attention to detail in the specification was not consistent. *Options*: peer reviews should focus on checking if requirements quality is high and consistent, *or* checklist entry to demonstrate requirements quality to be made compulsory. *Priority*: low.

Process Gap (PG)4 with associated rationale. Poor automation of RE and the subsequent phases of the SDLC which affect RE were creating significant time-bound communication problems with respect to requirements. *Criteria*: the tools used for SDLC management were estimation tools, defects trackers (database where defects are stored, and tracked for their status until they are fixed or cancelled) and general information management tools like spreadsheets. RE tools were not used to automate requirements management, CM and RM. *Options:* requirements management to be automated using tools, or CM and RM to be automated separately thereby automating part of RE. *Priority*: medium.

Process Gap (PG)5 with associated rationale. No clear distinction between requirements risks and issues. *Criteria*: risks were also logged as issues, which were usually the conclusions about requirement specification in a review. *Options*: when to log an issue as against a defect or a risk to be made consistent, *or* specificity of issues to be established and classified based on its significance. *Priority*: high.

19.6   Conclusion

While we have made the case for REPI rationale capture, we faced the following challenges in organization Z1: the benefit of rationale capture was initially perceived as a mechanism to certify REPI as a KPA; the use of natural language in the RE phase did not encourage structured and more formal notations for rationale; some people in Z1 thought that the level of detail expected in the rationale was too fine grained; the Cost Benefit Analysis (CBA) of recording rationale in addition to REPI was not calculated since metrics collection needed for CBA was a difficult exercise.

Rationale in process improvement provides reasoning behind an activity. If an organization is building systems integrated into repeatable, well-understood and controllable development processes, then continuous improvement of processes is inevitable, and rationale associated with improvement forms an important IP. Such claims are consistent with the experience of Z1, which is currently improving its RE process with extensive use of rationale generated through this research project. By describing the process improvement rationale, we can eliminate unclear ideas, and tentative ideas that are used to form further ideas that influence poor decision-making. Further, rationale helps to eliminate misconceptions that are common to any process improvement exercise. Well-structured rationale will provide satisfactory answers to the common questions in practitioners' minds "what is wrong with our RE process, and should we consider improving the RE process and roll out the new process now?" The approach we have offered guides an organization step by step to eliminate process gaps. By recording the rationale associated with each of the steps, and persistence of it, all parties involved in the process know not only *what* and *how* but also *why*. Knowing *why* is a critical part of process improvement that also allows for the inevitable changes associated with any living system or organization.

We have now reused the REPI rationale in Z1 for a project concerned with testing the effectiveness of the recommended improvements in reducing the number of defects that reach the customers. Further, we have reused the rationale behind REPI strategies to examine how an increase or decrease of certain parameters influences the testing process and achieve cost savings similar to REPI. We next want to examine if reuse of rationale will prompt proactive process improvement rather than the current tendency to improve processes reactively.

References

[1]   Aaen I (2003) Software Process improvement: Blueprints versus recipes. IEEE Software 3: pp. 86–93

[2]   Bratthall L, Johansson E, Regnell B (2000) Is a Design Rationale Vital when Predicting Change Impact? – A Controlled Experiment on Software Architecture Evolution. In: Proceedings of Conference on Product Focused Software Process Improvement. Berlin Heidelberg New York, Springer, June 20–22, Finland pp. 126–139

[3]   Çetin H, Satis B, Sokman BB (2005) Requirements Engineering and Team Development – Practical Process Improvement for Requirements Engineering. In: http://courses.cs.deu.edu.tr/cse518/Projects/Group1.doc

[4]   CHAOS (2004) The Standish Group Report 2004. The Standish Group, In: http://www.standishgroup.com/reports

[5]   Davis A, Overmyer S, Jordan K, Caruso J (1993) Identifying and measuring quality in a software requirement specification. In: Proceedings of the First International Software Metrics Symposium. Los Almitos, CA: IEEE Computer Society Press pp. 164–175

[6]   Dion R (1993) Process Improvement and the Corporate Balance Sheet. IEEE Software 10: pp. 28–35

[7]   Dutoit AH, McCall R, Mistrík I, Paech B (2006) Rationale management in software engineering. Berlin Heidelberg New York: Springer

[8]   Dutoit AH and Paech B (2000) Supporting Evolution: Using Rationale in Use Case Driven Software Development. In: Proceedings of 6th International Workshop on Requirements Engineering Foundation for Software Quality, REFSQ 2000, June 5–6, Stockholm, Sweden

[9]   Emam KE, Drouin J-N, Melo W (1997) SPICE: Theory and Practice of Software Process Improvement and Capability Determination. USA

[10] Fakharzadeh C (2000) Causal Analysis and Resolution. In: http://sunset.usc.edu/classes/cs577b_2000/EC/16/EC-16.pdf

[11] Hull MEC, Jackson K, Dick AJJ (2002) Requirements Engineering. Berlin Heidelberg New York: Springer. Brunel University, Uxbridge, UK

[12] Jeletic K, Pajerski R, Brown C (1996) Software Process Improvement Guidebook. Software Engineering Lab Series. NASA, USA

[13] Macaulay LA (1996) Requirements Engineering. Applied Computing. Manchester, UK, Berlin Heidelebrg New York: Springer,

[14] McDermott RE, Mikulak RJ, and Beauregard MR (2000) The Basics of FMEA. Productivity, USA

[15] Myers KL, Zumel NB, Garcia PE (1999) Automated Capture of Design Rationale. In: Proceedings of Eleventh National Conference on Innovative Applications of Artificial Intelligence 1999, July 18–22, USA

[16] Olson T, Beeson D (2002) How to Practically Improve Your Requirements Process Using the CMMI Framework. In: Proceedings of 2nd CMMISM Technology Conference, 2002, 11–14 November, India

[17] Palyagar B (2004) A Framework for Validating Process Improvements in Requirements Engineering. In: Proceedings of 12th International RE 04-IEEE Doctoral Symposium, September 7, Kyoto, Japan pp. 33–36

[18] Palyagar B (2004) Measuring and Influencing Requirements Engineering Processes. In: Proceedings of 9th Australian Workshop on Requirements Engineering, AWRE, December 6–7, Adelaide, Australia pp. 13.1–13.11

[19] Palyagar B, Richards D (2005) A Communication Protocol for Requirements Engineering Processes. In: Proceedings of the 11th International Workshop on Requirements Engineering – Foundation For Software Quality, REFSQ 2005, June 12–13, Porto, Portugal

[20] Pande PS, Neuman RP, Cavanagh R (2002) The Six Sigma Way Team Fieldbook: An Implementation Guide for Project Improvement Teams. New York, USA: McGraw-Hill

[21] Persse JR (2002) Implementing Capability Maturity Model. Wiley, USA

[22] Polyak ST, Tate A (1998) Rationale in Planning: Causality, Dependencies, and Decisions. Knowledge Engineering Review 13 (3): pp. 247-262

[23] Sawyer P, Sommerville I, Viller S (1997) Requirements Process Improvement Through the Phased Introduction of Good Practice. Software Process: Improvement and Practice 3: pp. 19-34

[24] Schaeffer MD (1998) Capability Maturity Model Process Improvement. Crosstalk The Journal of Defence Software Engineering pp. 4–5

[25] Shum S (1991) Cognitive Dimensions of Design Rationale. In: Proceedings of Human–Computer Interaction, 1991, August 20–23, UK pp. 331–344

[26] Sommerville I, Kotonya G (1998) Requirements Engineering Processes and Techniques.England: Wiley

[27] Sommerville I, Sawyer P Requirements Engineering a Good Practice Guide. England: Wiley

[28] Stelzer D, Mellis W (1998) Success Factors of Organizational Change in Software Process Improvement. Software Process - Improvement and Practice 4: pp. 227-250

[29] Verner JM, Evanco WM (2003) An Investigation into Software Development Process Knowledge. Managing Software Engineering Knowledge. New York: Springer, pp. 29-49

[30] Vinter O, Lauesen S, Pries-Heje J (1999) Process Improvement Experiment Final Report - A Methodology for Preventing Requirements Issues from Becoming Defects (PRIDE). European System and Software Initiative, Copenhagen, Denmark

[31] Wiegers K (2004) The Real World of Requirements Engineering. Requirenautics Quarterly The Newsletter of the BCS Requirements Engineering: pp. 5–8

[32] Wiegers KE (2003) Software Requirements. Microsoft Press, USA

20 Using Patterns for Sharing Requirements Engineering Process Rationales

L. Hagge, F. Houdek, K. Lappe, B. Paech

Abstract: This chapter introduces patterns as a means of supporting knowledge transfer in the requirements engineering (RE) domain. RE patterns capture and consolidate rationale for RE decisions which have been successfully taken in several comparable projects. Their main goal is to make these successful RE practices available to project teams on the job. The chapter describes a procedure for collecting patterns, presents three examples of RE patterns and discusses several applications of patterns, including process improvement.

Keywords: requirements engineering; rationale; patterns; process improvement

20.1 Introduction

Requirements engineering (RE) has been recognized as a critical success factor for nearly every systems or software engineering project [17], but no canonical approach to engineering requirements has been established in practice. Best-practice collections or software engineering methods captured in textbooks provide a framework of standard RE products and activities, yet it is often not possible to apply them directly because of conflicting project constraints. Also, the RE process depends on many individual project characteristics such as the project type and size or stakeholder groups [2,18].

For successful RE process implementation, practitioners need methodological and situational knowledge that has to be reliable and accessible on demand for the project teams [19]. The RE patterns presented in this chapter address this need for consolidated and structured knowledge. They are captured by reflecting and analyzing comparable situations (observations) of independent projects (case studies) with particular emphasis on the solution of conflicts underlying the situations. Those decisions or actions that were observed to be successful in at least two projects are recorded as patterns (Fig. 20.1).

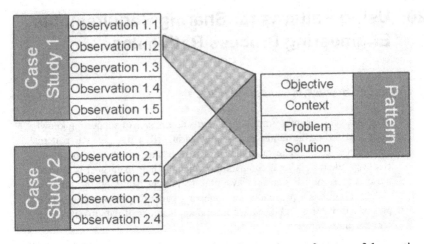

Fig. 20.1. RE Patterns comprise recurring observations of successful practices from different projects in an instructive format

RE patterns are described in an instructive format that makes the pattern content easily accessible. The patterns contain pairs of problems and solutions, enabling the selection of patterns for specific situations. They are reliable as they are obtained solely from proven real-life experience.

By definition, RE patterns support reuse of process knowledge. Furthermore, they can be employed for a variety of purposes in RE process improvement [10] [Chap. 1, Section 1.4 in this book]. Section 20.4. sets out how they were used to build consensus, to validate decisions, to support training, and to facilitate process assessment.

The rest of this chapter is structured as follows: Section 20.2 introduces the RE pattern format and describes the procedure for obtaining RE patterns. Section 20.3 presents three examples for RE patterns that have been identified using the described procedure with industrial project managers. They provide nonobvious advice from practical experience that is usually not covered by textbooks. Section 20.4 summarizes experience gained in working with RE patterns, including process improvement, teaching, and RE maturity assessment. Section 20.5 concludes with a discussion of RE patterns as reusable rationale.

20.2   Capturing Engineering Experience in Patterns

This section discusses patterns as a general way of collecting and sharing successful engineering practices and process rationale.

20.2.1 Background

Originally developed in civil engineering [1], patterns have been adopted by software engineers to be a means of providing well-formatted and instructive descriptions of good engineering practices. First their application focussed on design (e.g., [8,11]). Today, also process patterns are a well-known and established format for knowledge transfer commonly used in a variety of fields. Known examples are quality patterns [7,13], technology experience packages [5], process patterns [3], and anti-(process) patterns [6].

Pattern descriptions typically contain an objective to be achieved, the problem statement or context to which the pattern applies, and a recommended action for resolving the situation. Further elements include instructions for and experience from implementing the patterns and examples of known uses. Specifying problem statements explicitly in terms of underlying conflicting forces makes patterns more practicable as they directly address the situations encountered by project team managers.

Quality patterns (as RE patterns) employ the concept of providing prescriptive descriptions based on explicitly described empirical observations. The experience factory paradigm [4] is an example for a process improvement framework built on the same concept. It uses so-called "experience packages", which are comparable to patterns, to provide empirically established and thus trustworthy experience.

20.2.2 The Pattern Vector: Task, Forces and Action

The pattern vector is a compact pattern notation that combines an instruction for solving a problem with the conditions under which it should be used. It is best introduced using "a window place", a frequently quoted pattern from Christopher Alexander's "The Timeless Way of Building" [1], as an example:

In living rooms where people want to be comfortable, a sitting area should be located close to the windows. In rooms where the sitting area is not placed near the windows, people would be caught in a conflict: they would be drawn to the chairs to sit down and relax, but at the same time they would also be drawn towards the windows where the light is.

Using the window place pattern would resolve and prevent the stress situation.

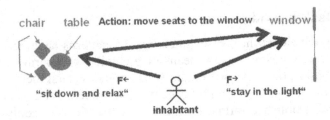

Fig. 20.2. Alexander's "A Window Place" pattern in the proposed pattern format

The underlying notion is that patterns help in resolving conflicts or stress situations – which are frequently perceived as "being torn apart by two forces". Figure 20.2 uses this metaphor to illustrate the window place pattern: people experience two opposing forces pulling them to the chairs and to the window.

Taking this picture as general reasoning, it has been proposed that patterns should be written as vectors [12]

$$P = (T, F^\leftarrow, F^\rightarrow, A),$$

where T is a task, $F^\leftarrow$ and $F^\rightarrow$ are the opposing forces generating the stress situation, and A is an action compensating the difference of $F^\leftarrow$ and $F^\rightarrow$, i.e., the stress. This pattern vector covers the pattern essence. The pattern statement can be created from the pattern vector using

IF $F^\leftarrow$ BUT $F^\rightarrow$ THEN A TO T.

It provides a short description of the pattern that helps readers to decide on the pattern's relevance and applicability for their purposes at a glance. For the "Window Place", the description reads as follows:

IF	people are drawn towards the chairs to sit down and relax
BUT	people are drawn towards the windows where the light is
THEN	move seats to the window
TO	design a comfortable living room

Using the same format for expressing RE experience underlines the general nature of the pattern vector, as is shown by the following example:

IF	a project has to step back to clarify the requirements
BUT	a project has to advance to meet the milestones
THEN	detail the specification documents by writing test cases
TO	elicit requirements optimizing completeness and the level of detail

For practical purposes, patterns have to be explained in a more elaborate format like in the established pattern collections, for example [11]. The task is split into an objective and a context, the forces are embedded into a problem description, and the action is called the solution. The solution can be illustrated by showing a model of its underlying structure and adding detailed instructions on how to implement the proposed solution. The usability of the solution can be supported by listing application areas and constraints for its successful implementation. Additionally, experience, known uses, and related patterns should be described. Section 20.3 sets out the full version of an RE pattern as an example.

20.2.3 Patterns and Rationale

Patterns are related to process rationale in the sense that they intend to capture reusable rationale for taking particular actions within processes. Figure 20.3 depicts the relation by mapping the pattern elements to the QOC notation (questions, options, and criteria [9,15]):

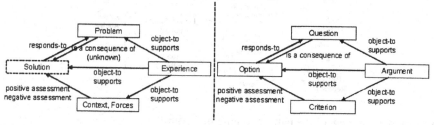

Fig. 20.3. Mapping RE patterns (*left*) to the QOC schema (*right*)

The problem description captures the decision to be taken, while the proposed solution offers one possible option for this decision. The objective, context description, and forces provide the qualities that help to evaluate the applicability of the proposed solution. Experience gained by using the pattern provides additional arguments in favor of the proposed solution.

While in QOC the entire set of options would be contained in one schema, each pattern proposes only a single option. The full set of options is given by a family of patterns addressing the same problem.

20.2.4 Obtaining Patterns from Analyzing Case Studies

Patterns are best captured nonintrusively, long after their proposed actions have been taken and their consequences have been observed [10] [Chap. 1, Sect. 1.2 in this book]. The procedure for discovering and documenting RE patterns consists of four major activities [14] (Fig. 20.4):

1. *Case studies* are collected from real-world projects. They contain accounts of important events and experience from projects.
2. The case studies are analyzed and reorganized into a set of *observations*, which describe events in the format of the pattern vector.
3. To identify patterns, the entire set of case studies is searched for identical observations from different projects. These observations are marked as *pattern candidates*.
4. The pattern candidates are elaborated into *pattern descriptions*, which are then published in a central pattern repository.

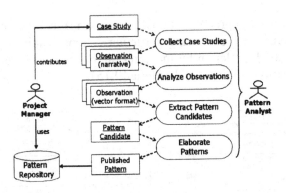

Fig. 20.4. Overview of the pattern mining procedure

A good way of capturing patterns is to organize a pattern workshop that follows the procedure above. Pattern workshops typically last around two to three hours and need a convenor, who should aim at bringing together six to twelve active participants.

20.2.5 Experience

To discover RE patterns, workshops have been successfully held on several occasions, ranging from working group meetings to international conferences [16,20]. Experience shows that such pattern workshops should be called for a previously agreed major topic, which should be specific enough to ensure that the attendees will be reporting comparable case studies but which, at the same time, should be general enough to allow for individual and diversified reports. Good examples for such topics were "RE in relations with subcontractors" or "tracing requirements in projects".

In most cases, the major challenge has been to identify adequate forces for describing the conflicts. Often, observers initially addressed the symptoms of a conflict, while the underlying conflict became clear only after discussion in the group. Also, frequently more than two forces seemed to apply to an observation, which often resolved into more than one conflict being addressed in an observation [14].

20.3   Examples for RE Patterns

This section introduces three RE patterns that have been identified in several workshops with participants from industry. They illustrate the pattern format and the variety of topics that are covered by a pattern collection. The first pattern is presented in the full RE pattern format, while the second and third are presented as extended abstracts only:

– "Detail the Specification by Writing Test Cases" addresses the RE process. It is applied when the specification turns out to be ambiguous or incomplete while a project is ongoing.
– "Organize Specification Along Project Structure" proposes an organizational measure. It recommends using the same structures for project management and requirements elicitation to minimize coordination efforts.
– "Provide Statements of Objective" improves the specification quality. The pattern recommends including requirements rationale into the specification to enable creativity and efficiency in the subsequent design.

The three patterns are examples taken from the Requirements Engineering Patterns Repository, REPARE, a constantly growing collection of RE patterns that is made available on the Web at http://repare.desy.de. The patterns are named and referred to by the action they propose. This taxonomy has been found to be efficient for communication and is also understandable for anyone without further knowledge of the RE pattern.

20.3.1 Detail the Specification by Writing Test Cases

If a specification turns out to be ambiguous or incomplete during the run of a project, this pattern describes a way of clarifying the specification without halting the implementation work (see also Fig. 20.5).

IF	the project has to step back to clarify the requirements
BUT	the project has to advance to meet the milestones
THEN	detail the specification documents by writing test cases
TO	elicit requirements optimizing completeness and level of detail

Objective. Usefulness (e.g., clarity, testability, coverage) of a specification is to be improved after it has already been frozen.

Context. Client and supplier have agreed on a specification that has been frozen, e.g., it is part of a contract, or because the project has progressed to the next phase. When using the specification for design, implementation, and test, the parties find that it is incomplete and ambiguous.

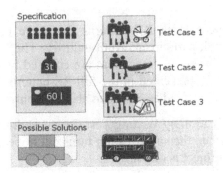

Fig. 20.5. Test cases offer a more detailed picture of the intended solution

Problem. The specification is in a state that endangers the project success, yet the necessary time and resources are not available for improving the specification.

Forces. The pattern is related to pushing the progress in the project:
– The project has to step back to improve the specification.
– The project has to move ahead to meet the milestones.

Solution. Leave the specification as it is and create test cases instead. The test cases should describe the usage and the expected output from an end user perspective. Provide the test cases to the implementation team, and agree that the test cases will become the criteria for approval and in this sense an appendix to the specification (see Fig. 20.6).

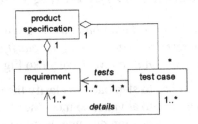

Fig. 20.6. Test cases contribute to the specification by detailing requirements

Structure. Test cases explain the context of requirements and provide examples for scenarios that rely on a requirement. They should contain an objective, preconditions, a course of events including exceptions and alternatives, and expected results for specific inputs. They can hence improve the level of detail, the clarity, the coverage, and the testability of requirements, for instance.

Instructions. The key to good test cases is the end user perspective. Test cases can be collected in different ways:
- Let key users describe use cases and concrete usage scenarios of the system and employ them as test cases.
- Let key users conduct tests and record their activities and their expectations.
- Let key users explain for each requirement in which situations the requirement is relevant to them, then create scenarios for each such situation.

Application Areas. This pattern has so far been observed in small and medium projects conducted by teams working to a great extent on a basis of understanding.

Constraints.
- Usually contracting is based on the initial specification, and the introduction of test cases later on can be seen as an attempt to extend or modify the project scope. This will therefore only work if both the client and supplier follow the same intention of improving the project quality.
- Ideally, the approach has to be established without affecting the project resources, implying that it should be applied to only a few requirements at a time.

Consequences.

➚ The test cases are used as a new basis for implementation.
➚ Hidden assumptions and wishes are revealed and made explicit before tests and approvals.
➘ Test cases can lead to unsolicited updates of the requirements specification from the client side.

Experience.
- Writing test cases cannot replace the requirements specification: generally both are needed to completely capture the different views of a project.

- It is easier to acquire resources for tests and test case specification than for requirements analysis, as the necessity of tests is generally acknowledged.
- Writing test cases helps to discover weak points in the specification.
- Test cases are best written by domain experts or end users who ideally act as multipliers in the project team.
- Test cases can be written in parallel by several independent persons.
- "Better late than never" – the availability of test cases for requirements always pays off in reduced development cycles.

Known Uses[22]. The pattern has been observed in the introduction of information systems.

- *Migration of an Information System (Logistics).* A logistics company's liability management application was to be replaced by a newly developed application. Management replaced the project leader after the specification was written. The new project leader found that the specification described the new system's functionality understandably and completely. He found a common understanding of what the new system should do had been established among all stakeholders. But he also found the specification unsuitable as a contractual basis due to the fact that the wording was ambiguous in too many places. The specification's authors resisted doing substantial rework because, if they did rework, they had to admit to mistakes in their prior work. For this reason, the new project leader convinced end users to specify and conduct tests. Clarifications took place when end users and developers discussed the test cases. This enabled the system to be introduced with the desired functionality.
- *Introduction of a Facility Management System.* To suit the purchasing of COTS components for a Facility Management System (FMS), user requirements were specified in an abstract, product-neutral style that was suitable for software selection and contracting. When customization started, more detailed issues arose and holes in the specification became apparent. Although the external developers provided features as specified, they were unable to envision the way the users intended to work with the FMS. The resulting system was functionally acceptable, but usability was low and user bias was high. As the specification could not be modified after contracting, both parties agreed to add test cases in order to better explain how the clients expected to work with the system. The

---

[22] Known uses refer to case studies from industry that have been reported in pattern workshops. Most of the material is unpublished.

developers employed the test cases as early as the module tests, thus being implicitly guided by the test cases. The result was an overall improvement of the system's ergonomics and user acceptance.

Related Patterns.

– "Bundle Requirements to Features" targets recording the relation of requirements and test cases.
– "Generate Approval Checklists" is used to record the test results.

20.3.2 Organize Specification Along Project Structure

This pattern recommends using the same structures for project management and requirements elicitation to minimize coordination efforts (see Fig. 20.7).

IF   domain experts have to negotiate requirements until mutual agreement has been reached

BUT   domain experts have to concentrate on technical work and thus are difficult to access for negotiation

THEN   organize the specification along the project structure

TO   negotiate requirements optimizing stakeholder involvement and agreement

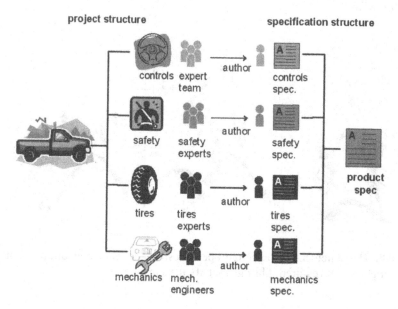

Fig. 20.7. Specification structure is in line with project structure

Summary. A project is organized according to a work breakdown structure (WBS). It should provide a single specification that covers the whole product and is agreed upon by the teams involved. Thus a collaborative working style is mandatory. However, groups of specialists tend to concentrate on the topics of their own immediate concern and may thus become too self-sufficient and difficult to access for negotiations.

Organizing the specification procedure in line with the project organization reduces communication overhead to a minimum. Each WBS team appoints an author that writes a specification from this team's view of the product. An "independent" requirements engineer creates an overall product specification from the partial ones. The requirements engineer takes responsibility for the specification progress and for ensuring requirements conflict resolution.

Known Uses. The pattern has been observed in an interdisciplinary plant construction project and in the introduction of COTS-based information systems.

20.3.3 Provide Statements of Objective With Each Requirement

Sometimes customers require technical features that seem convincing at first glance but turn out to be expensive or even impossible to realize later on. This pattern provides the ground for finding reasonable alternatives (see Fig. 20.8).

Fig. 20.8. The statement of objective opens design and implementation alternatives: wings are not required if bridges satisfy the same need

IF   the project should exploit existing solutions to benefit from their acceptance

BUT   the project has to use leading-edge technology for optimum results

THEN   provide statements of objective with each requirement

TO   analyze requirements optimizing the available design space

Summary. A customer orders the development of a new, innovative product, at the same time defining a vision that contains unacceptable technical details. Such statements frequently derive from transferring personal experience from other systems or domains to the problem at hand. Although perfectly justified, they often contain features that are unnecessary, expensive, or even detrimental.

By providing a statement of objective for each feature, a general specification of the user requirements and intentions can be obtained. For those features that correspond to impossible solutions, the statement of objective can be utilized to initiate alternative design activities.

Known Uses. The pattern has been reported from a defence project and from the introduction of an IT system for spare parts management.

20.4   Working With RE Patterns

This section cites examples for actively working with RE patterns in projects. It describes not only how patterns are made accessible on the Web but also how they have been used for process improvement, teaching students, and assessing requirements process maturity.

20.4.1 Making RE Patterns Accessible

Accessibility of RE patterns is a prerequisite to any pattern application. In most situations, readers are searching for suggestions that best fit their current circumstances. It is therefore important to make patterns searchable for the features that determine the situation's characteristics.

The pattern vector components provide an initial classification that can be used for filtering the pattern collection. Further analysis reveals additional dimensions: for example, the actors addressed by a pattern or the quality goals to be reached using a pattern. A pattern repository that implements these – and more structures – is available on the Web under the name REPARE: the Requirements Engineering Pattern Repository (repare.desy.de). It enables combinatorial queries and full text searches of patterns as well as navigation from case studies to their observed patterns and back.

In the following sections, it is assumed that patterns are available to project teams through a pattern repository.

20.4.2 RE Process Improvement: Guiding Project Teams

RE patterns are intended to guide project teams by helping them to make decisions concerning the RE process and by proposing adequate methods for the tasks they are facing. Ideally the teams simply read and use the patterns as they need them: The patterns provide coaching on the job; symbolically they replace an RE instructor (see also [10] [Chap. 1, Sect. 1.4 in this book]).

Practitioners involved in specification activities mainly refer to patterns describing RE methods and tools at a technical level such as "use requirements index cards" or "bundle requirements to features." These patterns also improve the accessibility of textbooks, which contain more exhaustive educational material, by acting as an index and thus delivering context-specific summaries and instructions.

Project leaders have been observed to first identify which of the forces from the pattern database reflect their current conditions and to then study the related patterns in order to understand how they would improve the situation. This approach yields patterns such as "organize specification along project structure" or "synchronize change requests" for setting up and managing a project.

20.4.3 RE Process Improvement: Decision Support

Another important application is usage of patterns as rationales in decision-making and reporting (see also [10] [Chap. 1, Sect. 1.4 in this book]): Explaining the patterns – especially the consequences and experience, supplemented with the known uses as proof – can convince clients and project managers of the necessity of certain RE activities and, in turn, make them provide the required resources. Also, letting the project manager then introduce the RE activities to the team (rather than an RE consultant, for instance) cuts bias against both the manager and the RE activities. The approach works for any type of patterns and has, for example, been employed to "organize the specification along the project structure" or to "generate approval checklists".

20.4.4 RE Process Improvement: Reflecting RE Skills

RE patterns are also valuable instruments for reflecting the RE skills of project teams and for challenging decisions taken by instinct. This application of patterns starts with a recent case study reported in terms of patterns: every RE activity performed is explained as the conflict it had to solve and the action taken. The conflict–action vectors can then be compared with the pattern collection: how far do they follow the patterns? Have all the recommendations of the pattern been implemented? Have the positive consequences, i.e., the pattern's potential been reached? This approach can be employed for self-reflection as well as for team discussion. It has led to very fruitful discussions in a variety of pattern analysis workshops.

20.4.5 Teaching Students

RE patterns offer a meaningful basis for supporting training through rationale as they combine technical and methodological instructions with information about specific application scenarios (see also [10] [Chap. 1, Sect. 1.4 in this book]).

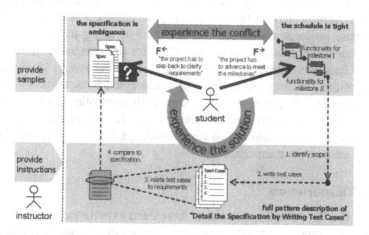

Fig. 20.9. Teaching students using the RE pattern "detail the specification by writing test cases"

Instructors should start by explaining a pattern's structure together with its relevance to practice. This should be followed by practical exercises based on material specifically created to simulate the pattern's conflict. The attendees are asked to resolve the situation by following the pattern's instructions. Examples for patterns that have been efficiently incorporated into such trainings include "use requirement index cards" and "detail the specification by writing test cases" (Fig. 20.9).

The adequacy of patterns for teaching purposes, however, depends on the pattern. Technical and methodological patterns are well suited as course teaching material, while organizational patterns such as "organize the specification along the project structure" tend to be more difficult to simulate.

20.4.6 Assessing Process Maturity

Patterns can be employed as an efficient foundation for assessing the requirements process maturity in an organization. First, it is determined whether the conflicts addressed by the patterns are present in the organization and if they are controlled. Then it is examined whether the conflicts are specifically controlled because of the patterns. The number of present and controlled conflicts serve as an indicator of the RE process quality, while conflicts purposefully controlled by patterns would indicate process reproducibility.

Figure 20.10 depicts the results of a pattern-based RE process evaluation. An initial survey covering eight projects in Germany from different sectors, including the automotive industries, transportation, and research, based on 15 RE patterns yielded that most of the conflicts addressed by the patterns were present in the projects (upper graph). Taking closer looks at individual projects underlines the potential of using patterns for process evaluations: a criticality can be computed for projects as the percentage of known conflicts relevant for the project. The awareness describes how many of the conflicts are purposefully addressed by actions with the maturity denoting the percentage of successfully controlled conflicts. By considering which RE activities the patterns refer to, the criticality, awareness, and maturity can be computed and visualized for the different phases of the RE process (bottom charts).

20.4.7 Experience

So far, the RE pattern applications have been experienced and observed in a limited number of industrial projects. Accessibility and the ability to offer applicable patterns were the critical success factors for any application. The pattern repository with its ability to search for patterns by the dimensions of the pattern vector was felt as an important improvement compared to pattern catalogues. But as the quality of the process improvement activities increases with the number of available options, and maturity assessment improves with better method coverage of the underlying patterns, extending the RE pattern collection remains the major challenge.

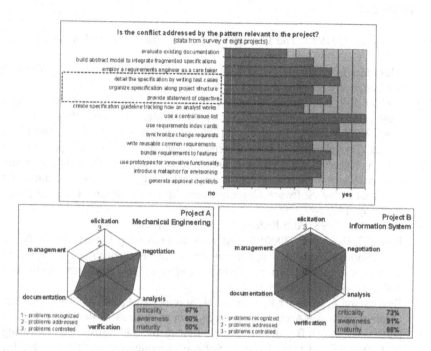

Fig. 20.10. Relevance of patterns to projects (*top*) and RE process maturity assessment based on patterns for two different projects (*bottom*)

20.5 Conclusion

RE patterns make reliable, successful RE practices available and accessible to project teams. In terms of rationale, patterns organize and deliver reusable knowledge in a generalized form that goes beyond individual cases.

RE patterns have been employed successfully for process improvement and other applications, as discussed in Section 20.4. Examples include the coaching of project teams on the job, providing arguments for justifying RE decisions teaching and training as well as evaluating RE processes. The RE pattern format and procedure for pattern search have shown to be highly useful and easy to teach Working with RE patterns is hence evolving into a powerful method for building, discussing, and transferring reusable RE process rationale.

References

[1] Alexander C (1979) The Timeless Way of Building. Oxford University Press, UK
[2] Alexander I, Maiden N (eds) (2004) Scenarios, Stories, Use Cases – Through the System Development Life Cycle. Wiley, New York
[3] Ambler SW, McGibbon B (eds) (1998) Process Patterns: Building large-scale systems using object technology. Cambridge University Press, UK
[4] Basili V, Caldiera G, Rombach D (2002) Experience Factory. In: Marciniack JJ (eds.) Encyclopedia on Software Engineering. Wiley, New York, pp. 511–519
[5] Birk A, Kröschel F (2000) A Knowledge management lifecycle for experience packages on software engineering technology. In: Ruhe G, Bomarius F (eds.) Learning Software Organizations. Springer, Berlin Heidelberg New York, pp. 142–160
[6] Brown WJ (1998) Anti Patterns. Wiley, New York
[7] Bunse C, Houdek F (2000) Transferring and Evolving Experience: A Practical Approach and Its Application on Software Inspections. In Ruhe G, Bomarius F (eds.) Learning Software Organizations. Springer, Berlin Heidelberg New York, pp. 210–226
[8] Buschmann F, Meunier R, Rohnert H, Sommerlad P, Stal M (1996) Pattern-Oriented Software Architecture – A System of Patterns. Wiley, New York
[9] Dutoit AH, Paech B (2001) Rationale Management in Software Engineering. In: Chang SK (ed.) Handbook of Software Engineering and Knowledge Engineering. World Scientific Publishing, Singapore, pp. 787–816
[10] Dutoit AH, McCall R, Mistrik, I, Paech B (2006) Rationale Management in Software Engineering. Vol. 1, Springer, Berlin Heidelberg New York
[11] Gamma E, Helm R, Johnson R, Vlissides J (1994) Design Patterns – Elements of Reusable Object-Oriented Systems. Addison Wesley, Reading, MA
[12] Hagge L, Lappe K (2005) Sharing Requirements Engineering Experience Using Patterns. IEEE Software 22(1):24–31
[13] Houdek F, Kempter H (1997) Quality patterns – an approach to packaging software engineering experience. ACM Software Engineering Notes 22(3): 81–88
[14] Lappe K and the Working Group on Requirements Engineering Patterns (WGREP) (2004) Requirements Engineering Patterns – An Approach to Capturing and Exchanging Requirements Engineering Experience. DESY 04-233, Hamburg, Germany
[15] MacLean A, Young RM, Bellotti V, Moran T (1991) Questions, options, and criteria: Elements of design space analysis. Human–Computer Interaction 6(3&4):201–250
[16] REP'04 International Workshop on Requirements Engineering Patterns, September 6, 2004, Kyoto, Japan. http://rep04.desy.de/
[17] Standish Group (1999) Extreme Chaos. http://standishgroup.com/sample_research/PDFpages/chaos1999.pdf
[18] Weber J, Weisbrod J (2003) Requirements engineering in automotive development: experiences and challenges. IEEE Software 22(1):16–24

[19] Wieser E, Schneider K, Houdek F (2000) Push or Pull: Two cognitive models of systematic experience transfer. In: Ruhe G, Bomarius F (eds.) Learning Software Organizations. Springer, Berlin Heidelberg New York, pp. 186–204

[20] Workshops in the German Working Group on RE Patterns (WGREP), http://repare.desy.de,"Share Experience / Pattern Workshops"

Index